Brutus: Caesar's Assassin

Brutus: Caesar's Assassin

Dr Kirsty Corrigan

Pen & Sword
MILITARY

First published in Great Britain in 2015 by
Pen & Sword Military
an imprint of
Pen & Sword Books Ltd
47 Church Street
Barnsley
South Yorkshire
S70 2AS

ISBN 978 1 84884 776 7

A CIP ca ie British
Library

Typeset in Ehrhardt by
Mac Style Ltd, Bridlington, East Yorkshire
Print Ltd,
Croydon, CR0 4YY

Pen & Sword Books Ltd incorporates the imprints of Pen & Sword Archaeology, Atlas, Aviation, Battleground, Discovery, Family History, History, Maritime, Military, Naval, Politics, Railways, Select, Transport, True Crime, and Fiction, Frontline Books, Leo Cooper, Praetorian Press, Seaforth Publishing and Wharncliffe.

For a complete list of Pen & Sword titles please contact
PEN & SWORD BOOKS LIMITED
47 Church Street, Barnsley, South Yorkshire, S70 2AS, England
E-mail: enquiries@pen-and-sword.co.uk
Website: www.pen-and-sword.co.uk

Contents

Acknowledgements

While responsibility for the work contained within this book remains entirely my own, a debt of gratitude is owed to several people who have helped this project come to fruition. Firstly, I must thank Arthur Keaveney for his initial suggestion to pursue an ancient history biography, which I would not have considered without his encouragement. Furthermore, he has continued to support me along the way with his practical advice on the subject, proofreading of chapters, allowing me free access to his book collection for research and, not least of all, his patience. I would also like to extend my thanks to those who have helped me source images for the book, which I would have had difficulty in obtaining otherwise: fellow Pen & Sword author, Nic Fields, swiftly and favourably responded to an out-of-the-blue email request to borrow an image which I had seen in his book, *Warlords of Republican Rome*, and generously supplied images of other relevant places which he had visited; Jenny Keaveney kindly agreed to take time out of her holiday in order to take a selection of specific photographs in Albania for me; the MoneyMuseum of Zürich were extremely helpful and prompt in their email responses, allowing me to use images of their coin collection; and the Torre Argentina Cat Sanctuary in Rome provided an image, and agreed to my use of photographs of the Republican temple complex which included some of their feline residents. Thanks and appreciation must also go to all those at Pen & Sword who helped in the production of this book. Finally I would like to say thank you to my cats, Roma, Nero and Isis, who have been my constant companions while researching and writing and, of course, to my husband, David, who has, as ever, wholly supported and encouraged me throughout this project.

Kirsty Corrigan,
September 2014.

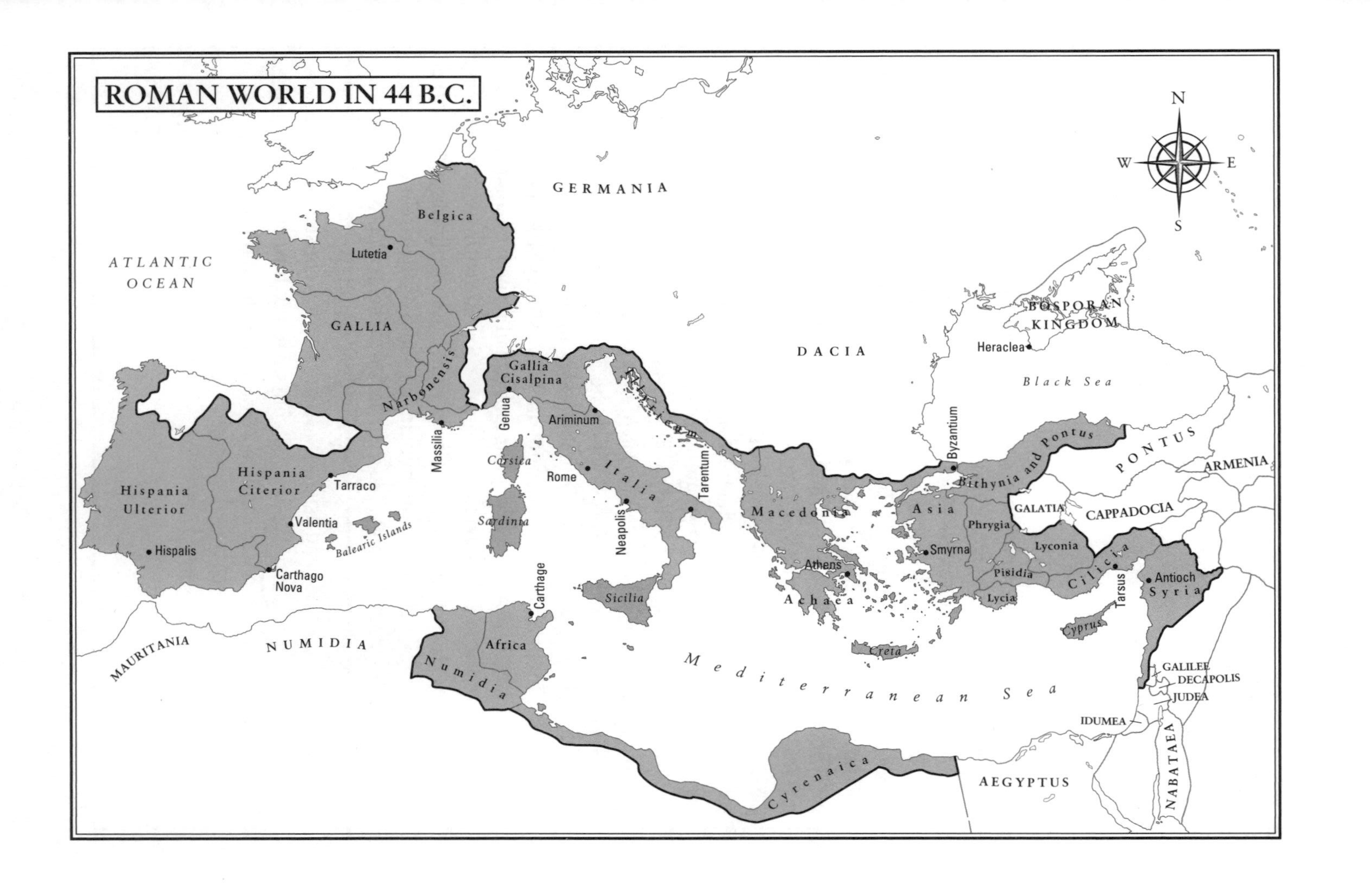

ROMAN WORLD IN 44 B.C.
N
W
E
S
GERMANIA
ATLANTIC OCEAN
Belgica
Lutetia
GALLIA
Narbonensis
Massilia
Hispania Ulterior
Hispania Citerior
Hispalis
Valentia
Tarraco
Carthago Nova
Balearic Islands
Gallia Cisalpina
Genua
Corsica
Sardinia
Ariminum
Rome
Italia
Neapolis
Tarentum
Sicilia
Carthage
Africa
Numidia
NUMIDIA
MAURITANIA
DACIA
Macedonia
Athens
Achaea
Creta
Byzantium
Bithynia and Pontus
Asia
Smyrna
Phrygia
Pisidia
Lycia
Lyconia
Cilicia
Tarsus
Cyprus
Antioch
Syria
GALATIA
CAPPADOCIA
PONTUS
ARMENIA
Heraclea
BOSPORAN KINGDOM
Black Sea
Mediterranean Sea
Cyrenaica
AEGYPTUS
IDUMEA
GALILEE
DECAPOLIS
JUDEA
NABATAEA

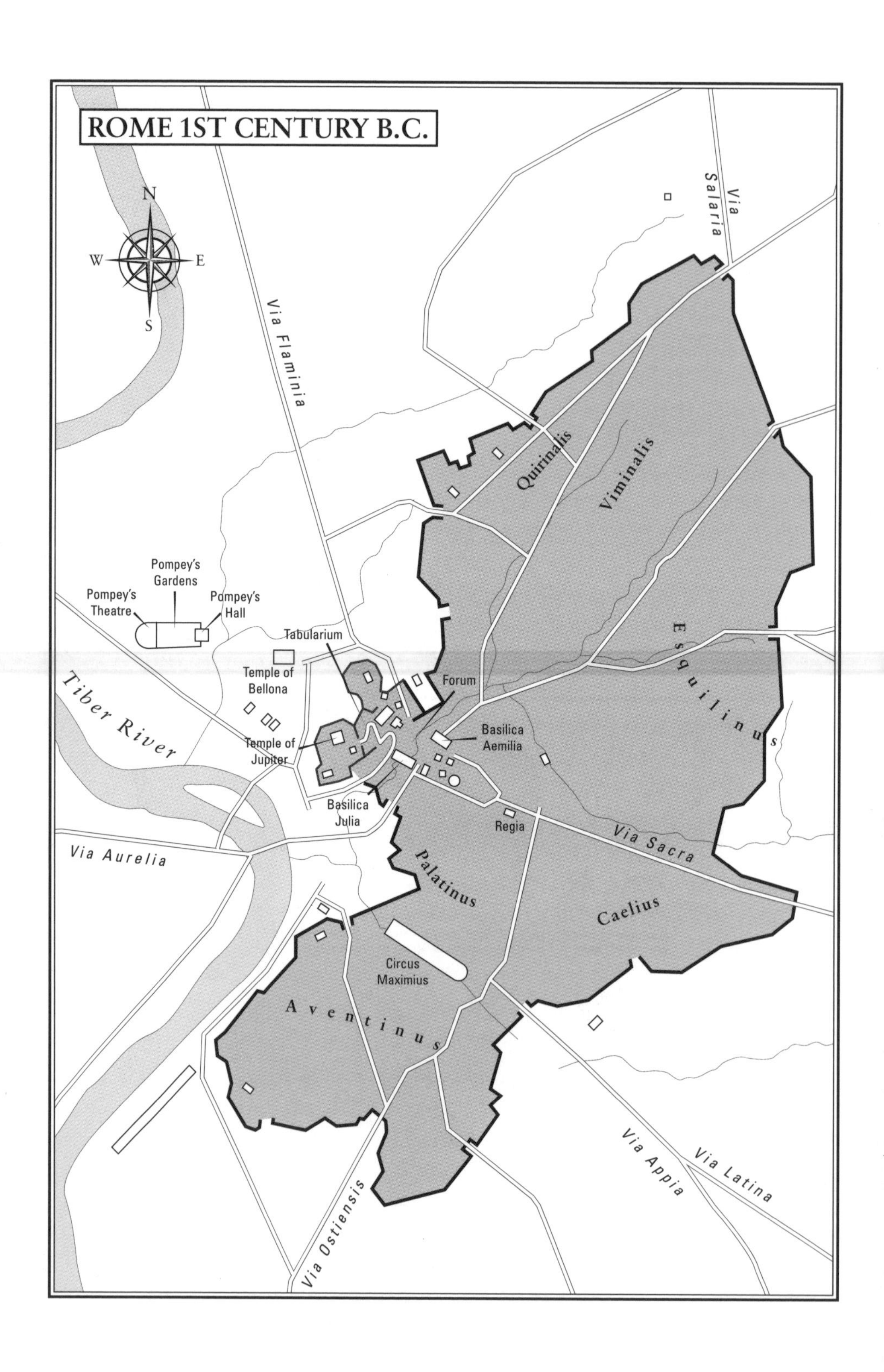
ROME 1ST CENTURY B.C.
N
W
E
S
Via Salaria
Via Flaminia
Quirinalis
Viminalis
Esquilinus
Pompey's Gardens
Pompey's Theatre
Pompey's Hall
Tabularium
Temple of Bellona
Forum
Basilica Aemilia
Temple of Jupiter
Tiber River
Basilica Julia
Regia
Via Sacra
Via Aurelia
Palatinus
Caelius
Circus Maximius
Aventinus
Via Appia
Via Latina
Via Ostiensis

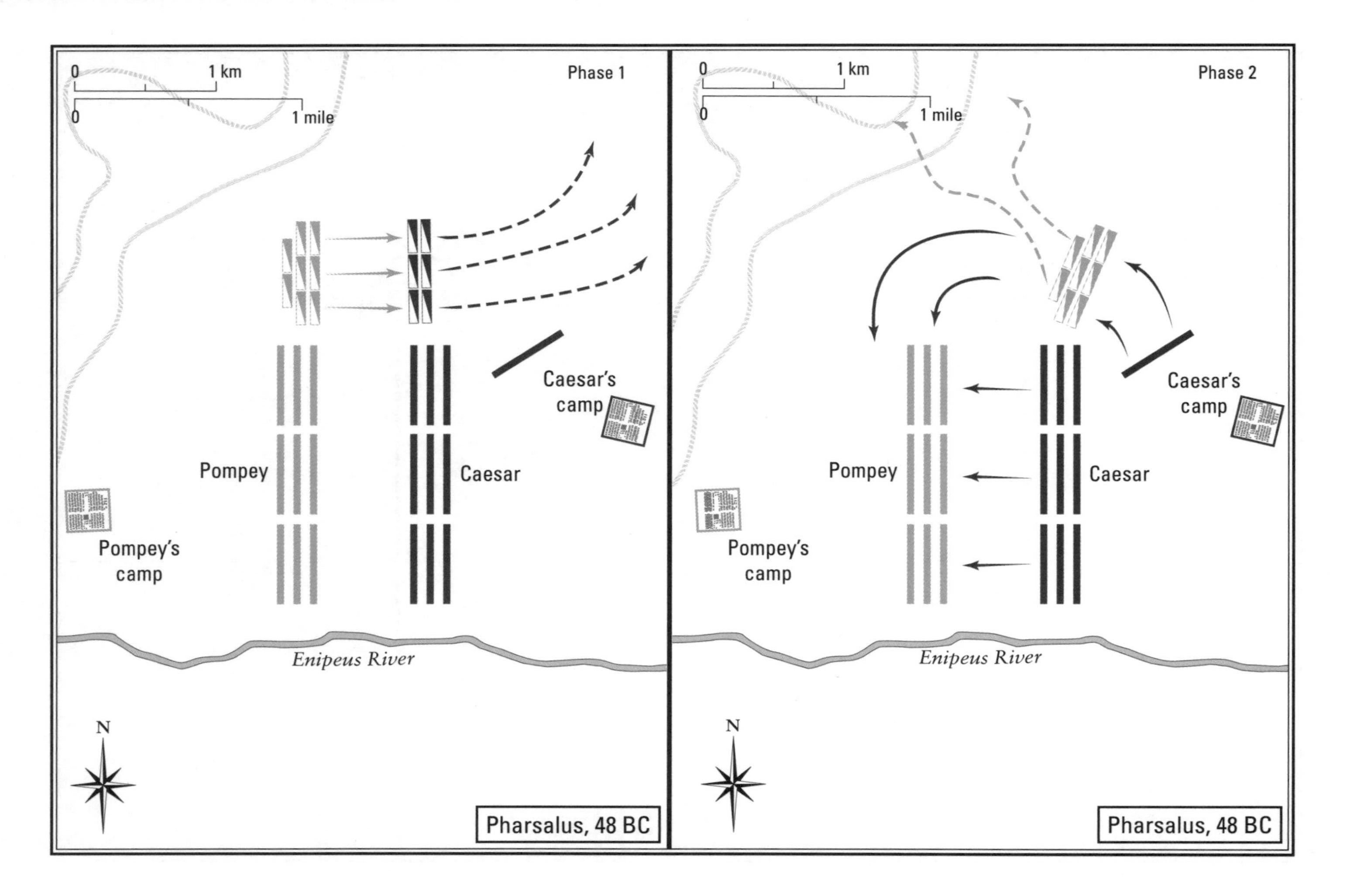
0
1 km
0
1 mile
Phase 1
Pompey
Caesar
Caesar's camp
Pompey's camp
Enipeus River
N
Pharsalus, 48 BC
0
1 km
0
1 mile
Phase 2
Pompey
Caesar
Caesar's camp
Pompey's camp
Enipeus River
N
Pharsalus, 48 BC

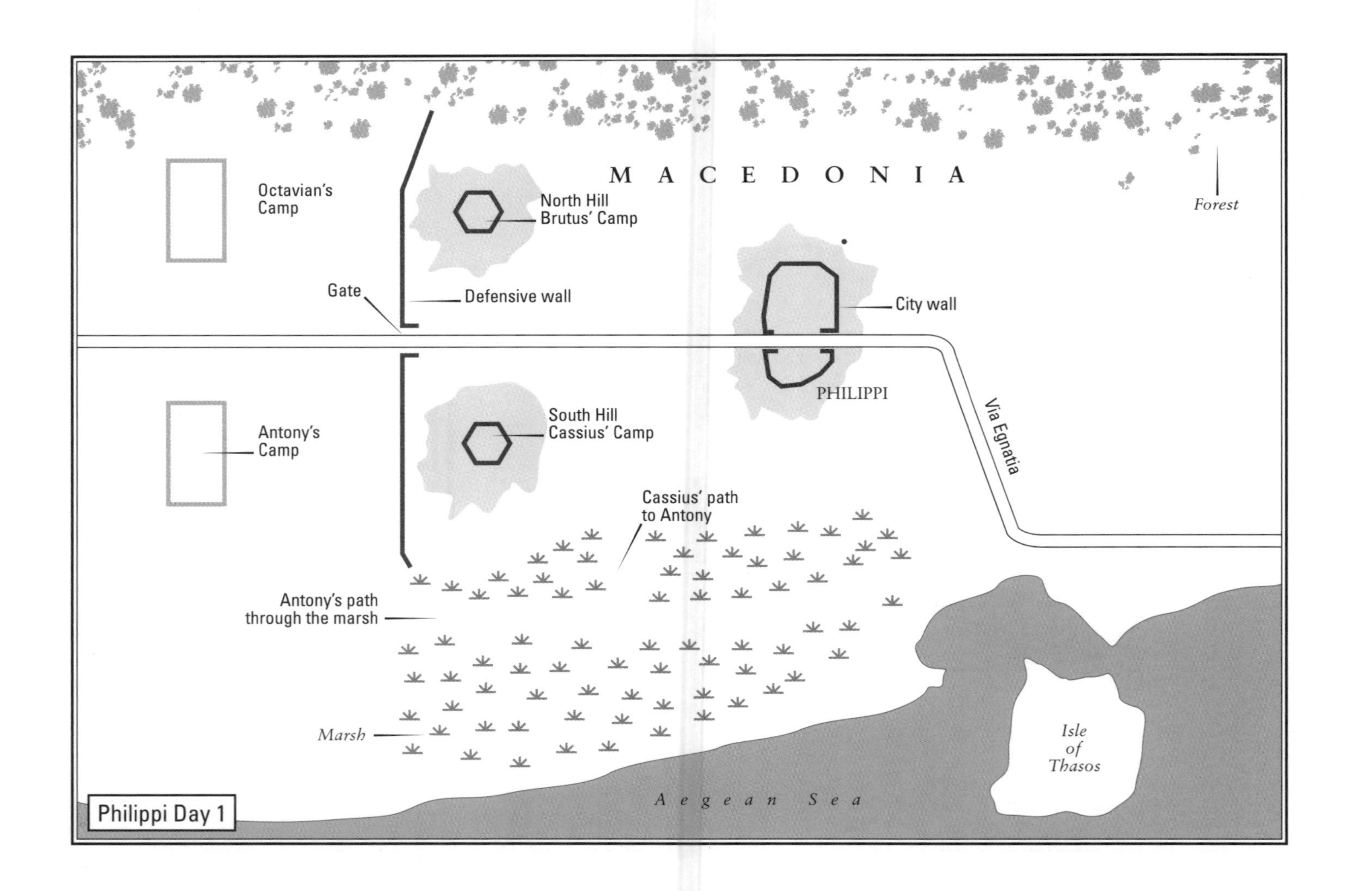
Philippi Day 1
MACEDONIA
Forest
Octavian's Camp
North Hill Brutus' Camp
Gate
Defensive wall
City wall
PHILIPPI
Via Egnatia
Antony's Camp
South Hill Cassius' Camp
Cassius' path to Antony
Antony's path through the marsh
Marsh
Aegean Sea
Isle of Thasos

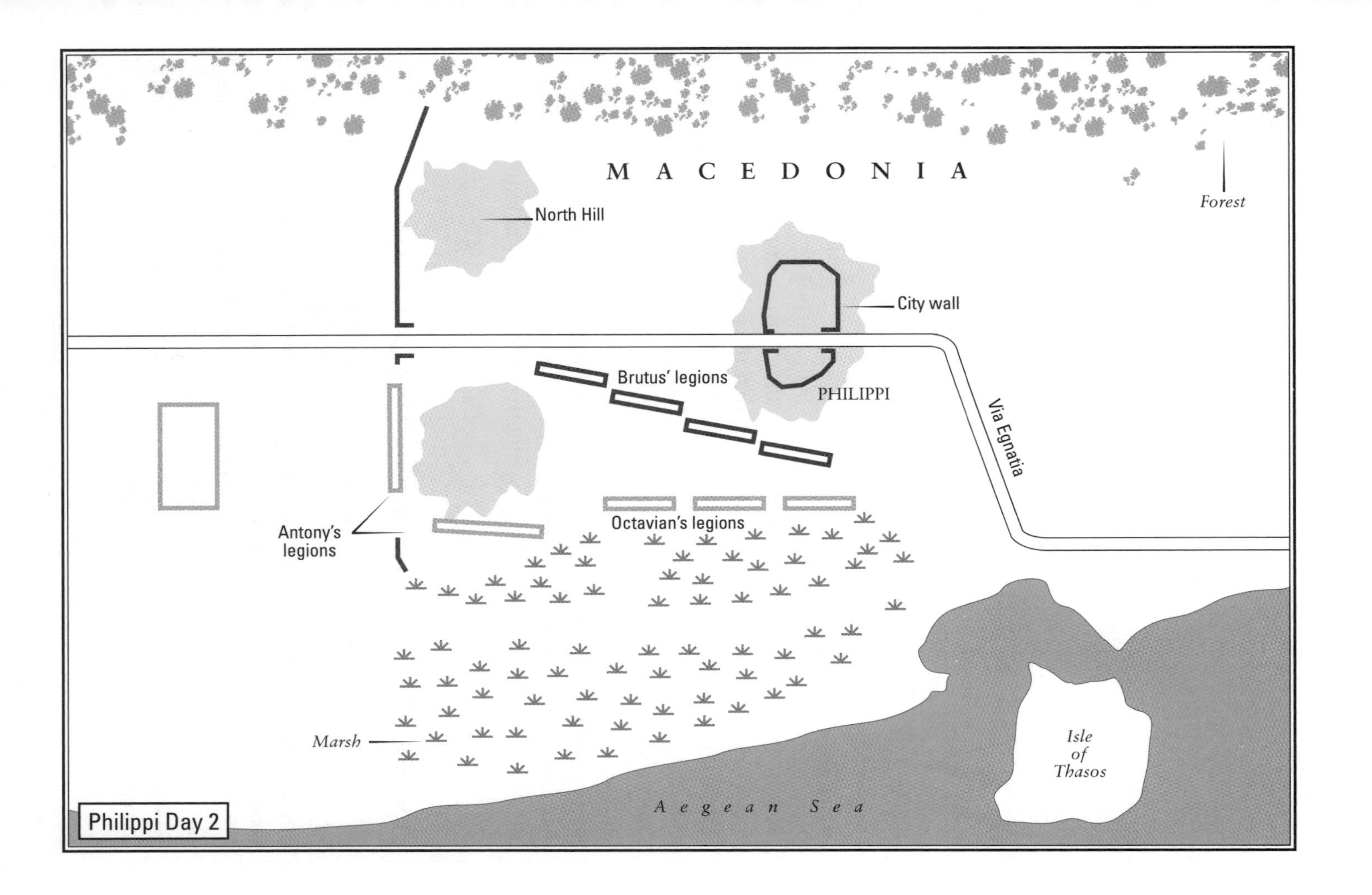
Philippi Day 2
MACEDONIA
Forest
North Hill
City wall
PHILIPPI
Via Egnatia
Brutus' legions
Octavian's legions
Antony's legions
Marsh
Isle of Thasos
Aegean Sea

Ancient Sources

While the following is not an exhaustive list of ancient sources referred to throughout this biography, it provides a summary of the principal texts which should be consulted when piecing together the life of Marcus Junius Brutus.

Appian, *Civil War*

Appian was an Alexandrian lawyer and historian, who compiled a narrative history of Rome in twenty-four books during the mid-second century AD. The sections on the civil wars of the late Republic have survived and are considered especially valuable. However, caution over the reliability of Appian's narrative should be urged, since his sources are uncertain and he was writing two centuries after the end of the Republic, meaning that he is considerably removed from the actual events of the period. Appian has a tendency to embellish details, which is most evident in the extended fictional speeches he places into the mouths of the historical figures about whom he is writing.

Augustus, *The Achievements of the Divine Augustus*

Also known by the Latin name of *Res Gestae*, this is a relatively brief record of the deeds of the Emperor Augustus, great-nephew and adopted son of Julius Caesar, which he had inscribed on his mausoleum, and copies of which were found on monuments in Galatia. Since this is Augustus' official record, intended for public consumption, it has an obvious propagandistic slant and therefore must be read with caution. Nevertheless, it is a valuable source, since it displays how Augustus, vanquisher of his adoptive father's assassins, wished events to be viewed.

Julius Caesar, *Civil War*

Caesar wrote a detailed commentary of the events of his successful war for supremacy against Pompey in 49–48 BC, in which Brutus was on the losing side. This is important as a contemporary document written by one of the protagonists, making it a rare first-hand account. However, it should also be borne in mind that this is a one-sided perspective of the proceedings, and so cannot be considered a balanced version of events. It is especially notable, in the context of this biography, that an important premise of this work is that Caesar portrays himself as protecting the state. Also in existence are anonymously authored records on other campaigns of his war against the Pompeians, written in a similar style and as a continuation of Caesar's work, including *The Alexandrian War* and *The African War*.

Cicero, *Brutus* and *Orator*

These works are both addressed to Brutus: the former is a history of orators which portrays Cicero, Brutus and Atticus participating in a fictional conversation; the latter is an outline of the best orator, in the form of a letter written by Cicero to Brutus. Various historical figures and Brutus' style and opinion of oratory are mentioned in the course of these works. We also gain a glimpse of some of Brutus' political viewpoints, at least as they exist according to Cicero. The elder statesman also dedicated several other works to Brutus, as a testament to his devotion to philosophy.

Cicero, *Letters*

A valuable ancient source is a historical figure's own words and personal thoughts. Therefore we are fortunate to have some of these preserved in Cicero's letters. These consist not only of Cicero's written words to Brutus, encouraging his fellow Republican to action, but also in the response of Brutus to several of these letters and exhortations. These offer a rare insight into the mind of the conspirator, his reasons for assassinating Julius Caesar, and his state of mind in the aftermath of the murder, as well as giving the background to the machinations and manoeuvrings of the politics at the end of the Republic. There is also a wealth of relevant correspondence between Cicero and other leading men of the day, revealing vital details of the contemporary political situation.

Cicero, *Philippics*

Cicero wrote this set of fourteen speeches attacking his arch-enemy, Mark Antony, between September 44 BC and April 43 BC. The political situation was precarious for the Liberators at this time, and these speeches are vital in providing us with many details about the events and changing fortunes of the Roman state during this turbulent and unstable period following Caesar's assassination. Not all of the *Philippicae* were delivered publically, but the unrelenting and vitriolic nature of these speeches, modelled on the *Philippics* which the Greek statesman, Demosthenes, delivered against Philip II of Macedon, undoubtedly contributed to Cicero's eventual death at the hands of Antony, during the proscriptions at the end of 43 BC.

Cornelius Nepos, *Atticus*

Nepos was a biographer, and contemporary and friend of both Cicero and Atticus. He wrote a life of Atticus, in which he touches on the turbulent politics of the end of the Republic, during which time his friend and subject managed to remain impartial. As a close associate of Atticus, Brutus is also a secondary topic in this biography.

Dio Cassius, *Roman History*

This historian was a Bithynian who had a prominent public career, acting both as Roman consul and governor. His chronological history of Rome, written in Greek and divided into eighty books, covers almost 1,400 years, from the foundation of Rome through to AD 229, a few years before Dio Cassius died. It was written over 200 years after the end of the Republic, and so the historian is considerably removed from the events of this period and his narration relies entirely on the sources of the intervening centuries. Like Appian, Dio Cassius' tendency towards embellishment of fact is revealed in the extended fictional speeches which he places into the mouths of the historical figures whom he is portraying.

Florus, *Epitome of Roman History*

This work is an abridgement of Roman history up to the age of Augustus, probably written by a poet and friend of the Emperor Hadrian in the second century AD. Florus wrote with particular emphasis on the wars of the Roman people in this rhetorical and concise version of history which, however, is not to be considered a particularly reliable source.

Livy, *History of Rome*

Livy is an Augustan historian who acts as our principal source for the early legends of Rome, and therefore depicts the important role of Brutus' legendary ancestors in the foundation of this mighty Empire. The first five books of his history of Rome were conceived as a whole and cover the period from the foundation of Rome to the early fourth century BC. Livy's moral tales particularly emphasise the character of leading figures from early Roman history, who are enlivened by speeches.

Lucan, *Civil War*

This epic poem is an account of the civil war between Caesar and Pompey at Pharsalus, written around a century later, during the reign of Nero. Although a work of fiction, *Civil War* includes the character of Brutus, and Lucan's depiction of him especially illuminates his relationship with his uncle, Cato the Younger, a hard-line Republican and Stoic who exerted much influence over his nephew. The poem is incomplete, and we cannot be certain how far Lucan would have taken his epic, nor the role Brutus would have played in it. Lucan, the nephew of Seneca the Younger, was forced to commit suicide for his alleged part in a conspiracy against the Emperor Nero, in AD 65.

Nicolaus of Damascus, *Life of Augustus*

Nicolaus was a Greek historian, living in the Augustan age. Among other historical works, he wrote a life of the first Roman Emperor, with whom he was acquainted, soon after his death. Much of this biography is lost, but the section describing the assassination of Caesar is extant: as an Augustan work, the author's sympathies are with the murdered leader.

Orosius, *Seven Books against the Pagans*

The church historian and priest Orosius was commissioned to write this history of the world down to his own day by St Augustine. As a late source, of the early fifth century AD, the sections dealing with the end of the Republic, almost 500 years earlier, including brief passages mentioning Brutus, are not to be considered particularly reliable.

Plutarch, *Lives*

Plutarch was a Greek biographer, historian and moral philosopher, who was writing during the height of the Roman Empire, over a century after Brutus had died. He wrote many biographies or lives of famous Greek and Roman figures, of which *Brutus* (and his comparison with the parallel *Dion*) was one, as well as *Antony*, *Caesar*, *Cato the Younger*, *Cicero* and *Pompey*. His approach is generally impartial, and the biographies contain much anecdotal information about the great historical characters he portrays, through which he especially drew out the moral nature of his subject, and which enliven these depictions and bring the figures to life.

Suetonius, *The Deified Julius* and *The Deified Augustus*

Suetonius was a Latin biographer of the first Roman Emperors, beginning with the life of Julius Caesar as a precursor before writing lives of the Julio-Claudians and Flavians, up to Vespasian. As secretary to the imperial household during the Emperor Hadrian's reign, in the early second century AD, Suetonius had rare access to imperial records and documents, unavailable to many of our other sources, making his own sources some of the most reliable. His purpose was not to write thorough chronological historical accounts, but biography with selected episodes and anecdotes for elaboration.

Tacitus, *Annals*

Tacitus was a historian who enjoyed a senatorial career under the Flavian Emperors, and lived on through the reigns of Nerva and Trajan. His experiences under the tyranny of Domitian coloured his works, so that his negative views about the Empire cannot be disguised. He was writing the *Annals* during the reign of Trajan, in the early second century AD, and this work covers the many cruelties of the Julio-Claudian era through its vivid portrayals of the Emperors of that period. The *Annals* include tales of the oppressed receiving punishment for alleged subversion in revering Brutus as a Republican hero.

Valerius Maximus, *Memorable Doings and Sayings*

During the early Roman Empire, Valerius Maximus compiled a handbook of notable deeds and sayings of historical figures, which he dedicated to the Emperor Tiberius. The nine volumes contain illustrative examples and anecdotes, often with a moral slant.

Velleius Paterculus, *Compendium of Roman History*

Velleius Paterculus was a Roman army officer compiling an epitome of Roman history to commemorate the consulship of his friend, Marcus Vinicius, in AD 30. Having lived during the early Empire and served under Tiberius, Velleius Paterculus appears to be in favour of the Empire which he experienced at first-hand and this, therefore, lends his writings a Caesarian slant. For example, he is extremely hostile towards Mark Antony, the enemy of his beloved Augustus; in the same vein, Velleius sympathises with the adoptive father of Augustus, Julius Caesar. This work, as is dictated by its nature, offers only a brief summary of the periods it covers, although some episodes are dealt with in more detail than others: the death of the Republic and birth of the Empire are periods that it dwells on only briefly.

Prologue

While Marcus Junius Brutus is a figure with whom most of us are familiar, this is chiefly as a product of the playwright, Shakespeare, as portrayed in his great tragedy, *Julius Caesar*. This book aims to reach further back than this celebrated Elizabethan version to consider instead the accounts of the ancient historians and biographers, in order to achieve, as far as possible, a historically accurate portrait of this pivotal figure of the late Roman Republic.

When writing, and indeed reading, a historical biography, particularly one concerning a figure from more than 2,000 years ago, we must be aware of many factors affecting the real truth.[1] The Greek and Latin writers had different reasons for writing their various accounts, and these undoubtedly colour their portrayals: they are often politically biased and so favour one of the protagonists in an episode over another; propaganda plays an important part since the surviving versions will mostly be those approved by the victorious, and so we do not often hear the views of the losers of history; accounts may simply be slanted towards one version of history because of the ancient sources to which they themselves had access, since we must remember that many of these ancient historians and biographers are not contemporaries but are writing more than a century after their subject's existence; furthermore, we must keep in mind that other accounts to which they refer may no longer exist for us to check and verify the details.

Since Brutus was one of history's losers, the ancient accounts of his life are often Augustan versions: Augustus, formerly known as Octavian, was the great-nephew of, and heir to, Julius Caesar. He was not only Brutus' successful opponent but also became the first Roman Emperor, and therefore it is easy to understand how this powerful man had much influence over the viewpoints and messages conveyed in the literature, art and architecture produced in the immediate aftermath of Caesar's assassination and Brutus' subsequent defeat and death. Later writers, although removed from the political events of the late Republic, would still, nonetheless, often be influenced by these earlier propagandistic versions of the truth.

Furthermore it should be kept in mind when reading this biography that many of the details about Brutus are fairly vague. Dealing with a less well-documented figure, perhaps, makes this an especially hazardous work to write. In some instances a 'fact' is reported, whether in an ancient or modern text, that has not been verified, or that is contradicted elsewhere, and it is not always possible to corroborate it with careful checking. Therefore, in order to fill the gaps of Brutus' life, it is necessary, at times, to take the source that is generally considered the most reliable and assume its validity.

The end of the Roman Republic is well known as a particularly turbulent and troubled period. It should also be added that it was a rather complicated one. As the leading men fought for supremacy, civil wars ensued, and the powerful Romans of the era seemingly freely swapped coalitions and allies. Indeed, few Romans of this period can be said to have followed the same path throughout their lives. Often this could be attributed to self-interest, self-preservation or self-promotion; sometimes, though, it could be derived instead from attempting to follow the morally correct path. Brutus can, possibly, be placed in this latter category, for we shall see that he, too, changed his alliances during his forty-three years. Brutus is certainly a true product of the troubled times in which he lived. We witness him navigating the politics and politicians of the late Republic, while trying, yet not always managing, to remain devoted to his principles. One point emerges clearly from this complicated and confusing period: the picture is not black and white, and there is no clear right or wrong side. Similarly, we shall see that no man was entirely good or evil: even Brutus, for all his reputation for great morality and high principles, cannot escape this era with his good name entirely intact and unscathed. However, this surely serves to make him a more interesting character, worthy of consideration in his own right, and earning his own biography.

The most infamous act of Brutus is, without any doubt, his leading role in the assassination of Julius Caesar, which thereby also inadvertently brought about the death of the Roman Republic: ironically, the very institution he was striving to protect. Discussions of Brutus, both ancient and modern, therefore tend to focus heavily on this aspect of his life. Furthermore, the ancient texts often contain much foreshadowing of this momentous event, no matter which period of his life they are considering. While unable to ignore or underestimate these events, this book will attempt to piece together as much information as possible from the ancient literature covering the entire life of this important figure, in order to offer a balanced biography of the mighty and noble Marcus Junius Brutus.

Chapter One

Background and Early Life

Ancestors

Marcus Junius Brutus was deeply conscious of his ancestral heritage and this awareness apparently greatly influenced his mightiest actions, as shall be discussed in due course. Therefore, before looking in more detail at Brutus himself, it will be useful to set the context of this biography by beginning with a summary of two important legendary figures from the early Roman Republic, from whom Brutus claimed descent. The first five books of the *History of Rome*, written by the Augustan historian Livy, act as the chief source for these legends.

Lucius Junius Brutus[1]

Lucius Junius Brutus, the first Brutus, was the nephew of the King of Rome, Tarquinius Superbus, or Tarquin the Proud as he is more commonly known. As the son of the King's sister, Tarquinia, he realised the danger of his position, especially having already witnessed many murders committed by the King, including that of his brother. For this reason, the astute young Brutus feigned obtuseness in order to protect himself, so as not to appear as any kind of threat to the monarch. Disguising his true character thus, he even accepted the cognomen of Brutus, which in Latin means 'Dullard'.

Brutus was sent to accompany two of the King's sons, Arruns and Titus, to the Delphic Oracle, with the cruel purpose of being a source of amusement to his cousins on their trip. However, Brutus' true character and future greatness was in evidence even then, although his cousins were not able to recognise it. Concerned foremost with their lust for power, Arruns and Titus asked the Oracle who would be the next King of Rome. Receiving the response that the first to kiss his mother would hold Rome in supreme authority, the cousins' reaction was to keep this information from their other brother; the shrewd Brutus, on the other hand, interpreted this answer differently and, pretending to trip, fell face first onto the ground to touch

Mother Earth with his lips. Clearly, in contrast to his arrogant royal cousins, Brutus' intelligence designated him for great things.[2]

Lucius Junius Brutus' rise to prominence came to pass through his heroic role in a tragic and notorious event of early Roman Republican history: the rape of the virtuous Lucretia. While on leave from the long siege at Ardea, during their leisure time, the young officers began discussing their wives, which created rivalry between them. Collatinus, the husband of Lucretia, suggested going to Rome in order to see their wives and judge whose was best. While the rest of the wives were found engaged in parties, Lucretia was the virtuous exception: she was found hard-working, spinning late at night by lamplight with her maids. Lucretia welcomed her husband and the princes, inviting them to dine. It was at this supper that Sextus Tarquinius conceived his unlawful lust for Lucretia, which was aroused by her rare chastity. The dishonourable prince visited Lucretia a few days later, alone and unannounced, and was again welcomed. Waiting for the opportune moment, once the household was sleeping, he went to Lucretia's chamber with a sword, threatening that if she did not yield to his sexual advances he would kill her and a slave, whose body he would place next to her in her bed, thereby disgracing her most-valued honour. Lucretia, having been thus raped, summoned her husband and father, asking that they bring a trusted friend: her father brought Publius Valerius while Brutus accompanied Collatinus. Lucretia requested that they pursue Sextus' punishment before nobly killing herself with a knife, ignoring their attempts to dissuade her because she refused to be held as an excuse for unchaste women.

At this point in the tale, Brutus springs into action: while the girl's husband and father were grieving, he pulled the knife from Lucretia's body, swearing on her spilled blood that he would avenge her by punishing all the Tarquins and preventing any man from ever being King in Rome again. This moment marks a change in the character of Brutus: no longer hiding his true nature, he suddenly emerges as a natural leader. Collatinus, Lucretius, and Valerius, astonished at his changed behaviour, and roused both by his speech and their anger at the tragic fate of Lucretia, now swore an oath to obey his command in a war against the Tarquins. Henceforth, Brutus would take control of the situation, exhibiting his true personality, and similarly inspiring action in the people. When the crowd gathered to see Lucretia's body, he incited them, as true Romans, to take up arms against the tyrants who had treated them as enemies. Leaving Lucretia's father to hold the town of Collatia, and posting guards to prevent news of the uprising from reaching the Tarquins, Brutus led the armed populace in their march on Rome.

At Rome the people were alarmed at the sight of an angry mob, but realised the serious nature of this uprising when they saw the men of distinction at its head. News of Lucretia's fate had also caused the same reaction in Rome as at Collatia, so the people crowded into the forum. Brutus convened a meeting and delivered yet another rousing speech, describing the horrific crime of Sextus Tarquinius against the noble Lucretia, in which he reminded the people of the general tyranny imposed upon the Romans by the royal family. This eloquence, alien to the character he had displayed previously, successfully inflamed the people so that they demanded the exile of the royal family; Tullia, the wife of the King, fled the palace. Leaving command at Rome to Lucretius, Brutus led an army of volunteers to the camp at Ardea to raise an army against the King. Brutus changed his route in order to avoid meeting the King, who travelled to Rome on learning of the rebellion so that he might restore order. While Tarquinius found the gates of Rome shut against him and his exile pronounced, Brutus the Liberator was received enthusiastically in the camp. Tarquinius' sons were expelled from the camp: two of them followed their father into exile at Caere (Cerveteri) in Etruria, but Sextus returned to his territory, Gabii, where he was assassinated for his previous unlawful behaviour.

Therefore, this is how twenty-five years of rule by Tarquinius Superbus, as well as 244 years of monarchy in Rome, was brought to an abrupt, yet just, end by Lucius Junius Brutus. Livy acknowledges, however, that Brutus would have done his country a disservice had he expelled any of the previous Kings out of his passion for liberty. Subsequent to the end of the monarchy, a new form of oligarchic government was necessarily established: henceforth two consuls were annually elected by popular vote under the presidency of prefect of the city. Thus in 509 BC the Republic was born and, along with the widowed husband of Lucretia, Lucius Tarquinius Collatinus, Brutus became the first consul of Rome. All rights and insignia of the Kings were transferred to the consuls, with the only exception being the rods, or fasces, which were permitted to only one of the pair: with his colleague's consent, Brutus was the first consul to possess the rods, and we are informed that he proved just as determined to preserve liberty now that he had established it.

Brutus' first act was to make the people swear an oath never to permit another King in Rome, thereby aiming to prevent anyone from succumbing to persuasion or bribery in order to assist in a restoration of the monarchy.

Next, he increased the number of the senate, which had been recently depleted by Tarquinius' bloody rule, to 300 men, recruiting largely from the equestrian rank. This was said to be the origin of the distinction between the fathers and the conscripts: the original members of the senate and these later enrolled recruits. Next, religious matters were addressed: previously, public sacrifices had been performed by the office of the King, so a new 'King of sacrifices' priesthood was created for this role, but it was made subordinate to the post of *pontifex*, in case the un-Republican sounding name of King (*rex*) caused offence.

This disquiet is also an indication of the general feeling regarding the safeguarding of the new Republic: the people extended their concern to Brutus' consular colleague, Lucius Tarquinius Collatinus, believing that he was a threat to liberty simply because he possessed the name Tarquinius. Brutus responded to this by calling the people to an assembly: he recalled the oath sworn never to allow the monarchy to be revived in Rome, and reluctantly requested that Collatinus complete the task he had begun in banishing the royal family, by offering him a deal to leave Rome with his possessions and some compensation, in order to remove the troubling name of Tarquinius from the state. Astonished at first, Collatinus was convinced by the people's entreaties and, mostly, that of his father-in-law: fearing for his life, he went into voluntary exile. Following this, Brutus proposed a decree banishing all Tarquins from Rome. Publius Valerius, who had assisted in the expulsion of the monarchy, was elected to replace Collatinus as Brutus' consular colleague for the remainder of the year.

However, discontent inevitably arose among some of the young aristocrats, who had been accustomed to more freedom under the monarchy, and who felt aggrieved that the new Republic brought more benefits for the lower classes, while prohibiting them from indulging in their pleasures. Therefore, when envoys from the Tarquins arrived on the pretext of seeking the recovery of the royal family's property, they found ready accomplices in a secret plot to steal the Tarquins back into Rome under cover of night, and gave letters from the Tarquins to the disillusioned young nobles whom they found favourable to their scheme. Meanwhile, the senate, who had been debating the matter, agreed to the return of the Tarquins' property, which allowed the envoys to stay and therefore gave them time to obtain letters confirming the intentions of those willing to be party to the conspiracy. Persuaded to join this plot were the two sons of Brutus, Titus and Tiberius, whose maternal uncles, the Vitellii, were chief conspirators along with the Aquilii.

The plot, however, was uncovered by a slave who overheard loose talk while the conspirators were dining at the house of the Vitellii, on the eve of the envoys' return to the royal family. Once the slave witnessed the exchange of correspondence, he informed the consuls, who at once arrested and imprisoned all involved and seized the letters. The slave informer was later freed and given money and citizenship as a reward. The traitors were duly punished, and Brutus faced the tragic task of inflicting the death penalty on his own sons: all eyes were on the scene of their deaths because of the terrible irony of the treachery. The lictors carried out the punishment, while the consuls watched from their seats on the tribunal: the guilty were stripped, flogged and beheaded. Brutus' anguish as a father was in evidence, as he nevertheless remained committed to his duty to the nation.[3]

In the meantime the senate had again voted on the matter of the return of the Tarquins' property, now deciding to leave it to the people to plunder, with the hope that this would prevent them from reconciling with the royal family. It was said that the Campus Martius was now created from the Tarquins' land between the Tiber and the city; and the crop from this land, thrown into the river, reportedly built up and became the foundation of Tiber Island.

Tarquinius, on learning of these events and realising treacherous routes were barred to him, decided upon war. On the pretext that he had been driven out of power by the conspiracy of a kinsman, he sought the aid of Etrurian cities. Veii and Tarquinii, with whom he particularly pleaded on the basis of having been born from the same blood, joined his cause. The consuls set out to meet the approaching forces: Valerius led the infantry, while Brutus went ahead with the cavalry. Tarquinius was at the head of the invading army's foot soldiers, while Arruns, his son, led the horsemen. Arruns, catching sight of the accompanying lictors, recognised his uncle and angrily charged straight at him, calling upon avengers of Kings. Brutus eagerly accepted the challenge and rushed at his nephew with equal violence. Neither one of them gave a thought to his own safety, as each was focused on wounding the other. This clash resulted in the death of both uncle and nephew, as each fell from his horse, impaled by the spear of the other, which had been driven through the shield and into the body. An evenly matched battle followed, with the Roman forces eventually emerging victorious when panic came over the enemy and led to the armies of Veii and Tarquinii withdrawing.

Valerius returned to Rome in triumph, where he celebrated his colleague's funeral with as much splendour as possible. Even greater tribute was paid to Brutus by the grief of the nation, and particularly the matrons, who mourned him for a year, as they would a father, because of his role as principal avenger of Lucretia's honour. These events all took place in the year of his consulship, 509 BC. The first Brutus thus died in the fight for *libertas*, or freedom, as his descendant and namesake, and the subject of this biography, also would, nearly 500 years later.

Gaius Servilius Ahala[4]

Gaius Servilius Ahala first enters Livy's Roman history in 439 BC, the year in which Lucius Quinctius Cincinnatus was made dictator, and appointed Ahala as his master of horse (*magister equitum*). This measure was taken because, at that time, a grain shortage gave Spurius Maelius the opportunity to win popular support by purchasing grain from Etruria and donating it to the poor. This led to Maelius developing consular and even monarchical ambitions: when these plots were uncovered by Lucius Minucius, the official prefect of the corn supply, the senate took drastic action by appointing the elderly dictator, who then enlisted the assistance of his younger colleague, Brutus' ancestor Ahala.

On the following day, Cincinnatus appeared in the forum, ordering Ahala to summon Maelius to him. When Maelius, afraid, inquired why, Ahala explained that he was required to stand trial to answer charges that had been brought against him. Maelius escaped from the grasp of Ahala's attendant with the help of the crowd and fled, calling on the people to protect him and claiming that he was in danger because he had aided them. However, Ahala caught Maelius and killed him, bespattering himself with his blood.[5] Guarded by a group of young nobles, Ahala returned to the dictator and reported that he had killed Maelius when he had tried to avoid arrest and stir up the populace: Cincinnatus congratulated Gaius Servilius Ahala, the ancestor of Brutus, for saving the Republic. The dictator then addressed and calmed the crowd, explaining that Maelius had been justly killed for using violence to resist arrest, whether or not he had kingly ambitions. According to Livy, Cincinnatus cited the example of Lucius Brutus killing his own sons for their attempts to overthrow the Republic which, the dictator claimed, Maelius would have known well. Insulted that a man of mere humble birth could dare to make such an attempt to buy Rome, Cincinnatus ordered that Maelius' house should be demolished, the goods confiscated, and the proceeds given to the public treasury.

Following this, charges were brought against both Ahala and Lucius Minucius that Maelius had been illegally executed. Firstly, in 438 BC, three of the tribunes, Quintus Caecilius, Quintus Junius and Sextus Titinius, made failed attempts to do so. Then, in 436 BC, a tribune whose name was also Spurius Maelius hoped to rouse trouble, knowing that his name had popular appeal: he appointed a day for the prosecution of Minucius, whom he claimed had made false accusations against his namesake, and proposed a law to confiscate Ahala's property because he killed a citizen who had not been condemned. However, his accusations were ignored.[6]

Marcus Junius Brutus and his Ancestry

It should be stressed that the stories of Lucius Junius Brutus and Gaius Servilius Ahala are indeed legends and cannot be taken as factual historical accounts, although it is probable that they are based on some truth. Indeed, the origin of many of the tales from Livy can be found in Greek history.[7] Similarly, therefore, the claims of Marcus Junius Brutus to these connections can be considered dubious. It has been observed, for example, that Lucius Junius Brutus had no offspring once his sons had been executed and, therefore, it is questioned how the line of descent can possibly be drawn down to Marcus Junius Brutus. However, these attempts to deny Brutus' heritage have been attributed to the hatred of his enemies, particularly that motivated by the assassination of Caesar, while the defence that Lucius Brutus had a third younger son has also been put forward.[8] Whatever the truth, such assertions do not derive purely from Brutus' desperate claims to fame, but would have existed in earlier centuries, as these legends of ancestry often did. Therefore, our Brutus was simply following the tradition that was already laid out for him.[9]

Whenever we are discussing Brutus, we should keep these legends in mind, just as he himself always did: these tales greatly influenced him and his actions. Regardless of whether or not such stories of ancestry were true, they played a prominent part in the life of the noble Roman, who turned to his most eminent ancestors, fictional or otherwise, in order thereby to emphasise his own glory. Furthermore, in Rome there were constant reminders all around of ancestors to whom one should look for inspiration and moral guidance. This was especially true for Brutus, who was surrounded by images and memories of the famous heroic actions of his ancestors: these were deeds that were fundamental to the Roman Republic in their original context, and would become pivotal for it once again in the hands of Brutus in the 40s BC. Brutus felt a responsibility to uphold these family standards, which can perhaps be considered at once both an advantage and a burden.[10]

A cautious reader may consider this emphasis on Brutus' awareness of his origins simply as a result of hindsight: his later infamous deed, in overthrowing a potential tyrant, is impossible to ignore and therefore makes it difficult to view any of Brutus' earlier actions without this in mind. However, reliable contemporary evidence clearly demonstrates the importance of family ancestry to Brutus. We know, for example, that Brutus requested that Titus Pomponius Atticus, his close friend and an antiquarian, draw up his family ancestry for him in detail.[11] His friend and associate, Marcus Tullius Cicero, reports that Brutus displayed busts of at least one of his legendary ancestors in his house, from which he claims that he was able to derive inspiration on a daily basis.[12] Important evidence is also to be found in the coins issued by Brutus himself: these proudly display images of his legendary ancestors, as well as the head of the goddess Liberty. It has been observed that he was the first Junius to display images of his ancestors on coins.[13] Some of these coins were minted as early as 54 BC, and so were in circulation at least a decade before his own act to liberate the Republic from a tyrant.[14] Following in the line of his two great ancestors apparently did dictate that Brutus would strongly support the Republic and oppose tyranny from birth.[15] Brutus' contemporaries also knew this all too well, so much so that they would play on his consciousness of family reputation in order to encourage him towards his act of tyrannicide; but more of this later.

Early Life and Family

Information about the early life of Marcus Junius Brutus, before he enters into his public career, is relatively sparse. However, it is possible to piece together some small details. The exact date of Brutus' birth is not known, but the year is usually given as 85 BC, according to a reference from his friend and contemporary Cicero, and therefore a reliable source on the matter.[16] We do know that he was born in Rome to parents who could both claim descent from legendary heroic figures of the Roman Republic, endowing Brutus with an illustrious and noble inheritance on both sides.

Brutus' father, also named Marcus Junius Brutus, was a purported descendant of the Lucius Junius Brutus who banished the Kings of Rome in the fifth century BC, and subsequently established the Roman Republic. He held the post of tribune of the plebs in 83 BC and it was most probably during this time that he attempted to establish a colony in Capua (Santa Maria Capua Vetere).[17] Cicero furnishes us with some minor details about the man:

in a fictional conversation about orators, he tells Brutus that his father was learned in both private and public law; we also learn that, as tribune, he interposed in the case of Quinctius, in order to delay proceedings.[18]

The most notable episode in the life of the elder Brutus occurred during the political struggles in the wake of Sulla's death, and led to his own demise.[19] Following Sulla's death in 78 BC, there was a split within his party, with the consul Marcus Aemilius Lepidus ostensibly taking up the cause of the enemies and victims of Sulla, and thereby attempting to overturn the recently established Sullan constitution and seize power through a revolt. At this stage, the senate gave extraordinary command to a Sullan adherent with proven military expertise, Gnaeus Pompeius Magnus, who would later become known as Pompey the Great, so that he could suppress the rebellion. The elder Brutus, who was Lepidus' colleague in this uprising, and probably his legate, had been placed in command of the forces in the province of Cisalpine Gaul. After having subdued the rebellious forces elsewhere with relative ease, at Mutina (Modena) Pompey was confronted with Brutus, who defended the besieged city for a long time. However, for unknown reasons, Brutus surrendered to Pompey, on condition that his life should be spared. Pompey agreed and gave Brutus a cavalry escort to accompany him to retirement in a small town on the River Po but, on the following day, Pompey sent a man named Geminius to execute him in cold blood.[20] And so, in 77 BC, aged only seven or eight, the young Brutus lost his father, whom Plutarch notes he was unlike in both wars and death.

Brutus' mother Servilia was said to be descended from the Gaius Servilius Ahala who had also performed a service in protecting the Republic, overthrowing a potential tyrant in the fourth century BC. Her immediate family was more politically prominent than that of her husband. She was the daughter of Quintus Servilius Caepio the Younger, a quaestor of 100 BC, and possibly also praetor in 91 BC: he died while serving as legate in the Social War of 90 BC, when commanding part of the consular army after the death of the consul, Rutilius. Servilia's mother was Livia, the sister of the tribune of the plebs who embarked on an extensive programme of political reform, Marcus Livius Drusus.[21]

Following his father's death, arrangements were made for Servilia's young son to be adopted by her brother,[22] Quintus Servilius Caepio: therefore, henceforth Brutus also became known by the name of Quintus Servilius Caepio Brutus. The widow Servilia was also married again, to Decimus Junius Silanus, the consul of 62 BC.[23] It is believed that this second marriage resulted in Brutus' three sisters.[24] Of the first sister, little is known except that she was possibly married to Publius Servilius Vatia Isauricus, who was consul in 48 BC.[25] The other two girls, maintaining the family's strong political connections, certainly married well. Junia Secunda was the wife of Marcus Aemilius Lepidus, the future Triumvir and son of the Lepidus who had led the rebellion in which Brutus' father had perished. One of their sons, Lepidus the Younger, was apparently destined to follow in his uncle's footsteps: he later plotted to assassinate Octavian, and paid with his life.[26] In a letter to his friend Atticus, dated 50 BC, Cicero scurrilously hinted that Junia Secunda was guilty of having an affair with a Publius Vedius.[27] Another of Brutus' sisters, Junia Tertia, also known affectionately as Tertulla, was married to Gaius Cassius Longinus, Brutus' fellow conspirator. They also had a son, recorded as being in his mid-teens in 44 BC,[28] and we know that Tertia suffered a miscarriage in the same year.[29] She long outlived her brother and husband, dying during the reign of Tiberius in AD 22: it is notable that, more than sixty years after the deaths of Brutus and Cassius, their images were conspicuously absent from her funeral, and clearly still considered as a form of threat.[30]

As we have already noted, Brutus' mother Servilia was extremely well connected. Therefore, it is not wholly surprising that we find her involved in political matters in Rome at various points during her son's prominence.[31] She is also known to have been involved intimately with one especially eminent Roman politician: Gaius Julius Caesar. This detail seems verified by the contemporary evidence of a broad hint in one of Cicero's letters dated 59 BC, and the affair is reported as fact by the later ancient writers, Plutarch and Suetonius.[32] Furthermore, Servilia was reputedly Caesar's favourite mistress, although one of many, according to the account of Suetonius: she received many extravagant gifts and favours from him, including a pearl of exorbitant cost and, following the civil war with Pompey, became the owner of property of the fallen at an extremely reduced price. Servilia, said by Plutarch to be madly in love with Caesar, was even rumoured to have given Caesar her daughter, Junia Tertia, as a lover.[33]

Servilia's affair is relevant, not only because Julius Caesar was to meet an untimely end at the hands of her son, but also because this well-known relationship was the source of a rumour that the real father of Brutus was Caesar himself. This story appears to have been fuelled by Caesar's final words as Brutus stabbed him which, as reported by Suetonius, were not the '*Et tu, Brute*' immortalised by Shakespeare in his tragedy *Julius Caesar*, but the Greek for 'You too, my son?'[34] According to Plutarch, Caesar himself suspected this to be the case, and the biographer gives this as the reason for his protectiveness towards Brutus. Appian's account also suggests that it was a rumour circulating during Brutus' lifetime. However, it should be emphasised that this story is extremely unlikely to have contained any truth: having been born in 100 BC, Caesar would have been only fifteen at the time of Brutus' birth; furthermore, the affair seems to have been embarked upon at a much later stage, since we certainly know from Cicero's letter that Caesar and Servilia were lovers more than twenty-five years after Brutus had been born. Ultimately, this appears to be a piece of gossip which was an opportunity too good to be ignored, given the additional pathos that could thus be attached to Brutus' later role as Caesar's assassin.[35] It can be stated, with more certainty, that his mother's illicit relationship with Caesar was a source of embarrassment and displeasure to Brutus and, therefore, it has been considered one motivation for his dislike of the man. This seems potentially borne out by his eventual choice to side instead with his long-term foe, Pompey, the man who was responsible for callously executing his real father; however, his political motivations and choices will be fully discussed in due course.

The Influence of Cato

Following her divorce from Servilia's father, Livia's remarriage to Marcus Porcius Cato Salonianus was to prove a particularly significant match for her grandson, Brutus. The son resulting from this marriage was Marcus Porcius Cato. Better known as Cato the Younger or Cato Uticensis, the maternal uncle of Brutus was ten years his senior, and was to be extremely influential in his nephew's life. Indeed, although after his father's death Brutus was adopted by Servilia's full brother, Caepio, from our sources Cato appears to have had much more significance in Brutus' life. It is, however, known that Caepio and Cato were close: Plutarch tells us of Cato's deep affection for his older half-brother, and therefore it is quite possible that they shared a role in Brutus' formative years.[36]

Certainly Brutus held Cato in high esteem: Plutarch describes him as admiring his uncle more than any other Roman alive.[37] Indeed the relationship of the austere and principled uncle who gave clear moral guidance to his nephew, the future tyrannicide, became legendary, and had an enduring appeal. For example, Lucan's incomplete Neronian epic about the civil war between Pompey and Caesar, written a century later, places emphasis on this relationship: although we cannot be certain how much further into late Roman Republican history the fictional *Civil War* would have stretched, the minor role of Brutus, as it stands, illustrates his reverential devotion to his uncle, and appears to exist principally to underscore Cato's unbending moral character and to validate his role in the war. Although Lucan's account is fictional, it nonetheless displays the long-existing belief about the nature of Brutus and Cato's relationship.[38]

Also relevant to Brutus is an anecdotal tale from his uncle's youth, narrated by Plutarch. When Cato was just thirteen, his tutor would often take him to the house of the dictator Sulla, who was a family friend. It was during the time of the proscriptions, and so the young Cato witnessed many people being led in for torture and execution. Observing this, Cato, angry and resolute, asked why no one had killed this man, and requested a sword so that he might thus liberate his country. Brutus apparently had yet another relative whom he could emulate in his later act of tyrannicide.[39]

Brutus' unwavering devotion to philosophy and renowned moral principles can also, perhaps, be attributed mainly to his uncle's influence. In more practical terms, Cato also helped launch his nephew's public career, when he allowed the young Brutus to accompany him on an expedition to Cyprus.[40] Cato's approach to politics was guided by his moral outlook, and he would always firmly stand by his principles. It is pertinent to the life of Brutus that Cato was a staunch defender of the Republic, and also that he developed a particular dislike of Julius Caesar and had a long-running feud with him.[41] This enmity seems to have been especially related to the infamous conspiracy of Catiline, in which he accused Caesar of being involved in the revolt against the Republic.[42] This bitter hatred was only further aggravated by Caesar's scandalous affair with Cato's half-sister, Servilia: there exists an anecdote in which, while debating in the senate, Caesar received a note that Cato suspected was from the conspirators and therefore forced him to read aloud; however, Cato was humiliated and angry when the contents revealed instead a love letter from Servilia. Since the conspiracy occurred in 63 BC, this offers further evidence that Servilia and Caesar were lovers many years after Brutus was born.[43]

Cato's implacable enmity towards Caesar can be traced in Plutarch's account of his life. Similarly, at first he also disliked Pompey. Essentially he was opposed to any possible tyranny, which he sensed would be the outcome of either one of these mighty men amassing too much individual power. However, he eventually joined sides with Pompey, once the latter had also recognised that Caesar was a threat to the state and realised the limits to his own power: Cato then felt that Pompey was the best option for the security of the state. This perhaps offers another explanation for Brutus' eventual choice of the cause of Pompey, his father's murderer, over that of Caesar, who had supported him politically over the years: the influence of Cato, his beloved uncle.[44]

Marriages

As is perhaps to be expected, given his reputation for unimpeachable morals, Brutus himself is not recorded as having been involved in any salacious affairs, unlike his mother. It should be noted, however, that there is one anonymous and relatively late text, which can probably be discounted as it is generally held to be unreliable, suggesting that he was once a lover of the notorious actress Cytheris.[45]

Indeed, relatively little is known about Brutus' personal life, although we do know that he had two wives.[46] The date of his first marriage is unknown, and it has been conjectured that they were wed in 54 BC, although it had certainly taken place by the middle of 51 BC. His wife was Claudia, the elder daughter of Appius Claudius Pulcher. This was a politically strong match since Brutus' father-in-law was descended from a distinguished family and was a prominent politician, who was one of the consuls of 54 BC. The marriage was also advantageous for the opportunistic Appius, whose younger daughter was later to be married to Pompey's son.[47]

However, in 45 BC, after several years of marriage, Brutus suddenly divorced Claudia amid general disapproval. We are not given the reasons for the divorce, but Brutus soon afterwards married Porcia.[48] She was the daughter of his recently deceased uncle Cato and the widow of Marcus Calpurnius Bibulus, both political opponents of Caesar.[49] Cicero does not appear to have shared the disapproval of Brutus' divorce from Claudia, and even seemed quite eager for this new match with Porcia, presumably for its political potential.[50]

It is notable that Servilia did not have a good relationship with her new daughter-in-law, who was also her niece: like her mother-in-law, Porcia never appeared to be far from the male world of politics at Rome, but she supported the cause of her father Cato, while Servilia favoured Caesar's interests over those of her half-brother. This undoubtedly caused friction, especially once Porcia became married to Brutus and was able to influence his political views, and possibly ensure that they were guided in a different direction from those of Servilia and her lover. It seems that even mighty Romans, such as Brutus, with crucial matters of state on their mind, could become embroiled in the familiar domestic trivia of petty rivalry between mother and daughter-in-law. Portraying a slightly, although perhaps unintentionally, amusing image of an unfortunate man caught between the two dominant women in his life, Cicero describes Brutus' situation as detestable (*perodiosum*), and reports that, in their hostility towards one another, 'the women' (*mulieres*) were behaving inconsiderately towards Brutus who, according to him, was dutiful to both.[51] While we cannot tell from this whether it was a rivalry that was politically, or simply domestically, driven, we may suspect the former.

Regardless of any personal difficulties this marriage may have caused, it has been suggested that there was genuine love between Brutus and Porcia, and that it may not have been in any way a political move. Porcia is described as a loyal and loving wife, who would prove herself worthy of both her father and her husband, as she bravely and dutifully supported Brutus in the plot to assassinate Caesar.[52] Porcia brought with her at least one son from her previous marriage, but it is uncertain whether Brutus fathered any children; however, if he had any offspring, we can assume that they did not survive to adulthood, since it is highly improbable that their existence could then have disappeared completely from the pages of history.[53]

Chapter Two

Early Career

Education

According to the ancient texts, Brutus was well educated and always dedicated to study, being particularly devoted to his interest in philosophy. Cicero compliments his friend on his unwavering devotion to learning, and the sources depict a man often to be found engaged in some form of study, or quoting the classics of literature, no matter what other important matter was imminent, whether public affairs, wars, or his own death.[1]

Suetonius tells us that, like his fellow chief conspirator, Cassius, Brutus had been a pupil of the Latin grammarian, Staberius Eros, an ex-slave who was freed for his devotion to literature. It is notable that Staberius was said to have taught the children of those proscribed by Sulla for free, a point that surely would have made him an appealing and appropriate teacher for the son of a man who had recently lost his life in a rebellion against the new Sullan constitution. Plutarch informs us that, in Latin, Brutus was well trained in both oratory and pleading.[2] He was also schooled in Greek literature and rhetoric and, as was customary for aristocratic Roman youths, was sent to Greece to continue his education. He pursued his studies in Athens, where his teacher was Pammenes, for whom Cicero expresses high praise indeed, designating him the most eloquent man of Greece. While learning with Pammenes, Brutus studied in detail a favourite of his tutor, the statesman and orator Demosthenes, and we know that his admiration was such that he later possessed a bronze bust of him in his villa at Tusculum.[3] One late and less reliable source suggests that he also studied in Rhodes, and he is known to have been acquainted with the rhetorician Empylus, who possibly hailed from the island, so that it has been suggested that he was Brutus' tutor there.[4] References to Brutus' later life also attest to his familiarity with Greek texts, since he is to be found readily quoting lines from epic and tragedy at pivotal moments. He was fluent enough in Greek to have authored a philosophical work, *Concerning Duty* (περὶ καθήκοντος), and his style of writing in the language was described as brief and epigrammatic.[5] His love of the Greek world also extended to his homes: at his villa in Lanuvium (Lanuvio), Brutus named the stream 'Eurotas', recalling the river on which Sparta lay, and also had a 'Persian Portico', as at Sparta, possibly even naming the villa 'Lacedaemon' after Sparta; similarly, at one of his houses, Brutus also had a library named the 'Parthenon'.[6]

Brutus' time in Greece was to prove extremely influential on the young Roman. It was in Athens that his love of philosophy developed. Plutarch tells us that there was scarcely any Greek philosopher with whom Brutus was unacquainted, and that he was most interested in the writings of the disciples of Plato. He followed the school of the Old Academy, often attending the lectures of its leader, Aristus, who was also a close friend, and a man reported to be less gifted than many philosophers but of good character.[7] Cicero also claimed to be a close acquaintance of Aristus, who had assumed leadership of the school from his brother, Antiochus of Ascalon. Antiochus had begun a revival of the original teachings of the school, and had numbered Cicero among his pupils.[8] Although bearing some similarities to Stoicism, the Old Academy taught different ways of thinking from the school to which Brutus' uncle Cato subscribed, generally being less severe and strict in approach.[9]

Cicero commends his friend's skills highly, both as a rhetorician and philosopher: as well as displaying his admiration and respect by dedicating several works to Brutus, in the *Brutus* he also encouraged him to continue to distinguish himself from ordinary orators by pursuing his studies. Furthermore, Cicero laments that the precarious political situation of the day has cut short the career of this promising orator, whom he considers has the talent to mark him out as a replacement for himself, which is high praise indeed.[10] However, later ancient sources were less complimentary about Brutus' rhetorical skills, although they showed greater appreciation for his philosophical works: Quintilian praises Brutus for the genuine nature of his writing and his gravity, matched to the serious subject matter; Tacitus, more damning, equates Brutus' skills with those of Caesar, saying that he is best suited to philosophy, and describing his speeches as dull and cold, although elsewhere he acknowledges that Brutus was eminent as a speaker of his day, and considers him the most earnest and free from envy.[11] Among his philosophical treatises were *Concerning Suffering* (*De Patientia*) and *Concerning Virtue* (*De Virtute*), but only a few words of each survive so that we are unable to assess their merit. It has also been recorded that Brutus epitomised various historical works, including those of Polybius, Caelius

Antipater and Fannius.[12] Another literary pursuit of his was composing poetry which, like that of Cicero, was not considered particularly successful, and has been lost completely to us.[13]

Clearly a well-educated and cultured man, Brutus' studious nature, especially his pursuit of philosophy, was renowned: Cicero puts into his friend's mouth the claim that he finds pleasure not in the results of eloquence itself, but in the study and devotion to thinking that it involves, and also refers to him as a most scrupulous historian; Plutarch introduces us to his character by describing his intellectual pursuits as contributing to his famous virtuous nature.[14]

Early Public Life (59–56 BC)

The date of Brutus' return to Rome, following his extended educational training in Greece, is unknown. The next we hear of him is in 59 BC: by this point, now in his mid-twenties, he is back in Rome and very much at the heart of public affairs.

The Vettius Affair (59 BC)

It may be something of a surprise to learn that the conspiracy to assassinate Julius Caesar was not the first such in which Brutus was implicated. A rather suspicious affair occurred in the summer of 59 BC, when Pompey was still at the height of his power as a part of the coalition with Caesar and Marcus Licinius Crassus, commonly referred to as the First Triumvirate:[15] several young nobles, including Brutus, were accused of conspiring to murder Pompey, although this story was eventually discredited. The true nature of this matter has never been fully resolved.

One of Cicero's letters, addressed to his friend Atticus, gives a detailed version of events.[16] In the letter, Cicero implies that Julius Caesar is behind these accusations, which he overtly suggests are fabricated. He claims that Caesar has employed the services of Lucius Vettius, who interestingly had previously turned informer for Cicero during the Catilinarian conspiracy, which was only a few years earlier: in an effort to be rid of the main opposition to the Triumviral party in the current elections, Vettius specifically insinuated himself with Gaius Scribonius Curio the Younger, who had been successfully electioneering on behalf of Caesar's political opponents. His eventual purpose was to bring Curio under some form of suspicion: this being, of course, conspiracy to murder Pompey. Vettius set about this by telling Curio that he had a plot to assassinate Pompey with the help of his slaves, believing that Curio would wish to join as a conspirator. It was understood that Vettius' ultimate aim was to be arrested along with his slaves, carrying weapons in the forum, and then to offer to turn informer. However, he had misread Curio, who instead reported the alleged conspiracy to his father. The elder Curio in turn passed this information back to Pompey himself and the case was brought before the senate.

Vettius' version of events was immediately questioned: at first he denied ever having spent any time with Curio, but then requested protection so that he could give evidence against him. Although the senate denied this request, he nonetheless proceeded to inform them that Curio was at the head of a group of young men that included Lucius Aemilius Lepidus Paullus, Lucius Lentulus[17] and, of most relevance here, Brutus. He added that Septimius, the secretary of the consul Marcus Calpurnius Bibulus,[18] had brought him a dagger from the consul: Cicero underscores that this is where Vettius' story begins to fall apart, since it is ridiculous to suggest that he could not have come by his own dagger; furthermore, Cicero comments, Bibulus was said to have warned Pompey about assassination plots recently, for which Pompey had thanked him. When Curio was brought into the senate to answer the accusations, Vettius' entire story was undermined on a specific point: Vettius had claimed that the group had planned to attack Pompey in the forum during Aulus Gabinius' gladiator show[19] with Paullus as ringleader, but Paullus was well known to have been in Macedonia at the time.

Subsequently Vettius was imprisoned for having confessed to carrying a dagger, and it was declared that any attempt to free him would be considered an act against the state.[20] The suspicious nature of this affair was augmented when, on the next day, Caesar led Vettius to the rostra in order to question him, and Vettius changed his story again: he now added names to the list of conspirators, including Lucius Licinius Lucullus, who was said to have sent Gaius Fannius to him, and Lucius Domitius Ahenobarbus, whose house was the supposed headquarters for the conspirators. Furthermore, although not explicitly identifying him, he also hinted at Cicero's complicity, interestingly intimating that the orator had said that what was needed was another Servilius Ahala or Lucius Brutus, Brutus' heroic tyrant-overthrowing ancestors. Vettius also named Cicero's son-in-law, Gaius Piso, along with Marcus Laterensis, when he was later questioned again by the tribune, Publius Vatinius.[21]

However, most important here is that Vettius now removed Brutus' name from the list of accomplices when questioned by Caesar: Cicero explicitly claims that Vettius must have been told what to say regarding the various changes to his story; furthermore, he states that it appeared 'a night and an appeal by night' had taken place since Vettius' original claim. It was, of course, well known that Brutus' mother was a favourite mistress of Caesar, so that this reference could easily be understood as a rather impertinent hint that Servilia must have used her feminine charms to intercede with Caesar on her son's behalf, still assuming that Caesar is behind the accusations.[22] This is notable as the earliest recorded instance we have of Caesar favouring Brutus, for whom he consistently displayed a fondness, apparently in order to please his lover Servilia.

At the time of Cicero's letter, charges of violence were being brought against Vettius, whom Cicero believed would be convicted and then would claim impunity as an informer, which would lead to prosecutions. Cicero treats this in a fairly trivial fashion, illustrating his belief that the accusations are without substance. However, events took a different turn, since Vettius was found dead in prison shortly afterwards, having been strangled: it was believed that those behind the whole fabricated plot had arranged his murder.[23] In a later prosecution, Cicero would shift the blame away from Caesar to Vatinius, the consistently ardent supporter of Caesar who had also questioned Vettius. Cicero now claimed that Vatinius was acting under the name of Caesar, but was in fact wholly responsible for various illicit actions, including using this alleged plot to bring down those 'most illustrious' men implicated, among whom Cicero declared that he was honoured to be numbered.[24] It is worth noting that, at this later point, Cicero does not mention Brutus as ever having been implicated.

With the uncertain nature of this whole affair,[25] we cannot say whether or not Brutus was truly involved in an assassination plot. However, the dubious nature of the evidence does suggest that the entire conspiracy was fabricated and, therefore, Brutus' implication in it must also have been fictional. However, regardless of the truth of the matter, it does tell us something about his political inclinations at the time: emerging into public life as a member of the optimates,[26] Brutus' loyalties were clearly opposed to the Triumvirate, otherwise Vettius would not have been able to implicate him realistically in the alleged conspiracy. Certainly his hatred for Pompey, derived from the cold-blooded execution of his father, was widely known, and this would have made Brutus a most credible suspect for attempts made against the Triumvir's life.[27] It also tells us that the Romans around him believed an assassination to be within Brutus' capability and character, and perhaps, therefore, we can say, with hindsight, that Caesar should have paid greater attention to this belief.

Annexation of Cyprus (58–56 BC)

In 58 BC, Cato took his nephew with him on an expedition to annex Cyprus, which was at that time part of the Ptolemaic kingdom, to the Roman Empire. Cato was allocated this task by the tribune, Publius Clodius Pulcher: he was working in league with the Triumvirate, who sought to remove Cato, their principal opponent, and a particularly dogged one at that, from the main political scene in Rome. While Cicero, another irritation to the Triumvirate, and nemesis of Clodius, was exiled, it was decided to manoeuvre Cato differently.[28] At first Clodius offered Cato this much sought-after role but, when he refused because he was fully aware of the true meaning of the offer, an edict was passed in the senate sending him on the mission, and he was assigned limited resources. Furthermore, Clodius added the less glorious task of restoring some exiles to Byzantium (Istanbul): Plutarch suggests that Clodius' intention was to keep Cato out of the way for the duration of his tribunate.[29]

Cato went to Rhodes, while he sent his friend, Canidius, ahead to Cyprus to negotiate with Ptolemy, who was then ruling the island.[30] However, Ptolemy committed suicide and left behind a vast amount of treasure. At this point, Cato decided to sail to Byzantium to settle the exiles there, before setting out for Cyprus himself. In the meantime, since he did not entirely trust Canidius, Cato wrote to Brutus instructing him to sail to Cyprus immediately, in order to confiscate the King's property. Clearly Brutus could, at that time, be trusted with financial affairs (however, as we shall see below, he would later be found involved in some more dubious monetary dealings[31]). At that point, Brutus was in Pamphylia (a region on the south coast of Asia Minor, located in modern southern Turkey), where he was recuperating from a severe illness, and only followed this order against his will. Plutarch gives two reasons for Brutus' reluctance, both displaying the reputation of his character: firstly, he had regard for Canidius, whom he felt had been swept aside ignominiously by his uncle; secondly, his studious nature dictated that Brutus felt such attention to matters of business were not worthy of himself.[32]

Despite this, we are informed, Brutus carried out his duty most effectively, earning Cato's praise in the process. The level of Brutus' involvement in the matter is not clear from Plutarch since he offers two accounts: in his *Brutus*, he is given much individual credit for successfully converting the King's property into money, before returning to Rome, shipping the bulk of the treasure back with him; in his *Cato*, however, although Brutus' involvement is acknowledged, Cato is the one who meticulously carries out all business arrangements.[33] It can therefore be judged, perhaps, that Brutus acted as an efficient assistant to his uncle in this business, and that he returned to Rome at the same time as Cato and the treasure, in 56 BC. Accompanying his uncle on this mission appears to have been Brutus' first role in official business, and so the true beginning of his public career.

First Official Role

Tresviri Monetales (54 BC)

Although the date remains uncertain, it was probably in 54 BC[34] that Brutus held his first official post, as one of the three moneyers, or *tresviri monetales*, a board of magistrates in charge of the Roman mint. This role tended to be occupied by young aristocrats who were about to embark on a public career.[35] While coins had originally been anonymous, the minting of them had now become a method of propaganda for the moneyer and his family connections. The purpose of this was both to make the moneyer well known and also associate him with Roman legends and heroes so that, when it came to elections for a public post, it would help to increase his votes.

Brutus, now in his early thirties, eagerly seized this opportunity to display his mighty ancestral heritage in order to aid his climbing of the political ladder. Indeed, Brutus was the first of the Junii clan to place images of his ancestors on a coin: he issued denominations featuring portraits of both the famous ancestors from whom he claimed descent, Lucius Junius Brutus and Gaius Servilius Ahala. As well as emphasising his familial connections, these choices have clear political motivations and underscore Brutus' Republican stance at this early stage in his career. One silver denarius, issued by him in 54 BC, depicts the head of Lucius Brutus on the obverse and that of Ahala on the reverse, and could be attributed simply to ancestral claims. However another, dated to the same time, displays on the reverse an image of Lucius Brutus walking between the lictors who were carrying the fasces (the bundle of rods with an axe, traditionally symbolising authority of the state), while the obverse, most importantly, illustrates the head of the goddess *Libertas*, or Liberty. This imagery has clear signals to the viewer of the coin: the combined depiction of Brutus' legendary ancestor who first established the Roman Republic by overthrowing a tyrant, appearing in his role as first consul, along with the personification of the goddess representing freedom, undoubtedly indicates that Brutus strongly supported the liberty of the Republic and was opposed to any sense of tyranny in Rome.[36]

It has been suggested that the images on these coins were produced in order to serve as a subtle warning to Pompey not to upset the status quo in the state: in 54 BC there were rumours of an impending dictatorship for him, about which Cicero expresses concern in letters to those closest to him.[37] Quintilian has also recorded a disapproving remark, supposedly made by Brutus on the topic of Pompey's potential dictatorship: 'for it is better to rule no man than to be the slave to any man: without the former, however, it is possible to live honourably; with the latter there is no condition for living'.[38] Although we are uncertain of the date of this comment, and are unable to verify its authenticity, once more it displays the unbending reputation of Brutus, which outlived him through antiquity and beyond. Furthermore, the implication of Brutus in the Vettius conspiracy has also been associated with the imagery employed on these coins.[39] Whatever the truth about the specific purpose behind the coins at the time, and their potential aim against one-man rule in Rome, it should be observed that they tell us a great deal about Brutus' political inclinations. Furthermore, although the exact dating of Brutus' role as one of the *tresviri monetales* has not been securely established, it is undoubtedly several years before Julius Caesar's assassination, Brutus' certain attempt to liberate the Republic from tyranny. Therefore, we are able to see that the principles that would later lead Brutus to his act of murder were inherent and firmly entrenched: he was always truly dedicated to his cause.

Moneylending Activities (53–50 BC)

The Salamis Affair

In 53 BC, Brutus had officially arrived when he served as quaestor, a financial administration role, and his first position held on the traditional *cursus honorum* (the course of honours, or sequence of public offices).[40] According to a source that is generally dismissed as unreliable, Brutus tellingly refused to serve under Julius Caesar on his campaign in Gaul. Instead, in 53 BC he accompanied Appius Claudius Pulcher, the governor of Cilicia, to his province. It is likely that Appius was his father-in-law by this time, since

Brutus was probably married to his elder daughter, Claudia, in the previous year.[41]

Little is known of Brutus' business while in Cilicia, except for the rather shady details of an extortion case involving the Cypriot city of Salamis, not at all compliant with the image of Brutus that is generally portrayed in the sources. Brutus lent the city, which was part of the province of Cilicia, money at an exceptionally high rate of interest. However, the murky and complicated details of these dealings only emerged once Cicero took over from Appius as proconsul of Cilicia, in 51 BC. Cicero's letters are unable to hide his disappointment in Brutus, for whom he otherwise always shows a great deal of respect and admiration.[42]

Following the return of Cato and Brutus to Rome after the annexation of Cyprus, the city of Salamis sent a deputation to their patrons requesting a loan. However, it had recently been made illegal to lend money to provincials at Rome.[43] Two Romans, Publius Matinius and Marcus Scaptius, agreed to lend the money if it could be done so legally. The Salaminians, desperate, sought the help of their patron Brutus to ensure that the transaction could take place: as a young senator, Brutus brought two resolutions, both of which were carried, in order to exempt this Salaminian deal from the law. We know from one of Cicero's letters to Atticus that these decrees stated that the governor of Cilicia should recognise the agreed bond in giving judgement, and that no action should be taken against the parties involved.[44]

Appius' behaviour as governor in the province was questionable, yet we have no evidence that Brutus played any part in this while there, other than turning a blind eye to his activities: he was in no position to challenge Appius on the matter, as his subordinate and junior. Appius' acts of extortion often left the communities unable to pay the current taxes, while still owing arrears for the previous tax period. One example of Appius' extortionate actions is found in his refraining from billeting troops in towns in return for large sums of money, as previous governors had also done: Cypriot cities paid 200 talents for this exemption. Needless to say, Cicero did not engage in this practice once he took up his governorship. According to Cicero, when he arrived in the province to take over as proconsul, Appius and Brutus took themselves off to the opposite end of the province, with the strong implication that they were trying to avoid the new governor, aware that he would disapprove of, and pass judgement on, how affairs had been managed. Cicero tells Atticus that he is too busy trying to repair the province to take this up with Appius, but suggests that Atticus should chastise their mutual friend, Brutus, for his impolite behaviour.[45]

In 52 BC, while Appius was still governor, one of the moneylenders, Scaptius, arrived in the province to collect the Salaminian debt: by now the city was in arrears. Appius appointed him as a prefect, with command of a cavalry, in order to aid his debt-collecting activities via methods of intimidation. Scaptius duly used the force at his command: he besieged the local councillors in the senate house, awaiting the funds; when they were finally released, five of them had apparently died of starvation.[46]

Cicero arrived in the province to take up his position in 51 BC, not long after Scaptius' harsh tactics, and promptly ordered the dismissal of his troops. He, nevertheless, audaciously sought the renewal of his prefecture from Cicero. Furthermore, and significant here, is that both he and Matinius came with high recommendation indeed: Scaptius brought letters of praise from Brutus.[47] Despite Cicero's eagerness to please both Brutus and their mutual friend Atticus, he could not bestow a prefecture on the despicable Scaptius, considering his recent behaviour. Cicero tactfully cited his regulation that no man with business dealings in the provinces could hold an official position there, an excuse he repeatedly offers in his correspondence to Atticus regarding the unsavoury affair.[48] However, Cicero promised to ensure that the Salaminians paid Scaptius: he ordered them to pay their debt, refusing to hear stories of Scaptius' misconduct. They agreed to pay at 12 per cent, a rate set by Cicero in the edict he issued, as was customary, before setting out to govern the province. However, Scaptius continued to press for the originally specified rate of 48 per cent, producing the two senatorial decrees of 56 BC, which Brutus had passed: the first was intended to circumvent the law forbidding the lending, and the second to ensure the bond was valid now that the law had been overruled. Cicero believed that this extortionate rate would ruin the city. Following some negotiations and calculations of each side's accounts, the amount owed was agreed, but Scaptius then requested that Cicero leave the matter there. Cicero believed that he had done all he could for Brutus at this stage, writing to Atticus that he expected their friend to be satisfied with this, and asking him to put his point of view to Brutus.[49]

A week later, Cicero wrote a follow-up letter to Atticus,[50] pleased that he had won the latter's approval for his approach used in handling the affairs of Appius and Brutus. However, Cicero apparently had not similarly pleased the former proconsul and his quaestor in his actions, whose letters to him reportedly displayed less satisfaction. It was at this point that Cicero, and, according to him, Atticus too, received the shocking revelation that it was Brutus himself who had lent the money and set up this unsavoury transaction: Scaptius was merely an agent in this messy affair, as proved by a letter from Brutus, which Scaptius had produced in a private interview with Cicero. Indeed, this new information contradicted a memorandum from Brutus, which had expressly stated that the Salaminians owed the money to his friends, Scaptius and Matinius, and that he was acting as guarantor for them. Cicero was not only dismayed, but disappointed to learn that this could be within the capability of the young man for whom he had, up until now, had a great deal of esteem, hope for the future, and a developing fondness. Finally Cicero, with a tone of exasperation, reveals his irritation with Brutus and his actions: Cicero openly declares to Atticus that, if Brutus thinks he should have made exceptions by handling his affairs differently from the specified conditions of his edict, which he was applying fairly in all other cases, then it is a shame to have displeased Brutus, but far worse to learn that he is not the man he believed him to be.[51]

This placed Cicero in an awkward situation, since not only did he and Brutus share a mutual close acquaintance, Atticus, but they had their own growing friendship which Cicero appeared keen to foster. It does not appear, however, that Brutus necessarily reciprocated this feeling: Cicero reports that Brutus adopts a rather abrupt and ill-mannered tone when writing to him, which he claims to find amusing rather than irritating. Brutus apparently used this approach, regardless of the content of his letters. This included when requesting a favour, such as asking that Scaptius be endowed with a prefecture, about which Cicero remained resolute, even though Atticus was urging the appointment too.[52]

Despite his disappointment in Brutus, Cicero continued to act in his interests: he brought this tricky case to resolution, by treading the middle ground, allowing the validity of the loan to stand, overruling the legal objection, and managing to persuade the Salaminians to overlook the matter that no interest should have accumulated because the money had been deposited in a temple. Furthermore, Scaptius was allowed to collect his debt, but only at the legal and more moderate interest rate of 12 per cent. However, if the Salaminians did not pay by a certain date, the original interest rate was to stand. A small note in Brutus' defence is that we learn that he was willing to accept a loss in order to reach a resolution.[53] Cicero apparently left the matter there, to be dealt with by his successor; however, he clearly was not completely comfortable with this, since he displays concern for the financial situation of the Salaminians at the hands of a new governor. Cicero, unlike Brutus it seems, found himself unable to abandon his principles entirely: in response to Atticus' comment that he should at least return from Cilicia with Brutus' goodwill, Cicero notes that this will not be at the expense of his own morality.[54] In following letters, Cicero assures Atticus that he has done all that can acceptably be done.[55]

When reading these letters, with Cicero's relentless attempts at justification of his acts, the impression conveyed is that Atticus was not altogether pleased with him, and instead favoured Brutus in this matter: for example, when Cicero had reached a resolution, and the Salaminians had agreed to pay Scaptius, Atticus intervened and asked Cicero to give Scaptius a prefecture to aid his debt collecting. Indeed Cicero says directly to Atticus that he believes him to have favoured Brutus over him in this matter.[56] This may strike us as odd, and it should therefore be noted at this point that Atticus was also an independent financier who managed Cato's business affairs, and quite probably also those of Cato's relatives, including those of his nephew, Brutus, who became a close friend of Atticus.[57] Therefore, Atticus' opinions on the Salamis affair were not necessarily selfless and disinterested, and this perhaps explains why he encouraged Cicero to look after Brutus' interests, and acted as an intermediary between them.[58]

Holding the post of quaestor, when serving with Appius in Cilicia, gave Brutus the opportunity to take measures to regain the money he lent. However, preferring still to remain shadily in the background, he persuaded Appius to appoint his agent Scaptius as prefect of cavalry, which thereby allowed him to pursue the recovery of the debt, even if that meant employing violent measures. It is somewhat surprising that such a supposed man of honour not only was able, but actually chose to manipulate the law and senate in passing these decrees, in order to exert power over a province, all for his own personal profit. Excuses have been sought for Brutus' actions, and judgements of misconduct made upon him as well. One point should be observed here: the actions of Brutus in lending the money secretly, and then doing his utmost to ensure he remained in the background, strongly suggest that he knew his behaviour to be somewhat reprehensible. Furthermore, it is also important to consider this situation in its context: and so it should be noted that Cicero, Brutus' contemporary, clearly disapproved of his actions. Such behaviour would certainly have been condemned, too, by the teachings of ancient philosophy, and so Brutus' actions appear to conflict with his professed ethics. Therefore, we can safely say that Brutus was not at all times the unbending, upright, moral character that he and history would perhaps have us believe.

Ariobarzanes

Nor was the Salamis affair a one-off moneylending activity:[59] Brutus also lent a large sum to Ariobarzanes III, King of Cappadocia, an area adjacent to Cilicia, and again we learn of this chiefly through the correspondence of Cicero. However, this does not appear to have tarnished his reputation as the Salamis affair did, at least not in the eyes of Cicero. He first mentions this in a letter to Atticus, where he is once again found strongly reassuring his friend that he is looking after Brutus' interests with more care than Brutus himself would and, furthermore, that he will satisfy the expectations of both of them.[60] Following a conspiracy against Ariobarzanes, the young monarch had been placed under Cicero's protection by the senate,[61] and Cicero thus claimed credit for saving his life and throne. Therefore he was in a position to negotiate with Ariobarzanes on behalf of Brutus, who had become abject regarding the return of his loaned money. Cicero reportedly consoled Brutus, for whom he claimed to have developed a fondness matching his feelings of friendship for Atticus.[62]

In February of the following year, Cicero is once more found dutifully promising Atticus that he has obliged Brutus, assuring that he has most carefully and willingly followed up all matters raised in a directive from him.[63] Ariobarzanes had offered Cicero money out of gratitude, which he instead persuaded the King to pay to Brutus as part of his debt. The repayment of the money was further complicated, however, because Ariobarzanes had also borrowed a sum from Pompey, whose agents were pressuring him. Cicero reports that Pompey was, however, acting reasonably in forgoing the original sum and only requesting that the interest be repaid: we should perhaps observe how apparently different this is from Brutus' approach with the Salaminian debt. Cicero nevertheless continued to correspond with the King in the vain hope of obtaining Brutus' money; and Deiotarus, a King in neighbouring Galatia and loyal Roman ally, also sent an envoy to Ariobarzanes on Brutus' behalf, but to no avail. Cicero genuinely believed that Ariobarzanes and his kingdom had been entirely stripped of all money, knowing that the King was forced to levy taxes from his people using methods like those of Appius, which, in any case, scarcely met the interest amount he owed Pompey: Brutus, therefore, must also have been aware that the Cappadocians were subject to harsh and exacting taxes, but nevertheless continued to press for the return of his loan.

Nor does this prevent Cicero from aiding Brutus further by bestowing prefectures on the agents working for him in Cappadocia, Lucius Gavius and a second Marcus Scaptius, as well as two further prefectures to men on Brutus' request. Cicero explains that making these appointments does not compromise his condition that no man engaged in business in his province could hold an official position, since their affairs are outside Cilicia. This Scaptius was apparently quite different in manner from his namesake and possible relative, whom we have seen involved in the murky dealings of the Salaminian affair: he reportedly had no complaints and subsequently declined the offer of the appointment. Gavius, on the other hand, behaved towards Cicero in a way that he found unacceptably arrogant and insulting. Cicero therefore considered his prefecture nullified and, when Gavius brusquely asked where he was to apply for his maintenance allowance, he simply retorted that he did not pay for services he had not received. Cicero tells Atticus that he has informed Brutus of this and, if Brutus prefers to listen to Gavius, then Atticus is welcome to his friendship alone.[64] Although Cicero here goes on to claim that he finds Brutus' own ungracious way of addressing him amusing, the tone of these comments suggests that Cicero is, perhaps understandably, becoming rather irritated by the demands of his so-called friend, Brutus.

Around two months later, the Ariobarzanes situation does not appear to have progressed any further, with Cicero merely repeating his assurances that he has done all he possibly can. However, Cicero later writes to Atticus again,[65] reporting that Ariobarzanes was just as eager to repay Brutus for Cicero's sake, as he was to pay Pompey for Pompey's sake. Being at some distance, in a different province, Cicero had some difficulty in being able to intervene only through correspondence; however, he had successfully managed to secure 100 talents for Brutus that year, which was proportionately a better return than Pompey received. This is the extent of our knowledge of this affair.

The Law Courts

The Trial of Milo (52 BC)

Brutus played a minor role in the fallout following the violent clashes between Publius Clodius Pulcher and Titus Annius Milo. Clodius, by now the uncle-in-law of Brutus, through his first wife Claudia, was Cicero's arch-enemy who had machinated the orator's exile in 58 BC and also arranged

Cato's expedition to Cyprus in that year: as we saw, both moves were carried out by the tribune with the knowledge of the Triumvirs, who wanted these inconveniences removed from Rome. However, Clodius afterwards surrounded himself with armed bands of men in order to maintain his power, generally menacing the public in the city and eventually threatening even Pompey. Consequently, the Triumvir secured the recall of Cicero from exile, particularly by supporting another tribune, Milo, who employed his own mob to counteract that of Clodius. The aggressive rivalry between Clodius and Milo continued, culminating in 53 BC, when Clodius was candidate for the position of praetor, while Milo was standing for the consulship. This resulted in violent disorder in the city between the two gangs until January 52 BC, when the ultimate skirmish broke out between them, leading to the death of Clodius. However, the city disturbances did not end there: rioting broke out, with Clodius' mob burning his body in the forum, and destroying the senate house in the process.[66]

With Crassus having been killed in Parthia in the previous year, and Caesar currently away commanding the war in Gaul, Pompey was appointed sole consul, with the approval of the optimates led by Cato: they had realised that Pompey was the lesser of two evils, and his appointment was now necessary for the sake of restoring law and order. The obvious place to begin his clean-up operation was with Milo who, although he had previously helped Pompey, was nevertheless dispensable, and became the consul's first target. The prosecution was brought against Milo,[67] with Cicero defending him out of obligation for his assistance in recalling him from exile,[68] but the orator was intimidated by the soldiers that Pompey had placed around the courtroom, as well as by the supporters of Clodius.[69] However, he had the strong support of Cato and his adherents: Cato himself had already delivered a speech in support of Milo after Clodius' death[70] and, most notable among his supporters for our purpose here, his nephew, Brutus, advised Cicero on the defence of Milo.

The defence of Milo was a difficult task, since not only were there plenty of witnesses supporting the evidence against him, but he also did not plead his innocence. Brutus' advice to Cicero was to argue that Clodius' death was of benefit to the state, but the orator preferred to take the less contentious line, which Cato's close friend, Marcus Favonius, had used as a witness to the incident: Milo was acting in self-defence.[71] However, Milo was convicted and went into exile at Massilia (Marseilles). Later, Cicero wrote a more vigorous version of the speech than he had managed to deliver in court, while Brutus similarly composed his own defence of Milo after the trial, purely as a rhetorical exercise, also entitled *pro Milone*, although this no longer survives.[72]

Although not yet at the forefront of the Roman political world, Brutus' limited involvement in this demonstrates that he was present just behind the scenes, and also confirms that he was following in his uncle Cato's footsteps as a member of the optimates. Significance perhaps can also be observed in Brutus' wish to defend assassination for the sake of the state.[73]

Defence of Appius Claudius Pulcher (50 BC)

Brutus was, by now, beginning to establish himself solidly as an advocate, pleading several important cases in the courts: according to Cicero, Brutus acted as his partner in some cases, while he pleaded others alone. Plutarch records that Brutus had the necessary skills for this, having been trained in Latin for both narrative and pleading. The details of the cases in which he was involved are, unfortunately, mostly lost to us. However, as well as his minor role in the trial of Milo, we do also know that he played a major role in defending his father-in-law, Appius Claudius Pulcher, following his return from Cilicia in 51 BC. Brutus defended Appius alongside the long-established and renowned orator, Hortensius, who died only a few days after the trial.[74]

Politically, Appius was an opportunistic and wily character who would frequently change his alliances to his advantage, and who would freely employ marriage connections for his advancement: the most significant of these, here, being the marriage of his daughter to Brutus. Appius' conduct as governor of Cilicia had been dubious, as we have already seen. Therefore, to find Appius facing a trial upon his return comes as no surprise: the prosecution was brought by Dolabella, soon to become Cicero's son-in-law.[75] It is also not surprising to find Appius' son-in-law, Brutus, a promising young advocate, who had to some extent shared in the questionable governorship of Cilicia, defending his actions. Pompey also lent his support.[76] With this combined powerful backing against the less respected prosecutor, the accusations of *maiestas* (treason or exceeding the bounds of authority) and *ambitus* (political corruption) were easily overturned:[77] indeed, the success of the defence can be seen in Appius shortly afterwards becoming censor.[78]

As well as defending his father-in-law, evidence of the relationship Brutus had with Appius, and his respect for him, can be found in his composing a *laudatio* in his honour. This was presumably written following Appius' death in 48 BC, but the contents of this eulogy are lost, and only known to us through a fragment quoted in a late Latin grammarian, Diomedes.[79]

Other Roles

Pontifex

Brutus also undertook the position of *pontifex*,[80] an office held for life, during the 50s BC. The exact year of his enrolment into this priesthood is uncertain, but we do know that one of his colleagues in this office was Quintus Caecilius Metellus Pius Scipio:[81] since Metellus Scipio fought and died on Pompey's side in the civil war, it has been recognised that Brutus must have served in the college with him at some point before the civil war began in 49 BC. Although we have no details about this aspect of Brutus' career, as a member of this pontifical college he had a responsibility for supervision of the Roman state religion. Since Julius Caesar showed Brutus favour at other times, it has been reasonably conjectured that he also owed this position to support from his mother's lover.[82]

With the arrival of the next decade, however, Brutus' promising political career was suddenly cut short by events of great magnitude for the Roman world: civil war.

Chapter Three

The Battle of Pharsalus

The early 40s BC brought the ascending public career of Brutus to an abrupt, but temporary, halt when state politics and a battle for supremacy between the two leading Romans of the day intervened.

Pompey versus Caesar (54–50 BC)

The End of the Alliance

Although this is not the place for a detailed discussion of the breach between Pompey and Caesar,[1] a brief summary of events will prove useful as background information regarding the politics and civil strife of the Rome in which Brutus was living and operating in the late 50s BC.

In 53 BC Crassus met an ignominious end, while on his disastrous military campaign against the Parthians, at the Battle of Carrhae.[2] With their fellow colleague dead, the remaining two leading men of Rome, Pompey and Caesar, were left in an alliance which, having been uneasy while Crassus was alive, became increasingly fragile. This compact had only transpired when the three men had been driven into unity by the dogged opposition of the optimates to each of them individually. The presence of a third person in this unofficial division of leadership had meant that there was never a balanced struggle for power between two men and, in this way, Crassus had been the link holding this unsanctioned Triumvirate together.

Furthermore, the familial connection between Pompey and Caesar had also been removed in the previous year: Pompey was married to Caesar's daughter, Julia, but she died in childbirth, along with the infant, in 54 BC, and so the personal link between the two no longer existed. These deaths, then, removed all connections and the way was open for the mutual political enmity between Pompey and Caesar to surface fully, at least according to the ancient sources.[3] The eventual and inevitable solution to this battle of giant political wills in Rome was for one of them to emerge triumphant, with the defeat of the other: there was room for only one of these men to exist at the forefront of public life in Rome, and a decisive outcome, fought out in the form of a civil war, became necessary.

Prelude to Civil War

With Caesar away fighting in the Gallic campaign, Pompey was declared sole consul of Rome in early 52 BC, as a measure designed to help bring the violent disorder in the city between Milo and Clodius back under control.[4] For the last five months of the year, Pompey chose a colleague to share his consulship, his new father-in-law, Quintus Caecilius Metellus Pius Scipio.[5] During his consulship, Pompey established various laws, with the outward aim of re-establishing order, including one forbidding election *in absentia*. This was a particular blow to Caesar, away in Gaul but waiting to come back to the city in dramatic fashion: he intended to return to celebrate a triumph on the same day as entering his second consulship, but his absence from Rome made it necessary for the latter to be voted on him *in absentia*, which was no longer possible. Although at first Pompey created an exception to this law, specifically with Caesar in mind, this privilege was later withdrawn. Caesar's opponents were determined to see his command in Gaul come to an end.[6] Furthermore, while Pompey's extraordinary command was extended for five years, a similar request from Caesar early in 51 BC, that his command should be extended until the beginning of his second consulship in 48 BC, was denied.

Despite the best efforts of the tribune Curio,[7] working in Rome on Caesar's behalf and proposing various compromises, events continued to conspire against Caesar, compelling him to make a choice.[8] His influential enemies, working together to manipulate the situation to appear as though Caesar was rebelling against the authority of the state, saw to it that he was to be frustrated in his wishes and, furthermore, endeavoured to diminish his sources of power, thus forcing his hand.

When the senate received an ultimatum from Caesar, Metellus Scipio responded with a demand that he should lay down his command by a fixed date or be declared an enemy of the state. Caesar realised that he must choose either the end of his political and public career, without the protection of which he knew he would also face prosecution and exile for earlier illicit actions, or war against the state. Finally, when the two tribunes, Marcus Antonius (better known to us as Mark Antony) and Quintus Cassius Longinus (probably the cousin of Cassius, the future assassin of Caesar), were forced to flee to him in Ravenna, Caesar had his pretext for war: defence of the tribunes, the voice of the people. When he crossed the Rubicon in January 49 BC to march on Rome with his forces, an act that was to become both significant and symbolic, he had made his decision: Rome was now in a state of civil war.[9]

Civil War (49–48 BC)[10]

The War in Italy

One month before Caesar committed Rome to war through his act of crossing the Rubicon, a river then acting as a natural and psychological barrier between Italy and Transalpine Gaul, Pompey had already taken the first physical steps towards martial action. In early December 50 BC, the consul Gaius Claudius Marcellus presented him with a sword and asked him to defend the Republic. Initially he ignored this but, after a short delay, Pompey went to the legions stationed in Capua, as if to prepare for war. These two legions had previously been fighting in Gaul, and herein was yet another affront to Caesar: both he and Pompey had been asked to supply a legion on the pretext of strengthening the army because of the threat from Parthia; Pompey nominated the one that he had already lent to Caesar in Gaul, thus depriving his rival's army of two legions altogether; furthermore, these troops were not sent to Syria as intended, but remained in Italy at Pompey's disposal. During a meeting with Cicero in Campania on 10 December, Pompey made it clear that civil war was now inevitable.[11]

Nevertheless, the first move of the war is attributed to Caesar on the night of 10 January 49 BC when, travelling from Ravenna to Ariminum (Rimini), he crossed the border into Italy: this was considered an invasion of the fatherland and, now that he had left his own province, he no longer had the authority to lead troops. This created an atmosphere of fear in Rome, where the memory of the recent civil wars, with the bloody actions of Marius, Caesar's uncle, and the Sullan proscriptions, were still alive.[12] This general feeling can be detected in the gloomy tone of Cicero's correspondence at the time, indicating both a sense of fear and despair.[13]

However, while Caesar led only one legion with him from Gaul, with the rest of his army to follow, Pompey had several based in both Spain and Italy and could also count on support from the east. Realising that it was imperative to move with speed rather than wait for the rest of his troops, Caesar swiftly advanced down the east side of Italy, seizing towns with little resistance, meaning that the expected bloodshed did not materialise. Although further attempts to negotiate were made, particularly on Caesar's side, it proved impossible to reach an agreement without further action. Caesar's rapid advance successfully took his opponents by surprise: not having had time to organise the troops to defend Rome, many of them hastily left the city for Campania on 23 January.[14]

The first clash between the two opposing sides took place at Corfinium (Corfinio), to the east of Rome in February. Lucius Domitius Ahenobarbus, a long-term enemy of Caesar who now replaced him as commander of the Gallic provinces, held the city: this was an act against the wishes of Pompey, who repeatedly urged him to bring his troops to join his own legions in the south. When Corfinium was then besieged by Caesar, who had now raised two legions, Pompey refused to send any aid. On learning that Ahenobarbus planned his own escape, his troops mutinied and surrendered. While most of the soldiers joined Caesar's army, Ahenobarbus and the other senators were allowed to go free: this was to be Caesar's first notable act of clemency, his famous quality which was to play an important role in later developments between him and Brutus.[15]

The War Leaves Italy

Pompey next made a strategic move, deciding to abandon the campaign in Italy and to travel to Epirus (a region encompassing areas of Greece and Albania): following the transferral of Ahenobarbus' army to Caesar, Pompey's men in Italy were now inferior in number and, furthermore, his only trained troops there had recently served under Caesar, making their loyalty in being led against their former commander doubtful; the eastern provinces, on the other hand, where Pompey had many clients and allies, could be relied upon to supply him with troops, and there he could raise and train an army with which to invade Italy.[16] Pompey therefore withdrew to Brundisium (Brindisi), on the east coast, from where he successfully and hastily crossed the Adriatic Sea to Greece, despite Caesar's attempt to block him with the construction of a mole at the harbour.

Since he did not possess a fleet with which to pursue Pompey, Caesar, now left as master of Italy, returned to Rome. There he attempted to assemble the remaining senate, seized the state treasury by force and, on 1 April, claimed the right to lead the state, with or without the senate's support. He then set out for Spain, encountering opposition from Massilia en route; he left his legates Gaius Trebonius and Decimus Junius Brutus Albinus, two of his future assassins, to conduct a siege, and the city was ready to surrender by the time Caesar returned. Once in Spain, he easily conquered Pompey's seven legions stationed there: within forty days, having been outmanoeuvred, Pompey's legates surrendered their five legions at Ilerda (Lérida, in the north-east), and the other two legions, based in the west, then also came over to Caesar. Some of the troops were added to Caesar's own, while others were disbanded, and the two previously Pompeian Spanish provinces now, in August 49 BC, belonged to Caesar.[17]

Elsewhere, however, Caesar's men had not met with the same success: Curio, who had been sent with two legions to secure Sardinia and Africa, having easily conquered Sicily, suffered a reversal of fortunes and was then annihilated near Utica (an ancient town located on the Tunisian coast) by King Juba of Numidia; Publius Cornelius Dolabella lost forty ships off the Dalmatian coast and his legate, Gaius Antonius, suffered defeat and was forced to surrender in the province of Illyricum. On his return journey from Spain, Caesar also had a mutiny to quell at Placentia (Piacenza).[18]

At the end of 49 BC, after having held a brief dictatorship in Rome of eleven days, which allowed him to secure his sought-after second consulship for the following year, Caesar moved south to Brundisium. There he joined his twelve somewhat depleted legions, with the aim of confronting Pompey in Epirus. Taking a risk, since he lacked a sufficient fleet with which to face that of Pompey, Caesar crossed the Adriatic with seven of the legions on 4 January 48 BC. He met with no opposition, since the winter made the crossing an unexpected move but, when Bibulus, the leader of Pompey's fleet and Caesar's long-term foe, realised, he blockaded Caesar and thereby prevented Antony from bringing over the remaining five legions. Furthermore, Pompey had by now had ample time to recruit a full army and carefully organise supplies, so that Caesar's troops were both severely outnumbered and lacking provisions in comparison. Given Caesar's weakness, he could not risk a clash, but instead made further, but unsuccessful, negotiation attempts.[19]

After three months, on 10 April, Antony was finally able to join Caesar in Epirus. Strengthened, but still inferior, Caesar made an attack on Pompey's supply base of Dyrrachium (Durrës on the Albanian coast, which was located at the beginning of the Via Egnatia leading to Macedonia), attempting to draw Pompey into battle, but only minor skirmishes followed. Pompey had established a fortified line of defence along the coast, in response to which Caesar built an outer line of fortifications which enclosed Pompey against the sea. Fortunes were varied, but Pompey held the major advantage: Caesar's supplies began to run short and he was forced to break away.

However, having just made a failed attack himself, Pompey did not capitalise on a disastrous attempt at assault by Caesar and, instead of seizing victory, inexplicably allowed his foe to escape.[20]

Battle of Pharsalus: The Final Clash

Having withdrawn from Dyrrachium, Caesar headed south-east into the region of Greece known as Thessaly, in search of provisions. Pompey, retaining his superiority in numbers and, believing that this would guarantee his victory, pursued him to Pharsalus (Farsala). Caesar occupied the fertile plains, and Pompey set up camp on higher ground opposite. However, still preferring to avoid conflict, he declined to engage in the battle which Caesar offered, instead attempting to deprive him of supplies and thus force him to surrender. However, all the senators with Pompey, except for Cato, applied pressure to him to bring this civil war to a swift end and to meet with the enemy in a final clash. Yielding to their wishes, on 9 August, as Caesar was preparing to move camp to find supplies, Pompey advanced on to the plain to confront his enemy. Despite Pompey's far larger army, his soldiers lacked the experience of Caesar's battle-hardened veterans.[21]

Following an unsuccessful engagement, in which his inexperienced army collapsed as their lines fell into disorder and they gradually began to retreat, Pompey fled the battlefield, and set out for Egypt. On arrival there, he met an ignominious end when he was treacherously stabbed by a man who had once served under him and who was now on the staff of the young Pharaoh, Ptolemy XIII. Pompey's head was cut off and later presented to Caesar, while his body was left unburied on the shore.[22]

Brutus' Choice: Pompey or Caesar?

The reason for here narrating the main events of the civil war between Pompey and Caesar is that Brutus, as is to be expected, since he was by now in his mid-thirties and therefore operating fully in the political world of Rome, became a participant in the unavoidable and momentous clash between the two most prominent Romans of the day. Brutus had a decision to make regarding whose side he would choose: that of Pompey or Caesar? This was by no means a straightforward choice for him.

Brutus was, of course, to be found numbered among the supporters of his uncle Cato's circle, the optimates. The breach between Pompey and Caesar had been fostered by Cato and his group, who were manoeuvring behind Pompey and encouraging opposition to Caesar. They had decided, reluctantly, that Pompey was the lesser of two evils and so chose him to help them defend the cause of the Republic.[23] This support had initially transpired while Caesar was away in Gaul, when the optimates decided to back Pompey in gaining the sole consulship. Following this, they realised they could, to some extent, employ and manipulate Pompey for the sake of their mission against the growing military might of Caesar, and certainly that they could encourage the break-up of the coalition.

It was the optimates who had remained determined that Caesar must return to Rome as a private citizen so that they could see him prosecuted for his dubious behaviour during his first consulship. This stubbornness ultimately forced the state into civil war: they repeatedly rejected the compromises Caesar offered, including one that both he and Pompey should give up their commands, which could have averted the disastrous clash of arms, and which the vast majority of the senate would have preferred to accept. Indeed, it seems that it was only the optimates who wanted this: Caesar repeatedly attempted negotiations, Pompey remained hesitant for some time, and the rest of the senate, an overwhelming majority of 370 against just 22, voted for this compromise. This behaviour, and particularly their overriding of the tribunician veto, which forced the tribunes, Antony and Cassius, to flee Rome, made the optimates' claims to be defending high principles, legality and the liberty of the state, somewhat dubious.[24] However, there is no indication in the ancient sources of whether or not Brutus was playing any active part in these political machinations: as a relatively young senator still, it can be assumed that he remained fairly peripheral in any manoeuvrings at this stage, although we may surmise that he was one of the 22 rather than the 370. Nevertheless, we can say with certainty that Brutus had a strong political inclination, and that it sat firmly with the optimates: he was Republican through and through.

This was not a straightforward choice for Brutus, however, for two principal reasons. Firstly he harboured a deep-seated hatred of Pompey, which derived from the leader's cold-blooded murder of his father while Brutus was still only a child: indeed, he was said never to have spoken to Pompey for this reason and, furthermore, had a certain Roman obligation of enmity (*inimicitiae*) towards him on behalf of his murdered father. Secondly, Brutus' mother, Servilia, as Caesar's lover, instead favoured his cause and encouraged her son similarly to follow and support it. According to Plutarch, at least, he was expected to side with Caesar.[25] There were reports at the time that Caesar was making claims to be avenging the deaths of Brutus' father and other victims of Pompey during the Sullan period:[26] this may have led to such an expectation that Brutus would be more inclined towards Caesar. However, Brutus was a man of strong principles, and this naturally involved him choosing to place the welfare of the state before any personal feelings: Caesar's domination was not considered to be in the best interests of Rome. Furthermore, his mother's relationship with Caesar would not have endeared him to Brutus, but rather would have been a major source of embarrassment to him.[27] Faced with an unenviable choice between two political leaders, neither of whom he liked in either a personal or political capacity, Brutus put aside his personal feelings and opted to follow the cause that could be considered closest to the moral benefit of the state. And so, following his uncle's lead, Brutus threw in his lot with Pompey, the man whom he had never, until this point, acknowledged.[28]

Brutus' Role in the War

Having placed himself under the leadership of his enemy, Pompey, Brutus first took up the post of legate to Publius Sestius, a friend of Cicero who had taken over from him as proconsul of Cilicia. However, having sailed to the province, Brutus realised that there was little to be done there, and soon decided instead to join Pompey's forces in Macedonia, in preparation for the impending clash of arms. Plutarch reports that Pompey was so delighted to see Brutus join his side that he rose from his seat to greet and embrace him as a superior before all. The implication of this characteristic Plutarchean anecdote is that Brutus was adding prestige and moral vigour to Pompey's cause by his very presence: his honourable nature, having thus become suitable as a legendary topic, indicates the outstanding reputation of Brutus.[29]

Further adding to his respected reputation, and his image as a learned man devoted to study, are the reported activities of Brutus while he was in the camp: he was said to have spent any spare part of the day, which was not taken up with Pompey and the campaign, on books and literature. However, that is not to suggest that he was trying to avoid the fighting: according to Cicero, whose late and reluctant attachment to Pompey's side and absence from the battlefield are both notable, Brutus eagerly engaged in the cause once he had decided to support Pompey.[30] Nevertheless, even on the eve of the final clash at Pharsalus, while others were resting or worrying about the approaching battle, Brutus was reportedly to be found busy in the honourable occupation of studying: we are informed that he endured a long and tiring day in the heat of high summer in their marshy encampment, since the soldiers carrying his tent, which would provide some shade, had taken some time to arrive; nevertheless, although it was almost midday before he anointed himself and ate just a small amount of food, he worked on into the evening composing an epitome of *The Histories* of Polybius.[31]

We have no record of the role that Brutus played during the fighting of the final clash. All we know for certain is that he was on the losing side and, after Pompey had fled the battlefield and the camp was besieged, Brutus managed to escape through a gate which led into a waterlogged and reedy swamp. From there he travelled overnight to safety in nearby Larissa (Larisa).[32]

Events After the War (48–47 BC)

Caesar's Clemency

Brutus had escaped safely but, in any case, it is said that, for the sake of his mother, Brutus was to be preserved at all costs by the opposing side: Plutarch reports that Caesar was most concerned for the safety of his lover's son during the battle, ordering that no violence should be done towards Brutus, so that he should only be taken prisoner if he gave himself up willingly, and that he must not be killed on any account. Furthermore, as Caesar surveyed the fallen on the battlefield, lamenting that the optimates had wanted it this way, he was said to have been distressed when Brutus could not be found.[33]

From Caesar's purported attitude towards Brutus, we can assume that he would have warmly welcomed him, just as Pompey did, had Brutus initially chosen to fight on his side in the civil war. However, Caesar need not have worried about his would-be protégé's welfare and choice of leader, since Brutus had escaped the war unharmed and was soon to transfer his allegiances to the victor of Pharsalus. This desire to preserve Brutus and win him over should surely be attributed to the principled reputation of this nephew of Cato, as much as to the identity of the man's mother, since such a man could only lend political weight to his chosen side and leader.[34] When Caesar received a letter from Brutus in Larissa, he was thus overjoyed to learn of his safety, and invited Brutus to come to him. Brutus then became the fortunate beneficiary of Caesar's famous *clementia*, or mercy, when Caesar not only gladly pardoned him but also made him a favoured companion. Indeed, Caesar also extended this clemency beyond his favourites, sparing the lives of many others at Brutus' request. The only person explicitly named among these is Cassius, the future fellow conspirator of Brutus, on whose behalf Plutarch claims Brutus successfully petitioned Caesar.[35]

Plutarch relates the story, somewhat undercutting Brutus' usual good reputation in the Greek biographer's work, that he became the informant of Pompey's whereabouts. According to his account, Caesar, having received conflicting reports about Pompey's likely location, took a walk alone with Brutus in order to ascertain his opinion on the matter. Believing him to be the most reliable source, Caesar immediately acted on Brutus' suggestion that Pompey had gone to Egypt, but reached the country too late, after Pompey had been assassinated. However, caution should be urged here: this seems an improbable tale, in view of Caesar's own version of events, where he reports that he set out for Egypt, guessing the kingdom to be Pompey's intended destination when he heard that his opponent had been seen in Cyprus, and knowing that he had connections there. What Plutarch's account does, perhaps, illustrate is the belief that Brutus had now shifted his allegiances entirely from Pompey to Caesar.[36]

Defence of Deiotarus

Brutus did not return to Rome immediately after the war and his reconciliation with Caesar, but remained in Asia Minor. Once more the details of his activities during this period are limited. We do know, however, that Brutus took up his advocacy role again, in the defence of his own and Rome's old ally, Deiotarus, King of Galatia (a region of Asia Minor). Like Brutus himself, Deiotarus had at first supported Pompey, but switched his allegiances to Caesar after Pharsalus. When Caesar arrived in Asia Minor near his kingdom, Deiotarus went to him as a suppliant, and the victor, displaying his characteristic clemency once more, pardoned Deiotarus and allowed him to retain his kingship.[37] However, Caesar forced the tetrarch to give up portions of his kingdom, following complaints received from neighbouring Galatian princes, who were disputing his position as tetrarch over the entire kingdom of Galatia, claiming parts of it as their own. It was on this point that Brutus interceded before Caesar on behalf of Deiotarus, in the summer of 47 BC at Nicaea (Iznik). We are told that Brutus, although not entirely successful, aided the monarch in retaining some of these areas.[38]

To his credit, this displays that Brutus, despite having recently changed sides, nevertheless remained committed to a cause and continued to speak up for what he believed, even when it contradicted the views of his new and powerful friend, Caesar. Indeed, it is in this context that Plutarch confirms

Brutus' commitment to morally worthwhile causes only, noting that he would refuse to grant petitions on an unjust basis, but would forcefully argue his point on high-principled grounds. Therefore, Brutus' moral nature and selectiveness meant that whenever he undertook a case, his very involvement lent his side a weighty and convincing argument. Brutus' strength of conviction was such that he supposedly criticised those who generally found themselves unable to refuse anything, harshly declaring that they must have been corrupted in their youth.[39]

As is so often the case with Brutus, we lack much of the evidence, since the speech for Deiotarus is no longer extant; however, some opinions on its quality have been passed down to us. During the case, Caesar himself commented on how Brutus spoke vigorously and freely, and was also reported as observing that 'what he wants is of the greatest importance; but whatever he wants, he wants badly'.[40] Cicero also described the speech as most ornate and abundant, although this was in the context of a work dedicated to Brutus and containing, therefore, a note of flattery. Elsewhere, later opinion has not been so kind: in Tacitus, the speech was condemned as dull and tepid.[41]

Perhaps also worth noting here is the existence of a speech of Cicero, addressed to Caesar in 45 BC, defending the same Deiotarus.[42] This charge, brought by Deiotarus' grandson, interestingly accuses the King of an attempted assassination of Caesar, while he was staying in Galatia after the civil war. The matter was never fully resolved since, before Caesar could investigate further, he instead met his end at the hands of real assassins much closer to home; however, it was generally believed that Deiotarus' grandson was bringing a false accusation because of a hostile family feud.

Brutus' Greek Encounters

Before his return to Rome after the civil war, we know of two stops that Brutus made in Greece, both of which involved meetings with statesmen who had been prominent in Roman politics during the turbulent period leading up to the civil war. We learn of these encounters from Cicero's fictional conversation with Brutus on the history of orators: this was a work addressed to him which was eponymously entitled *Brutus*.

During a sojourn at Mytilene on the island of Lesbos, Brutus visited Marcus Claudius Marcellus who, as consul in 51 BC, had been one of the foremost men strongly opposed to Caesar and was among those actively obstructing him at that time.[43] As a follower of Pompey, Marcellus withdrew into self-imposed exile in the Greek town after having fought on the unsuccessful side at Pharsalus. While visiting Marcellus in Mytilene, Brutus heard him speak and, according to the words that Cicero has put in Brutus' mouth, he was much impressed with the former consul's oratorical skill.[44] Cicero also has Brutus add political comment here, praising Marcellus for his ability to console himself in these times, with his integrity and renewed literary pursuits. Cicero's fictional portrayal seems borne out by Brutus' real views: he is known to have written an essay on virtue, *de Virtute*, in which he praised Marcellus for his keen pursuit of literature while in exile, and observed that the man seemed most happy and was thus fortunate in his exilic position; indeed, Brutus seemed disappointed to leave him, saying that he felt that it was he himself going into exile by doing so.[45]

Brutus made another Greek stopover, this time on the Greek island of Samos, where he met with the other consul of 51 BC, Servius Sulpicius Rufus. Sulpicius had attempted to remain more neutral during the civil strife between Pompey and Caesar, although unable to avoid the clash altogether, and had withdrawn to the island after the war.[46] He was an eminent and much-respected jurist, and the comments attributed to Brutus by Cicero are suitably complimentary.[47] Given Sulpicius' reputation, Brutus sought instruction from him on pontifical law in connection with matters of civil law, which undoubtedly proved interesting and useful to him, given his role as *pontifex*.[48] In the fictional conversation between Cicero and Brutus, the latter claims to have heard Sulpicius speak, both often and eagerly while on Samos. Again inserting a political comment, in addition to some flattery of himself, Cicero has Brutus lament that the state has lately been deprived of Sulpicius' advice and Cicero's voice. To portray Brutus thus complimenting him is, perhaps, evidence of Cicero's respect for the man and his opinions on oratory, as is the work itself, which is not only dedicated to Brutus, but also depicts him, Cicero and Atticus engaged in an educated and equal discussion of the subject.

Before he returned to Rome, then, Brutus took further time away in order to make these visits to learned men and hear them speak. This perhaps adds to the impression that Brutus was more interested in study than matters of state, although it has been feasibly suggested that his purpose in visiting these two ex-consuls was motivated by an attempt to reconcile them with Caesar, with whom he himself was now on good terms. It is notable here that Brutus later wrote to Cicero exculpating Caesar from Marcellus' murder, which took place as he was returning from exile in 45 BC. Brutus was inevitably drawn into the world of politics and war, which currently engulfed him and the Roman world, whether he liked it or not.[49]

Chapter Four

Cato: Death of the Ultimate Republican

With Pompey defeated at the Battle of Pharsalus, and soon after murdered treacherously in Egypt, the path to power seemed to have been cleared for Caesar. However, before he could be declared the undoubted victor and emerge as the most prominent Roman of the day, the smouldering embers of the civil war needed to be extinguished. No sooner had Caesar returned to Rome after settling matters in the east, in late 47 BC, than he found it necessary to set out again, before the year was out, on a new campaign: this time in North Africa.

The War in Africa (47–46 BC)

Cato's Role in the Civil War

Pockets of resistance to Caesar still remained, one of which consisted of those resolute Republicans who had neither surrendered nor sought Caesar's pardon after the battle. One of the leaders of this opposition was, once more, Cato, Brutus' uncle and steadfast enemy of Caesar. Cato had been foremost among those senators who had been determined to deny Caesar's wishes, and thereby played a large role in initially forcing Rome into a state of civil war.

When the war between Pompey and Caesar had broken out, Cato set out for his allotted province of Sicily. He had been given command of the island, and was making preparations for war there, but put up little resistance when Caesar sent Curio to seize Sicily on his way to Africa: on learning of his approach, Cato swiftly abandoned the island, realising he could not hope to match Curio in a battle, and intending thereby to avoid unnecessary bloodshed for the Sicilians.[1] After having joined Pompey, Cato was dispatched to Asia, but found he was not needed there. Cato played a part in raising a fleet for Pompey, when he persuaded the Greek island of Rhodes to supply ships to the Pompeians. Pompey was said to have been on the point of giving command of the fleet to Cato, until he remembered, or was reminded, that this would concentrate enough power in Cato's hands to enable him to seek the liberty he wanted for his country, by ordering the victor to lay down his command after the war. The staunch Republican is also reported to have delivered a rousing and effective speech to the soldiers at Dyrrachium. When Pompey set out from Dyrrachium to Thessaly, in pursuit of Caesar, Cato did not go to Pharsalus to take part in the fighting, as his nephew Brutus did: instead he was left behind and put in command of the camp and all its possessions, since Pompey was said both to have trusted and feared Cato.[2]

On learning of Pompey's defeat, Cato resolved to join him and set out for Africa, where he expected to find the vanquished leader. However, on arriving in Libya he met Pompey's son, Sextus, who informed him that his father had met his tragic end in Egypt. Cato then decided to join forces with Pompey's father-in-law, Metellus Scipio, who had managed to raise a large army in North Africa, with the support of King Juba.[3] Caesar hastily left Rome for Africa, after having returned to the city only shortly before, in order to put down this resistance. After a hard-fought struggle, on 6 April 46 BC Caesar defeated Metellus Scipio to win the Battle of Thapsus (an ancient city located on the coast of Tunisia).[4]

Cato Uticensis

Meanwhile, Cato was stationed in the Caesarian city of Utica, north of Thapsus, and was, therefore, once again nowhere to be found in the fighting, as Metellus Scipio pointedly observed. Cato had prevented him from putting to death all the citizens in order to please King Juba, and so had been given the duty of guarding the city, which suited both the citizens and Metellus Scipio. While there, Cato set about making the city a supplies store for the Pompeians, simultaneously protecting the citizens, but Plutarch reports that he felt despair regarding his side's chance of victory, and rightly so.[5]

However, when news of the defeat at Thapsus reached Cato, he did not immediately give up all hope, summoning together and exhorting his senate along with the senators from Rome who were present in the city. It was proposed that they should free their slaves in order to aid defence of Utica. The 300 men who made up his senate were businessmen, however, and so their loyalty to the cause was not strong; suspecting this, Cato advised King Juba and Metellus Scipio to keep away from Utica. In the meantime, the cavalry who had escaped from Thapsus had approached the city but were also wavering: Cato went out with the senators in order to persuade them to join him in defending Utica, but they distrusted the citizens and left while

Cato returned to the 300 men, who had by now become restless and decided that seeking Caesar's mercy was the best option. Finally accepting that all was lost, Cato worked to secure the safety of the senators, supplying ships for their escape.[6]

Caesar hurried to Utica after his victory at Thapsus, but was frustrated in his hopes of taking his Republican arch-enemy alive, for Cato had committed suicide. Cato, recognising the futility of resisting any longer, advised others to seek Caesar's mercy but he himself, by pursuing his own death, purposely and honourably avoided receiving his long-term foe's famous clemency. He calmly went to bed and, after having read some of Plato's philosophy, a habit of studying literature at moments of crisis that his nephew clearly inherited, stabbed himself; although friends had tried to dissuade him and bound up the wound, he was determined to meet his death and, since this wound did not prove fatal, he secretly opened it up again and eventually died. The citizens of Utica buried Cato with honours, in gratitude for his treatment of the city, and he henceforth became known as Cato Uticensis.[7]

Cato's suicide was a last attempt at resistance of, and opposition to, Caesar, which was clearly effective since it proved a source of irritation to the victor: according to Plutarch, Caesar, on learning of Cato's suicide, exclaimed that he begrudged Cato his death, as Cato had begrudged him the opportunity to save his life. Indeed, the ancient sources portray this as a deliberate act of defiance, with Cato denying Caesar the chance to pardon him, which he believed would have meant yielding to the victor's tyranny.[8]

After Cato's Death (46–45 BC)

Influence After Death

Even from beyond the grave, Cato was able to continue to harass Caesar, as he had done, relentlessly, in life. When Caesar was celebrating his quadruple triumph in 46 BC, ostensibly over four of his recently defeated foreign enemies, he foolishly also displayed images of the deaths of some Roman foes who had died in the course of the civil war, including one of Cato committing suicide.[9] However, Caesar had misjudged the situation, since this insensitive move provoked a groan from the disappointed and grieving spectators: Cato had won once more.

Initially Brutus was said to have disapproved of Cato's suicide, believing it to be a cowardly act, although he later re-evaluated this opinion in light of his own similar situation.[10] Nevertheless, it is reasonable to suppose that he felt a sense of great loss at the death of the uncle to whom he had always been close, and also, given the reported general reaction, that he was affronted by the inappropriate display at Caesar's triumph.

Soon after Cato's death, and despite his recently formed attachment to Caesar, Brutus defiantly showed his respect for his beloved uncle by requesting that Cicero should write an eponymous eulogy of him.[11] This also proved to be a source of annoyance to Caesar, who considered it to be a denunciation of himself, and so countered the *Cato* angrily in the following year with an *Anti-Cato*, containing many charges against his dead enemy, whom he portrayed most negatively.[12] The victor of the civil war thus revealed that Cato continued to be his nemesis, even after death. Cicero had perhaps predicted this reaction, when he was keen to put down in writing, publicly, that he had authored the *Cato* only at the instigation of Brutus, clearly wanting him to share responsibility for this work.[13] Brutus, patently not concerned about offending Caesar, afterwards decided to add his own voice to this matter of personal importance, when he followed Cicero's version up with his own encomium of his uncle; this, in turn, caused Cicero offence because, according to the elder statesman, the content gave Cato too much credit for his role in suppressing the Catilinarian conspiracy, thereby diminishing Cicero's own proud claims to have saved the state.[14]

Caesar's repeated displays of inappropriate behaviour, in continuing to fight a war against a dead man while others were revering him as a hero of the state, revealed that Cato was the one man who could truly get under his skin, and also that Caesar was emerging as the loser in this particular, moral, battle. These actions did nothing to enhance his own reputation and also cast doubt over his famous clemency.[15] Caesar, however, did not appear to take great offence at the writers of the eulogies personally, only the content of the writing, since his relationships with Cicero and Brutus were maintained as before. Indeed, Caesar's recorded comments about the works seem diplomatic in making reference only to the style: he claimed that repeatedly reading Cicero's eulogy improved his own style, while he was less complimentary about Brutus' work, finding himself eloquent in comparison with his style of writing.[16] Later, however, Augustus, presumably feeling it necessary to defend the honour of his slaughtered adoptive father, wrote a *Reply to Brutus on Cato*.[17]

Once dead, Cato's steadfast values immortalised him as a hero of the Republic, and he remained an icon to which hopeful or oppressed Republicans could cling ever after, as the ultimate example to be emulated.

For Cato was held as a hero not only in the immediate civil strife following the defeat of the Pompeians, but also during the early days of the Roman Empire which emerged from the civil wars.[18] Given this lasting influence, the death of Cato undoubtedly had a powerful impact on Brutus, and the effect of his uncle's honourable reputation must surely have played some part in inspiring and encouraging his future Republican actions.

Brutus' Advancement (47–45 BC)

An obvious question to be addressed at this point is, if Brutus was so eager to support his now-deceased uncle and his Republican values, where was he when Cato was fighting and dying in Africa? For, at that time, Brutus was not to be found supportively beside his uncle, as we might expect, but was instead enjoying the benefits of his newfound reconciliation with the merciful Caesar, as he picked up his public career from where it had been abruptly cut short by the civil war.

Governorship of Cisalpine Gaul

In 47 BC, Caesar designated Brutus as the governor of Cisalpine Gaul for the following year.[19] This was an open demonstration of Caesar's faith that Brutus had transferred his allegiances to him from Pompey, Cato and the Republicans, after Pharsalus, or, at least, it displayed Caesar's hope that he had won Brutus over and was his attempt thereby to secure his loyalty. Not only had Caesar pardoned Brutus, following his support of the wrong side in the civil war, but he now bestowed this privilege upon him, which can perhaps be considered evidence of his fondness and respect for Brutus, since this position of command, probably as a *legatus pro praetore*, was quite an honour. The highest position Brutus had held previously on the political ladder was that of quaestor, the most junior administrative role of the *cursus honorum*. His new role as propraetor, an office which involved governing a province, was normally taken up only after a full year as praetor had been served, and the role of praetor was expected to follow a term as aedile. Therefore, by placing Brutus in this office, Caesar was helping him to make a significant career leap upwards, although such moves were not entirely without precedent.[20]

Furthermore, this was an exceptional office to give to a relatively inexperienced politician because of the province chosen. Cisalpine Gaul was an area approximately corresponding to that of North Italy between the Rubicon River and the Alps. Not only was its proximity to Rome of positional significance, but it was an important province to Caesar himself: he had spent several years governing Cisalpine Gaul, with much of that time fighting in and conquering further Gaul, and could rely on the area for loyal troops. It was also, of course, from this region that Caesar had crossed the Rubicon and invaded Italy, thereby beginning the civil war and, while Brutus was commanding this province, the remnants of that war were still lingering on in Africa in the form of his uncle Cato and the other committed Republicans. It is also notable that significant provinces, such as Cisalpine Gaul, would often be governed by an ex-consul, as proconsul, meaning that Brutus had received an even greater privilege through this command.

Brutus thus followed in his father's footsteps as governor of Cisalpine Gaul, for it was in this province, thirty years earlier, that the elder Brutus had met his untimely end at the hands of the treacherous Pompey, while leading the forces of the region in the rebellion against the Sullan constitution.[21] Brutus left for the province in early 46 BC and continued as governor there into the spring of the following year, when his return to Rome was anticipated.[22] Marcus Terentius Varro Gibba, who later fought and died with the Liberators at Philippi, was assigned to him as his quaestor.[23]

While in post in Gaul, Brutus received a series of letters from Cicero,[24] seeking to secure his favour for friends and acquaintances, especially men from his home town of Arpinum (Arpino), recommending them to Brutus by focusing on aspects of their character which were calculated to impress him. These letters concerned matters of money owed and rent collection from estates in Cisalpine Gaul: as governor, Brutus would have had a judicial capacity over such affairs. Whether or not these letters had any influence on Brutus we do not know, although, given his occasional open display of disrespect for Cicero and his inherent stubbornness, we may suspect that he made his own judgements on the worthiness of such causes.

Whatever the outcome of Cicero's correspondence, it seems certain that Brutus governed the province with success and fairness, since the accounts are unanimous in recording the gratitude of the people of Cisalpine Gaul for his treatment of them. Singing Brutus' praises as a most venerable and agreeable character, Cicero claims that the province's fortune in uniquely not being involved in the civil war is thanks to their governor.[25] Similarly, Plutarch reports that Brutus' governorship was most fortunate for the province, since he brought relief and consolation to the people following their previous misfortunes. It has been suggested that this may have been, in part, due to

Brutus not demanding the full quota of military levies: in recent years Caesar had often relied on the province as a source of troops for his various wars, so a break from providing young men for Roman armies would have been an overdue and welcome relief.[26] Furthermore, Plutarch notes that this was exceptional behaviour by Brutus, since it was in contrast to most other governors of provinces, whose greed in pursuit of financial opportunities he compares to the ruthless plundering of the vanquished in war. This now seems a quite different man from the Brutus who, several years ago, as quaestor of Cilicia, had subjected the city of Salamis to extortion.[27] Confirming its gratitude, the city of Mediolanum (Milan) erected a bronze statue of Brutus to acknowledge the benefits that the people had received while under his governorship, and it was said to be of impressive craftsmanship and a good likeness of the man. Furthermore, this statue stood the test of time, unlike the man himself: it was still in place during Augustus' reign as Emperor, being called upon by men in the name of freedom.[28]

According to Plutarch, Brutus ensured that the people of Cisalpine Gaul realised that they owed much not only to himself, but also to Caesar and, in consequence, the latter was most pleased to discover the contented cities of the province when he visited them upon his return from the war in Africa. Despite previous significant differences between the two men, and despite Cato's lasting opposition to Caesar until his death during this period, Brutus' successful governorship seemed to attach him to Caesar even more closely: Plutarch records that Caesar was delighted to have Brutus as a companion at this time.[29] Overall, then, Brutus' governorship of Gaul can be considered a success and credit to him.

Cicero's Dedications to Brutus

It was during this period that Cicero addressed two of his written works to Brutus, a sure sign of the orator's respect and admiration for the man. These dedications were perhaps also an indication of Cicero's hopes for the Roman Republic, which he seemingly invested in Brutus, and maybe now more so than ever before. Brutus was currently enjoying the favour of the leading Roman of the day, and perhaps it was assumed that he thus was also able to exert some influence on Caesar. Cicero's dedicatory works were the *Brutus* and the *Orator*, both of which can be dated to 46 BC from clear references to events contained within them.

The *Brutus* is a history of oratory, presented in the form of a fictional dialogue between Brutus, Atticus and Cicero. It was written in early 46 BC, before Brutus had departed for his post as governor in Gaul and, in it, Cicero honours his two friends for recent kindnesses. By the end of 48 BC, Cicero had descended into despondency following his choices regarding the civil war, as a series of his letters to Atticus reveal.[30] Having been caught in uncertainty between the two sides of the civil war, in these letters we find a man who is often seeking approval for his actions, as well as petitioning for help in gaining Caesar's favour: Cicero eventually abandoned the Pompeians after Pharsalus in order to return to Italy and, from late 48 BC, he nervously remained in Brundisium for some months; with the Pompeians gathering strength in Africa, Cicero was now unsure that Caesar, the winner at Pharsalus, would become the victor of the entire civil war, and he was concerned that he would be considered a traitor by whichever side won.

According to this dialogue, it took an encouraging and admonishing letter of advice and consolation from Brutus to revive Cicero and bring him back to his old self. Indeed, Cicero speaks of its effects in restoring him from his serious state of depression and despair in terms scarcely short of the miraculous:[31] Brutus' ability to turn Cicero's mood so dramatically must testify, once more, to the respect and admiration the elder statesman felt for this up-and-coming politician, and quite probably also to the hope for the future that he placed in him. It seems that, on this occasion, Brutus extended more kindness and respect towards Cicero than he had done at previous times: the letter, which is described as affectionate, appears to have been considerately calculated to win Cicero around, since we are told that, in it, Brutus reminded Cicero of his many achievements and benefits to the state, which would live on after his death.[32] Brutus, exercising his judgement, must have known very well that Cicero was a proud man to whom reputation and honour, particularly in relation to the state, were matters of the utmost importance. It has also been reasonably suggested that the purpose of the letter was, at least in part, to aid reconciliation between Cicero and Caesar, with whom we know that Brutus had, by now, made his peace.[33] Although we cannot say if Brutus and his letter played any part in it, we certainly do know that in late September 47 BC Caesar greeted Cicero warmly at a meeting in Brundisium and subsequently, by the beginning of October, Cicero was on his way back home; having received Caesar's famous clemency, it seems that the two men thereafter held a mutual respect for each other.[34]

Brutus sent the crucial letter from Asia Minor, where he spent some time on his return from Pharsalus, and it has been posited that it was, in fact, the *De Virtute* treatise that Brutus wrote following his visit to Marcellus in

Mytilene, although this view has not been fully accepted.[35] Whatever the full nature of this letter to Cicero, in genuinely grateful response, the recipient produced this dedicatory work for Brutus. Atticus is also honoured by his appearance in this dialogue because he had recently put together valuable historical annals, which he had dedicated to Cicero, who acknowledges that these detailed chronological lists had made this current historical work possible.[36] Both Brutus' letter and Atticus' annals seem to have encouraged Cicero to return to literary pursuits and given him some drive and purpose again, and for that he is evidently grateful to both men. Cicero therefore speaks to, and of, Brutus in respectful and affectionate terms throughout the piece, revealing his own fondness, and also that of Atticus, for him. There is also, as is perhaps to be expected from the fraught political situation in which they found themselves, some comment on current affairs of the state in the dialogue: Cicero credits Brutus with certain opinions in accord with his own, although we cannot, of course, be certain that he necessarily held or agreed with these views.

In the course of the dialogue, we are also furnished with some incidental details about Brutus, whose biography, as we have seen, is relatively thin and patchy up until the mid-40s BC. Brutus mentions contemporaries and acquaintances: he notes that he was friends with the tribune of 54 BC, Quintus Mucius Scaevola, at whose house he would often meet Gaius Rutilius; he says that he was pleased to have heard Licinia, daughter of the great orator Lucius Crassus, speak; and he laments the recent deaths of two Pompeians in the civil war, Lucius Torquatus and Valerius Triarius. We discover that Brutus would often attend conferences between Cicero and the renowned orator, Hortensius, before cases on which they worked together, and that in some cases Brutus also had a role, whether jointly with them or alone. Cicero also mentions that he and Brutus are neighbours in Tusculum, in the Alban hills just outside Rome, and it is clear from the setting of the dialogue that Brutus, as well as Atticus, would visit Cicero at his different villas.[37]

Brutus also speaks of Calvus, the leader of the Atticists, as being their mutual good friend.[38] Atticism was a simpler oratorical style, favoured by Brutus over the more ornate manner of the Asiatic style, of which Cicero was an exponent. It was from this point of difference that the *Orator*, also dedicated to Brutus, took its departure. Written later in 46 BC, as a response to repeated requests from Brutus,[39] the work takes the form of a letter addressed to him. In it Cicero delineates the perfect orator, while defending his own traditional style of rhetoric against the criticisms of the more restrained Atticists: it is apparent that such criticisms also came from Brutus. He has often been considered an Atticist, and Cicero tells us that his aim was to imitate the Attic models, but it is not clear whether Brutus actually subscribed to the school or simply possessed Attic tendencies in his style.[40] Despite the stance of defending himself, Cicero remains warm and affectionate, as well as fulsomely complimentary, towards his addressee and friend throughout. However, it has been suggested that Cicero had an ulterior, political, motive in this, since Brutus was currently in favour with Caesar. Reportedly, Brutus responded to both Cicero and Atticus to say that he could not agree with Cicero's view of the best style of oratory.[41]

Brutus was devoted to philosophy, and Cicero flatteringly claims that he was one of the most learned in the field.[42] Brutus had encouraged Cicero's pursuits in this field, as well as devoting his own *de Virtute* to him, so that Cicero, in turn, felt obliged to return the compliment.[43] These were the reasons Cicero gave for dedicating several philosophical works to Brutus during this period: the *Paradoxa Stoicorum* (*Paradoxes of the Stoics*) appears to have been written while Cato was still alive, probably in 46 BC, while the *de Finibus Bonorum et Malorum* (*On the Ends of Good and Evil*), *de Natura Deorum* (*On the Nature of the Gods)*, and *Disputationes Tusculanae* (*Tusculan Disputations*) were all composed in 45 BC, following the death of Cicero's beloved daughter, Tullia, early in that year. As well as underscoring Brutus' interest in philosophy, since he was Cicero's inspiration for writing these philosophical works, and offering a glimpse of the nature of the relationship between the two men, we also learn something of Brutus' views and beliefs from these dedicatory philosophical works. In particular, book five of the *Disputationes Tusculanae* takes its departure from Brutus' claim, in his *de Virtute* (*On Virtue*), that virtue was sufficient for a contented life: the book contains a fictional discussion on the matter, in which Cicero puts opposing arguments into the mouths of others, thereby allowing him to avoid offending Brutus, towards whom he so often appears deferential.

During 45 BC, however, there is a sense that relations between Cicero and Brutus became slightly strained once more. Writing these philosophical works provided Cicero with some distraction from his bereavement, and consolation in his grief, which was apparently quite unlike the letter that he received from Brutus on Tullia's death: although described as sensible and friendly, this was reportedly somewhat cold and insensitive, provoking tears from the recipient, with its reproachful tone telling the mournful father simply to stop grieving and carry on with life; nonetheless, Cicero writes to Atticus in March, saying that he wishes that both he and Brutus could be with him to help alleviate his distress. In May of the same year, Cicero asks Atticus to chide Brutus for declining an invitation to stay at his villa at Cumae (Cuma), although we know neither Brutus' reason, nor the weight of Cicero's comment. A month later, Cicero mentions not being able to visit Brutus, who had wanted to see him daily at his own country villa, and had reportedly lost enjoyment of it because of this: the probable reason for Cicero's refusal here was his period of mourning, and he speaks of them soon meeting up at Tusculum, where they both owned villas. In July, Cicero tells Atticus that he would have preferred to have visited Brutus in Rome, rather than have him come to Tusculum, noting that their states of mind were such that they could not currently live in each other's company. However, simultaneously Cicero was preparing the dedicatory works for Brutus, since he mentions, in the same letter, one of them as being with the copyist. Perhaps their relationship was a little difficult at this time, but there was certainly nothing seriously wrong, nor was it beyond repair: only a couple of days later, when writing to Atticus, Cicero was eagerly seeking to learn of Brutus' affections for him. Furthermore, both of them had personal matters that would have been creating a distraction from their normal concerns at this time.[44]

Marriage to Cato's Daughter[45]

As a man on the up, thanks in no small part to his transferred allegiances, Brutus' next move is a somewhat surprising and pointed one: it seems that he was unable to neglect his roots and principles entirely, perhaps, we may speculate, never having been able to forget that he was not faithfully by his uncle's side when he died, since it was at this point that he married his cousin, Porcia. This appears to have been a fairly deliberate move, since it was necessary for Brutus first to divorce Appius' daughter, Claudia, and his second marriage then took place soon after, causing something of a stir. Indeed it all seemed to happen quickly, since Cicero was writing of the divorce in mid-June and, from his comments, the marriage had clearly taken place by early July.[46] Of course, while we cannot be certain of his reasons for the match, and it should not necessarily be read as an act of defiance towards Caesar, it does, nevertheless, seem proof that Brutus cannot have transferred his allegiances to Caesar entirely or, at least, was socialising and operating in the circles of those who had not: his new wife was the daughter of Cato and widow of another of Caesar's long-term enemies,

Bibulus. This marriage may not have damaged his career, but surely cannot have benefitted it, since he was happily enjoying the advantages of a recent reconciliation with Caesar: perhaps it is this that has caused a reluctance in some to see this as a political move and led them to believe that it must have been motivated by love instead which, of course, is a possibility.[47] Regardless of his original reasons for marrying her, Porcia would contribute to Brutus' future Republican actions through her support and encouragement in that direction.

A Conflict of Interests

The source of Brutus' rising success in his public career, Julius Caesar, was simultaneously the cause of his uncle Cato's demise. It has been suggested that Brutus perhaps waited to discover the outcome of Pharsalus, in the hope that the Republic would live on in the victor, as both Cicero and Cassius, Brutus' future fellow conspirator, seem to have done to differing extents.[48] Brutus, as we have seen, was personally fond of neither Pompey nor Caesar but, with the former gone, an alliance with the latter undeniably offered him new and immediate opportunities.[49]

However, we perhaps should not judge Brutus too harshly for his choices in this difficult conflict of interests: before his suicide, Cato sent his own son to obtain a pardon from Caesar,[50] and so we may reasonably assume that he would have wanted the same for his beloved nephew and protégé. The uncompromising Cato, as the ultimate Republican, realised that he had no place in the new Roman Empire that Caesar was building, but perhaps he believed that the next generation of Republicans could both exist in that world and also continue pursuing the best interests of the state, and maybe he fostered hopes that they could yet make a real difference through their actions.

Brutus certainly remained loyal to the cause despite his new political alliances, and this was not only through stubbornly writing a eulogy of his beloved uncle, nor by sensationally marrying his uncle's daughter. Whether motivated purely by genuine Republican ideals, or prodded into action by a sense of shame at his lack of support for his uncle's cause, we cannot say for certain. However, we do know that Brutus, through his Republican actions, was soon to make a momentous impact on the Roman world, and history.

Chapter Five

Prelude to Conspiracy

At this point the ancient sources become more detailed on Brutus' life than they have been thus far: this is understandable with the approaching assassination of Julius Caesar, the infamous action that secured Brutus' place in history. Before examining that incident in detail, however, we must first consider the events leading up to the murder.

Significant Alliances (45–44 BC)

Association with Caesar

The last we saw of Brutus, although retaining his Republican stance and some degree of defiance against Caesar, he was nonetheless enjoying the benefits of reconciliation with the man who had emerged as the leader of Rome. Brutus' career was advancing and, indeed, it continued to do so, thanks to his association with Caesar.

In 45 BC, Caesar designated Brutus as the urban praetor (*praetor urbanus*) for the following year, with Cassius, Brutus' soon-to-be fellow conspirator, assigned to the post of peregrine praetor (*praetor peregrinus*). The praetorship was one of the most venerable offices of the state, since its purpose was to hold authority in the absence of the consuls.[1] These particular posts were the most senior praetorships available, and Caesar put them into the hands of two former Pompeians who were, or had been, personal enemies: this perhaps now seems something of an oversight on Caesar's behalf, given our knowledge that these men would soon lead the conspiracy against him but, at the time, Caesar may have been making a calculated move by bestowing favours upon two prominent Romans whose loyalty and obligation he thereby aimed to secure. Caesar's favouritism towards Brutus was evident here once again, and not only in his choice to appoint him to the praetorship. The post of *praetor urbanus* was the traditional, and therefore more distinguished, of the two, and Caesar awarded this to Brutus on the basis of his fame and virtue alone, despite Cassius being the more senior and experienced man, who had gained significant military distinction. Plutarch speculates on the rivalry that this caused between Brutus and Cassius, even suggesting that Caesar had purposely fostered such competition, by leading both to believe that they were in line for the position: according to Plutarch, Caesar acknowledged that Cassius had a greater claim on the city praetor role, but nonetheless openly chose to place Brutus in the more distinguished office.[2]

Plutarch suggests that Brutus could have been elevated further still.[3] The biographer claims that he was in a position to become the most influential among Caesar's friends which, if true, would surely have been a more sensible route to take than the path that he ultimately chose. Certainly it seems that Brutus had, at first, hoped to use his influence and Cicero's powers of persuasion on Caesar, in order to ensure that the Republican form of government continued: in July 45 BC, Brutus had visited Cicero at his Tusculan villa and urged that he write 'something' to Caesar; although Cicero had agreed initially, it seems that he was distracted by other matters and did not carry out this request.[4] In the following month, Cicero is to be found expressing concerns about Brutus' current association with Caesar, whom Brutus had gone to meet on his return from the last battle of the civil war, which had taken place at Munda in southern Spain.[5] In the same month, Cicero sceptically dismisses as naive Brutus' belief that Caesar has now joined the optimates: in a letter to Atticus, Cicero wryly comments that Caesar would have to walk among the dead to find any of those men to join, by which he means that, following the recent civil war in which Caesar was leader of the opposition, so many of them had lost their lives.[6] It seems that there was a concern that Brutus had lost sight of his principles but, instead of having abandoned them, Brutus appeared to hold the hope that he could secure the Republican constitution through his good relations with Caesar, which seems a worthy approach and undertaking, fully compatible with his political stance.

Furthermore, Plutarch even suggests that Brutus could have become the first man in Rome eventually, if he had been patient and served out his time as a deputy to Caesar. If the reports of Caesar's favouritism towards Brutus are to be believed, this is perhaps not an unfounded claim from Plutarch: Caesar may well have continued to push Brutus in an upward direction and reserve the best political positions for him. Indeed we know that, in 45 BC, Caesar also designated Brutus, along with Cassius, as consul for 41 BC; however, thanks to their actions, neither Caesar nor they themselves would live long enough to see this fulfilled.[7]

Therefore, Brutus' political career was secure and positive at this point, and the state was relatively stable. Of course, in a period following civil strife, it could never be completely settled, but we must address the question of exactly what went wrong as far as Brutus was concerned: what made him upset this state of affairs to advance suddenly from enjoying Caesar's favour to becoming his assassin? Naturally, this was not an easy decision for Brutus; for the ever-serious man, it could not have arisen without good and genuine reason, as well as much deliberation.

Influence of Cassius

That Brutus chose not to follow the more moderate courses open to him has been attributed by the sources to his relationship with Cassius: despite their political rivalry, Brutus apparently heeded the warnings of Cassius' friends against trusting Caesar, and was steered away from his association with the Roman leader and the advantages that it brought; seemingly rather easily influenced, Brutus believed their claims that these benefits were not intended to reward his virtue, but to destroy his purpose and spirit.[8]

Gaius Cassius Longinus was the brother-in-law of Brutus, married to his half-sister, Junia Tertia, or Tertulla as she was also known. We know that they had at least one son, since we are told that the boy was due to assume the *toga virilis* on the day of Caesar's assassination, making him in his mid-teens in 44 BC, and suggesting that their marriage had been a relatively long-lasting one; Tertia also suffered a miscarriage in that year.[9]

As a child, Cassius was said to have been taught by the same principled Latin grammarian, Staberius, as Brutus, which perhaps helps to explain their similar views in later life.[10] Also like Brutus, Cassius spent some time pursuing his education in Rhodes. Plutarch offers an anecdote from Cassius' childhood, intended to illustrate that he was always inherently opposed to tyranny, as well as emphasising the violent temper that he was said to possess: he attended the same school as Faustus, Sulla's son, who, when he was bragging about his father's absolute power, found himself on the end of Cassius' fists; when the boys were brought before Pompey, who preferred to keep this out of court despite the requests of Faustus' family, the fearless Cassius threatened to do the same again if Faustus repeated his boasts.[11]

As an adult, Cassius continued to demonstrate his brave and bold nature, distinguishing himself through military commands. Notably, he was assigned as quaestor to Crassus, when he was proconsul of Syria, and took part in his disastrous campaign against the Parthians, in 53 BC. At the Battle of Carrhae, Cassius was one of those officers who urged Crassus to call off the campaign and, having failed in that, advised him, in vain, on the most sensible manoeuvres; he is portrayed as being able to see through the eastern deceit that was to lead to the defeat of the Roman army, unlike Crassus himself. When Crassus was rendered completely ineffective, having been crippled by despair over his son's death and the terrible predicament of his army, Cassius and the legate Octavius together seized the initiative and led the retreat.[12] After the final defeat, with the soldiers willingly accepting him as their commander, Cassius is credited with saving what was left of Crassus' legions, by leading them into the safety of Syria. He took control of the province, becoming its proquaestor until 51 BC, and successfully defended it from two Parthian attempts at invasion during this time.[13]

In 49 BC, as the civil war was breaking out, Cassius held the post of tribune of the plebs and was openly anti-Caesarian.[14] On 7 February that year, it was Cassius who carried Pompey's order to the consuls that they should go to Rome to remove the money from the treasury. Therefore, it is no surprise that he joined the Pompeian forces: given his recent military experience, he was made commander of the Syrian squadron of Pompey's fleet. At about the same time as the Battle of Pharsalus was drawing to a close, Cassius led the Syrian, Phoenician and Cilician fleets to Sicily and launched a successful attack on Caesar's ships there; however, following a counter-attack in which he was nearly captured, and on learning of the Pompeian defeat at Pharsalus, Cassius led the fleets away from Sicily.[15]

Later on, Cassius, like Brutus, obtained Caesar's pardon; indeed, Plutarch claims that it was thanks to Brutus' request that this transpired.[16] Having been reconciled with Caesar, Cassius, with his fleet, joined Caesar's forces in the east as his legate. In a letter to Cassius, Cicero suggests that he himself and his addressee both waited to discover the outcome of the war before ultimately deciding which side to choose. However, elsewhere, Cicero makes the unique claim that, while in Cilicia in 47 BC, Cassius considered turning against Caesar in order to destroy him.[17]

There exists warm correspondence from Cicero to Cassius,[18] and he was also to be found staying with Cicero at Formiae (Formia) in February 49 BC, at the time that Rome was being thrown into a state of civil war.[19] Their friendship demonstrates that Brutus and Cassius, as well as being related by marriage, were operating in the same circles. This was despite having a different moral and ethical outlook: Cassius had abandoned the severe school of Stoicism in order to become a follower of Epicureanism instead which, with its living for the moment approach, stood in opposition to the former. Although Brutus was a follower of the Old Academy, Stoicism was nearer to his beliefs than Epicureanism.[20] Clearly their personalities, motivated by their philosophical views, affected their approaches to the assassination, since Cassius is portrayed as ready to seize the day and more a man of action, while Brutus is the deep thinker who prefers to weigh matters up carefully before making his move.

Despite their kinship through marriage, there were these obvious differences between Brutus and Cassius, and a rivalry did arise. Plutarch records the rumour that disputes had already occurred between the brothers-in-law, and that they were particularly inflamed by Caesar overtly favouring Brutus, somewhat unfairly given Cassius' seniority and greater experience; the biographer does, however, also note the possibility that this competition for the senior praetorship was the original cause of their rivalry. Nevertheless, in time Brutus and Cassius became sufficiently reconciled to be able to unite and lead the conspiracy against Caesar, although a certain mutual resentment and mistrust of each other continued to simmer under the surface long into the future.[21]

These differences between the lead co-conspirators did also appear to remain where the conspiracy was concerned: their motives for the assassination were reported to be different since, while Brutus was believed to be opposed to the very institution of tyranny, there were suggestions that Cassius was driven by a personal grudge against Caesar the man. However, Plutarch reports Cassius' private resentment, only to dismiss it.[22] Generally in the sources Cassius is portrayed as always having been opposed to any form of tyranny, even from childhood, and indeed his family were said to be the same.[23] However, there exists a letter in his own words, speaking of Caesar's war in Spain, the Battle of Munda, against the son of Pompey, Gnaeus, which explicitly states that he would prefer the old, merciful master, rather than a new and cruel one, perhaps suggesting that he could have, after all, tolerated tyranny from the lesser of two evils.[24] Nevertheless, his involvement in the assassination of Caesar seems to bear out the more widely believed view that he was unable to endure either tyranny or the tyrant.

Caesar the Tyrant (46–44 BC)

A man such as Brutus cannot have been influenced simply by the hostility of his brother-in-law, with whom he clearly was not always in agreement, to turn his rather comfortable life upside down through an act of murder: there must have been far more significant motivation for the highly principled

Brutus to consider the assassination of a close and beneficial associate to be a wise move.[25] Admittedly, we have seen how some of Caesar's actions troubled him and how he put up a certain amount of resistance to these, such as writing the eulogy for his uncle Cato, and marrying his daughter, Porcia; however, we have also witnessed how Brutus was seemingly accepting of Caesar's position, and very much enjoyed the benefits of it, even hoping that Caesar could somehow be persuaded, through his influence, to support and foster the Republican constitution. However, Brutus' hopes gradually faded, as it emerged that Caesar's monarchical tendencies had a greater hold on him than any desire to preserve the Republic. In essence Brutus' reasons for assassination derived from this strong belief in the Roman Republic as the best form of government, and in Caesar's actions, which appeared to contradict, and indeed attack, the very foundations of the state.[26]

Catalogue of Errors: Caesar's Offences[27]

Julius Caesar had never had an easy relationship with the optimates,[28] so his effective sole leadership, from 46 BC up until his death in 44 BC, standing in conflict with what they held dear, simply could not have been a completely unopposed one. His errors and offences against the Roman state and, perhaps more accurately, the nobility of the senate, both of whom are represented in the *Senatus Populusque Romanus* (the familiar *SPQR* which is displayed in public areas of Rome to this day, and means 'the Senate and Roman people'), have been variously and frequently recorded. It is important for us to consider these cumulative offences committed in the final years of Caesar's life, in order to give a full contextual setting to the conspiracy and murder.

The mistakes that Caesar made, which seemingly became more frequent towards the end of his life and would thus ultimately lead to his downfall, read in the ancient sources like a long and inevitable list; however, as so often, this owes much to the power of hindsight and the imposition of later knowledge of events upon these actions. At the immediate time, it was unlikely that all of Caesar's moves were read as such obvious and open attempts at tyranny: as we shall see, some may have been foolish errors on his behalf, rather than deliberate steps towards sole power; in some instances, he may have been purposely set up for a fall by his enemies; and we must also bear in mind that others may simply be constructed falsehoods about his intentions. Nevertheless, Caesar was murdered and this was ultimately because of the kingly desires that he was perceived to be holding at the time. The sources are particularly plentiful at this point in enumerating the increasingly monarchical tendencies of Caesar which would bring about his demise. We should understand that the exact timing of many of these acts cannot be ascertained: we can only be sure that these incidents occurred during the period between the end of the Battle of Thapsus and Caesar's death.

It was once the embers of the civil war had finally been extinguished that events descended so far that the future of the Republic was revealed as bleak and beyond repair, and any hope that it might be otherwise was rapidly vanishing. With the troubles of war over, and the return of Caesar to Rome, attention was naturally turned to settling the state and form of government: what was most concerning for the senate was that all power now seemed to be concentrated in the hands of one man and, furthermore, that this was a man who displayed scant regard for their existing Republican law and constitution. Caesar, while simultaneously being appointed dictator for ten years, was consul each year from 46 to 44 BC, and in 45 BC held the consulship alone for the majority of the year, before abdicating from the position. A sole consulship was not without precedent, since Pompey had held the same office in 52 BC: however, on that occasion the specific situation of violent disorder in the city had demanded it, while the office of dictator was originally designed for such times of crisis in the state. Furthermore, Pompey had been elected with the approval and support of the optimates, who had believed that they could control state affairs through him.[29] However, Caesar's disregard for the constitution was especially apparent with regard to the consulships of 45 BC: firstly, his nonchalant attitude was revealed when he took up the office before arriving back in Rome, only to give it up on his return without valid reason;[30] then, when one of the two men who took over the consulship from him for the last few months of the year died on the final day of his position, Caesar simply appointed a man who wished to be consul for the remaining few hours, instead of following law and procedure.[31] This was an outright insult to the senate, since they had been neither consulted nor involved in the decision about who would become one of the most senior statesmen of Rome; Cicero's acerbic comment, that the replacement consul was so alert as not ever to fall asleep during his consulship, reveals, in humorous manner, the typical feeling that this disrespect aroused among the leading men of Rome. As Suetonius observes, it seemed that Caesar now viewed consulships as relatively insignificant next to his power as dictator.[32]

Nor was this Caesar's only unprecedented and illegal action during this period: among other unconstitutional acts, at least according to the ancient sources, he designated magistrates several years in advance; he endowed several ex-praetors with consular rank; he enlarged the numbers of the senate with men who did not necessarily possess the required status; he left his own selected prefects in charge of the city in his absence, instead of the duly elected praetors;[33] he entrusted some of the care of public finances to his own slaves; and he put the son of one of his freedmen in command of his three legions in Alexandria.[34] Whether or not these, and other similar reported deeds, are factual, Caesar attacked the Republican constitution by repeatedly ignoring and bypassing the senate, and the laws and precedents it valued highly, thereby rendering the Republican government ineffective and worthless. Caesar appeared to believe that, as dictator, he had the right to act as he pleased and, indeed, he frequently appeared to do so. One Suetonian anecdote, the truth of which, of course, we cannot determine, claims that Caesar made a derogatory remark labelling Sulla as foolish for having abdicated from his dictatorship.[35] Such monarchical behaviour could only be tolerated for so long without yet another clash between Caesar and the other leading men of Rome.

As well as his disrespect for the constitution, Caesar made it evident that he had not learned from his former mistakes. Following his success at the Battle of Munda, the final battle of the civil war and, indeed, Caesar's final ever battle, he celebrated another triumph. In his quadruple triumph of 46 BC, he had, as we saw, aroused the revilement of the people when he displayed images of the deaths of his Roman foes in the civil war, with that of Cato particularly causing offence; although Caesar attempted to display this Spanish triumph in 45 BC as a victory over a foreign country, which had incidentally included some treacherous Romans, the people instead saw this triumph for what it was: an insensitive and tragic celebration of the defeat of yet more Romans. However, according to Plutarch, the people grudgingly accepted this since they were relieved to have some respite from civil strife at last.[36]

Furthermore, in response to the successful conclusion of Munda, the senate began voting excessive victory honours to Caesar. In 46 BC, after the campaign in Africa, his victory had been rewarded in a similar fashion, with various honours being given, including the dictatorship for ten years in succession. These earlier honours were now further augmented and, in early 44 BC, Caesar's dictatorship was extended for life.[37] He was also bestowed with honorific titles: he was now to be called *imperator* (commander) at all times, and not just when leading an army, and this was also to be extended to his descendants;[38] he received the title *pater* or *parens patriae* (father of his country); he was appointed to the role of censor of public morals; and he was granted tribunician sacrosanctity. Also, Caesar's birth month, Quintilis, was renamed after him: this was one honour that was to remain for posterity, with the month of July existing to this day.[39]

Besides these honours, which could mostly be viewed as obsequious extensions of privileges that were already in existence, there were others that appeared more monarchical, or sometimes even godlike, in essence. For example, Caesar was given the distinct privilege of being allowed to wear triumphal dress on all occasions, along with the laurel wreath. Coins from this time began to depict images of him explicitly wearing the latter: this was an unprecedented move since he was the first living Roman to have his portrait displayed on coinage, which was a custom that, up until now, had belonged instead to Hellenistic monarchs, who were worshipped as gods. Furthermore, Caesar's birthday itself was to be celebrated with public sacrifices, and prayers offered to him annually, and Mark Antony was appointed as his priest, endowing Caesar with a status akin to the gods. He was called Liberator, rather ironically, given the same claims that the conspirators would soon make for themselves upon assassinating him, and a Temple of Liberty was to be built. Other temples were dedicated in his honour, including one decreed to Clemency as a thanks-offering for his trait of mercy, and a Temple of New Concord (*Concordia Nova*), along with an accompanying festival, to celebrate the newfound peace which he had brought to the city. Statues of the man were to be set up, in a dangerously hubristic manner: two on the rostra were to be crowned with insignia to distinguish him as saviour of his country; an ivory one was to appear in a chariot, alongside those of the gods in the procession at the games in the Circus; another was to stand on the Capitol, next to those of the legendary Kings of Rome and, ironically, the one of the tyrant-banishing and inspirational ancestor of Brutus, Lucius Brutus; and a further one, inscribed 'to the invincible god' (*deo invicto*), was to be placed in the Temple of Quirinus. In one speech, Cicero comments on the unpopularity of these statues, which he attributes to the malicious gossip of envious men, and he also defends Caesar from accusations of tyranny; elsewhere, however, we have seen that Cicero appears disillusioned and holds similar beliefs to those of the other jealous and resentful nobles.[40]

As well as simply accepting such honours, Caesar actively committed deeds that overstepped the boundaries of acceptability and, in some cases, could even be considered as betraying his kingly desires. Admittedly, some of his acts were innocent and beneficial to Rome, but were nonetheless perceived as being an offence against the Republic: for example, his reorganisation of the calendar was viewed by his enemies with suspicion. This demonstrates the mood in Rome at the time, and the readiness of the optimates to see the worst in Caesar's every move. However, other deeds, with more overtly monarchical connotations, cannot be excused, nor dismissed, so easily. For example, Caesar now sat on a raised couch at the theatre; he carried out business from a gold and ivory throne; and this latter, along with his gilded and bejewelled crown, was carried into the games along with his chariot and statue.[41] As a member of the Julian clan, Caesar claimed descent from the goddess Venus, through her grandson Iulus, who was the son of the hero Aeneas: Iulus was the legendary first King of Alba Longa (an ancient city in Latium, now Lazio, the region in which Rome is also located). This type of claim by men of leading Roman families was not, in itself, exceptional; however, Caesar imitated the clothing of Iulus, which had royal connotations, since his high red boots reminded the people of those of the early Kings, and therefore were yet another cause of offence.[42]

There were also more overt indications in Caesar's actions that the many honours had begun to go to his head, and that he was, rather foolishly, warming to the idea of a kingship for himself. One such event reportedly occurred on a day on which he had been voted various extravagant honours by all in the senate, except for a few, notably including Cassius; on this particular day, Caesar did not rise from his seat to receive the consuls and senate; this, understandably, was viewed as an arrogant insult to the state by both the senate and the people. Afterwards, ill health was cited as an excuse, but clearly not believed by the ancient historians and biographers, although Plutarch instead places the blame on one of Caesar's sly detractors, claiming that he had discouraged him from standing, as he had intended to do. Suetonius also acknowledges this possibility, while recording the opposing version, that Caesar was angry with the man who had suggested he ought to rise; furthermore, Suetonius notes the hypocrisy of Caesar's arrogance, since he himself had been incensed on another occasion, when the tribune, Pontius Aquila, had not stood up as he had ridden past in triumphal procession: Caesar sulkily overreacted to this affront, refusing to make any promises for several days after the event without sarcastically noting that he must consult Aquila first. If another anecdotal tale is to be believed, Caesar must have realised the gravity of his error in not rising to receive the deputation: as if predicting his very near future, he left for home immediately, dramatically baring his throat as an offering for anyone who wished to kill him.[43]

Such behaviour led to the public belief that Caesar aspired to be a monarch, and he began to be addressed, or treated, as a King. Indeed, the sources record several anecdotes demonstrating this, and show that this provided an opportunity for his enemies to encourage him in this direction, in order to accelerate his downfall. For example, one of his statues on the rostra was crowned with a royal diadem, secretly at night; when two tribunes removed this crown and led those responsible to prison, Caesar supposedly reacted angrily, claiming that they had denied him the opportunity to refuse this himself. It appears that this event is linked with another, soon after this, when the crowd hailed Caesar as King (*rex*), as he was returning to the city from Alba Longa; Caesar openly rejected this, but was reportedly disappointed when the people then fell silent. The same tribunes were responsible for bringing to trial the man who began shouting this, and it was at this point that Caesar became truly enraged and acted against them: he accused them of plotting this in order to incite rebellion against him, expelled them from their office and, in some versions of events, sent them into exile. It is particularly relevant here that he was said to be especially aggrieved because the tribunes' actions were received well by the crowd, who hailed them as Brutuses, with reference to the tyrant banisher and legendary ancestor of Brutus.[44]

It was in this atmosphere, at the festival of the Lupercalia in February 44 BC, precisely one month before his assassination, that Caesar was involved in what was to be perhaps his ultimate gravely misjudged situation. An additional priestly college for the Lupercalia, the Julian, had been initiated in Caesar's honour, and so he was present in his capacity as supervisor of the festival. As consul, Antony was one of the participants in the race, and he entered the forum carrying a royal crown to place on the head of Caesar who, seated on his throne, did not appear displeased at this presentation; the crowd reacted with a groan, and so Caesar rejected the diadem, this time to the people's open delight; this whole scene was played out repeatedly until Caesar sent the crown to the Capitol as an offering to Jupiter; finally, he ordered his refusal to be recorded in the annals. While sources hostile to Antony place the blame for this piece of theatrical display instead on him, generally the ancient texts suggest that this was Caesar's not-so-subtle attempt to gauge the people's response which, it may be imagined, was not that which he had hoped.[45]

When all this was combined with Caesar's plans for the east, it proved to be one indication of tyranny too many. It was recorded in the oracular Sibylline books, which were consulted by the Roman state at times of crisis, that Parthia could be conquered only by a King. Since Caesar was currently busy preparing for a campaign against this long-standing and bitter enemy of Rome, and with the memory of Crassus' crushing defeat by this foe still being painfully raw, rumours began to circulate that it would be proposed in the senate that he should officially be given the title of King to ensure his success, although this was only to apply in the provinces and not in Rome. Nevertheless, this cause of offence was augmented since Caesar was about to depart for the east, and his future acts were therefore all to be declared valid. This did indeed prove to be the final straw, since the proposal for granting the title of *rex*, or King, was supposed to take place on 15 March 44 BC, better known as the Ides, and the infamous and fateful day of Caesar's assassination. In order to prevent any further unbearable acts becoming a reality, the conspirators decided that it was now imperative to strike.[46]

This is not intended as an exhaustive list of Caesar's offences and miscalculations as recorded in the sources, but the sheer amount given here should suffice to demonstrate why the true Republicans were so affronted and frustrated at this time and, more importantly, why they believed that they must take whatever action necessary to stop Caesar in his tracks. It would have been difficult to view many of these signs, some of which had such an extravagant nature, as anything but an indication of foolish arrogance in the very least, and tyranny at worst. In these deeds, Caesar was often demonstrating some of the hallmarks of Hellenistic monarchs with their ruler cults, or at least willingly having signs of this mantle imposed upon him: alarmingly, these tyrants were worshipped as gods and, indeed, Dio Cassius goes so far as to accuse Caesar of behaving as if he were immortal.[47] This blatant disrespect for the traditional law and order was an insult to the institution of the Republic, and those who still firmly believed in that dying form of government were understandably troubled. The consular and jurist Servius Sulpicius Rufus, whom Brutus had visited in Samos on his return from Pharsalus, perhaps captures the general mood of the time among the aristocracy, in his lament that they had lost country, honour, rank and every political distinction.[48] Indeed, their worst fears seemed to be confirmed in Caesar's reputed comment that the Republic was nothing but a name without form or substance. Brutus certainly believed that Caesar had kingly desires, for he explicitly says so in a letter addressed to Cicero after the assassination, and it was clearly this belief that drove him to murder.[49]

However, we should also remember that it was during this period that he was bestowing on Brutus and Cassius, among others, privileged offices several years in advance of the traditional time, so that they were receiving the benefits that were perhaps simultaneously being used as a pretext for his murder in some ways. Furthermore, the ancient sources speculate that it was actually Caesar's enemies who were behind many of these honours, hoping to render him a truly despised man so that it would be received well by all when he was eventually brought down.[50] That the assassination was really being plotted so carefully from this early stage is, perhaps, somewhat unlikely, but it is more than reasonable to assume that the general jealousy of those senior statesmen around him did have some part to play in this effort to tarnish his image and, of course, that the resentment of these men had a major role in instigating the conspiracy and assassination.[51]

Chapter Six

Conspiracy

Brutus the Tyrannicide

Descendant of Republican Heroes

As we have already seen, Marcus Junius Brutus was keenly aware and proud of his legendary ancestry, as well as his more recent family legacy, and felt a moral obligation to uphold the Republican standards which he had inherited, and which had been recorded for posterity. Equally conscious, it seems, were his fellow Romans: knowing this vulnerable point in the man all too well, they began to exploit Brutus' sense of familial duty and pride in order to urge him to action. Indeed, this now became a crucial motivation in driving Brutus on to the extreme measure of assassination.[1]

The ancient sources tell us that, in the unhealthy atmosphere of jealousy and resentment that had now been created in the unsettled Roman state thanks to the apparently tyrannical behaviour of Julius Caesar, references were made to Lucius Brutus, the legendary hero who had banished the first Kings of Rome and established the Republic.[2] It followed that thoughts naturally began to turn to the potential of the descendant of this tyrant banisher who had strong Republican tendencies, the highly principled Brutus. Such thoughts led to messages being left which seemed intended either to encourage or shame Brutus into action. These hortatory notes were put up in secret, at night, like companion pieces to the crowns secretly placed on Caesar's statues: indeed, as Plutarch suggests, it is quite possible that the same people were responsible for both, hoping thereby to force the issue of Caesar's tyranny and, more importantly, Brutus' obligation to rescue the state from it.[3]

On the Capitol, next to the statues of the Kings of Rome, there was a bronze effigy of Lucius Brutus, holding aloft his drawn sword.[4] Comments were left on the base of this statue, expressing wishes that he were now alive, or that there could be another Lucius, with the implication that he could then rescue Rome from its latest tyrant. Similarly, on the base of Caesar's statue which, it should be remembered, stood alongside those of Lucius and the Kings, a cutting two-line verse was inscribed:

Brutus, since he drove out the Kings, was made the first consul;
This man, since he drove out the consuls, finally has been made King.[5]

Less subtle exhortations to Brutus were also attached to the tribunal and chair, which belonged to him in his role as praetor. These remarks had the intention of wounding his pride and thus spurring him on to act, and included gibes such as: 'are you sleeping, Brutus?'; 'you are not Brutus'; 'are you bribed, Brutus?'; 'are you dead, Brutus?'; and 'you are not his descendant'. Dio Cassius records that similar comments were also distributed in pamphlets, questioning Brutus' descent from Lucius, since the legend recorded that he had ended his own family line when he had his only sons killed. However, it was currently in the interest of the majority to accept that Marcus Junius Brutus was, indeed, a descendant of Lucius, in the hope that he could be persuaded to follow a similar path. Therefore, the people also cried out to him in person, repeating his name so laden with significance, and exclaiming that they needed a Brutus. Dio Cassius also suggests that some people were more direct and approached him in person. Thus, unable to escape his own legacy, Brutus was greatly pressurised by external forces.[6]

Closer Influences

Brutus was also the recipient of more personal, although subtle, appeals from his friend Cicero, who made frequent hinting references to his ancestry. In his *Brutus*, written in 46 BC, Cicero imagines addressing his friend on the subject of the Republic: lamenting that Brutus' career was suddenly cut short by the turmoil of the state, he expresses the idealistic hope that the rising statesman Brutus can find a Republic in which he can flourish politically, as he deserves, and where he will be able, not only to live up to, but also to increase the fame of his ancestors. In other works also dedicated to Brutus around this time, Cicero makes further passing references to his friend's ancestors having delivered Rome from tyranny out of an honourable sense of duty.[7] At the point when Brutus was, somewhat naively, hopeful that Caesar could be persuaded to re-establish the Republic, Cicero also makes an ironic and suggestive comment on his ancestry to Atticus: referring to the family history that Atticus created at Brutus' request, which illustrates the importance that he placed on his family line, Cicero wryly asks what happened to this work, implying that Brutus has now forgotten his legacy and abandoned his duty as a descendant of Republican heroes.[8]

It would be going too far to suggest that Cicero, who was often quite cynical about Caesar, was attempting to incite Brutus to murder with such references: indeed, following the assassination, he strongly defends himself from Antony's accusations that he was the instigator.[9] Cicero, like so many, including Brutus, clearly had idealistic wishes for the traditional Republic to be re-established: understandably, the Republican and morally solid Brutus, of such a famous and noble pedigree, became the focus of such hopes, both for Cicero and like-minded Roman citizens in general. A similar example of a personal appeal to Brutus comes from the hints of another close friend, Ligarius, who had been pardoned by Caesar, but resented this: when Brutus visited him on his sickbed, Ligarius claimed he would be well again if his friend had a purpose worthy of himself.[10]

Eventually, Brutus himself was persuaded to become the focus of his own hopes for this restitution of Republican government, too, although perhaps not in a way that Cicero had contemplated. According to the sources, it was Cassius, forevermore to be paired with Brutus as his partner in crime, who played the biggest role in convincing his brother-in-law to join the conspiracy to assassinate the tyrant Caesar. As we have seen,[11] the circle of Cassius had already been able to influence Brutus with their warnings not to be taken in by Caesar's favours, even though the relationship between the brothers-in-law had, at that time, somewhat broken down. Now Cassius realised the importance of having his noble relation by marriage involved in such a conspiracy. Indeed he could not ignore this, for Plutarch reports that friends of his explicitly declared that they would join the conspiracy only if Brutus took a leading role in it: it was considered that Brutus' involvement would enhance and even justify the act of assassination, lending to it a sense of just honour which would be absent if he declined to participate. This is very revealing about Brutus' noble reputation and the impact his purported virtue had on those around him: indeed, even sources hostile to the conspirators acknowledge that Brutus was highly esteemed. Plutarch also suggests that it was when he perceived that the messages about Brutus' ancestry were beginning to have an effect on him that Cassius then capitalised on this opportunity to recruit him to the conspiracy.[12]

Cassius thus found a reason to renew his relationship with Brutus, and visited him with the purpose of recruiting him to the plot. The crucial point, at this stage, was the imminent proposal in the senate that Caesar should be named King: a conversation between Cassius and Brutus is reported to have taken place on the subject, in which Brutus told Cassius he would not attend the senate on the day of the proposal but, if summoned there as praetor, he would do his duty by defending his country and dying for liberty. Cassius happily received this response from Brutus, and encouraged him further by informing him that he would have the full support of the nobility, assuring him that they had been the ones responsible for leaving the messages about his heritage, since they sought from him the emulation of his ancestors in this pressing matter.[13]

Although the two men approached this from different angles, they came together in their strong shared belief that Caesar, who would be King, must be permanently removed as soon as possible. The generally held belief in the sources is that Cassius was motivated by personal hatred of Caesar the man. Brutus, on the other hand, was held to have the most honourable of intentions: he was opposed to the very institution of tyranny, a stance that was inherent in him due to his ancestry. It should be remembered here, however, that Brutus did previously feel personal hostility towards Caesar: he shared the views of his uncle Cato, although not his extreme animosity towards Caesar, in his disapproval of his mother's illicit affair with the man whose political views were similarly not to his taste. Therefore, although the prevailing view is that Brutus acted out of devotion to the state, the sources do briefly speculate on the possibility that his decision to join the conspiracy was motivated instead by these personal reasons. However, the ancient texts always portray Caesar as openly fond of his lover's son and, following Pharsalus, it appeared that he had eventually, more or less, succeeded in winning Brutus over with his kindness and favours: Brutus had been reconciled with Caesar, and so it seems unlikely that his part in the assassination is to be attributed to personal feelings.[14]

This understandably caused something of a moral dilemma for Brutus, and Plutarch acknowledges the predicament that now arose for him. This was no easy decision, since he knew that he had received many benefits from Caesar and, furthermore, he was aware that he had gained Caesar's confidence and realised that such an abuse of this trust would be an act of extreme ingratitude.[15] On the other hand, Brutus bore the weight of the future security of the Roman state on his shoulders, knowing, as Cassius had emphasised to him, that many men were depending on him. The indications of the inner turmoil to which this led appear to have been outwardly visible, at least to one of those closest to him: his wife, Porcia. This woman's role in supporting her husband in carrying out the assassination has become legendary, proving her to be worthy, both as wife of Brutus and daughter of the late Cato. While Brutus remained composed when outside of the home, he was said to be particularly troubled at night. Porcia observed this anxiety in her husband, and chose to perform a somewhat drastic deed in order to demonstrate her worthiness and strong physical nature to Brutus, before questioning him about the source of his current angst. Having dismissed her attendants from her room, Porcia took a small barbers' knife used for cutting finger nails and dramatically inflicted a deep wound on her thigh. Following the pain and illness that this caused, either at the height of her pain when Brutus had become concerned for her health, or once she had passed through the worst of it, she then broached the subject with him: at this point she is credited with a speech reminding Brutus of her parentage and assuring him that, since she could overcome pain, she was no weak-natured woman, but she could and should be trusted to share all burdens with him; one source even has her claim that she would prefer to die than be distrusted by him. When Porcia then revealed her self-inflicted wound to Brutus, he disclosed the plot to her and found the resolve to commit himself to the mission: he reportedly prayed to the gods that he would succeed and thereby prove himself worthy of his wife, before helping her to recover.[16]

Greek Examples

Some modern scholars attribute Brutus' act of tyrannicide, in part, to the influence of Greece, where he had spent valuable time studying.[17] Cicero observed how the Greeks revered tyrant slayers, ironically almost as gods,[18] and in Athens the examples of men who had abolished tyranny were visible for Brutus to behold. Statues of Harmodius and Aristogeiton were on display in the agora of the learned city, as well as at home in Rome, and would have acted as an inspiration to an impressionable young scholar. Their tale is narrated by the Greek historian, Thucydides: Harmodius had rejected the advances of Hipparchus, the younger brother of the tyrant Hippias; in revenge, he publicly insulted Harmodius' sister, so Harmodius and Aristogeiton responded by attempting to overthrow the tyranny at a festival, but failed, although they succeeded in killing the cruel Hipparchus instead; despite their failure and Hippias' increased tyranny following the deed, they were hailed as heroes by the Athenians.[19] Indeed Brutus was later to achieve the same heroic status when bronze statues of him and Cassius were erected after Caesar's assassination, close to those of Harmodius and Aristogeiton.[20] Interestingly, it should be noted that we have no record of

Brutus objecting to such worship, despite all his professed moral values, although this information may simply be missing from our scant accounts.

Brutus' philosophical beliefs also appear to have contributed to his decision to kill the tyrant, particularly his learning from the school of Antiochus, which followed Plato's Old Academy. The Platonic viewpoint, equating life under a tyranny to a form of slavery, was rehearsed by Brutus on various occasions, both before and after the assassination. For example, we saw such a moral stance supposedly expressed earlier in his life, at the threat of Pompey's dictatorship, and frequent references are made to his liberating Rome from slavery, both around the time, and in the aftermath, of the assassination, and often in his own words. Indeed the conspirators were to become known as the Liberators (*Liberatores*) committed to preserving the freedom, or liberty (*libertas*), of the Roman people, in the same vein as Brutus' legendary ancestors. It was not only his family history he could look to, however, since there was also a celebrated Platonist whose actions Brutus could emulate, proving that the abolition of tyranny existed within the principles of his philosophical school: Chion, the assassin of Clearchus of Heraclea.[21] It is perhaps also relevant here to mention Plutarch's interesting pairing of the lives of Brutus and Dion: this brother-in-law of Dionysius I, at the Syracusan court, was an acquaintance of Plato; thus introduced to philosophy, he was opposed to tyranny and, as guardian of the rule of his nephew, Dionysius II, in vain hoped to create a moderate leader; instead Dionysius II, suspicious, banished his uncle, only for him to return later and overthrow the tyranny.

Therefore Brutus' education had surrounded him with suitable examples to follow, as well as his family legends. It is also possible that the topic of tyranny was a part of his Greek education, as an appropriate subject for declamation in rhetorical training. Surely such a wealth of experiences, influences and legends were prominent in the mind of Brutus when Caesar became too tyrannical to bear, and aided his decision to act.

The Plot

Co-Conspirators: Safety in Numbers

And so, with various influences and pressures on Brutus, the stage was set for this conspiracy to be plotted in full and for one of the most notorious assassinations in history to be carried out. Frustrated and unable to stop Caesar's tyranny in any other way, Brutus and Cassius now drew together several of the leading members of the senate in order to form a conspiracy against him. This conspiracy, and the assassination to which it led, has been aptly described as 'a continuation of the civil war by other means':[22] indeed, it involved several of those men who had fought on Pompey's side against Caesar, only to be pardoned and welcomed back into Roman politics by him after Pharsalus. This can only be termed as ingratitude and, therefore, makes their actions appear less than honourable, but the presence of one man, despite such hypocrisy, seemed to endow the murder with a lofty and noble status: for, if Brutus were to be involved, the people would surely understand this killing to have been committed for the greater good of the Roman state.

Brutus and Cassius set about their mission carefully, gathering co-conspirators by secretly testing out the feelings of friends and confidants, as well as those whom they considered to be bold and unafraid of death. Their caution was a wise move in the precarious atmosphere of the time, when men would freely switch allegiances, and indeed already had, as no example can be more pertinent than that of the two men themselves. Other notables joined who had, like Brutus and Cassius, received benefits from Caesar, including Decimus Brutus and Gaius Trebonius. That these two men feature so prominently in the sources among the other named conspirators can perhaps be attributed to the fact that, unlike Brutus and Cassius, they had been consistently allied with Caesar for some time: both had served for several years in his Gallic campaign and fought on his side in the civil war against Pompey, with Trebonius also having publicly supported the Triumvirate before that. Caesar's trust in these men is apparent in their level of command under him: notably, during the civil war, he left them to lead the siege against Massilia, with Trebonius in charge of land operations, and Decimus commanding the fleet.[23]

Suetonius credits Decimus Brutus as being one of the leaders of the conspiracy, and certainly Cicero, at one point, places him first on an abbreviated list of the conspirators; we shall also see that he does have a prominent role in the action, especially in the aftermath of the assassination.[24] Caesar had made Decimus proconsul of Cisalpine Gaul for 44–43 BC, and designated him as consul for 42 BC, and it was Decimus, not Marcus, Brutus who was named as a secondary heir in Caesar's will, proving that there must have been a certain closeness between them.[25] Indeed, Plutarch reports that, since Decimus was considered neither bold nor enterprising, he was chosen as a recruit precisely because he had Caesar's confidence, and also, more practically, because he possessed a large band of gladiators for shows, which gave him power and could prove useful in the aftermath of the assassination. However, Decimus would not agree to join the conspiracy until he had spoken privately with his distant kinsman, Brutus: reportedly, like many of the co-conspirators, it was only on discovery that the noble Brutus was one of the leaders that Decimus decided to sign up, and then eagerly so.[26]

The other prominent conspirator in the sources, Trebonius, was one of the two men who replaced Caesar as suffect consul, when the latter disrespectfully gave up his sole consulship in the middle of 45 BC. When his colleague died on the last day of the year, Caesar simply appointed a replacement co-consul suffectus without following due process, and it has been considered that Trebonius must have felt this insult most keenly. At the time of Caesar's death, he had been made a proconsul of Asia.[27] Despite his long-term support of Caesar, the assassination was not the first time Trebonius had been involved in a plot against the dictator. Just a year before the successful assassination attempt, in the atmosphere of dissatisfaction and mistrust that pervaded 45 BC, which spread even to men he could consider his supporters, plans were formed to remove Caesar. These plans were believed to have emanated from his inner circle, and Mark Antony was one of those implicated; however, this accusation is perhaps only to be attributed to his highly prejudiced arch-enemy, Cicero. On Caesar's return from Spain, following the Battle of Munda, despite recently having fallen into disfavour with him, Antony nonetheless travelled out to meet the dictator at Narbo (Narbonne), in Gaul. While there he also met with Trebonius, who suggested forming a conspiracy against Caesar, but Antony declined to respond to this proposition. According to Plutarch, it was for this reason that Antony, although perhaps surprisingly considered as a co-conspirator, was excluded from the current assassination plot, on Trebonius' advice. Most interestingly, although Antony's relationship with Caesar seemed to be repaired, he chose not to reveal Trebonius' plot to the intended target.[28] Furthermore, it should be noted that Plutarch records an anecdote in which Antony was also accused of plotting against Caesar along with Dolabella, the former son-in-law of Cicero; this report was swiftly dismissed by the dictator when news of it reached his ears.[29]

As far as the sources indicate, these were the two main conspirators in addition to Brutus and Cassius. Other names are mentioned, although it does not seem to be possible to gather together a full inventory of those involved. Cicero's abbreviated list should be consulted first, since its contemporary nature makes it a reliable source for the identity of the conspirators.[30] Here we find Gnaeus Domitius Ahenobarbus mentioned before Trebonius: his father was Lucius, the long-term opponent of Caesar who was implicated in the Vettius affair, and who held Corfinium in the civil war, ignoring the commands of Pompey on whose side he was fighting. Like Brutus, Ahenobarbus was a nephew of Cato: the Republican stalwart's sister, Porcia, was his mother. Therefore, Ahenobarbus had a firm background in the opposition of Caesar, and unsurprisingly was to be found with his father both at the siege of Corfinium and the Battle of Pharsalus, and he was yet another man pardoned by Caesar after the civil war. Ironically, given his strongly Republican background and actions, his grandson would become one of the most notorious tyrants in history: the future Roman Emperor, Nero.

Another name cited by Cicero is Lucius Tillius Cimber, a supporter of Caesar, who was known to have had some influence with the dictator. Caesar had made him governor of the province of Bithynia and Pontus in 44 BC, but this did not prevent him becoming an integral member of the conspiracy, quite possibly motivated by the exile of his brother.[31] Finally, Cicero refers to the two Servilii: these were the brothers Publius and Gaius Servilius Casca who, like so many of the conspirators, were adherents of Caesar. The latter was a tribune of the plebs in 44 BC, and his brother was to take up this role in the year following Caesar's murder.

That Cicero's list, although reliable, was merely an abbreviated one is apparent in his comments that it would take a long time to enumerate the rest, and that he felt it to be a blessing for the Republic that so many had been involved.[32] It can be safely assumed that those whom he names are principal offenders, integral to the conspiracy and assassination. None of the extant ancient sources provides a full list of the conspirators, but they all clearly indicate that there were numerous Roman senators involved. Certainly, this was by no means to be the small undertaking of a few men: one source states that there were in excess of sixty men involved, while another increases this figure to more than eighty.[33]

While including most of those men already identified by Cicero, Appian offers the names of several more senators who were purportedly involved in the plot. He divides his list into friends of Brutus and Cassius, and friends of Caesar. The only new name among the latter is Minucius Basilus, who had fought with Caesar as a commander in Gaul, and held a praetorship in 45 BC. In that year, Caesar denied him a province, giving him money instead, and his decision to join the conspiracy is attributed to this insult.[34] Of significance among the listed associates of Brutus and Cassius is Lucius Pontius Aquila, who was the tribune in 45 BC who had declined to stand at Caesar's triumph, angering the dictator.[35] Interestingly, his villa in Naples was one of those confiscated by Caesar in the aftermath of the civil war against Pompey, and sold at a minimal price to Servilia, Brutus' mother, who was still in possession of it after the assassination.[36] Also of note is Servius Sulpicius Galba, who served as a legate under Caesar in Gaul from 58–56 BC, and was praetor in 54 BC. Although formerly an adherent of Caesar, he now felt resentment towards the dictator, who had prevented him attaining the consulship, and so decided to enrol in the assassination. He was the great-grandfather of the future Emperor, Galba.[37] Another relevant name featured on the list is Quintus Ligarius, who fought against Caesar in Africa and received his pardon following Cato's suicide, but was nonetheless exiled for treason by the dictator, who labelled him 'a villain and an enemy'; Cicero interceded with Caesar on Ligarius' behalf, in person and through a defence speech, with eventual success. It was this Ligarius who, from his sickbed, had played a role in encouraging Brutus towards the conspiracy.[38] According to Plutarch's version of events, there was another friend of Brutus, Pacuvius Antistius Labeo, who was also involved: this jurist had been privy to the plot quite early on, attempting, with Cassius, to convince Decimus Brutus to enlist.[39]

Perhaps even more notable than the list of those men included in the conspiracy is one glaring omission: that of Cicero. Plutarch claims that Brutus and Cassius kept the plot from Cicero, despite his despair at the current state of affairs in Rome, because they felt that his old age and tendency towards careful calculation would hinder their necessary swift and decisive action. His continual wavering throughout the civil war period does suggest that they were right to judge that Cicero did not truly have the heart for such a momentous deed. However, he was not the only close friend of Brutus and Cassius to be excluded from the conspiracy. Plutarch reports that, when testing out their feelings through a philosophical debate, Brutus found that the views of two friends, Statilius, the Epicurean, and Favonius, who was an adherent of Cato, were not concordant with the assassination plot. The former declared that a wise man should not endanger himself for foolish people, while the latter believed that civil war was worse than an illegal monarchy. Therefore Brutus chose not to include them in this conspiracy, about which he revealed nothing at this stage. Labeo, however, had argued against them both, and so the plot was later disclosed to him, and he eagerly enrolled.[40]

Various reasons are given for these men deciding to enlist in the plot to assassinate Caesar. Many of these men were his enemies, who had formerly fought alongside Pompey in the civil war and, although pardoned by Caesar, had not been truly reconciled with the dictator. Naturally, his tyrannical behaviour had proved abhorrent to these Republicans, as it had to Brutus, but it also proved unbearable to some of those whom Caesar had counted as friends. Others had more personal grudges against him, such as the loss of property: these personal reasons could sometimes be petty, such as jealousy at being overlooked for honours or irritation at being obstructed in attempts to attain political posts. It has also been suggested that some men had their eyes on becoming powerful leaders themselves.[41]

Once they had recruited enough men to their plot, all the conspirators swore to secrecy, and were said to be surprisingly successful in maintaining discretion, managing not to raise any suspicion, nor to reveal their plan. Their achievement may perhaps be measured in the fact that the secret plot never reached the ears of Cicero. Dio Cassius does, however, suggest that the plot was almost detected because of their large number, and also because they reportedly delayed, ironically through fear of discovery and punishment. Nevertheless they were careful, and were said to have held their planning meetings at each other's houses, with only a few men attending at a time.[42]

Other Victims

As well as being considered as a member of the conspiracy, Mark Antony was also a potential victim of this plot. Some of the conspirators, Cassius being the only one explicitly named, wished to kill Antony along with Caesar, for they feared his power both politically, as Caesar's fellow consul in 44 BC, and also militarily because of his influence with the Roman army. According to Dio Cassius, Marcus Aemilius Lepidus was also a possible target: he was the brother-in-law of both Brutus and Cassius, since he was married to Brutus' sister and Cassius' sister-in-law, Junia Secunda. Lepidus had been master of horse to Caesar's dictator since 46 BC, and presumably was considered to pose a threat as one of the dictator's right-hand men. It was his father who had led the post-Sullan rebellion, in which Brutus' father had perished at the hands of Pompey.[43] Along with Antony and Octavian, Lepidus would soon become one of the future Triumvirs.

However, Brutus' noble nature was instrumental here: he refused to turn this honourable assassination of a tyrant into a bloodbath of any sort. He is reported to have claimed that glory could arise from tyrannicide alone, and that to kill any of Caesar's friends as well would have made their motivation appear nothing more than personal enmity associated with the faction of Pompey. For Brutus this was a far higher calling than the base murder of those he disliked, and indeed he no longer seemed to consider Caesar a personal foe: this was to be the death of a tyrant for the sake of the liberty of the Roman Republic. Similarly, he added that the conspirators should not want to convey the incorrect impression that they were simply aiming to seize power themselves. It was Brutus' influential opinion that prevailed, unsurprisingly given that his participation was considered essential by many of the conspirators: Caesar, as tyrant, was to be the only target for their swords.[44] Whether this was a mistake or not, only time would tell. Certainly Cicero, driven by his personal hatred of Antony, believed so, and would not let the conspirators forget this in the aftermath of the assassination: he incessantly complained that this deed had been left half done, stating that the tyranny had survived in the form of Antony; and he also claimed, with the wise words of hindsight, that he would not have left Antony alive, had he only been party to the assassination.[45]

Time and Location

Given the sheer number of men committed to this undertaking, it was necessary to give due thought to finding a suitable location and opportunity for assassination that would not arouse suspicion. Different choices were explored: the elections in the Campus Martius were proposed as one possibility, with the conspirators dividing into two groups, so that one half was engaged in forcing Caesar off the planks that formed the temporary voters' bridge while the other half waited below to kill him when he fell; another option discussed was attacking the dictator when he took one of his frequent walks along the Via Sacra; a third known consideration was to set upon him just outside the theatre; yet another suggestion was the approaching gladiator shows, where men could be armed without suspicion.

A final decision was reached, however: the murder was to take place at the senate meeting on the notorious Ides of March, the fifteenth of the month.[46] As we saw earlier, it was this senate meeting that ultimately forced their hand to assassinate Caesar, or certainly rushed their need to act: for it was here that it was to be proposed that the dictator should now receive the title of

King, before he shortly set out for his campaign against Parthia, on the basis that the prophetic Sibylline books pronounced that only a monarch could conquer that land; and this was the act of tyranny that proved to be one too many for the optimates to endure. A senate meeting was also felt to be suitable for other reasons: Caesar would be most vulnerable to their attack there, not expecting it; only senators could enter, and many of the senators were members of the conspiracy; it was also hoped that others, not privy to the plot, would join the fray once they realised what was happening, and that all would support the mission of liberty after the deed; here, they were able to conceal their swords easily, either under their togas or in document boxes; it was also felt to be a safer location, since any men in opposition to the murder were unlikely to be carrying weapons although, to safeguard themselves, they stationed armed gladiators nearby in case of any violent resistance; somewhat naively, they believed that, by committing the act in a public place, rather than as a private conspiracy, they would prove that this was being carried out for the greater good and that it would be received as such.[47]

During this period, senate meetings were being held in a temporary location, since the senate house in the forum had been burnt down eight years previously by the riotous mob at the funeral of Clodius. The current site was a curia, or hall, located in the porticoes attached to the mighty theatre of Pompey, the first permanent one in the city, which was opened in 55 BC with magnificent games on a massive scale to celebrate its dedication:[48] this meant that Caesar was to fall on the site of what was perhaps his enemy's finest legacy to Rome. The irony of this was not lost on the ancient authors, some of whom attributed it to divine retribution.[49]

And so the final plans were in place: the stage was now set for one of the most infamous assassinations ever and, most importantly, for the deed that was to earn Brutus his indelible place in the annals of history.

Chapter Seven

Assassination: Liberty Recovered

Beware the Ides of March

The plot to kill the dictator Caesar seems to have been planned with such care and attention to detail that, despite the sheer number of conspirators involved, it went undetected. It was perhaps for this reason that Caesar chose to ignore various foreboding omens, as well as more earthly warnings, which occurred in the period leading up to his assassination.

Of the many supernatural portents, Cicero records the details of an ill-omened sacrifice performed by Caesar, where a sacrificial ox was found to have no heart. According to Cicero this took place when Caesar first sat on the golden throne and wore purple robes:[1] since Cicero was a contemporary of the dictator, it is reasonable to assume that there is some truth to the story of a portentous sacrifice having taken place, but it may perhaps be suspected that these particular details are an elaboration attempting to forge a link between Caesar's monarchical and hubristic actions and his murder. Caesar took no notice of this portent, but Spurinna, the haruspex inspecting the entrails, warned him to beware in case his thought and life should fail him. Cicero does not include the specific detail that Caesar should 'beware the Ides of March', which has perhaps gained most fame from Shakespeare's tragedy, but this does exist in several other ancient accounts.[2] Sacrifices are again performed on the next day, and are found to be equally unfavourable, because the assassination had, by now, become inevitable. Further sacrifices of ill-omened outcome were carried out on the inauspicious day itself, at the entrance to the temporary senate house.

Various other omens are listed in the sources, with Suetonius and Plutarch providing particularly full and detailed lists.[3] Suetonius records one especially predictive anecdote, which he credits as truthful since its source was Cornelius Balbus, a close and trusted friend of Caesar.[4] A few months before his death, in the process of building country houses in the colony of Capua for the veterans settling there, many ancient tombs were destroyed;

the tomb of Capys, the founder of Capua and grandfather of Aeneas, was discovered, containing a bronze tablet inscribed in Greek: the prophetic words stated that, when the bones of Capys were disturbed, a descendant of his (which Caesar was purported to be through his legendary ancestor Aeneas[5]) would be murdered by kin, and later would be avenged at a heavy cost to Italy.

Other accounts of portents include the bizarre behaviour of animals and nature, such as the horses that Caesar had dedicated to the River Rubicon, at the start of the civil war against Pompey, now refusing to graze and witnessed weeping; or the so-called 'King-bird' which, on the day before the assassination, flew into the hall where the senate was due to meet, carrying a piece of laurel, only to be pursued by various other birds who tore it to pieces there in the ill-fated room. There were also reports of lights in the sky, crashing sounds through the night, and birds of omen flying into the forum. Strange fire-related apparitions were also witnessed, including the vision of multitudes of men on fire, and a soldier's slave emitting a flame from his hand, but displaying no injury when the blaze subsided.[6]

Aside from the supernatural phenomena, there were more reliable warnings from the mortal world for Caesar to heed, and he was by no means ignorant of these manifest signs. The most blatant indication came in the form of men accused of plotting against him. In late 46 BC, Cicero addressed a defence speech to Caesar in which he spoke of a plot against his life, which was clearly known to both of them, although the identity of those responsible appears to have remained a mystery. Two years later, and several months after Caesar's assassination, in one of his vitriolic speeches against Antony, Cicero again mentions a plot that had been known to Caesar: he recalls how a story had been circulating that an assassin with a dagger, who had supposedly been sent by Antony, was arrested at Caesar's house; following this, according to Cicero, Caesar had accused Antony in the senate.[7] It is doubtful that we can trust Antony's bitter enemy to be reporting reliably on his involvement in such a conspiracy, but it does appear from these two accounts that there were earlier plots against Caesar's life, and that he was fully aware of the threats to his life. According to other sources Antony was, indeed, implicated in at least one earlier conspiracy: we have already seen how Trebonius approached him in Gaul, when forming a plot;[8] and Plutarch also records how he was accused of planning a revolution with Dolabella. When Caesar heard these reports, he dismissed them, claiming that it was not such fat and long-haired men he feared, but the thin and pale ones:

Plutarch states that Caesar was here alluding to Brutus and Cassius. Caesar was also reported to have made a similar comment about his suspicions of Cassius, asking his friends what they thought he wanted, and saying that he did not like him because he was too pale. However, his view of Brutus was more contradictory: Plutarch informs us that he feared Brutus' lofty spirit, his reputation and his friends, but that he had faith in his character. Apparently trusting more in Brutus than Cassius, Caesar was said to have rejected accusations made to him about Brutus' murderous designs, not believing that such an honourable man would thus debase himself, when he would soon succeed to his power by legal means. If true, this last comment displays that Caesar had completely misunderstood Brutus: for it was not Caesar's power and position that Brutus sought by his assassination but, as everyone else seemed to know, the restoration of his beloved Republic.[9]

On top of all this Caesar was, of course, very aware that he was a hated man: not only did he have a long-standing history of hostility between himself and the optimate party at Rome, having consciously acted against their sacred form of government on many occasions, but he also knew that he was alienating those who were perhaps of a milder disposition and more favourable towards him. Cicero records the incident where he himself had gone to visit Caesar at his house, but was made to sit and wait to be summoned: Caesar reportedly remarked that he could not doubt that he was deeply disliked when a man such as Cicero could not see him at his convenience, adding that he would be a fool not to realise that Cicero, despite his good nature, must detest him.[10]

Despite all these signs which now, with the power of hindsight, seem to be all too obvious warnings of impending murder, Caesar nevertheless dismissed his personal bodyguard of Spanish cohorts during this period. This may seem extremely imprudent, but it has been suggested that Caesar felt that the security of his bodyguard was no longer necessary, since one of the special honours voted to him was an oath pledged by all senators to protect his person. Furthermore, Caesar was said to have explicitly refused a bodyguard when advised, stating that he preferred a sudden death to a life living in fear.[11] He was known to have expressed this opinion about death on other occasions too. Suetonius reports that Caesar, on reading how Cyrus the Great gave his own funeral directions while dying of an illness, was said to have hated the idea of a long and lingering death, expressing a wish for a quick and sudden one.[12] Indeed one reason given for his negligence towards personal security was that his failing health meant he no longer wished to live. More relevantly, several of the ancient sources record the anecdote in which Caesar was dining at the home of Lepidus, his master of horse, on the eve of the assassination: in macabre and eerily predictive fashion, discussion at the dinner couches turned to consideration of the best form of death and, in response, Caesar swiftly interjected: 'that which is unexpected'. Decimus Brutus, his trusted friend and soon-to-be assassin, who was also present in one version of events, was clearly paying attention: the dictator's wish was about to be granted thanks to him and his fellow conspirators. Another important source of Caesar's disregard for his safety was his misguided judgement that his enemies would believe that he was more beneficial to Rome alive than dead: he reportedly thought that they would prefer his powerful presence to their state being torn asunder by yet more political turmoil, which he believed was what his death would bring. In the end, of course, he underestimated the strength of their Republican inclination, while they similarly misjudged the stability that he had recently brought to the state: they did not appear to think through what would emerge in the wake of his assassination, somehow idealistically expecting an automatic and smooth return to the previous Republican form of government.[13]

The eve of the inauspicious day, unsurprisingly, brought further and increased signs of impending doom to the house of Caesar. That night both the dictator and his wife, Calpurnia,[14] were plagued by bizarre dreams. Caesar dreamed that he was flying above the clouds, clutching the hand of the King of the gods, Jupiter, in a vision foretelling his supposed deification. Meanwhile Calpurnia was suffering more troubling nightmares: Caesar, confused, and feeling faint as well according to one version, having been woken by the strange occurrence of the doors and windows of the room suddenly flying open of their own accord, and most probably also by the reported unexpected noise made by the weapons of Mars which were being stored in his house presently, looked upon his wife in the moonlight and saw her murmuring and groaning in her sleep. Accounts vary, but Calpurnia was being disturbed by distressing visions of her husband's demise: she was dreaming that she was weeping, holding the bloody and wounded body of Caesar, who had been stabbed; alternatively, or in addition, Calpurnia had either seen their home fall in ruins, or an honorary gable ornament, voted to Caesar's house by the senate and indicative of his status, torn down.[15] Whichever of these visions Calpurnia had, the portents were not promising for Caesar, and accurately so.

The Ides of March

The fateful and notorious day, 15 March 44 BC, finally arrived. The ancient texts are replete with details of how this day's events unfolded, and it is an amalgamation of these accounts that will be rehearsed here. However, it is timely here to remind ourselves that caution must be urged regarding the reliability of the various anecdotal tales emerging from this momentous event: they are naturally subject to elaboration, confusion and literary convention as they are retold over time. Ultimately, while reported as fact, we cannot necessarily take them at face value, although we can accept that there is some truth in their account of the proceedings of the day and, of course, in the final outcome.

The Morning Before: Caesar

On the morning of the Ides of March, deeply distressed by the previous night's occurrences and what they might portend, Calpurnia begged her husband not to go out that day, and to postpone the meeting of the senate. If Caesar would pay no heed to her dreams, she asked that he at least check the auspices by other means before setting out. Caesar was alarmed at this uncharacteristically anxious behaviour exhibited by his normally rational wife, and so did as she asked; the augury did not bring any better results. Although previously Caesar was undisturbed by the many signs and warnings, this clearly now troubled him, since he began to hesitate and was even prepared to postpone the senate meeting: indeed, because of these concerns, as well as reported ill health, he had reached the sensible decision to send Antony to cancel it.[16]

With the delay in waiting for Caesar, and learning that he may not attend at all, the conspirators began to worry that their plan had been thwarted and might thus be detected. At this point Decimus Brutus, Caesar's trusted friend and secondary heir, stepped in with an act that can only be termed as treachery. He went to the house of Caesar to persuade him, successfully of course, to attend the senate meeting. According to the sources, he applied pressure, playing on the dictator's pride: Decimus pointed out to Caesar that he was laying himself open to accusations of tyranny, not to mention derision, for calling together this meeting of the willing senate so that he could be declared King outside of Italy, only to cancel it on a whim because of his wife's dreams; Decimus slyly added that, if he truly felt it to be an inauspicious day, then at the very least he should go to the senate to postpone the day's business in person. Decimus then proceeded to lead Caesar off physically.[17]

At this point there were further warnings for Caesar to heed, both supernatural and mortal. Firstly, an image of Caesar, in the entrance hall to his house, fell and shattered to pieces. Shortly after Caesar's departure from the house, either another man's slave or one of Caesar's close acquaintances, attempting but failing to reach the dictator because of the multitude surrounding him, forced his way into the house and found Calpurnia; this man waited for Caesar's return, claiming to have urgent business to relate to him, but clearly not in possession of all the details of the assassination plot, otherwise he would have realised the futility of remaining there. Another man also attempted to inform Caesar that there was a plot afoot before he reached the senate. Artemidorus, a Greek philosopher who was acquainted with Brutus' circle and therefore privy to the conspiracy, and who had also entertained Caesar in his home at Cnidus (Knidos), approached the doomed dictator with a document, pleading with him to read this one quickly, for it contained vital information. Caesar took this one scroll, while all others handed to him were passed straight on to his attendants, but he never had an opportunity to read it because so many people were demanding his attention: he entered the senate carrying it, and it was still in his hand as he was struck down. However, in one version Artemidorus reached the senate too late, and it was another man's note found in the dead man's hand.[18]

Caesar was also given another type of warning before reaching the senate, in the form of the soothsayer, Spurinna. Despite his previous doubts about the day, Caesar now confidently adopted his nonchalant attitude once more: either meeting with Spurinna as he was proceeding to the senate, or while performing further sacrifices before entering the meeting, Caesar jokingly brushed aside his earlier warning about the Ides, now that the day had come; the soothsayer ominously replied that the Ides may have arrived, but they had not yet gone. In spite of this gloomy prophecy and the unfavourable results of the sacrifices performed on the day, Caesar nonetheless proceeded to the fateful meeting.[19]

The Morning Before: The Conspirators

Returning to our principal subject, Brutus, we are furnished with the detail that, before leaving his home that morning, he put on his dagger in preparation for the momentous deed. Meanwhile, the other conspirators convened at the house of Cassius in order to lead his son, Brutus' nephew, in procession to the forum, since he had come of age and it was the day on which he was to assume the *toga virilis*. The conspirators, noted as being remarkably composed considering the magnitude of their fast-approaching undertaking, then proceeded to the location of the assassination, the temporary senate house in the porticoes of Pompey's theatre. Gladiators, presumably the ones belonging to Decimus Brutus, had been stationed around the theatre in case they were needed as protection, ostensibly on the basis that they would be fighting there in the games scheduled for that day. Here the group of conspirators must have been reunited with Brutus. In their role as praetors, Brutus and Cassius calmly went about their business, listening to petitions and bestowing judgements. The purported composure of Brutus is illustrated in a Plutarchean anecdote: when one of his pronouncements was challenged by a man who instead appealed to Caesar, Brutus defiantly proclaimed that Caesar did not, and would not, prevent him from acting according to the laws. This unshaken and confident manner serves to underscore that Brutus held a firm belief in the moral rectitude of the murderous deed he was soon to perform.[20]

Contradictory reports, however, suggest that the conspirators did become anxious and unsettled, at least in the delay while waiting for the arrival of their intended victim. For example, we know that they decided to send Decimus to fetch Caesar, by treacherous and deceitful means, in case the dictator should postpone the meeting and their plot should then be discovered. Other occurrences provide evidence that they had become anxious. One of the Casca brothers was understandably shaken by the unfortunately ambiguous comment of an unidentified man: he accused Casca of hiding a secret, but claimed that Brutus had told him everything. Unnerved, Casca assumed that he was making reference to the assassination plot, and was on the point of revealing everything, when the man jokingly explained that he was wondering how Casca had suddenly become rich enough to stand for the aedileship. Another disconcerting moment came when Brutus and Cassius were approached by the senator Popilius Laenas, who made a similarly alarming remark to them: he whispered that he, too, hoped they would succeed in their plan, and urged them not to delay since men were now talking about it. That this comment had rattled the chief conspirators can be seen in their reaction to what happened next: their fear was increased when they witnessed Laenas rushing up to speak at length with Caesar as he alighted from his litter. Believing that he was in the course of disclosing their plot, the conspirators exchanged looks between themselves to give a sign that they were prepared to avoid arrest by killing themselves on the spot; indeed, their hands were poised on the daggers they wore hidden under their clothing. When Brutus realised that Laenas was merely requesting something from Caesar, he indicated that there was nothing to be concerned about to his fellow conspirators with a change in his demeanour, so that no one unnecessarily committed suicide.[21]

It was not only the conspirators who were troubled by the awareness of what would come to pass that day. Back at the house of Brutus, his wife was working herself up into a frenzy with the burden of the knowledge of her husband's impending mission. Quite unlike the strong-willed character she claimed to be when she previously displayed her unfeminine resolve to her husband so that he would reveal this plot to her, Porcia now became the epitome of a feeble woman, suggesting to us that perhaps Brutus should not, after all, have shared the source of his anxiety with her. In a constant condition of distress, she panicked at every noise, and kept sending messengers to discover the state of affairs with Brutus. Her womanly weakness was revealed in her physical inability to endure this high anxiety: she was overcome with faintness, and those present incorrectly believed she had collapsed in death. A messenger rushed to Brutus to deliver the sad news of his wife's demise although, unbeknown to him she had, in fact, revived: however, as to be expected of a man so dedicated to his cause, he refused to allow this to interfere with his important mission, remaining focused on his public duty to defend his beloved Republic.[22]

Honourable Murder: Death of a Tyrant

Now that Caesar had arrived for the senate meeting, the moment for murder was rapidly approaching and it was time for the conspirators to be roused to action. While all the senators proceeded into the hall, Trebonius detained Caesar's fellow consul, Antony, outside in conversation. Almost a year later, Cicero can still be found grumbling at Trebonius as the one responsible for having kept Antony, the source of his trouble, alive. However, the conspirators feared the strength of Antony, both physically, as an experienced soldier described as robust by one of the sources, and politically, given that he was Caesar's fellow consul. Therefore, since Brutus had decided that Antony should not be killed as well, they wisely judged it best to employ one of their number to keep him out of the way of the action instead.[23]

At this juncture, the members of the senate respectfully rose from their seats as Caesar entered the curia. Once Caesar had been seated, the band of conspirators surrounded his chair: some took their seats behind him, while others approached him in a gesture of petition. Tillius Cimber then instigated the assassination by approaching Caesar with a plea for the return of his exiled brother. The other conspirators supported him in his supplication, physically imploring Caesar, reportedly clasping his hand and kissing his head and breast. However, Caesar haughtily dismissed them, deferring the matter for another time, but the assassins persisted: they would not accept this rejection and Caesar, becoming angry, found that he was unable to free himself from their grip, even by force. Now Tillius gave the sign for the attack to commence: with both hands, he tore the purple toga off the shoulders of the beleaguered dictator, thus exposing his neck and, in one version, cried aloud to his fellow assassins: 'Friends, what are you waiting for?' Meanwhile, Caesar exclaimed at the violence being enacted upon him, but to no avail: with the sign given to attack, the first blow was struck.[24]

The exact details of how the bloody murder unfolded vary slightly in the texts, but all sources agree that it was one of the Casca brothers who was the first to draw his dagger in order to stab Caesar. From his position somewhere behind Caesar, he inflicted a wound that was not deep, either at the base of his neck or in his shoulder. One account differs in suggesting that he was aiming at Caesar's throat but missed and instead struck him in the breast. Wherever it was, the wound was not a serious one, allowing Caesar to fight back in some way: he either grabbed the handle of the dagger, holding onto it and, in his shock, imploring the 'impious Casca', asked what he was doing; or, it was Casca whom Caesar took hold of, using his writing stylus to stab him in the arm; another version reports that Caesar snatched his toga back from Tillius, and then took hold of Casca's hand to throw him back with force. In whatever way Caesar resisted, the next precise detail that we are given is that Casca summoned his brother, in Greek, to come to his aid. The blows now rained down upon Caesar from all sides: as he was turning, outstretched and repelling Casca, he was struck in the side, possibly by the other Casca brother; Cassius wounded him in the face; Brutus struck his groin; Decimus Brutus slashed his thigh; and another conspirator, named Bucilianus, literally stabbed him in the back. In the general confusion of the mêlée, several of the conspirators were accidentally wounded by each other, showing just how frenzied and disorganised the nature of their attack was: Brutus received a blow to the hand, possibly from Cassius aiming his dagger at Caesar for a second time; Minucius also missed his target, finding instead the thigh of his fellow-conspirator, a man named Rubrius Ruga. It seems that the conspirators had decided that each of them should strike a blow to demonstrate their equal and united involvement. The scene was thus one of butchery, leaving them all spattered with blood, both that of the dictator and their own. The stab wounds were numerous, with the number being given as twenty-three by the majority of sources, although one text records it as thirty-five; some of these were cruelly inflicted even after he fell down in death. According to the physician, Antistius, who reportedly examined Caesar's body, there was only one fatal wound among so many: the second stabbing of the dictator's breast.[25]

However, according to tradition, the deepest cut was not a physical but an emotional one, and it came from the hand of Brutus. For when Caesar realised that even his beloved Brutus had betrayed him, seeing him approach with his dagger drawn, he gave up then and there. Until that point Caesar, although met with a hail of blows in whichever direction he went, had frantically sought a way to escape from the assailants surrounding him, portrayed like vulnerable prey set upon by a pack of wild animals. When he saw Brutus, however, this changed. Caesar did not speak the immortal words '*Et tu, Brute?*', as Shakespeare would have it, but possibly uttered the similar phrase 'You too, my son?' in Greek. These were the final words of the powerful dictator, and they have reinforced belief in the story that Brutus was his own offspring. Despite this having been proved as extremely improbable, as we have already seen, it is easy to see why this has been an attractive theory, especially for thus increasing the poignancy of Caesar's final moments.[26] An alternative account claims that after his initial groan at the first strike Caesar remained silent throughout the entire ordeal. However, the ancient authors do agree that, once he had seen Brutus, Caesar gave up resisting, sank down, and covered his head and lower body with his toga, simply accepting the blows and resigning himself to his premature death: it was as if he, too, recognised that Brutus' role in his assassination defined this as an honourable and just murder.[27]

In this way Caesar the tyrant was overthrown, slaughtered at the hands of friend and foe alike. He was found still clutching the warning note in his hand, and reputedly met his tragic demise under the eyes of Pompey, in what seemed to be an act of divine justice, according to the ancient authors. For, since this assassination took place in one of the porticoes attached to the magnificent theatre of Pompey, there was a statue of this enemy of Caesar, here in this very hall. Cassius was reported to have looked at the image of Pompey and invoked it immediately before the murder, which was uncharacteristic behaviour for this usually cool and calm Epicurean, motivated by the magnitude of the deed he was about to commit. And, adding to the drama of this tale of murder, when Caesar fell, it was said to be at Pompey's feet: this is a detail that does not appear to be fictional, since it is verified by the contemporary Cicero. Caesar's body ended up ignominiously slumped against the blood-soaked pedestal of this statue, although it is uncertain whether he simply fell onto it in his death throes or was purposely pushed there by the assassins realising the sweetness of the irony. The reputed site of this momentous historical event, on the edge of Pompey's theatre complex, can still be visited today, in the Largo Argentina area of the city.[28]

For his part, once he had stabbed Caesar, and carried out his honourable and obligatory deed of tyrannicide, Brutus reportedly held aloft his dagger, in a pose akin to that of the statue of his tyrant-ridding ancestor, Lucius Brutus, and called upon Cicero, crying out that liberty had been recovered.[29]

Chapter Eight

Assassination Aftermath: The Rise and Fall of the Liberators

The Ides of March Continued

Immediate Aftermath

During the preceding furore, no one from the rest of the senate came forth to aid Caesar: in shock and horror, they stood by and did nothing as he was butchered, reportedly even stunned into silence. Only two senators proved to be the brave exception: Gaius Calvisius Sabinus, a governor of Africa Vetus, and Lucius Marcius Censorinus, who would become consul with Calvisius in 39 BC. They both loyally attempted to defend Caesar from the attack, but the sheer number of the conspirators rendered them unable to assist and forced them to flee along with the rest. Brutus attempted to make a speech to alleviate the fears of the rest of the senators, still believing in the power of the moral and just nature of the crime he had just committed. However, panic and chaos ensued in the senate hall: all the senators fled in terror and panic, seeking a place to hide. Since they were operating in the name of liberty, the conspirators had no intention of pursuing those fleeing. The general pandemonium nevertheless spread throughout the city to those who witnessed it: houses were shut up, markets were plundered, businesses were abandoned, and, according to one account, there was even murder during the uproar.[1]

Amid all the chaos, Caesar's body was left, most unceremoniously, where it had been struck down, beneath Pompey's statue. It finally took the good grace and courage of three slaves to carry him home in a litter: we are furnished with the additional and unfortunate detail that Caesar was carried off with one arm hanging down. Caesar, the tyrant, was dead, but it was certainly not to be a fitting and glorious end for the most powerful Roman of the time: the mighty had not just fallen, but had been entirely annihilated.[2] According to one account, the conspirators had initially planned to drag the tyrant's corpse to the River Tiber, as well as confiscate his property and annul his decrees, but fear of Antony and Lepidus prevented this. The conspirators need not have feared Antony at this stage, however, since he incorrectly believed himself to be a target for the assassins: at first, disguising himself as a slave, he fled into hiding at night, taking refuge at the house of a friend; later, he returned to his own home, which he took measures to secure against attack. Lepidus, Caesar's other right-hand man at this time, desiring revenge for the murdered dictator, took a more practical approach to the crisis: he hastened to Tiber Island, where he had troops stationed since he had been about to leave for command of his province of Narbonese Gaul and Nearer Spain. Overnight, he transferred the soldiers from Tiber Island to the Campus Martius and forum area, to await the command of Antony, and supposedly delivered a speech against the assassins at dawn the next day.[3]

In the meantime, Brutus and the rest of the conspirators marched, via the forum, up to the Capitol, escorted by Decimus' band of gladiators, so that they might pray to the gods. They were said to be confident and exultant, still covered in the blood of the murdered dictator and with their daggers on display as they went, crying out that they had slaughtered the tyrant. However, a conflicting account suggests that they adopted a defensive pose, using their togas as makeshift shields, by wrapping them around their arms. The conspirators, or Liberators as they now fashioned themselves, exhorted the people, calling upon liberty, the restoration of the Republican government, and the memory of Lucius Brutus. One version of events claims that they were also calling for Cicero as they proceeded. It is not clear exactly when Cicero enrolled in the Liberators' cause, although his support must have been assumed, but it seems that he did not join them on the Capitol: in his correspondence, he speaks as if slightly detached from the Liberators and, in the ancient sources, he is soon to be found arguing on their behalf elsewhere, while they remained ensconced there. However, he must have been in contact, and associated, with them, since he recalls offering them the wisdom of his advice almost immediately after they seized the Capitol.[4]

They did succeed in enrolling some sympathisers to their cause en route, with several names given in the ancient texts. The accounts are fairly disparaging in accusing these men of wanting a share of the glory without the bravery and resolve to commit the deed. However, we must remember that Brutus and Cassius were extremely careful about whom they recruited to their assassination plot, and we know that some men were explicitly excluded at the planning stage: Favonius is named as one of the men who now joined them, but Brutus had tested out his feelings before the assassination and decided that he did not possess the required qualities to be a co-conspirator.

It can be assumed that similar tests and verdicts were applied to other men. Now that the dangerous action was over, they gladly welcomed these new members to their mission to restore liberty and the Republic. Other men of note who joined the Liberators at this point include Publius Cornelius Lentulus Spinther, son of the consul who had been a supporter of Caesar initially, but who later came over to the optimates. Spinther the younger would fight in the civil war against Antony and Octavian, and produced coins in support of the Liberators at that time, some of which survive. Lucius Staius Murcus also now associated himself with the Liberators: he had been a legate under Caesar in Gaul and Africa, but would play an integral role in the aftermath of the assassination, as proconsul in Syria and then fleet commander alongside the conspirator Ahenobarbus.[5]

One other relevant name mentioned as now backing the Liberators, but whose motives were more questionable than those of others, is Dolabella. This detested former son-in-law of Cicero, who had fought with Caesar against Pompey, saw an opportunity for himself: since he had been designated by the dictator to replace him as consul in 44 BC, when he soon departed for his Parthian campaign, Dolabella wasted no time in seizing the office that had been left empty by his assassination instead. He was something of a reprobate who could not be trusted and whose principal driving forces appeared to be self-preservation and self-promotion. An accusation of plotting against Caesar had also been laid at his door previously. Therefore it was not altogether surprising that, having seized the insignia of the office, Dolabella now aligned himself with the Liberators: he reportedly headed up to join them on the Capitol after making a short speech on the current state of affairs, in which he was rumoured to have claimed that he had been party to the conspiracy and that the day should henceforth be celebrated as the birthday of the Republic. The Liberators were said to be pleased to have won this man over to their side, particularly hoping that he could provide strong opposition to Antony. However, unsurprisingly, Dolabella would soon be found simultaneously negotiating with Antony, with whom he had recently clashed publicly, and who had vociferously opposed the suffect consulship being given to him. This slippery character would later prove to be an instrumental thorn in the side of the Liberators, since he would eventually be bought by Antony's offer of a command against the Parthians and the province of Syria, and thus would become a lethal enemy of the Liberators in battle.[6]

It was beginning to become apparent that the Liberators had not given any serious thought to the repercussions of Caesar's murder, since there is no evidence of any real plan or policy as to what should happen next, particularly in the event of their idealistic hopes not being realised, which was not something that they seemed to have taken into consideration. In effect they had won the battle but not the war: they had succeeded in their mission to slay the tyrant, but their ultimate intention of restoring the Republic was a different matter, which would involve much more strategy than they had deployed. One theory put forward attributes this lack of preparation to the conspirators' need for absolute secrecy before the assassination, but a straightforward deficiency of good judgement and foresight must also be held accountable.[7] They merely responded to the evolving situations, which often seemed to take them by surprise, making it up as they went along, rather than controlling matters. It can safely be assumed that, having convened on the Capitol, the Liberators began discussing a plan of action, but now it was too late to implement anything useful: it all appeared to depend on the actions of others, especially as they had no military support in the city, other than Decimus' gladiators. Cicero urged that they summon the senate to the Capitoline Temple, and thus take control, but they chose not to follow this advice.[8] The Liberators remained occupying the Capitol throughout the night of the Ides of March.

The Following Days

Calm Restored, Reconciliation, and Amnesty

The exact sequence of events in the days following the eventful Ides of March cannot be reconstructed with complete certainty, since the ancient accounts sometimes present conflicting and confused details at this point. However, it does seem certain that a level of calm and order was restored in the city of Rome after its initial panic, once it became clear that the Liberators had no intention of committing a mass slaughter, or of beginning a plundering spree. On the day after the assassination, 16 March, many of the senators and people, feeling thus reassured, assembled on the Capitol. Here, Brutus delivered a well-calculated speech, which won over this crowd. Appian suggests that bribery also played a part in swaying the opinion of the people at this stage: according to him, the Liberators had hoped that a love of liberty and the Republic, combined with bribery, would prove persuasive, but he dismisses the two things as incompatible; the people, won over by whichever means, were said to have been too afraid to praise the murder, and instead called for general peace in order to secure the safety of the Liberators.

The success of Brutus' speech can, perhaps, be measured in his desire to publish it: two months later, he sent a written version to Cicero for editing before publication, and the recipient judged it to be perfectly polished and without need of any amendment, but nonetheless claims that he would have written it with more fire than style, given the crucial circumstances; Atticus, however, appears to have felt differently, and was quite insistent that Cicero should make some changes.

Plutarch reports that Brutus' audience, in response to this speech, applauded him and encouraged the Liberators to come down from the Capitol, which they then did. His anecdote depicts Brutus surrounded by the most distinguished citizens, being treated almost as a hero: he was singled out to be escorted with great honour to the rostra in the forum, while the rest of the Liberators followed alone. The multitude in the forum, who were reportedly ready to begin demonstrating their displeasure at the assassination, were struck with awe at the very sight of Brutus, proving both the power of his honourable reputation and why it was so vital for the other conspirators that he was a leader of the assassination. As Brutus began addressing the crowd, with his hand still bleeding from the wound inflicted upon him during the frenzied attack on Caesar, he was met with silence: this is interpreted as an indication both of pity for Caesar and respect for Brutus. Appian offers a summary of this speech which, in his account, is shared with Cassius: reportedly, the lead conspirators praised each other and their deed in honourable terms; they gave a special vote of thanks to Decimus for providing his gladiators at the crucial time; and they once more cited the example of their tyrant-banishing forefathers, encouraging the populace to follow their lead. They also supposedly made more practical political suggestions. One was to recall Pompey's son Sextus from Spain, where he was continuing his father's civil war against Caesar's men. The other was to secure the return from exile of the two tribunes whom Caesar had latterly deposed in a fit of tyrannical pique, when he took offence at what he believed were challenges to his potential kingly status; however, this had possibly been proposed before Caesar's death.[9]

Two other men are recorded as having spoken in the forum at this time, on behalf of the conspirators. One was the new replacement consul, Dolabella, who possibly now declared the birth of the new Republic: witnessing a consul coming out in support of the Liberators and opposing the murdered dictator was said to have given the hesitant crowd courage to do the same. However, in contrast with the effect of the other speakers, when a certain

Lucius Cornelius Cinna began denouncing Caesar, the crowd reacted with anger. Cinna's father had been a supporter of Marius, Caesar's uncle, while his sister had been Caesar's first wife. Caesar had secured his recall from exile, and Cinna had therefore been one of his adherents. However, Cinna is recorded as being the one who recently sponsored the recall of the two tribunes deposed by Caesar, so he was already known to have opposed the dictator publicly. It has generally been considered that this praetor was not part of the assassination, but a sympathiser who joined the Liberators afterwards, despite the sources offering some evidence to the contrary. Either way, Cinna certainly possessed Republican sympathies, which he chose to demonstrate in dramatic fashion now: he theatrically cast off his robe of office, since it had been bestowed upon him by the dictator, declared that Caesar was a tyrant and the conspirators were tyrannicides like their ancestors, and suggested rewarding them with honours. Cinna instantly became the focus of the crowd's latent hatred, and the uprising that this caused forced the Liberators to retreat once more to the Capitol. In another noble act, Brutus reportedly sent away the most eminent men who had not been involved in the conspiracy, to keep the guiltless free from the potential danger of a siege.[10]

Realising that Caesar's assassins meant him no harm and so there was no threat posed to his life after all, Antony now recovered his courage. That Lepidus had gathered his forces together will, doubtless, also have rallied Antony, although they were both said to be harbouring concerns about the army to which Decimus had access as governor of Cisalpine Gaul. Nevertheless, Antony took the decision to seize political control and obtained Caesar's official papers and money from his grieving widow, Calpurnia. The overembellished account of Appian offers some additional information here which does not form part of the narrative in the other principal reconstructions of these events; this is possibly because these details are purely fictional, but it is nonetheless useful to acknowledge them. According to Appian, Brutus and Cassius sent messengers from among their accompanying friends to enter into negotiations with Antony and Lepidus on the night of 16 March: these ambassadors requested reconciliation, liberty, and peace for the state, but they did not dare to praise the murder of Caesar, asking instead for toleration of the deed. Antony returned a non-committal answer, and agreed to consider the best course at a meeting of the senate. Overnight, Antony stationed guards about the city, and there were also watchfires which allowed the conspirators' friends to move about freely, visiting the houses of the senators in order to entreat on behalf of the assassins and the Republic.[11]

Returning to the generally accepted reconstruction of events, early on the morning of 17 March, Antony summoned a meeting of the senate in the Temple of Tellus. This alternative temporary site for senate meetings was conveniently located near to his home and, in this unsettled political crisis, this location must have seemed a wise choice, since he would be able to make a quick getaway to safety in the event of violence breaking out once more. As an added measure, armed guards were posted around the entrances to the temple precinct. However, the only disturbances that broke out were as a result of Cinna's presence, reclothed, as he now was, in the praetor's robe that he had publicly discarded the day before: the enraged supporters of Caesar were so incensed that they threw stones at him; they pursued him to his house; and they would have set fire to it, had Lepidus not arrived with his soldiers to intervene. Previously having called for vengeance, Lepidus now played an integral role in restoring order and in aiding Antony to control the political turmoil: these services to the state were widely appreciated and, for this, he was hastily rewarded with the role of *pontifex maximus*, which had been made vacant by Caesar's death.[12]

Other than the uproar surrounding Cinna, there was generally a spirit of reconciliation at this meeting, and hopes were even raised that liberty and the Republic might still yet be restored. The Liberators were not present at the meeting, but most of the senators were believed to have had some sympathy for them. As to be expected, Cicero spoke up on their behalf but, more surprisingly, Antony was also said to have done the same. A third man noted as coming out in favour of Brutus, Cassius and the rest, was Lucius Munatius Plancus, the current proconsul of Transalpine Gaul, who had formerly served as a long-term legate under Caesar, both in the Gallic campaign and in Spain and Africa during the civil war. He was another man who would successfully, and ruthlessly, manoeuvre through this dangerous and unsettled period by reading the situation and responding accordingly, constantly shifting his allegiances in the name of self-preservation: in this current uncertain political crisis he was, therefore, to be found supporting a safe middle ground. At this meeting, the thorny question of how to deal with Caesar's decrees arose: on the one hand, if he were to be declared a tyrant, this would invalidate all his acts and, since this would have included the current and designated magistracies, political chaos would have ensued; on the other hand, if Caesar were not to be considered a tyrant, it would be necessary for the conspirators to face justice as murderers. This dilemma understandably caused concern: it was reportedly now that Dolabella first chose to switch sides for fear of losing the consulship for which he was legally too young but clearly very eager. In order to reach a compromise, it was decided to declare all of Caesar's decrees valid, including consideration of those which were only in draft form, while the conspirators were to be granted an amnesty. Cicero, a definite friend of the conspirators, proposed the amnesty, citing the example of the Athenians: this reference to the restoration of democracy in 403 BC by Thrasybulus, recalled the general amnesty granted after he overthrew the new oligarchic government, known as the Thirty Tyrants, which had been established by Sparta following Athens' defeat in the Peloponnesian War. At this point, Dio Cassius places a fictional speech in the mouth of Cicero: based on what he proposed at this time, the speech is of a conciliatory tone and Cicero is presented as urging that now was the opportune moment to act for the sake of peace in the state. Whatever the content of his long speech in reality, it was clearly convincing, since accounts agree that the senate passed the decree granting immunity to the conspirators. Furthermore, special honours were proposed for the tyrannicides by Tiberius Claudius Nero: this man had recently served as quaestor to Caesar in Alexandria, and would soon become the father of the future Emperor, Tiberius; a few years later he would be forced to give up his pregnant wife, Livia, and infant child to the rapacious Octavian. Accounts differ as to whether or not the conspirators received these honours.[13]

Although unverified by other accounts, Dio Cassius suggests that, while the meeting of the senate deciding their fate was taking place, the conspirators were seizing an opportunity to win over the soldiers: Caesar's veterans were disgruntled, concerned that they would lose their settlements of land in the colonies, so the conspirators reassured them that they would not revoke any of the dictator's acts. They then similarly addressed a crowd at the foot of the Capitol, and sent a note to the forum, making promises to the same effect. At this point, Appian, in an unlikely section of his text, given the spirit of reconciliation that had been fostered at the senate meeting, imagines Antony, supposedly wearing protective body armour, leaving the Temple of Tellus along with Lepidus, in order to speak to the masses with words seemingly intended to incite. Appian then also depicts Brutus addressing a crowd, including the soldiers, at the Capitol: this speech may be no more reliable, since its principal purpose is as a literary device intended to balance the words of his opponents who went before, but it should be noted as containing general perceptions of the chief assassin.[14] The tone is defensive, enumerating the offences of Caesar, and it raises the theme of living in servitude under a tyrant, which was known as a particular concern of Brutus the Liberator. After he finished speaking, it is noted that all judged his words as entirely just, and that there was general admiration for the conspirators.[15]

Following the apparently successful conciliatory meeting, the senate dispersed from the Temple of Tellus, having made optimistic decisions for the future. Antony's handling of these difficult matters was appreciated as masterful by all, for his moderate actions were thought, at the time, to have averted further political strife in the city and ended civil war for the state. Continuing in this peacemaking vein, negotiations were now entered into between Antony and Lepidus, and Brutus and Cassius: in order to assure their safety, Antony sent his young son as a hostage to the conspirators; one account suggests that Lepidus made a similar pledge by sending his son, or sons, who were, incidentally, the nephews of Brutus. The conspirators were thus persuaded to come down from the Capitol, and were greeted warmly with applause. The populace demanded a public demonstration of the new concord, and so the opposing leaders shook hands. As a further gesture of their goodwill, Antony invited Cassius to dine with him that night, while Lepidus, despite his alleged ongoing desire for vengeance and revolution, hosted his brother-in-law, Brutus. These banquets cannot have been an easy situation for any of the parties involved: one anecdote narrates how Antony asked Cassius if he carried a knife, to which the chief assassin's reply was affirmative, adding, in a threatening manner, that it was a large one if Antony now wished to play the tyrant. Nonetheless, the leaders of the opposing factions appeared to be making an effort to keep the peace, and the future of the state now looked promising. However, this was to prove very short-lived indeed.[16]

Caesar's Will and Funeral

Although Plutarch states that the senate reconvened early on the following day, 18 March, to decide on the distribution of provinces, these were not allocated until later in the year. The decisions that were actually made on this day were to cause a disastrous turn of events for the Liberators. Caesar's father-in-law, Lucius Piso, now spoke up in favour of publishing the details of the will, with which he had been entrusted, and of giving the murdered state leader a public funeral. Plutarch depicts Antony supporting this on the one hand, with Cassius opposing it on the other, while he describes the moderate Brutus yielding to Antony, and thereby committing a fatal error: his second after refusing to make Antony a target for assassination, according to the biographer. The senate passed this motion, and both Cicero and Atticus were immediately alarmed for the welfare of their friends and the state, realising what such a public display to the mob would likely mean: in the event, they were to be proved right, and Cicero could still be found uttering his despair at this over a month later.[17]

The will was opened and read at the house of Antony. Having regained political control, and some stability for the state, Antony was now in a strong position to begin manoeuvring matters in his favour. He had already secured the money and official papers of the assassinated dictator, and now had access to his will, believing that this would be beneficial to himself. However, the will contained catastrophic news for both sides. Firstly, there was the matter of the heirs: it may not have been apparent yet, but Caesar's naming of his shrewd young great-nephew, Gaius Octavius, better known to us as Octavian, not only as principal heir to his fortune, but also as his adopted son, was to spell the end for the Liberators, for Antony, and for the Republic. Of more immediate effect, the people were appalled to learn that Decimus Brutus, the treacherous friend of Caesar, was named as an heir in the second degree; several of the other assassins had also been named as guardians of his son if one had been born to him, and Antony was to be found merely among this group. The factor causing the most instant impact, however, was that Caesar had bequeathed generous gifts to the populace: every Roman was to receive the sum of 300 sesterces, and he had also left them his private gardens near the Tiber for their pleasure. The public favour which the Liberators had recently been enjoying for their tyrannicidal act was now swiftly swept aside by the slaughtered dictator's final wishes. This act of unexpected kindness, understandably, made the fickle people forget the acts of tyranny and feel a renewed compassion towards Caesar, their benefactor who evidently did love Rome and its people, and in turn this aroused and unleashed great public anger at his murder.[18]

Antony seized the opportunity to capitalise on this mob fever, with a very theatrical public display at the funeral of Caesar, which was held on 20 March. This was a public relations disaster for Brutus, Cassius and the rest of the Liberators. The butchered and pitiable corpse of Caesar, with multiple wounds and clothed in a tattered and bloodstained toga, was carried into the forum and placed on the rostra, before the eyes of the crowd: this very visual reminder of the brutality of his murder was sufficient alone to rouse the anger and grief of the people. Antony augmented this by purposely playing on these raw emotions of the crowd, using powerful rhetoric in his eulogy over the body of the murdered man. This may be most familiar to us from Shakespeare's version of events, but his was not the first fictional account of this oration, since Appian and Dio Cassius both produced funeral speeches by Antony in their texts. The ancient sources concur that, realising the effects of his words and responding to the reaction of the people, Antony increased his tone of compassion for Caesar: he employed methods such as recalling the dictator's quality of clemency, as well as his services to the Roman state; contrasting his current pitiable condition with his former glorious one; and simultaneously denouncing the conspirators as villainous and traitorous murderers. Furthermore, he dramatically lifted up the bloody robe and pointed out each and every one of the many stab wounds. Suetonius claims that suitably provocative words from Roman tragedy were quoted during the funeral proceedings, including an especially apt line by Pacuvius: 'Did I save them so that they might murder me?'[19] Antony also had the decrees recited which listed the many honours voted to Caesar by the senate, selectively emphasising those calculated to incite the crowd against the treachery of the assassins, including the oath to protect his person, which particularly recalled their unjust betrayal of Caesar.[20]

The sincerity, or lack thereof, of Antony's desire for reconciliation and calm in the state was now apparent: the mob completely swallowed the bait that he dangled before them and were worked up into a frenzied state. Public outpourings of grief and wailing developed into anger and violence. A funeral pyre had been set up for Caesar on the Campus Martius, near the tomb of his beloved daughter, Julia. However, before this could be utilised, the populace began rioting, as they had after Clodius' death several years before, and built a makeshift funeral pyre out of furniture torn from nearby buildings. Caesar's body was thus cremated in the middle of the forum, amid disorder and violent chaos. The populace soon after honoured their murdered leader by setting up a marble column on the site, inscribed 'to the father of his country', and worshipping there. This spot in the forum is still marked to this day by the remains of an altar which was incorporated into the Temple of the Divine Julius, built by Octavian in memory of his adoptive father. In their rage, some of the crowd, brandishing lit firebrands snatched from the funeral pyre, proceeded to the houses of the assassins, intending to set them alight; others went in search of the assassins themselves, meaning to murder them. Cicero remarks that it was necessary for them to take up arms to repel the attacks and defend their property. One house was burned down, but none of the conspirators was harmed, having securely barricaded themselves in their homes. However, those hungry for blood succeeded in finding one victim who was, unfortunately, merely an innocent bystander who had come to pay respects to his dead friend. Cinna had become the focus of the crowd's odium, following his public denouncement of Caesar on the day after his murder. The name of this man had not been forgotten: in their enraged state, when the undiscerning mob came across a tribune named Gaius Helvius Cinna, they did not hesitate long enough to realise that this was not the praetor who had offended their beloved dead leader, and tore him to pieces. Indeed, one account claims that the attack was so frenzied that it was impossible to recover his body afterwards, while another text states that his head was paraded on a stake. According to Dio Cassius, a certain tribune named Casca, fearing a similar fate, made an announcement denying any involvement in the assassination. This Casca has been identified as Gaius Servilius, one of the two Casca brothers but, if this is the case, it would mean that either the murder was not committed by both brothers, as the accounts record, or that Gaius was now simply lying to preserve himself.[21]

Brutus, Cassius and the rest of the conspirators were extremely alarmed by these violent protests, of which they were the targets. A strong wave of panic, understandably, ran through their ranks. A letter from Decimus to Brutus and Cassius, most probably written following these threatening disturbances, reveals the nervous state of the assassins at this time.[22] The tension is palpable in Decimus' report on the current precarious situation to his friends, following a visit from Aulus Hirtius, who was to prove a vital player in the manoeuvrings between the factions. Hirtius was a supporter of Caesar, who had fought with him since Gaul and so was to be found on the side of Antony against Caesar's assassins: clearly, however, he was behaving moderately in choosing to keep on good terms with Decimus. In the letter, Hirtius has just informed Decimus that Antony is most treacherous and is denying Decimus his designated province of Cisalpine Gaul; Antony has also declared that the conspirators are not safe in the city, but Decimus and Hirtius are mistrustful of his motives, realising that he really wants them out of the way in case they regain the upper hand; Decimus tells his co-conspirators that he has requested commissions abroad for them all, but thinks they are unlikely to be granted, since he expects that they will soon be declared public enemies; sounding utterly desperate, he advises that they leave Italy, but then he suddenly changes his tone to state that he will demand that they be allowed to stay in Rome with a bodyguard. Clearly this final request was not met since, for the sake of their safety, they were left with no other option but to withdraw from the city as soon as possible. Within a few days of the funeral Brutus and Cassius had left Rome, but remained in the region of Latium, hoping that the public fury and political uproar would eventually abate so that they could return. As city praetor, Brutus could not legally leave Rome for longer than ten days, making it necessary for Antony to grant him a special dispensation to do so.[23]

Brutus, with his noblest of intentions, had seriously underestimated the potential hostility of the masses, believing that, if they killed only the tyrant, the people and Caesar's supporters would accept their moral actions readily. The Liberators appear to have suffered an almost insurmountable setback. Furthermore, Brutus' refusal to assassinate Antony at the same time as Caesar did now seem a terrible error of judgement. Brutus had misjudged Antony, who had now swung the political situation back in his favour, and looked set to seize power: Cicero could now lament sanctimoniously, with the marvellous power of hindsight, that the tyrant was dead, but the tyranny lived on, and that the deed had been carried out with manly courage but childlike purpose.[24] However, in Brutus' defence, it should be noted that, in any sudden absence of political leadership, it is extremely likely that some other candidate will soon step forward to seize control of the political situation: had they killed Antony, then another usurper would have risen to the fore. In the event, this is exactly what would happen anyway, even with Antony's powerful presence: the Liberators, and Antony, would discover in time that they had a force far more formidable than the fickle and easily swayed mob to fear. It would come in the form of the heir of Julius Caesar: Octavian, Caesar's great-nephew and adopted son would reach Rome by early May.

Chapter Nine

Liberty Lost: Countdown to the End of the Republic

Liberty on the Run

Withdrawal from Rome (March–May 44 BC)

Before the arrival of Octavian, bringing with him his determination to seek vengeance for his adoptive father, the Liberators had already found their position in the city untenable, having been forced to withdraw by the danger posed to them from the mob uprising in Rome. Brutus and Cassius chose to remain in the vicinity of Latium, merely retreating to Antium (Anzio) on the coast, approximately thirty-five miles south of Rome. They hoped that the populace's emotions would eventually subside, allowing them to return: sadly, however, neither Brutus nor Cassius would ever again see their beloved city.[1] In such municipal towns, the Liberators were received well, finding sympathisers to their cause from among the local landowners. The disillusioned and disappointed Cicero had similarly taken the decision to withdraw from Rome, leaving in early April and informing Atticus how the men of these towns eagerly flocked to hear him deliver news about the state of the Republic, while elsewhere he speaks of the Liberators receiving the support of Italy, and specifically names two towns near Naples, Teanum Sidicinum (Teano) and Puteoli (Pozzuoli), which chose the chief Liberators as their patrons. Brutus and Cassius, then, spent several months away from the city in this fashion, waiting and assessing the political situation. We know that at or around this time several other assassins also departed from Rome: Decimus, Trebonius and Cimber all had provinces assigned to them by Caesar, to which they now hastened for their own safety. One thing that is patently clear is that the Liberators were very passive in their behaviour: not having seized control in the city, they allowed themselves to be driven out of Rome, and were now completely dependent upon the actions of others, and particularly those of Antony.[2]

We are extremely fortunate to have, for this period, Cicero's frequent, if biased, correspondence to Atticus, who at first remained behind in Rome and from whom Cicero was therefore always eager for news. These letters begin on 7 April, while Cicero is staying at a friend's house at the start of his journey out of the city. Their regularity, running from the spring through to the summer of 44 BC, is valuable in aiding historians' attempts to trace the political situation in the months following Caesar's assassination and these are, therefore, an extremely useful place to start. Furthermore, they are of inestimable value here, since they offer a real insight into the mind of a man firmly on the side of the Liberators, and in a similar position of absence from the city, often making this correspondence the closest we can hope to get to the perspective of Brutus and Cassius themselves at this time.[3]

At first the state of affairs seemed quite hopeless, especially since Cicero's earliest post-assassination correspondence reports the biased viewpoint of his host, Gaius Matius, who felt that no one could fix the Roman state if even Caesar himself had failed, and who spoke gleefully of an expected uprising from the legions in Gaul.[4] Matius' comments, then, clearly unnerved Cicero, and generally there is an anxious tone to these letters. This perhaps was a strange choice of host en route for Cicero at this time, fleeing the fraught situation as he was, since Matius was not only a Caesarian, but was described by Cicero as most hostile to Brutus, and the feeling was apparently a mutual one. In a later exchange of correspondence with Cicero, Matius offers a quite different view of the assassins, whose actions have clearly not brought liberty to everyone, and whose ingratitude with regard to his dear friend Caesar clearly disgusts him.[5] But for Cicero, Brutus was the representative of public peace: indeed Cicero several times throughout his correspondence refers to the Liberators as 'our heroes', or even gods, and speaks of their achievement on the Ides of March as bringing them eternal glory, as well as consolation to himself. Furthermore, he often shows concern for their safety, as well as speaking of his desire to protect them. This all demonstrates that he had definitely thrown his lot in with them.[6]

However, there are also more hopeful times, and we do get brief glimpses of a more relaxed and happy Cicero. For example, in early April he speaks of promising signs that the fickle mob have calmed down, since they were now found enjoying a mime at the theatre and even applauding Lucius Cassius, brother of the chief assassin.[7] Also on a positive note for the Liberators, not long before 12 April 44 BC, Antony met with Brutus and Cassius and, although we have no record of what was discussed, it must have been in the spirit of reconciliation, since Cicero describes the conversation as 'not disagreeable'. It is reasonable to assume that Brutus and Cassius were more buoyed by this meeting with Antony than the often-pessimistic Cicero who, in the remainder of this letter to Atticus, speaks with his familiar tone of despair.[8] Another piece of good news for the Liberators in April, which unsurprisingly was extremely pleasing to Cicero, was that, among other legislation, Antony abolished the office of dictator: this was surely a most hopeful sign for the restoration of the Republican constitution.[9] A further promising indication of the ongoing reconciliation between the Republicans and Caesarians was that lines of communication clearly remained open between Brutus and his brother-in-law, Lepidus: Junia Secunda delivered a 'moderate and friendly' letter from her husband to her brother sometime before the middle of April, and we may imagine that familial connections played a role in helping maintain this relationship. Around this time, Brutus moved from Antium inland to Lanuvium and so, at approximately only twenty miles away, was now closer to Rome: he stayed here for a while, to the disappointment of Cicero, who clearly had hoped that Brutus would have achieved more by his noble deed than simply being forced to skulk outside Rome. Another positive event comes in mid-April, when Cicero's cheerfulness, since Antony had secured the approval of Brutus, is evident.[10] This presumably refers to the pleasing news that Cicero has just mentioned: at some point in the last few days, Antony had executed an impostor pretending to be the grandson of Marius, Caesar's uncle. Following the assassination, Amatius or Herophilus, as he was known, using his purported status as a relative of Caesar, had been violently denouncing the murdered dictator's enemies at the altar erected on the site of his cremation in the forum, and had gathered a menacing gang of men together in order to hunt down the assassins. On discovery of this plot, Antony moved hastily to put a stop to this dissension, executing Amatius without trial. This execution led to further disturbances in the forum, which Antony suppressed with the deployment of soldiers. This act has been attributed to Antony's desire to have any possible heir to Caesar removed but, at the time, the Liberators, including even Antony's foe, Cicero, clearly interpreted this as a sign of the consul's commitment to keeping peace in the state.[11]

What can perhaps be gathered from Cicero's occasional shifting in mood, and particularly his tendency towards despondency, is the effect of the uncertainty about affairs in Rome, which not only he, but also Brutus and Cassius, must have experienced at their respective distances from the city: it can be assumed that such a prolonged absence from Rome, and its accompanying lack of knowledge about the crucial happenings there without

Lucius Brutus/Libertas coin: Denarius issued by Brutus as moneyer in 54 BC. The obverse shows the head of the goddess Liberty. The reverse shows his legendary ancestor, Lucius Junius Brutus, as the first consul. *(By kind permission of the MoneyMuseum, Zürich)*

Lucius Brutus/Ahala coin: Denarius issued by Brutus as moneyer in 54 BC, showing the heads of his legendary ancestors, Lucius Junius Brutus on the obverse and Gaius Servilius Ahala on the reverse, both heroes of the Republic, as Brutus would also aspire to be. *(By kind permission of the MoneyMuseum, Zürich)*

Salamis: A Roman colonnaded street in Salamis, Cyprus. It was this city that suffered extortion at the hands of Brutus when he carried out corrupt money-lending activities there during his early career. *(Courtesy of Nic Fields)*

Julius Caesar: Statue of Julius Caesar in Via dei Fori Imperiali, Rome, with base showing the familiar abbreviation, SPQR (*senatus populusque Romanus*: the Senate and Roman people), and his status as *Dictator Perpetuus* (Dictator for Life). The photograph was taken on the Ides of March, and a wreath to commemorate the anniversary of his assassination has been placed at his feet. *(Kirsty Corrigan)*

Pharsalus: View of the plains at Pharsalus where the final battle of the civil war between Caesar and Pompey took place in 48 BC, and at which Brutus fought on the side of the defeated Pompey. *(Courtesy of Nic Fields)*

Temple of Venus Genetrix in the Forum of Caesar: Three columns are all that remains of the temple vowed by Caesar to Venus Genetrix, his mythical ancestress and protecting deity, at the Battle of Pharsalus. *(Kirsty Corrigan)*

Caesar Dictator coin: Obverse of a denarius minted in 44 BC, shortly before Caesar's assassination. Caesar was the first Roman to have his portrait on a coin during his lifetime, which was interpreted as another indication of his kingly desires. The inscription reads 'Caesar, Dictator for Life'. *(By kind permission of the MoneyMuseum, Zürich)*

Theatre of Pompey: The outline of the first permanent stone theatre built in Rome has been preserved in the curvature of the buildings in Via di Grotta Pinta. Perhaps Pompey's finest legacy to Rome, it was in a hall in the porticoes attached to this theatre that Brutus and the other conspirators would strike Caesar down. *(Kirsty Corrigan)*

Largo di Torre Argentina: The archaeological site of Largo di Torre Argentina contains the remains of four Republican temples and part of the portico of the Theatre of Pompey, the reputed location of Caesar's assassination. *(Kirsty Corrigan)*

Theatre of Pompey Portico: At the rear of the circular temple (Temple B) at the Largo di Torre Argentina archaeological complex, the remains of part of the portico of the Theatre of Pompey can be seen: this was the temporary meeting place for the senate on 15 March 44 BC and is the reputed site of Caesar's assassination. Image taken on the Ides of March 2013. *(Kirsty Corrigan)*

The Forum: A view of the Roman forum from the Capitoline hill. *(Kirsty Corrigan)*

The Rostra: The remains of the speaker's platform known as the rostra, in the Roman forum, which was a focus of much important activity during the dying years of the Republic. It was here that hubristic statues of Caesar were set up, and from here that Brutus delivered his speech to the multitude on the day after the assassination. This is also where Antony displayed the dictator's dead body at his public funeral, and later the head and hand of the proscribed Cicero. *(Kirsty Corrigan)*

The Altar of the Divine Julius: The remains of the Altar of the Divine Julius, which was later erected on the site where Caesar's body had been cremated in the forum by the frenzied mob. *(Kirsty Corrigan)*

Brundisium: A view of the inner harbour of Brundisium (modern-day Brindisi) on the Adriatic coast of Italy. This strategic port, located at the end of the Via Appia, acted as the main departure point for those travelling east to fight in the civil wars at Pharsalus and Philippi. *(Kirsty Corrigan)*

Brutus the Cat: The archaeological site of Torre Argentina, location of Caesar's murder, now houses a cat sanctuary. The residents are often to be found sunbathing or wandering among the ruins: Brutus, namesake of our subject, is one of these sanctuary cats. *(By kind permission of Torre Argentina Cat Sanctuary, www.romancats.com)*

Dyrrachium: A view out to sea at Dyrrachium, a strategically important port on the coast of Illyricum (modern Dürres, Albania). Many of the Romans who fought in the civil wars of the late Republic in the east passed through here, on the way to or from Italy. It was one of the first cities that Brutus captured in the east. Some accounts suggest that, after his suicide at Philippi, his head was thrown overboard during a stormy crossing from here. *(Courtesy of Jenny Keaveney)*

Apollonia: A view of ancient Apollonia, Illyricum (in modern-day Albania). Brutus besieged Antony's brother, Gaius, and his army here before taking him prisoner and seizing the city. Gaius was later executed when Brutus discovered that Cicero had been killed in the Triumvirs' proscriptions. *(Courtesy of Jenny Keaveney)*

Via Aemilia, Mutina: A view of the Roman road running through Modena, the ancient Mutina in Cisalpine Gaul. It was in this town that Brutus' father was besieged by Pompey in 77 BC, and Decimus Brutus was besieged by Antony for several months in early 43 BC. In 46 BC, Brutus was governor of this province. *(Courtesy of Nic Fields)*

Brutus/Spinther coin: The reverse of a denarius, minted in Asia Minor in 43 BC by Brutus and Lentulus Spinther, who joined the Liberators after Caesar's assassination, to pay the soldiers joining the fight for the Republic. This coin shows religious insignia associated with Brutus' role as a member of the pontifical college. *(By kind permission of the MoneyMuseum, Zürich)*

Temple of Mars Ultor: The Temple of Mars Ultor, Mars the Avenger, within the forum of Augustus in Rome, was vowed by Octavian at the Battle of Philippi, to commemorate the vengeance he inflicted upon his adoptive father's assassins. *(Kirsty Corrigan)*

Philippi: A view of the plains of Philippi in ancient Macedonia (now Filippoi in Greece), where Brutus and Cassius were defeated by Octavian and Antony in 42 BC, before both committed suicide. *(Courtesy of Nic Fields)*

Augustus: A statue of Augustus, formerly known as Octavian, in the so-called Prima Porta pose. Located in the Via dei Fori Imperiali, with the Forum of Augustus and Temple of Mars Ultor in the background. *(Kirsty Corrigan)*

them, often would have led to a fear of the worst for the Liberators. This absence also explains Cicero's eagerness to learn news from Atticus, which is so often evident in these letters. Several times he seems keen to hear about Brutus in particular, thus demonstrating the regard in which he continued to hold this outstanding champion of Roman principles: in one letter he reveals his affection for the chief conspirator when he declares to Atticus that he will not fail this man of unique and unparalleled virtue; he is equally complimentary in a letter to Dolabella, where he describes Brutus as having the best temperament, a most agreeable character, and being of unique uprightness and steadfastness.[12]

Antony, on the other hand, was for Cicero the very antithesis of Brutus, as his greatest source of irritation and anxiety by far. It was now that he began tirelessly expressing his opinion that it was an almost unforgivable oversight that the tyranny, in the form of Antony, was still living. Clearly his criticisms of the mistakes of Brutus, Cassius and Decimus eventually became so much that Atticus felt it necessary to defend the chief conspirators, causing Cicero to deny that he was blaming them. Cicero can be found repeatedly complaining that the tyrant's acts are being upheld, and lamenting the state of affairs, which he claims to have found easier to deal with under Caesar himself. He accuses Antony of bribery, embezzlement, forgery and corruption. One of Cicero's greatest bugbears was that Antony allegedly carried out various illicit acts for which he falsely claimed the authority of Caesar's decrees, while another condemnable deed, for example, was his plundering of the Temple of Ops for the vast public wealth stored there. It was this political atmosphere that had Cicero often appearing convinced that all hope was lost and, at times, finding it so unbearable that he even seemed ready to turn his back on Roman politics altogether, or melodramatically wished that he had died alongside Caesar. Despite such hostility, on the surface at least, Antony and Cicero maintained conciliatory relations: in the latter half of April, there exists an exchange of correspondence between the two men, which has the appearance of politeness and courtesy. However, Antony's letter, seeking Cicero's approval for one of his supposed illicit acts carried out in the name of Caesar, the recall of a certain exile, does contain a veiled threat to Cicero regarding his safety, although the tone is, outwardly, extremely polite. Therefore, despite being considerately consulted on the matter, Cicero is under no illusion that Antony will go ahead without his approval, and he tells Atticus how outraged he is about this disgraceful behaviour; yet he writes Antony a reply in quite fulsome terms that do not betray his true feelings, although the latent tone of sarcasm surely could not be missed. We do not have the details of Antony's reply, but it was, according to Cicero, straightforward and not inflammatory.[13]

However, on the whole, during April matters did seem to calm and slightly improve, and Antony must be acknowledged for playing his part in maintaining a level of reconciliation between the Caesarian and Republican parties, for the sake of keeping order in the state. At the end of April, Cicero is under the impression that the situation may be an improving one, because of the content of letters that he has seen from Brutus to Antony and Atticus.[14] Nonetheless, he remains in his usual pessimistic mood but, on 1 May, the new month brings news to Cicero which causes a complete turnaround in his outlook. Antony had not entirely succeeded in quelling the disturbances caused in the wake of Amatius' execution, and it took the consul suffectus, Dolabella, to put a stop to the rebellion once and for all: soon after Antony left Rome, in late April, he tore down the altar and pillar to Caesar, thereby removing the focal point for the worship of the dead man, and put many of the rioters to death. To the Liberators this illegal act was a promising sign in their favour, but the excitable Cicero got too carried away by this news: he foolishly believed that Brutus could now walk safely and boldly through the forum. Furthermore, on the basis of this, Cicero, who had previously loathed his former son-in-law, was able to write of his 'wonderful Dolabella', whom he also labelled heroic for these actions. Within a few days, he would write directly to Dolabella, congratulating him in the most fulsome manner: Cicero allows himself some credit for influencing the praiseworthy character of this new guardian of the Republic, whom he even claims is a rival to Brutus with his honourable reputation. Cicero was so excessive in his praises of Dolabella that Atticus clearly felt the need to try to temper his friend in a letter. This event had so turned Cicero's mood that he never sounded more hopeful about the fate of the Liberators, and it would be reasonable to assume that Brutus and Cassius at first shared this optimism to a certain extent, although undoubtedly they would have been more restrained and cautious, in the manner of the moderate Atticus.[15]

Proof of this restraint soon came, when Brutus wrote within a few days to inform Cicero that, far from feeling optimistic, he was instead contemplating exile. Cicero was deeply disheartened once more. Now, with Brutus seemingly having given up, Cicero's emotions took another dramatic turnabout and, despairing and contemplating civil war, he began speaking of death as preferable in his old age. The despondent elder statesman, who had been considering going to Greece for some time to visit his son there, now more seriously contemplates it, in the light of Brutus' talk of exile. Furthermore, on learning that the 'extraordinary Brutus' will not be attending the forthcoming senate meeting on 1 June, he wonders how their dear friend can now continue to lead a public life. Cicero clearly believed that the re-establishment of the Republican constitution depended on Brutus and his associates, which again demonstrates the respect that this man could command, and also indicates that he was regarded as the leader of the Liberators. Elsewhere, similarly, Cicero encourages Cassius to action by telling him that the country's only hope rests on him, Brutus and Decimus. Atticus, however, does not appear to have shared Cicero's belief that Brutus could be the saviour of the Republic, although we do not know his exact reasons for this: maybe he felt that Cicero was again getting too carried away in his overestimation of one man, or perhaps his more neutral position simply gave him a different perspective on the current political situation. This did not mean that Atticus had entirely given up faith in Brutus politically, however, since he advised Cicero to prepare both a speech and an edict for him. With Brutus having recently rejected Cicero's edict in favour of his and Cassius' own gentle-toned version, of which both Atticus and Cicero approved and felt hopeful, Cicero did not think writing Brutus a speech was a good idea, since the Liberator clearly preferred his own intellectual and polished style. Besides, Cicero felt, disappointingly, that Brutus could not be safe enough in Rome to deliver any speech. Further unfortunate news, of a more personal note, reached Cicero at this time: Cassius' wife and Brutus' sister, Junia Tertia, had suffered a miscarriage. Cicero, always thinking of politics first, remarked that they needed to keep up their stock of Cassii and Bruti now.[16]

Brutus and Cicero's defeatist attitudes were not entirely erroneous, since civil war was becoming a real danger. Cicero felt that all was lost if war broke out, and this caused a most gloomy outlook in his correspondence henceforth: at one point, he remarked that no one but losers would follow Brutus in war, although this was more an indication of his pessimism than reality, and at other points he again spoke of death as a preferable option. Certainly, however, a major and valid source of anxiety recurring throughout Cicero's letters is the military might of the opponents of the Liberators: it can be assumed that such matters were similarly weighing heavily on the minds of Brutus and Cassius. Several times Cicero expresses concern over the line that Pompey's son, Sextus, might take, being equally troubled by the prospect of a civil war between him and the Caesarians and by the possibility of them coming to terms, as well as speaking of the threat of a potential uprising by the legions in Gaul and perhaps Spain too. A more pressing worry was the sizeable and menacing bodyguard with which Antony had surrounded himself since Caesar's assassination. These men, stationed in and around the outskirts of Rome, were said by Appian to have grown eventually to 6,000 in number and to have consisted of battle-hardened soldiers. Antony, evidently judging that the city was now in a stable enough condition to leave, had departed from Rome towards the end of April, in order to settle the veterans of Caesar in Campania. While doing so, he successfully recruited many of these men to the Caesarian cause, asking them to swear an oath to support Caesar's acts and to ensure that they all remained armed. Cicero had interpreted Antony's failure to meet with him en route, while visiting the Bay of Naples where it was known that he was residing, as a bad sign, but when he heard about these actions of Antony, he felt sure that his worst fears were confirmed and that they were heading for war: his irascibility at the fact that Antony had not been assassinated reveals itself most strongly at this point. Also concerning for the Liberators was that there were other forces available in provinces under governors who were likely to come down on the side of the Caesarians in the event of a civil war. Notably, Asinius Pollio was currently continuing the war against Sextus Pompey in Further Spain; Plancus, who had been a friend of Caesar, but had supported the amnesty for the assassins, was proconsul of Transalpine Gaul; and Lepidus, who had now departed to Narbonese Gaul and Nearer Spain.[17] The Liberators had nothing with which to match these potential forces of Antony, and no funds with which to obtain them. Although the conspirators, Trebonius and Cimber, had their provinces of Asia and Bithynia and Pontus respectively, they did not have an army to go with them. This left Decimus as the only Liberator to possess any troops, in the form of his three legions stationed in Cisalpine Gaul; he set out to join them in the latter half of April. When Cicero mentions this in his correspondence he, quite despondently, states his belief that Decimus is their best hope militarily.[18]

On 3 May, the critical Cicero wrote to Cassius full of exhortations to act, directed at the three chief Liberators, but, for all his words of wisdom and the clarity that comes with hindsight, Cicero offered them no practical advice and appeared to be at a loss as to how to counsel them to advance. Indeed, a week later, the most he can suggest to Atticus is that they must adapt to the circumstances which change hourly; Atticus seemed to be in the same quandary too; and in mid-May Cicero appeared reluctant to meet Brutus, despairingly admitting that, as he does not know what to do himself, he cannot help him. Again this illustrates that they were entirely dependent on the actions of others. Nonetheless, despite fears about the Caesarians' military power and Brutus' talk of exile, neither he nor Cassius simply gave up. Instead they were seemingly looking to the future: around this time, they were asking Cicero to exert his influence on the consul designate for 43 BC, Hirtius, who was also then sojourning on the Bay of Naples. According to Cicero, both he and his future colleague, Pansa, were affable and appeared to be of a moderate nature. This was in spite of their regret at the death of Caesar, to whom they were attached, and who they believed had made himself vulnerable through his clemency; and furthermore, this was a loss which they viewed, not incorrectly, as having thrown the state into turmoil. The views of these more neutral figures reveal a less biased perspective on the state of affairs: it should, therefore, be noted that such men saw, and feared, the danger of violence not only in Antony, but also the Liberators. Furthermore, in his despair, Cicero even seemed to be turning on Brutus slightly, tetchily commenting that he had done more for personal glory than the common peace. Cicero's mood swings should not be interpreted as indicative of the general attitude but, coupled with the feeling of more moderate characters such as Hirtius and Pansa, it is quite easy to see how Brutus and his fellow conspirators could also be viewed as villains bringing chaos to the Roman state. However, Cicero underestimated his friends, believing them to be deficient in the necessary spirit for warmongering, while the consuls designate had not entirely misread the abilities of Brutus and Cassius.[19]

What becomes abundantly clear from reading this period through the correspondence, and eyes, of Cicero, with his changes of mood, are the ups and downs: the fortunes of the Liberators were entirely at the mercy of the vagaries of others. Due to their lack of post-assassination preparations, and freedom from desire to seize control of the state, they were completely dependent on those who did wish to take the political lead in Rome. And this continued to be the case as they were forced out not just of Rome, but eventually Italy too. However, before this happened, a new dominant force was about to make his mighty presence felt in Rome.

Arrival of Octavian

A hitherto overlooked, yet extremely significant, factor was quietly coming into play: Octavian. At first dismissed as insignificant, it soon emerged that both Antony and the Liberators should have been keeping a closer watch on this sickly, yet shrewd, young man, who was to prove the biggest danger to them all. Having carefully gauged the state of affairs and weighed up his options, once the great-nephew and heir of Caesar reached Rome, it did not take long before he had manoeuvred the situation so that matters in the state hinged on his actions, rather than those of Antony, but no one at the time comprehended the magnitude of his advent. Through Cicero's letters we learn of his arrival. Initially, in the first half of April, Cicero merely expresses curiosity about the young man's arrival in Italy from Apollonia (in the region of Illyricum, in modern-day Albania), wondering if he has intentions of staging some sort of coup d'état, but this is quickly forgotten amid other more pressing matters. According to Appian, Octavian was received well by the soldiers and veterans as he travelled across Italy. On 18 April, having obtained money from Caesar's funds in Asia, Octavian arrived in Naples, and Cicero was staying nearby. He then learned that the young man intended to accept the inheritance of, and adoption by, Caesar: justifiably, concerns about a struggle with Antony thus began to be raised. Within a few days, Cicero had met Caesar's heir, who was residing in the neighbouring villa, belonging to his step-father: initially, Cicero arrogantly and foolishly claimed that Octavian was dedicated to him; this did not, however, prevent him from judging that the young man, while respectful and friendly, was not to be trusted and was potentially dangerous to the Liberators, although he underestimates Octavian's character in attributing this principally to those who surround him.[20]

The heir of Caesar then seems to have dropped from the forefront of Cicero's mind for the next few weeks, at least in terms of the extant correspondence. Nonetheless, during this time important events were occurring. In early May, Octavian reached Rome, where he was supposedly hailed by a glorious supernatural omen: allegedly, his arrival coincided with a halo appearing around the sun. He wasted no time in formally announcing the acceptance of his adoption, on the following day.[21] By 18 May, some news of Octavian's arrival and reception in Rome had reached Cicero, who was not pleased with a speech made by Octavian at a meeting in the forum. Cicero does not explain why he disliked this speech, but it should be noted here that, according to one source, Octavian, as soon as he arrived in Rome, made no secret of his intention to avenge the murder of Caesar: indeed, as his adoptive son, he had a certain obligation to do so.[22] Whatever the contents of his speech, Octavian had quickly begun to make himself noticed, and Cicero recognised that he was a potential menace to the Liberators; he now remarks that he does not like Octavian's preparations for the games to be held in honour of Caesar, nor his choice of Caesarians as agents. At about this time, Antony returned to Rome, presumably having received troubling news of Octavian's instant impact on the people and city. The first meeting of the two men did not go well: Antony attempted to snub the youth, and refused him access to the funds which would allow him to pay Caesar's legacies to the people; in return, Octavian reproached him for failing to punish Caesar's assassins, an indication of his intentions for the future regarding the Liberators. Despite Antony's attempt to delay his adoption, Octavian, already recognising the power both of the mob and the name which he now bore, demonstrated how he revered his adoptive father's memory: he wished to display Caesar's gilded throne and diadem in the Circus, but this public relations opportunity was denied, much to the pleasure of Cicero.[23]

In June, Cicero recognised the spirit and intelligence inherent in Octavian but, following his step-father's view, was doubtful that too much faith could be put in him. Nonetheless, it was at this point that Cicero appeared, for the first time, to be conceiving a plan involving Octavian: he cautioned that he should be kept away from Antony, which was not a current concern given how they had initially received each other, and presumably it was now that he first had the idea of fostering an enmity between the two men; simultaneously, he thought that the young man should be encouraged in the right direction, in other words that of the Liberators, towards whom he believed Octavian was well disposed. In this belief Cicero had made one of his gravest errors of judgement.[24]

Liberty Banished

Removal from Italy: Honourable Exile (June–July 44 BC)

Meanwhile, Cicero was cautious about returning to Rome at the beginning of June for the senate meeting, which Antony reportedly wanted him to attend: in mid-May Cicero tells Atticus that he needs to assess the situation before re-entering the city, since he has received warnings that Antony has been gathering his soldiers together with the purpose of surrounding the senate meeting on the day, thereby making it unsafe for the Liberators and their associates, and anyone who wanted to oppose him, to attend; by the latter part of May, Cicero is making a show of resistance to going. Brutus, who was staying at Cicero's villa in Astura (Torre Astura) at this time, hoped to meet with Cicero, who was also now in Latium, before the 1 June, presumably to discuss matters pertaining to the meeting. However, in mid-May, the pessimistic Cicero was reluctant to do even this, feeling that he had nothing to offer him; although later in the month he seems more resolved to meeting and helping his friend again. By the end of the month, Cicero had again considered going to the senate meeting on 1 June, before changing his mind back once more. His indecision is understandable since the political situation was evidently volatile: even the moderate Caesarian, Hirtius, had chosen to stay away from the senate meeting, and strongly advised Cicero to do the same; on the day, Hirtius' colleague, Pansa, would also be absent. Brutus and Cassius, now in Lanuvium, were clearly becoming agitated about this situation in Rome, and sought advice from Cicero, but he was also beset with doubts. At the end of May, the chief assassins addressed a letter to Antony, the slightly abrupt tone of which perhaps reveals both their anxiety and annoyance. The essence of this invaluable letter is that the chief conspirators are seeking assurances that it is safe for them to return to Rome for the senate meeting. They have been warned by friends that the large numbers of armed men about the city pose a threat to them and, furthermore, there exists a rumour that these veterans are considering replacing the altar to Caesar. It appears that Brutus and Cassius had been under the impression that relations between themselves and Antony were fair, having put their trust in him until this point, and apparently even having dismissed their supporters from the municipal towns as an act of goodwill. However, now they were unsure of his intentions, and the reconciliation was fragile once more.[25]

The contents of the senate meeting itself were also of concern to Cicero and the Liberators. Not only was it where Antony was due to report on the acts of Caesar, which he had supposedly been investigating as part of a committee, but which Cicero accuses him of never having convened, thereby leaving him free to make all the decisions according to his own preference and advantage, but the redistribution of the provinces was also to be discussed. Antony and Dolabella had been assigned the provinces of Macedonia and Syria respectively for 43 BC, at some time in the first half of April. However, it had been known since late April that Antony had intended to exchange Macedonia for the whole of the strategically vital Gaul. Cicero interpreted this as meaning that Decimus Brutus would be deprived of his province, Cisalpine Gaul, which would, of course, spell disaster for the Liberators, whose only military support came from Decimus' legions there: Cicero was correct to judge that a clash of arms was thus inevitable, since Decimus could not simply give up his assigned province to Antony without putting up some resistance. It was also believed that the senate meeting would bring attacks on the Liberators, and notably on Decimus by Lucius, Antony's brother. The day of the meeting arrived, but there was no Brutus, Cassius or Cicero present, who all wisely kept away from the city, and presumably no other Liberator attended either. The biased Cicero reports that the senate meeting was poorly attended, which was understandable given the threat of the sizeable armed guard outside. As had been expected, among other acts, Antony passed a tribunician law, against the will of the senate, which granted him governorship of Gaul for five years in exchange for Macedonia. It also allowed him to retain the legions from Macedonia, which had been stationed there in preparation for Caesar's Parthian campaign. This meant that Antony could then transfer these trained soldiers to Gaul. Indisputably, this was Antony making due preparations to shore up his position with military strength.[26]

Following this meeting, a despondent Brutus continued to seek the advice of his beloved elder friend, Atticus, and wrote letters which were, to Cicero at least, distressing. Despite this closeness between Atticus and Brutus, it was at about this time that the rich banker, striving to remain neutral as ever, refused to take the lead in a plan for the creation of a fund for the Liberators from the wealth of the equestrian order, and would not contribute money to their cause. However, he did say that Brutus, as a friend and individual, was welcome to access his funds privately and later, as Brutus was departing from Italy, Atticus was said to have sent 100,000 sesterces as a gift to his friend, adding a further 300,000 when Brutus was in Epirus. He was also reported later to have left a ready supply of money in Epirus for any of the proscribed who were fleeing the Triumvirs, and given permission for them to reside there.[27] On 2 or 3 June, Atticus was planning what, in the end, turned out to be an abortive visit to Brutus at his villa in Lanuvium. Cicero once more shrugged his shoulders, wondering what advice Atticus could possibly offer, now that there was no way out, beset by forces on all sides as they were.

At this time, information reached Cicero of the plans for another meeting of the senate, which would be held on 5 June. At this meeting, Antony, who, clearly still fearing the threat of the chief assassins, wished for them to be removed from Italy but without being able to obtain power abroad, effectively arranged their departure on an official but flimsy pretext.

Brutus and Cassius were ungenerously assigned the supervision of the corn supply in Asia and Sicily respectively, which involved them purchasing and monitoring the export of grain to Rome from these provinces: this move has been aptly described as an 'honourable pretext for exile',[28] and it was designed to neutralise them. Cicero was appalled that such a lowly office should be assigned to these two great men and, furthermore, by Antony, although he does admit that it was better than them simply sitting idly in their suburban villas waiting for something to happen. However, this set off another dilemma for the chief assassins and their closest friends: whether to accept these menial posts, in their usual passive manner, or to act. Cicero, erroneously, did not believe they had the courage or power for the latter, and was unable to see how they could possibly advance from here.

To this end a family conference was held at Antium, where Brutus and Cassius had now returned, on 8 June: also present were Brutus' mother, Servilia; his wife, Porcia; his sister, and the wife of Cassius, Junia Tertia; Favonius, the supporter of Cato who had been excluded from the assassination by Brutus; and Cicero, whose letter to Atticus on the subject of this conference provides us with details of the proceedings. We can imagine how fraught a meeting this must have been at times, with no love lost between Servilia, the lover of Caesar, and Porcia, her daughter-in-law and niece, and the daughter of Cato, who would doubtless have wanted quite opposing things for Brutus. Nor were relations good between Servilia and Cicero: before arriving, Cicero seemed irritated that Brutus was taking his mother's advice, and while he was there this dominant woman poured scorn on some of his usual words of wisdom about the way in which the plot and assassination had been mishandled, silencing the normally verbose man. Brutus, on the other hand, was reportedly pleased to see Cicero and sought his advice: the despondent Cicero recommended that he should accept the corn commission, urging him to protect himself, since the defence of the Republic rested on him. However, it was not only Cicero who was offended by the insult of this lowly office that Antony was hoping to foist on the chief assassins. When Cassius walked in and overheard Cicero's defeatist attitude, his eyes were so full of determination that Cicero commented that he appeared as if 'breathing war': he defiantly declared that he had no intention whatsoever of being packed off to Sicily, and would be setting out for Greece instead. At this point, Brutus announced that he, instead of leaving for Asia, would go to Rome, if Cicero was in agreement: he was not, of course, given that it would not be safe for Brutus to return to the volatile city in the current political climate. Indeed, this seemed a rather foolhardy intention. Further discussion of a political nature followed, in which Cassius was especially regretful about opportunities lost throughout the whole affair, and was particularly critical of Decimus Brutus for not using the legions at his disposal wisely. The outcome of the conference was that Servilia agreed to exert her political influence, which she evidently believed lived on beyond her relationship with Caesar, in order to have the corn commission removed from the decree; Cassius remained determined to depart for Greece; and Brutus was persuaded to drop his foolish idea of going to Rome, meaning instead to set out for Asia soon.[29]

In short, although he was glad to have had the opportunity to see Brutus before his expected departure, Cicero was disappointed by the meeting, which he felt was a further indication of the chief Liberators' lack of plan, method and order. On this basis, he was finally reconciled to the decision to leave Italy himself: for the past two months, he had been seeking the advice and approval of Atticus in his characteristic deliberation over whether he could leave Rome in her hour of need, while still retaining his honour, or whether he was obliged to stay and ride out the political crisis, hoping to aid the Republic by his presence but thereby putting his life at risk. He did have justifiable reasons for departing from Italy: he wanted to visit his son, Marcus, in Athens, and he also had the opportunity of a commissioner role, as legate under Dolabella. At the end of May he had written to both Dolabella and Antony, so as not to offend the latter, confirming that he wanted to take up the post and, at the time of the conference at Antium, he had just received the news that he was appointed to Dolabella's staff, which suited his current frame of mind. His deliberation over the matter remained a recurrent theme of his letters to Atticus for the next two months. Some financial matters in mid-June delayed the departure of Cicero, who then seemed eager to leave in case of violence breaking out, with particular regard to potential hostilities between Sextus Pompeius and Antony. However, Cicero then hesitated further, delaying for another month, eventually setting out in mid-July, with a plan to return by the beginning of the following January, when Antony would no longer be consul.[30]

Public Games (July 44 BC)

Brutus' extended absence from the city, and decision to heed the advice of Cicero not to return to Rome now, meant that he was unable to uphold his duty as urban praetor in relation to organising the games of Apollo, due to be held from 6–13 July. At the family conference, Brutus decided, therefore, that they should be held in his absence, but under his name. Instead, Antony's brother, Gaius, who was also a praetor in 44 BC, presided over these games. As the sponsor, Brutus remained keen to lay on lavish games, which he hoped would help sway popular opinion back in favour of the Liberators. His friend, Atticus, and possibly also his influential mother, Servilia, helped Brutus with the arrangements, and kept him involved from a distance, and Brutus expressly delayed leaving for Asia until the games were complete, vainly waiting to see if they could bring about a change of situation in Rome. When Brutus asked Cicero to attend the games, he, unsurprisingly, dismissed this idea outright as foolish: for he, himself, out of the same concern for personal security, had not returned to Rome since his departure following the assassination. Nonetheless he was equally anxious for them to be well attended, and requested full accounts of the proceedings from Atticus. A Plutarchean anecdote reports that, in Naples, Brutus busied himself meeting several potential actors, and asked the friends of a certain famous actor, Canutius, to try to persuade him to go to Rome for his games, since no Greek would go.

Given Brutus' keen interest in holding these games as a potential means for turning the opinion of the mob, he was deeply offended when he learned that an announcement about them was using the new name for the month, Iulius, instead of the traditional Quintilis: this was one of the many honours voted to Caesar before his death because it was his month of birth. Cicero found this unsuitable, and reported that Brutus, who was very distracted with concerns about these games, was quite troubled by this: according to Cicero, he was going to write instructing that the advertisement for the hunt, which would take place on the day after the games and for which he had provided many wild animals, should be announced as taking place on 14 Quintilis. A further blow came when, at the opening of the games, which were not well attended, the planned performance of Accius' tragedy, *Brutus*, was replaced instead with the less contentious *Tereus*. The implications of the *Brutus*, narrating the legend of his ancestor, Lucius Brutus, nobly and heroically banishing a tyrant, were obvious and could not be missed. Brutus had clung to this legendary ancestry keenly in his attempt to emulate it through Caesar's assassination, and would have wished, through this play, to remind the audience of the similar nobility of his recent act, committed for the sake of the state, and of the benefits that he had thus brought. However, the people responded well to the inferences contained within the *Tereus*, applauding and clamouring for Brutus, and he was, unsurprisingly, said to be delighted with their reported reaction.[31]

A week later, however, Octavian easily outdid Brutus' games of Apollo with those he held in honour of the victories of his murdered adoptive father. Octavian, refusing to be cast aside so easily by Antony, decided that he must use his own resources to raise money for the purpose of buying popular support: this enabled him to lay on the lavish games for which he had been preparing over the past two months, and also allowed him to distribute Caesar's legacies to the people, according to the terms of his will. Having already gained the backing of Caesar's veterans, who were willing to follow him as the inheritor of that powerful commander's name, he also used a speech in the forum to exhort the people to support him. Although Octavian was once more frustrated by Antony in his attempt to display Caesar's throne and crown at the games, he nonetheless, with some supernatural assistance, successfully managed to turn this into an excellent public relations exercise: when a comet appeared before sunset on seven successive days of the games, it was believed to be a sign of Caesar's apotheosis, and Octavian used this opportunity to place a statue of Caesar, with a star above his head, in the murdered dictator's recently constructed Temple of Venus Genetrix, which he had vowed before Pharsalus. Although the games at first caused further friction between Antony and Octavian, the pair came under pressure from Caesar's soldiers: it was vital for both to keep their troops on side, and so this led to a superficial and temporary reconciliation.[32]

Preparations for Departure (June–August 44 BC)

Meanwhile, the games of Apollo were not Brutus' only concern: following the conference at Antium in early June, and his decision made there to depart for Asia, he busied himself with preparations for leaving Italy. Although he did not intend to leave until after the plans for the games were in place, and in the end delayed even longer, he wasted no time in getting a fleet together: on 10 June, only two days after the conference, he was already to be found gathering ships. In the meantime he and Cassius would remain in the area. At some time between 12 and 20 June, Cicero had again seen Brutus and Cassius, this time at Lanuvium, along with Atticus; however, this meeting left Cicero in one of his gloomy moods, since they supposedly had given up hope of anything other than that which Antony had offered them. Cicero, consequently speaking pessimistically of suicide, not for the first time blames Brutus for this state of affairs, although he does not explain exactly what he expected him to have done differently. Over the next two weeks Brutus himself sunk into despondency: on 2 July, Cicero notes that a letter from Brutus, while of ambiguous tone, still displays some sparks of manly spirit; but, on 6 July, he forwards Brutus' most recent letter to Atticus, remarking on the helplessness contained within it. Whatever caused his sudden despair, Brutus nonetheless continued with his proactive plans for departure. On 8 July he was staying on the islet Nesis (Nisida), in the Bay of Naples, where he received a visit from Cicero and his nephew, Quintus. Recently this fickle young man, who was also the nephew of Atticus, had decided to switch allegiances, formerly having been a supporter of Antony, much to the disappointment of his uncle Cicero. Brutus received Quintus extremely well, and they were reconciled, as the young man had hoped: even the doubtful Cicero believed that there had been a change in the character of his brother's son. For the sake of protection, Cicero had been hoping that he could share his planned voyage abroad with Brutus; however, when he met him at Nesis, Brutus, distracted by the games, reportedly did not pick up on Cicero's hints, and Cicero then discovered that he intended to delay departure as long as possible, in the futile hope of an advantageous change of situation in Rome. Cicero had expected Brutus to possess only small vessels, and so was surprised to discover that he had a well-equipped fleet: reportedly, both Brutus and Ahenobarbus, fellow conspirator and commander of the Liberators' fleet, had some good double-banked galleys, while others, such as Brutus' proquaestor, Lucius Sestius, and Bucilianus, one of the assassins, also had fine vessels ready. The fleet of Cassius was said to be an even finer affair; his fleet had arrived in the Bay of Naples by 11 July, but Sestius, who was expected, had not. Cicero had clearly underestimated the chief Liberators: they were advanced in their preparations to leave Italy. Ostensibly they were preparing for their new corn commissioner roles, but the possibility that they were equipping themselves in case of a future clash of arms should also be acknowledged.[33]

On 17 July, Cicero gave up waiting for Brutus, who was still to be found at Nesis, while Cassius was at nearby Naples, and he finally set out on his own. Having vacillated for as long as he had, even then Cicero continued to tarry around the Italian coast, unsure that he was following the right course. Finally departing from Italy on 6 August, in the end adverse weather forced him back to the mainland, where he received hopeful news from Rome which made him decide to stay in the country, and henceforth he was to remain in his beloved homeland until his death. A group of prominent men, including a friend of Brutus who had just left him in Naples, where he continued to reside for the moment, brought several pieces of news to Cicero. He received a copy of a pleasing speech which Antony had recently delivered to the people: this possibly refers to an address given in mid-July, when Antony was attempting to foil Octavian's extravagant plans for the games in honour of Caesar. Cicero interpreted this public clash between the Caesarians as a promising sign for the future. He also now read a copy of the manifesto that Brutus and Cassius, seemingly having gained some confidence, issued probably in the latter half of July, and with which Cicero claimed to be satisfied: this has been identified as the edict in which the chief Liberators agreed to withdraw into permanent exile if they could be assured that the state was secure, and on the proviso that their public duties regarding the corn commission were revoked.[34] Evidently Brutus' mother, Servilia, had not been able to exert her political influence successfully to arrange this after all. Cicero judged this manifesto as fair. Furthermore, Brutus and Cassius were issuing letters to ex-consuls and ex-praetors, encouraging them to attend a senate meeting on 1 August, where their edict would be discussed. It was rumoured that, at this meeting, Antony would give up his claim on the Gallic provinces and submit to the authority of the senate: Cicero was hopeful that this signalled that a compromise would be reached and the Liberators would soon be able to return to Rome. Cicero, also hearing that the people were missing him, was thus eager to turn back home.[35]

On his return journey, on 17 August, Cicero stopped at Velia, in Campania, where he met with Brutus, who had ships stationed at the nearby river mouth. Cicero now learned that he had been misinformed about the senate meeting which, by the time he had received news of it, had already taken place. Brutus was, according to Cicero, delighted that he had returned and, despite previous reports of the political situation being overly optimistic, nonetheless encouraged him to proceed to Rome as planned. Brutus, rather hypocritically, told Cicero of his disappointment that he had left Italy, thereby abandoning the Republic: previously he had kept his true feelings hidden, and Cicero was shocked to learn that Atticus had done the same. Brutus was particularly disappointed that he had not been present at the senate meeting, where matters had not gone as expected. It was possibly at this meeting that Brutus and Cassius were designated their proconsular provinces, over which there is some confusion in the sources: Brutus certainly received Crete, while Cassius was probably given Cyrene (modern eastern Libya). Piso, the father-in-law of Caesar, had spoken against Antony at this meeting, but had received no backing in the senate. Furthermore, Antony had not reacted well to the manifesto of Brutus and Cassius, publicly rejecting it and writing a harsh edict and letter in reply. The forthright missive of Brutus and Cassius in response to Antony, dated 4 August, has fortunately been preserved for posterity: in it, they observe the unwarranted offensive and menacing tone of Antony's edict and letter. They deny his accusations that they have been levying troops and money, tampering with the armies, and sending couriers overseas. Antony has also apparently angrily attacked them regarding Caesar's murder, something that we may strongly suspect had long been simmering under the surface and was bound to explode in their face in time. Defiantly, they refuse to be intimidated by his hostile threats, rather audaciously reminding him that he owes his freedom to them. Making it clear that they have no regrets concerning their murderous actions, in sum they choose their freedom over his friendship. They sign off in terms couched in threats of their own, reminding Antony of the fate of the last tyrant. This letter demonstrates that relations between the Liberators and Antony had finally broken down irreparably and thus signals the coming civil war, something that they themselves now acknowledge is a possibility. For Brutus, this made him accept that there was no longer any point in remaining in Italy, fruitlessly waiting for the political situation in Rome to change: realising the struggle for his beloved Republic was futile here, he finally resolved to set out from Italian shores sometime before the end of August 44 BC, with the hope of pursuing the cause of liberty elsewhere.[36]

Chapter Ten

Prelude to Civil War

August–November 44 BC

Brutus Departs for Athens

Plutarch narrates an anecdotal event which reportedly took place before Brutus' departure from Italy, concerning his wife, Porcia: on the point of returning to Rome, distressed at having to part from her husband who was now preparing to leave the country, she burst into tears on catching sight of a painting of Andromache bidding farewell to her husband, the Trojan hero Hector, on his way to battle. The tragic overtones and foreboding contained therein are patent, with the great and noble couple doomed by war in the east. The supposedly strong-spirited Porcia would reportedly return to the painting daily and weep before it. In a similar foreboding anecdote, Brutus maintained that his wife had the mental strength of a man, nonetheless: when a friend recited the famous lines of Andromache declaring that Hector was everything to her, Brutus smiled and said that he would not dream of addressing Porcia with Hector's well-known words to his wife, in which he ordered her to return to the loom and her maids. This was reportedly because Brutus believed that Porcia, the daughter of Cato, had the same spirit to fight nobly for her country as the men did.[1]

Despite his wife's angst, Brutus, as always obeying his sense of duty above all else, set out from Velia for Athens sometime after his meeting with Cicero, but before the end of August. Ostensibly he was travelling to his designated province, but in reality he was setting out for the east, as decided at the family conference in June. Cassius remained in Italy for another month, but would follow suit in late September or early October, travelling via Asia to Syria.[2] Crete and Cyrene were presumably chosen as relatively harmless provinces with which to appease the chief Liberators, while getting them out of the way. However, Brutus and Cassius, as became obvious from the family conference, had no intention of being manoeuvred by Antony and the Caesarians. Indeed, away from Italy matters seemed much improved: for, once he reached Athens, Brutus received a warm welcome from the citizens, who showed appreciation for his heroic act of liberation. Plutarch reports that he was even paid public honours as a tyrannicide, including the setting up of bronze statues of him and Cassius next to those of the tyrant slayers, Harmodius and Aristogeiton, in the agora.[3] The studious and erudite Brutus was very much at home in this intellectual city, where he had earlier received his educational training. While staying here with a friend, he took the opportunity to pursue his interests, reportedly attending the lectures of two philosophers in the city at the time, Theomnestus and Cratippus, and enjoying engaging in philosophical discussion with them both.[4] Apparently occupied by such literary activities, it was not realised that he was simultaneously making plans for war. Brutus was secretly recruiting to his cause many of the like-minded young men currently studying in Athens. Notably, among these were Cicero's son, Marcus, whom Brutus praised for his noble spirit and hatred of tyranny, and Quintus Horatius Flaccus, better known as the future Augustan poet, Horace, who would later sing of his time as tribune of the soldiers, on the wrong side at the Battle of Philippi.[5]

As well as influencing young Republicans to fill out the ranks of his army while he was in Athens, Plutarch reports that Brutus sent one of his men, a certain Herostratus, into Macedonia. Demonstrating strategic ability that he had, up until now, seemed to be lacking, Brutus wanted to act quickly to secure this region before the arrival of Antony's brother, Gaius, who was to be proconsul of this province for the next year. Therefore, Herostratus' mission was to try to win over the commanders of the Roman army in the region. No longer hiding his intentions, Brutus seems to have achieved his aims to gather forces and funds for war over the next few months. His position in Greece gave him useful access to the east, and to the Roman officials travelling to and from their provinces. In this way he successfully obtained funds and loyalty from Gaius Antistius Vetus, the departing quaestor of Syria. Similarly, when the retiring proquaestor of Asia, Marcus Appuleius, was on his return journey from the province, Brutus intercepted him at Carystus (Karistos) on the Greek island of Euboea and secured the troops, vessels and treasure that he had brought with him.[6] His co-conspirator, Trebonius, also sent him money from his province of Asia, and Cimber, another of Caesar's assassins, offered aid from Bithynia, raising a fleet and money for the Republican cause. Furthermore, former troops of Pompey, supposedly remnants from the Battle of Pharsalus wandering about Thessaly, now enrolled in the cause of Brutus. He also took action by seizing the cavalry soldiers whom Dolabella's quaestor, Cinna, was leading to Syria, and by sailing up the Greek coast to Demetrias (near the modern city of Volos), in order to appropriate some weapons, which Caesar had prepared there for his war against Parthia, and which were being conveyed to Antony at the time.[7]

At this point in Brutus' life, with the approaching civil war, the ancient texts begin to record tales portending his death, just as Caesar's demise was similarly foretold by omens in the sources. Plutarch recounts one such anecdote of foreboding: once Brutus had successfully negotiated with Appuleius, they celebrated the Liberator's birthday together, proposing toasts of 'Victory to Brutus' and 'Liberty for Rome'. Brutus then called for a larger bowl of wine, in order to encourage the celebrations, and spontaneously recited the dying words of Homer's Patroclus, claiming that fate and Apollo were responsible for his death. This gloomy quotation has more recently been interpreted as referring to Brutus' inability to hold the games of Apollo, but Plutarch records the belief that this was instead an inadvertent premonition of his approaching doom: one of the reported watchwords given to his soldiers at the fateful last battle at Philippi was 'Apollo', and this god was also, ironically, Octavian's patron deity.[8]

Events in Rome: Antony versus his Enemies[9]

Meanwhile, trouble was brewing back in Rome. Cicero, following Brutus' hypocritical advice, had returned to the city at the end of August, where he was welcomed warmly, but where relations between him and Antony subsequently broke down to such an extent that he now became more fixated than ever on this personal enmity. Antony required Cicero to attend the senate meeting to be held on 1 September, but Cicero declined, using the excuse that he was weary from his journey, having only just arrived. In reality, he was afraid of the threat of violence from his nemesis and, furthermore, he could not agree with the sacrilegious motion that was to be proposed: a day was to be added to all festivals of thanksgiving in honour of Caesar. Antony, resorting to force, was on the point of sending armed men to Cicero's Tusculan villa to coerce him to attend but, in the event, he was dissuaded from violence by others. Cicero now embarked on a dangerous war of words with Antony, which would spill over into violence and would eventually lead to the execution of the elder statesman. For, on 2 September, at another meeting held in Antony's absence, Cicero, at his first appearance in the senate since March, delivered the first of his fourteen famous speeches against his foe, known as the *Philippics*.

We are fortunate to have these, despite their overt biased nature, because of the detail of political events of the relevant period contained therein. This first one, although containing many open criticisms and recriminations of Antony, was less vitriolic in tone than those following, even acknowledging the beneficial acts he had carried out in the wake of Caesar's assassination. Reportedly, Cassius informed Cicero that he approved of this speech, and so it is reasonable to surmise that Brutus would have felt the same.[10]

In consequence, the insulted Antony spent the next two weeks formulating an angry reply, in which he declared Cicero his enemy and attacked his career. He delivered this invective in a senate meeting called especially on 19 September, but which Cicero again did not feel safe to attend, since armed guards surrounded the location, which was, ironically, the Temple of Concord. Reportedly, two others were also no longer able to enter the senate for having spoken their minds: Piso, who had attacked Antony on 1 August, and Publius Servilius Vatia Isauricus, who was possibly the husband of Brutus' sister, Junia Prima, and who apparently also criticised Antony at some point after Cicero. The contents of Antony's reply are chiefly known from Cicero's following response, the second *Philippic*, which is the most well-known of these speeches, since it is the most sustained, long and venomous of his attacks upon his foe, with the condemnations often of a personal nature. Cicero was busy writing this speech far into October, and it was never read out publicly, although it was written as if delivered in the senate on 19 September. Cicero sent copies to both Brutus and Atticus, leaving the latter to pass judgement on it and decide when, if ever, would be a suitable time to publish it.[11] Among other accusations, Antony charged Cicero with having instigated the murder of Caesar: Cicero, believing that Antony's intention is thereby to incite the veterans against him, firmly denies this in the second *Philippic*, but notes that he would be honoured to be included among the Liberators. Furthermore, he informs Antony that he would have assassinated him too, as he frequently claimed elsewhere. He also retorts by reminding Antony that he had shown Brutus and the rest respect, and therefore claims that he could not truly hold them as murderers, while also recalling Antony's supposed involvement in an earlier conspiracy against Caesar. Of course, this speech was not delivered to Antony in reality. In the light of Antony's actual speech against him, when writing to Cassius soon after the meeting on 19 September, Cicero once more declares that all hopes rest on him and Brutus, and he hopefully speaks of them planning something worthy of their glory.[12]

Cicero seemingly achieved nothing with such hostility, other than inflaming an already volatile situation for the Liberators. Now, Antony finally came around to the idea of vengeance for Caesar, something that he had previously dismissed for the sake of reconciliation and harmony in the state. Other issues may have played a part in this, but Cicero's insistence on relentlessly goading Antony must also be considered as a contributing factor. For, in early October, before he had finished writing the second *Philippic*, Cicero learned that Antony had inscribed a statue of Caesar, which he had set up on the rostra, with the words 'To the Father for his Eminent Services'. Although the title of 'Father of his Country' had been bestowed upon Caesar as one of the many honours during his lifetime,[13] Cicero suggests that Antony is thereby implying that the assassins were not just murderers, but parricides. Furthermore, on 2 October, Antony addressed the people, condemning the assassins as betrayers of their country who had no place in the community of Rome, and holding Cicero responsible for their actions. In a letter informing Cassius of this state of affairs, Cicero also mentions how Cassius' legate has been deprived of his travelling allowance on the basis of their public enemy status. His tone is, once again, defeatist, now acknowledging that the use of violence is all that is left to them, and he places his hopes in the courage of his addressee, and presumably also in his partner in crime, Brutus. Cicero, apparently unable to help himself, could not always see beyond his personal cause for resentment to the bigger issue at stake.[14]

However, within a week there was yet another turn of events: following Antony's move to block Octavian from illegally holding the tribuneship, with which it was feared he would try to prosecute Caesar's assassins, Antony was forced to suspend the election due to popular resentment;[15] soon afterwards, in Appian's sequence of events,[16] Octavian was accused of an attempt on Antony's life, via Antony's own bodyguards. According to Cicero, although the people thought this was a false charge by Antony, believing that he hoped thereby to obtain Octavian's money, it was considered to be a welcome truth by those in the know. Cicero now more firmly, and naively, began to put his hopes in the young Octavian, foreseeing the possibility of their joining forces, and hoping thereby to change the situation in favour of the Liberators.[17]

Antony, with his consulship approaching its end, was seemingly being attacked on two fronts: both by the Republicans, and by Octavian and the Caesarians who had joined him. According to the biased Cicero, Antony sensed his loss of popularity, and so set out for Brundisium on 9 October. There he intended to collect Caesar's four Macedonian legions, which he had arranged to be allocated to himself on 1 June, and which he wanted to transfer to Cisalpine Gaul, the province which he had designated for himself at the same time, but which was currently under the governorship of the Liberator, Decimus Brutus.[18] This act of bringing troops into Italy was interpreted as a martial move threatening Rome, not only by the Republicans, but also by Antony's latest foe, Octavian, who decided that he must act quickly and set out for Campania. Octavian and Cicero now became united in their hatred of a common enemy, as Cicero had hoped: he aimed to capitalise on this opportunity, underestimating Octavian and unaware that the young Caesar would be the one using him, not vice versa. Cicero was receiving letters from Octavian on a daily basis, and his final extant correspondence to Atticus, dated to the first half of November, describes these events soon after they unfold.[19] On 1 November, Cicero, currently at Puteoli, received a letter from Octavian detailing his plans: having already won over the veterans in two of the colonies, by making large payments to each man, he now planned to visit the other colonies. Octavian was also gaining popularity in the municipal towns, where he was received well. Antony, meanwhile, was advancing on Rome with one of the legions. He had not enjoyed the successes of Octavian: one legion had not arrived in Italy yet, and the others reportedly confronted him angrily, protesting that he had neglected to avenge Caesar's murder, and dismissing the paltry offer of a donative that he made. Antony was forced to execute the ringleaders in order to prevent dissension, and temporarily won the rest over with a promise of further largesse when they reached Cisalpine Gaul. He then ordered the legions to march up the east coast of Italy to Ariminum, on the border of Cisalpine Gaul, while he returned to the city.[20]

With a war between Antony and Octavian seemingly on the point of breaking out, Cicero somewhat foolishly dismisses Octavian when the energetic young man seeks an interview with him for strategic advice, apparently feeling uncertain that this inexperienced youth had a hope of holding out against the battle-hardened Antony. Instead he sent him advice to return to Rome, where the people would support him, with the 3,000 veterans whose loyalty he had already obtained. In his letter to Atticus, Cicero calls on Brutus, wishing he was present to make the most of this opportunity. Cicero is beset once more with doubts about what he himself should do, lacking confidence in Octavian because of his inexperience, and unsure whether to oblige the youth who, in another letter of early November, has requested his return to Rome, where he wishes to operate through the senate and thus Cicero's presence and backing would be extremely advantageous to him. However, Cicero did not believe that this would be a good idea until the beginning of 43 BC, when Antony would no longer be consul, so that he and his menacing armed guard would no longer be present. Nonetheless, on November 10, having returned to Rome, Octavian occupied the Temple of Castor and Pollux and the surrounding area of the forum with the veterans, and from there he made an address. Cicero's concerns were heightened when he read the contents of the speech that the new Caesar had delivered, and learned how he dramatically reached out to a statue of the dictator, declaring his hopes to attain his father's honours. Octavian, however, now made a mistake: he promised to oppose Antony, misreading the many soldiers who had recently served under him, and were not therefore prepared to fight against him. Octavian necessarily backtracked, allowing those who wished to return home to do so, and promising further rewards. Octavian, realising that he did not have a force with which to oppose the might of Antony, withdrew from Rome in order to raise more troops.[21] Nevertheless, Atticus and Cicero clearly foresaw the potential danger latent in Octavian, fearing that he would be hostile to Brutus and the other assassins. They believed Octavian's true intentions would be revealed when the assassin, Publius Servilius Casca, came to assume his tribuneship in the following month.[22] However, in speeches he would soon make against Antony, Cicero casts Octavian as a saviour of the Republic, protecting the Roman state from the wicked public enemy and aggressor, Antony.[23] Cicero was mistaken: in truth, the supreme manipulator, Octavian, was raising an army with which he would eventually, cleverly biding his time, avenge the death of his adoptive father and simultaneously take up Caesar's position at the head of the state.

Next, Antony returned to Rome, leaving most of his troops stationed at Tibur (Tivoli), and therefore not leading the assault on the city as Cicero would have us believe, although reportedly bringing armed men with him. Once back in the city, he issued manifestos containing insults aimed at Octavian, in response to the speech that the young man had recently delivered against him. He also called a senate meeting on 24 November, with the intention of there declaring Caesar's heir a public enemy; reportedly having warned that anyone failing to attend would be considered his enemy, Antony himself then postponed the meeting. Cicero scurrilously suggests that Antony was unable to attend on the initial date because he was too busy drinking and banqueting. However, a more probable reason for his absence is his return to his troops at Tibur, which was possibly motivated by the unwelcome news that one of his legions had defected to Octavian. Antony then hurried back to Rome, and the senate convened on the Capitol on 28 November. At this meeting provinces were distributed, reportedly to the advantage of Antony's supporters: men such as the Caesarian Sabinus, who was one of the two senators who attempted to defend the beleaguered Caesar, were rewarded; loyal Republicans, such as the Cinna who had dramatically denounced Caesar soon after his death, refused to share in the allocation; and Antony banned others, such as Cassius' brother Lucius, from attending at all. Also, the official provinces of Brutus and Cassius, Crete and Cyrene, were now removed from them. However, the proceedings were interrupted by further bad news summoning Antony away: another of his legions had deserted to Octavian. Antony immediately departed from the city to rejoin his troops at Tibur: in Cicero's depiction he was ignominiously running away, but reportedly many influential men also went there to swear their allegiance to him. Antony then set out for Ariminum, from where he would cross into Cisalpine Gaul, the strategically vital province that he intended to take for himself.[24]

December 44 BC–March 43 BC

Decimus Brutus: the Fight for Cisalpine Gaul

As one of the lead conspirators, Decimus Brutus had set out for his province of Cisalpine Gaul soon after the assassination, once it had become apparent that it was untenable for the murderers of Caesar to remain in the city. However, he had not merely retreated into hiding: by December 44 BC, having spent several months in the province that Caesar had designated to him, he had readied himself for a potential clash with Antony. During the summer and autumn of 44 BC, he recruited fresh troops in addition to his current legions stationed in Cisalpine Gaul, and made successful expeditions against Alpine tribes in order to train his soldiers ready for a battle with Antony. He also thereby won the loyalty of his men by proving his military worth to them, and was thus acclaimed *imperator*. Cicero reassured Decimus that he would have his support in the senate, both when these actions were not received entirely favourably and when Antony was marching with his troops towards Cisalpine Gaul. As he had with Brutus and Cassius, Cicero placed high hopes for the restoration of the Republic in Decimus, and encouraged him in this direction. He even urged him to act without waiting for the official approval of the senate, which, of course, would not happen for the remainder of 44 BC, while Antony still held the consulship.[25]

In the senate meeting that had taken place at the beginning of June, Antony had negotiated for himself to receive command of Cisalpine Gaul, an action that Cicero had interpreted as likely to lead to a conflict and, indeed, Antony had already tried to deny Decimus the province immediately after the murder.[26] However, Antony only now, caught as he was on the wrong side of both Octavian and the Republicans, set out to wrest this important province from Decimus. When Antony arrived in Cisalpine Gaul, he ordered Decimus to surrender his command of the province, which he was legally entitled to do as incoming governor. The current proconsul, however, resisted, intending to defend his province with the army that he had prepared for such an event. His first defiant move was to send Antony a copy of the instructions that he had received from the senate when he took up office, and simultaneously to issue a manifesto stating that he would retain Cisalpine Gaul on behalf of the senate and people of Rome. In the third and fourth *Philippics*, delivered on 20 December in the senate and at a subsequent public gathering, Cicero presents Antony's actions as an illegal invasion and claims that he is next planning a move against Rome. Indeed, the purpose of the meeting was to ensure the provision of an armed guard at the forthcoming meeting in the new year, in fear of possible violence from Antony's supporters. Cicero had not intended to attend this senate meeting of 20 December, but did so upon receipt of the dispatch from Decimus.[27] This was too good an opportunity for Cicero to miss, and he now, after a long absence, seemed to return to his former glory, once more publicly declaiming on the preservation of his beloved Republic. Cicero used this meeting to deliver his speech against Antony, whom he depicted as the tyrant to Decimus Brutus' tyrant banisher, recalling Lucius Brutus, the legendary ancestor of both Decimus and Marcus Brutus.[28] Cicero also made more practical and immediate proposals: he called for Antony to be declared a public enemy; asked that Decimus' actions in Gaul should be confirmed; suggested that the current governors should retain their provinces on behalf of Rome until replacement governors were appointed by the senate; and proposed that the new saviour of the Republic, Octavian, and the legions who had defected to him, should be supported and honoured. The senate approved and passed Cicero's resolutions, which effectively reversed the assignment of provinces that had taken place in early June and at the end of November.[29]

However, before the end of the year Decimus, realising that he was not strong enough to face Antony in open battle, moved south towards Italy until he reached the city of Mutina, where he made preparations for a long siege.

Antony's soldiers soon had the city surrounded, and thus civil war in effect began once more for the Romans. With Decimus and his army now besieged, it was time for the senate to step in and help the commander who was legally representing and defending Rome and one of its important provinces, according to the recent decree proposed by Cicero. The senate duly met on 1 January 43 BC, the day on which Aulus Hirtius and Gaius Vibius Pansa took up their posts as consuls, and the political situation was discussed, with the matter of Antony and Decimus high on the agenda. The suggestion was made that an embassy should be sent to Antony with demands to end the siege and withdraw from Cisalpine Gaul, with war being declared if he refused to comply with the wishes of the senate and people of Rome. However, Cicero, seemingly driven by personal hatred of Antony once more, objected to this moderate approach, wishing instead to declare war immediately on this worst of public enemies, and this gave rise to the main premise of his fifth *Philippic*, delivered that day. In the course of this speech, when proposing honours for Octavian for his assistance against Antony, including currently having gone to Decimus' aid in Cisalpine Gaul, he most foolishly dismisses wider concerns that Octavian still harbours a dangerous resentment against Caesar's assassins, misguidedly believing instead that the heir of Caesar has devoted himself wholeheartedly to the cause of the Republic.[30] The debate lasted four days, with Piso arguing against Cicero, at least according to Appian's narrative, with an integral and valid point being made that it was Decimus who was behaving illegally and not Antony.[31] The result was to take the more moderate approach: envoys were to be sent to Antony. Cicero was more successful in obtaining the honours that he had proposed for various men on 20 December: these included Octavian being made propraetor, despite his young age, so that he could officially command an army, and the envoys going to meet with Decimus in order to pass on a formal vote of thanks from the senate. Soon after the discussion concluded, Cicero addressed a public gathering, delivering his sixth *Philippic*: in this, he presented the proceedings of the senatorial debate, glossing over his defeat there and presenting the situation as frustratingly delaying the inevitable war upon the villain Antony.[32]

There was an anxious wait for news from the envoys. Before their return, however, it was decided in Rome that action should be taken by the consuls: Hirtius was to depart for Cisalpine Gaul in order to lend aid to Decimus, and Pansa was to remain behind to make preparations for the approaching war, including holding a levy of troops throughout Italy. Hirtius set out immediately, despite suffering from a long-term illness at the time. In mid-January a routine senate meeting offered Cicero an opportunity to enunciate once more on his suggested policy for war against Antony, in the form of his seventh *Philippic*.[33] Before the end of the month, while waiting for the return of the envoys, Cicero wrote a letter of encouragement to Decimus, reassuring him that Rome was firmly behind him.[34] Cicero was deeply disappointed when the envoys finally returned at the beginning of February and, instead of having declared war on Antony, as had been decided if he declined to agree to the terms, they brought back Antony's own envoy making demands. Antony, clearly not cowed by the threat, had understandably stood firm and refused both to end the siege of Mutina and to withdraw from the province. Antony was, however, willing to consider the senate's terms, if certain of his own demands were met including, among others, that he should receive Transalpine Gaul, with his legions being supplemented by men from Decimus' army, for the next five years: in other words for as long as Brutus and Cassius should also hold provinces. Although attention had been temporarily diverted from these two chief Liberators, while their co-conspirator Decimus was at the forefront of matters nearer to Rome, they were clearly still on the minds of some in the city. This concern was not misplaced, since Brutus and Cassius, although away in the east, would very soon return to the political scene, in a far stronger position than when they left Italy.[35]

Antony's refusal to comply with the conditions set out by the senate furnished Cicero with a further opportunity to rehearse his favourite theme to the assassins: on learning of his enemy's demands, he immediately wrote letters to Cassius and Trebonius, complaining that they had not also killed Antony on the Ides of March.[36] Following receipt of Antony's instructions, a senate meeting was promptly convened on 2 February to discuss the matter, with Cicero arguing that war must be declared, while others called for a second embassy to Antony. In the end a compromise was reached with a state of public emergency declared, instead of war. Another meeting was held on the following day so that Pansa could read out a report which had arrived from Hirtius, in Cisalpine Gaul. It was during this meeting that Cicero delivered his eighth *Philippic*. In this he interpreted Hirtius' military report as proof that war had already begun, while proposing that any who defected from Antony by 15 March would be exempt from punishment, and he also contemptuously dismissed Antony's demands as arrogant and intolerable.[37] Shortly afterwards followed the ninth *Philippic*, dealing with honours due to Servius Sulpicius Rufus, a member of the embassy who had died while en route to make terms with Antony. Cicero did not miss an opportunity to speak out against his foe: since Sulpicius, the eminent jurist whom Brutus had visited on Samos on his return journey from Pharsalus, was on an important mission for the Roman Republic when he died, Cicero held Antony responsible for his death.[38]

In Cisalpine Gaul, the situation remained fairly stable while the winter prevented any serious fighting. Reportedly, following a battle in which some lives were lost, Hirtius had taken possession of the town of Claterna, which lay between Forum Cornelium (Imola), which Octavian held, and Bononia (Bologna), which Antony had taken with a large garrison. All of these towns were situated along the Via Aemilia, the road running north-west to Mutina, where Decimus was besieged. From north of the River Po came supplies of money, troops and weapons, with Patavium (Padua) being distinguished for having ejected and barred Antony's men. Further up the Via Aemilia, beyond Mutina, two towns were known to be loyal to Antony, Regium Lepidi (Reggio Emilia) and Parma, but Cicero wrote to Cassius in mid-February, gladly informing him that the rest of the province was behind the Republic.[39]

Brutus and Cassius Control the East

In early February 43 BC, while all eyes were on Cisalpine Gaul, unexpected but promising news came from Brutus in the east. His secret plans for military action had apparently come to fruition without the knowledge of Rome which, if intentional as it appears, was a clever move on his part. From the evidence of the extant sources, it seems that Brutus and Cassius had been largely forgotten for the time being, amid the current conflict closer to home. In late October, neither Cicero nor Atticus seemed to be in possession of much news of Brutus or Cassius: at that time, Cicero wrote to Atticus that he was soon to visit Servilia, who would be able to update him, since she still appeared to be at the centre of matters concerning her son, and was expecting a visit from her son's agent, Scaptius.[40] None of the extant letters provides details of what Cicero there learned about Brutus and, after this, despite his eagerness for further news, it seems that only unconfirmed rumours reached him about the exact whereabouts and actions of the chief Liberators outside of Italy. However, Brutus and Cassius had, in fact, both been busy in the east, and confirmation of Brutus' practical actions now arrived in the city in the form of an unexpected dispatch from the man himself, declaring that he had brought Macedonia, Illyricum and Greece under his sway and, since he was always acting in the service of the Republic, he declared that these regions were now in the control of the senate and people of Rome.[41]

It seems that Brutus, after spending several months in Athens raising men and supplies, had marched to occupy Macedonia with his newly formed army. It is probable that he made this strategic move swiftly in order to secure the province late in 44 BC, after the distribution of the provinces on 28 November, in which Antony's brother, Gaius Antonius, had been allocated Macedonia for 43 BC. Firstly Brutus sent his representative, Herostratus, ahead to win over the army commanders stationed there, and he himself must have followed with his army fairly soon afterwards, in order to arrive before Antonius. Presumably Brutus collected the funds that Atticus had deposited for him in Epirus, while en route to Macedonia.[42] The current governor of Macedonia was Quintus Hortensius Hortalus, the son of the renowned orator with whom Brutus had defended Appius Claudius in 50 BC.[43] He was amenable to Brutus, and worked with him to secure the region for the Republican cause, agreeing to hand Macedonia over to him instead of Antonius, and holding a levy in the province in order to raise troops. Meanwhile Brutus' fellow conspirator, Ahenobarbus, succeeded in drawing over part of Dolabella's cavalry in Macedonia, which was en route to his province of Syria. Once established in Macedonia, and reportedly earning the support of the local monarchs and leaders, Brutus learned that Antonius was approaching the neighbouring province of Illyricum, with a plan of uniting forces with those of the proconsul there, Publius Vatinius.[44] Brutus therefore moved hastily to take the province and troops himself. Traversing the difficult terrain of the region despite the harsh winter conditions, Brutus now fell prey to an illness brought on by a combination of cold, hunger and exhaustion. Plutarch here narrates how, having gone ahead of the supply train, the men had no food to give their weak leader as they reached the port of Dyrrachium, and so they were forced to go to the gate of the city to ask the guards for supplies: on learning of Brutus' plight, these men brought food to him themselves and so, when this city later surrendered to him, Brutus treated the people with kindness. Cicero credits the proconsul Vatinius for having opened the gates of Dyrrachium and handed over his army to Brutus, although Plutarch's version suggests that there was some initial resistance, while other sources claim that Vatinius' men disliked their leader and willingly went over to the other side. In whichever way he captured Dyrrachium and the soldiers holding the city, Brutus afterwards led his superior army south down the coast to the city of Apollonia, which Antonius, having failed to win over Vatinius' soldiers, was holding with seven cohorts. There followed some fighting in the area between the two sides, with Brutus' troops enjoying some success. This included Cicero's son, who had joined Brutus at Athens, now seizing control of a legion which was under the command of one of Antonius' legates. It was at this point, with Antonius besieged in the city, that Brutus wrote informing Rome that he had successfully gained control of Greece, Macedonia and Illyricum.[45]

After receipt of Brutus' letter, the senate called another meeting, at which Cicero delivered his tenth *Philippic*. The success of Brutus had generally been received favourably in Rome, although some supporters of Antony believed that, since he was, in truth, acting illegally in seizing these provinces, he ought to surrender his legions:[46] Cicero's speech counters these views, and exalts Brutus and his achievements for the Republic. Cicero claims that Brutus had withdrawn from Italy to avoid civil war and patiently remained abroad until the senate had decreed, on 20 December, that the allocation of provinces made on 28 November should be annulled, thereby making Gaius Antonius' attempt to take proconsular control of Macedonia the illegal action. Only then did Brutus act and, of course, for the sake of his beloved Republic, to which all Rome's armies belonged. Furthermore, Cicero argues that these regions would have become a place from which Antony could have launched an attack on Rome if his brother had gained command there, and so Brutus was defending the state. Cicero also answers concerns that Caesar's veterans will be displeased that Brutus has an army: he objects on the basis that they have supported Decimus, whose part in the assassination was interpreted as more of a betrayal since he was closer to Caesar. In summing up, Cicero proposes that Brutus should receive the official support of the senate in taking command of the region for the protection of the Republic, just as Decimus and Octavian had recently done in Cisalpine Gaul, and also that Hortensius should continue governing Macedonia under the general command of Brutus, until the senate should appoint his replacement. Cicero's proposals were approved.[47]

Before the end of the month, however, further news arrived from the east, which was in great contrast to the dispatch from Brutus: the conspirator, Trebonius, was dead. He was the first of Caesar's assassins to die, and it happened at the hands of Dolabella, who had entered Asia in January, en route to his own province of Syria. While there, Dolabella treacherously engineered Trebonius' murder. As proconsul, Trebonius agreed to cooperate and provide Dolabella's troops with supplies, although he exercised caution and refused them admission to any stronghold in his province. When the pair met at Smyrna (Izmir), they were on good terms, but Dolabella falsely informed Trebonius that he was proceeding to Ephesus (Efes) to supervise the embarkation of his troops, and at night he turned back to capture the city by stealth, seizing Trebonius and having him cruelly tortured, before ordering his beheading and treating his remains with disrespect. Dolabella was not, after all, to prove the mighty saviour of the Republic, second only to Brutus, as his former father-in-law, Cicero, had fulsomely pronounced less than a year previously.[48] On receipt of this news, the senate immediately convened and promptly declared Dolabella a public enemy. A debate then took place, in which it was discussed how war should be waged against Dolabella. Here, Cicero delivered his eleventh *Philippic*, seizing the opportunity to equate Antony and Dolabella: indeed Antony claimed in a later letter that he approved of Dolabella's actions and had arranged with him to execute Trebonius, whom he viewed as thus receiving just punishment for his act of parricide. Cicero proposed in his speech that Cassius, who was already in Syria, should be given the task to lead this campaign against Dolabella. He suggested that Cassius should be made proconsul of the province, and should also receive an extraordinary command extending over the provinces of Asia and Bithynia and Pontus for the purpose of this war, taking over the armies of the current governors, and being given the right to raise money, supplies and men throughout the region. Cassius' mother, brother and notorious mother-in-law, Servilia, were all said to be opposed to Cicero making this motion; Cicero claimed that Brutus' mother was nervous and concerned. In the event, the senate voted against Cicero's proposal, possibly concerned that bestowing such a large portion of the east upon one of Caesar's chief assassins was imprudent. They decided instead that the consuls should take the provinces of Syria and Asia in order to pursue Dolabella, but only once Decimus had been rescued.[49]

However, the senate's decision was not to stop Cassius, who would act with the encouragement of Cicero to proceed without their authority, just as Cicero had also advised Decimus to advance in Cisalpine Gaul. For Cassius had gathered formidable forces and was not to be prevented from using them to pursue and exact justice for his murdered fellow Liberator. However, it was clear that, when writing to Cassius in February, Cicero was not party to his exact whereabouts and actions, although he was eager for news and had heard reports that the Liberator was in Syria in command of troops: Cicero's speech in the senate therefore must have been based largely on assumptions and rumours, which did prove to be correct. After his departure from Italy in the latter months of 44 BC, Cassius had set about raising troops and supplies, just as Brutus had, and did so with great success. Reportedly, he went first to Trebonius in Asia to secure money and troops from his co-conspirator, and drew over some of Dolabella's cavalry to himself, with the aid of Trebonius' quaestor, the younger Spinther, who had joined the Liberators after the assassination, and who also levied troops for Cassius. He also gained supplies from another of Caesar's assassins, Cimber, in Bithynia, as well as obtaining the support of local people from Asia and Cilicia. Cassius also succeeded in making an alliance with King Tarcondimotus and the people of Tarsus (the capital of Cilicia), although it was said to be against the will of the latter, who were supporters of Caesar. Cassius then proceeded to Syria, which he had chosen as his destination because the people were known to be well disposed towards him, following his time there as quaestor under Crassus keeping the Parthians at bay.[50] In Syria, the proconsul for 44 BC, Lucius Staius Murcus, who had associated himself with the Liberators after Caesar's assassination, and the retiring governor of Bithynia and Pontus, Quintus Marcius Crispus, joined Cassius with their armies, cooperating fully with him. He also acquired troops from one of Dolabella's legates, Aulus Allienus, who willingly handed his legions over, and from Quintus Caecilius Bassus, a rebel Pompeian who was being besieged in Apamea by Murcus and Crispus, and whose legion mutinied and went over to Cassius against the commander's wishes. Cassius confirmed that he had taken these actions in Syria in a letter to Cicero dated 7 March 43 BC, meaning that Brutus and he had established themselves securely in the east over approximately the same period of time in the winter of 44 to 43 BC, and were now both in a very strong position. Cassius had also, like Brutus, sent a dispatch to be read to the senate confirming his position in command of all armies in Syria. However, it never reached Cicero, who was to approve it first, and it was presumed to have been intercepted by Dolabella. Brutus also requested approval from Cicero at this stage, as so often before, concerned at how the news of Cassius would be received by Caesarians in Rome: he had written to his sister, Junia Tertia, the wife of Cassius, as well as his mother, asking them not to make Cassius' success public until Cicero had been consulted on the matter.[51]

Outside Rome, a deadlock had thus been reached while the state was poised on the threshold of a civil war on three fronts, now that the chief Liberators held strategic positions across the Roman world: Decimus, although besieged north of Italy, in Cisalpine Gaul, had the support of Octavian and the consul Pansa in opposing Antony; Brutus dominated the provinces located immediately east of Italy, holding Greece, Macedonia and Illyricum, and had Antony's brother, Gaius, besieged in the latter; and Cassius, whose power, although not sanctioned, nonetheless extended across the further east, since Syria and the nearby Asian provinces were under his influence, and he was ready to hunt down and punish the outlaw Dolabella with his forces. Exactly one year on from the assassination of Caesar, then, the Liberators, now that they had finally taken decisive action, found themselves in their strongest position yet. However, it was becoming clear that this was at the cost of peace: far from what Brutus had intended or wanted for the state, civil strife was looking inevitable in deciding the fate of his beloved Roman Republic.

Chapter Eleven

Civil War in the West

March–December 43 BC

The Western Provinces

With Rome teetering precariously on the brink of civil strife that no one wanted, further final attempts at negotiation were made. In early March, there were reports in the city that Antony now wished to come to terms, and the senate therefore decided to send a second embassy to him, which was to include none other than Cicero. However, this plan fell through, with the consul Pansa then reconsidering his peace-seeking stance, and Cicero delivering his twelfth *Philippic*, criticising the very concept of sending an embassy to Antony and arguing that it would be a futile act, while once more listing Antony's misdemeanours and depicting the intolerable idea of his return to the city. Cicero defends his own surprising role as ambassador by claiming that he had been falsely led to believe that Antony had changed his stance and was to withdraw from Mutina, and also that concern for Decimus had impaired his judgement. Although naturally unwilling, he does not refuse to go on the mission altogether.[1]

At this point, the governors of the western provinces, who had up until now remained quiet as far as we can tell from the sources, came into play. We may remember that Pollio was in Further Spain, Plancus was in Transalpine Gaul, and Lepidus was in Narbonese Gaul and Nearer Spain.[2] It seems that they had kept out of the current uncertain conflict, possibly waiting and assessing the situation before deciding which side to support, and it is notable that all three men would successfully navigate the civil wars and emerge with their lives. In mid-March, Pollio, a Caesarian who was to become involved in the literary circles of Octavian when the latter had become the Emperor Augustus, wrote to Cicero, although the letter was not sent for another month. Pollio notes his honest devotion to peace and liberty, and complains that he has only now received instructions from Rome, in the form of Pansa's request that he place his armies at the disposal of the senate. However, he explains that he is unable to influence matters, blocked off as he is by Lepidus' province, and he has been resisting Lepidus' pressure to hand over one of his legions. For it seems, from Pollio's correspondence, that Lepidus, Caesar's former master of horse, and the brother-in-law of Brutus and Cassius, had been openly backing Antony, which is perhaps not altogether surprising given his immediate reaction when Caesar was murdered. At about this time, communications were received in Rome from both Lepidus and Plancus, proposing a peaceful settlement with Antony: Cicero's negative reaction to Lepidus' proposal specifically is recorded in his thirteenth *Philippic*, delivered in the senate on 20 March. Following the lead of Servilius, possibly married to Brutus' eldest sister, he did not believe peace could be considered until Antony withdrew from Mutina and laid down his arms.[3]

This speech also quotes and refutes the points of a letter from Antony, which Hirtius had recently forwarded to Cicero. In this correspondence, among other comments, Antony resorted to denouncing Caesar's assassins: it is here that Antony records his support for Dolabella in having put Trebonius to death, and he also, menacingly, speaks openly of avenging Caesar's death. Furthermore, he complains that Brutus and Cassius are receiving support from the senate for their illegal usurpation of the east, and that Brutus was given money by Appuleius. We also learn here that, while taking over the eastern provinces, Brutus had executed two prominent Greek locals, Menedemus of Macedonia and Petraeus of Thessaly, who had been active supporters of Caesar during the civil war against Pompey, and who had been granted Roman citizenship. Cicero simply dismisses this as something irrelevant and trivial, but this casts a somewhat less glorious light on his hero, Brutus: we do not know the nature of events behind these executions, but may surmise that these Caesarians attempted to resist the takeover of the area by one of Caesar's chief assassins. Antony also raises questions over Casca being allowed to assume the tribuneship, and Galba being present in the camp of the senate. Cicero appears to enjoy sparring with Antony, even though many of his foe's points were justified, making his argument in defence of the Liberators sometimes flimsy at best.[4]

In his manifesto, Antony speaks of Lepidus and Plancus as his allies, but Cicero simply, and hopefully, dismisses this. His thirteenth *Philippic* is mostly polite in tone towards these two governors, who were holding the important western provinces closest to Cisalpine Gaul: he could not afford to alienate men with the power to turn the fortunes of the Republic by joining forces with the wrong side. When he went home from the senate on 20 March, Cicero set about writing to both men on the subject of their peace-seeking and loyalties, and made his true feelings more patent. He clearly was not aware that Lepidus had already openly allied himself with Antony, as Pollio's letter was to inform him when it eventually arrived.[5] Cicero was under no illusion about the nature of these two men, however, and knew that they could not be entirely relied upon in the service of the state. He seemed to be slightly more confident that Plancus could be swayed: since September, Cicero had been in correspondence with him, in the vain hope that encouragement would make him loyal to the Republic. Plancus' duplicitous nature had been revealed when his letter proposing peace with Antony arrived at approximately the same time that his legate appeared in the city, contradicting the contents of this letter with a pledge of loyalty to the senate, directly from the man himself. However, the untrustworthy Plancus, who was also busy writing on 20 March, explained away this discrepancy, for he sent an official dispatch to the senate and a private letter to Cicero on this day, before he could have received Cicero's correspondence to him.[6] In these communications, Plancus makes his fairly feeble and transparent excuses for not having supported the Republic outright, claiming that he was forced to feign his allegiance with Antony for fear of danger otherwise, and accusing Antony of trying to win over his men with bribes. Assuring the senate and Cicero that he, his legions and province are all firmly behind the state, he declares that it is safer to send confirmation of his true loyalties verbally via messenger, than commit his intentions in writing. Clearly this opportunist was attempting to keep his options open with what would prove to be nothing more than empty promises. No one can have been completely deceived by his words. Nevertheless, Cicero continues to pursue his policy of writing to Plancus in friendly and often flattering terms, in an attempt to secure his loyalty to the Republic, and requests that he go to the aid of Decimus at Mutina.[7] Furthermore, when writing to Brutus in April, Cicero seems to hold out genuine hope for Plancus' loyalty, while openly denouncing Lepidus, the addressee's brother-in-law, as an enemy of the Republic. He informs Brutus that he has even come into conflict over Plancus with his fellow consular, and the possible other brother-in-law of Brutus, Servilius, who clearly refused to be fooled by his hollow missive.[8]

The Battle of Forum Gallorum

Now that spring had arrived, the ceasefire in Cisalpine Gaul ended and military action advanced rapidly. Shortly before the senate meeting on 20

March, Pansa had set out to join his colleague, Hirtius, as well as Octavian, in bringing aid to the besieged Decimus Brutus: for, he and his army were beginning to suffer from hunger after the long winter shut up in Mutina and the situation could not be sustained much longer. In receipt of unfavourable messages and rumours from Cisalpine Gaul, Cicero sent anxious letters to Brutus and Cassius during the first half of April: concerned about the crisis in Mutina, he was again looking to the chief Liberators as the ultimate saviours of the state, and as a refuge to which the Republicans could flock should events in Cisalpine Gaul not go well. Meanwhile, Octavian continued to work with Hirtius, agreeing to share his stronger men with him, although he was biding his time, reportedly aware that he was simply being used against Antony until he should be defeated. Hirtius and Octavian advanced together from their respective camps further south-east on the Via Aemilia towards Mutina, in fear that Decimus' weak army should surrender out of desperation to Antony. Meanwhile Antony, unable both to maintain the siege and keep the garrison at Bononia, was forced to abandon the latter, which Hirtius and Octavian consequently took en route. Once outside Mutina, they succeeded in getting messages to Decimus, so that he was made aware that relief was at hand. However, they avoided entering into battle with Antony, waiting instead for Pansa and his army to arrive and increase their strength. Appian and Dio Cassius report that there were some cavalry engagements, however, and that Antony, leaving his brother, Lucius, in charge of the siege, went out to face his opponents. This led to some clashes, in which Antony emerged victorious, and which gave him the confidence to attempt to take Hirtius and Octavian's camp before Pansa could bring them support.[9]

A letter to Cicero from Servius Sulpicius Galba,[10] one of Caesar's assassins, preserves a first-hand account of the important clash that took place on marshy and woody ground around the village of Forum Gallorum (near the modern town of Castelfranco Emilia, situated between Bologna and Modena) on 14 or 15 April 43 BC.[11] As a legate of Hirtius, Galba had gone to join Pansa in the relief mission, and he describes how Antony came out to intercept them, unaware that Hirtius had, on the previous night, sent a legion and cohorts to escort them, foreseeing Antony's move. For Antony, having left his brother to create diversionary attacks on Hirtius and Octavian, was intending to ambush Pansa and his inexperienced recruits, by concealing his men in the marshes on either side of a narrow stretch of the Via Aemilia, in order to prevent Pansa's forces joining up with the rest of the Republicans. On seeing Antony approaching, Hirtius' escorting reinforcements, including the Martian legion which had previously angrily deserted Antony, advanced without awaiting command, causing others to follow in a disorganised fashion. Antony had kept his main army concealed back at Forum Gallorum, so that he could launch a surprise attack on the Republican forces pursuing him, which led to a fierce battle, particularly as it involved Antony's current men versus his deserting troops. The right wing, which Galba was leading, had some success in advancing at first, but was then forced to fall back when Antony's cavalry tried to surround it. Octavian's cohorts were stationed on the Via Aemilia, where a long struggle took place, and the weaker left wing was forced to give ground when it began to be outflanked by Antony's strong arm of cavalry. Meanwhile Octavian himself remained in command of defending the camp near Mutina from Lucius Antonius, which he did successfully. All Republican ranks withdrew and Antony, believing he was victorious, failed in an attempt to capture their camp. On Antony's return to his own camp, Hirtius, having learned of the earlier events, led his veterans out to meet his opponent's battle-weary troops and successfully destroyed or routed all of them in the same area where the clash had taken place earlier that day, forcing the defeated Antony to withdraw to his camp outside Mutina. It was a victory for the Republicans, but at the cost of many fatalities, including that of Pansa, who had been taken to Bononia, suffering from wounds that would lead to his death a week later.[12]

A report of the battle by each of the three commanders was sent to Rome, where Cicero praised them for their success in his fourteenth and final extant *Philippic*, delivered in the senate on 21 April. Having been in a state of panic following the circulation of a false report of Antony's victory for the past few days, which presumably had come about on the basis of his initial success against Pansa, Cicero and Rome were now overjoyed. A day of celebration and public thanksgiving was proposed, but Cicero argued in his speech that Antony should officially be declared a public enemy before that should happen, and also felt it inappropriate while Decimus remained besieged in Mutina. This did not, however, prevent Cicero from proposing similar honours for the three victorious generals, including that a monument should be erected to the memory of their fallen soldiers and that they themselves should be hailed as *imperatores*. Significantly for the future, this led to Octavian being acclaimed as *imperator* for the first time.[13] Cicero also wrote to Brutus on current affairs in jubilant mood on this day: he records, as he also does in the fourteenth *Philippic*, how the people of Rome had publicly revered him as saviour of the state the day before, escorting him to the Capitol and then to the rostra. Cicero here praises Octavian, and misguidedly expresses hopes that he can continue to influence 'the boy' (*puer*), which even he admits may not be an easy task. Furthermore, he now begins requesting that Brutus return to the city, informing him that the people seek this: had Brutus now returned, the situation may have changed in favour of the Liberators, but he was cautious, aware that the assassins of Caesar still did not enjoy widespread popularity.[14]

The Battle of Mutina

However, this was not yet the time for rejoicing, since Decimus still remained besieged in Mutina, and there was more fighting to come. Unfortunately, there are not such detailed and reliable sources available for the Battle of Mutina.[15] We do know that, a week after the Battle of Forum Gallorum, on 21 April, the same day that Cicero was delivering his last surviving *Philippic* in the senate, Antony decided to risk a battle. With Hirtius and Octavian threatening to break through the siege lines, he hoped to avoid losing his hold on Mutina, and the two sides came to blows outside the besieged town. Despite his army's weakness, it seems that Decimus managed to make an effective sortie from Mutina in order to aid the attack on Antony. Hirtius' forces succeeded in defeating those of Antony. Having lost the battle, and despite advice from friends to continue the siege, Antony was forced to withdraw, and thus Decimus was finally relieved after several months shut up in Mutina. On learning of the success at Mutina, Brutus expresses his joy in a letter to Cicero in early May: he is particularly pleased that the sortie of his fellow Liberator, Decimus, made a valuable contribution to the victory. Cicero was also, unsurprisingly, delighted at Antony's defeat, prematurely believing that the Republic was now saved. In the senate he proposed honours for the victors: since the battle had happened to take place on Decimus' birthday, one suggestion was that his name be entered in the calendar on that day of significance, although this was rejected.[16]

However, the battle had not been without losses, and Cicero also proposed honours for the fallen. Notable among them was Hirtius, who had been cut down in battle, supposedly in the camp of Antony, near his tent. Also killed was one of Caesar's assassins, Pontius Aquila, who was a legate under Decimus. A report got about that Octavian fell there too: Pollio, writing to Cicero from Spain in early June, had heard that this was the case, but it was, unfortunately for the Liberators and Antony, nothing more than a false rumour. It was also at this time that accusations of Octavian's cowardice in battle began to come about: although attributed to Antony, this was a taint on his character from which Octavian could never fully escape, and which lived on in the sources. Furthermore, accusations of foul play were now made against Octavian, which were also passed down through the sources for posterity. Hirtius had reportedly been killed by the enemy in battle a day or two before his colleague Pansa was to die of his wounds: the death of the two consuls, leaving behind their forces and vacant positions at the head of the state, was deemed extremely convenient for Octavian, since it left the young heir to Caesar in a strong position to usurp power, as indeed he soon would. Pansa's physician, Glyco, was arrested for having poisoned the consul, and this was linked back to Octavian. Brutus felt compelled to write a letter to Cicero on behalf of this doctor, who was married to the sister of his friend, Achilleus, in order to vouch for him and implore Cicero to get him out of custody.[17]

Following his defeat, Antony gathered the remnants of his troops and marched further into Gaul, towards the Alps. He had hope of joining forces with Lepidus, Plancus and Pollio, and sent envoys to all three. However, at this time, Plancus, continuing to keep his options open, was writing to Cicero with assurances of loyalty to the state: firstly he wrote that he was marching his army towards Mutina, as he had been instructed to do by the senate, and claimed that he would oppose Lepidus if he tried to obstruct his access; then, having learned of Antony's defeat and approach, he decided to stay where he was, supposedly so that he could block Antony's route, and also claimed to be encouraging Lepidus to join him in this mission.[18] Meanwhile, the praetor Publius Ventidius Bassus joined Antony on the Ligurian coast, having traversed a difficult route with his legions made up of fresh troops: he would be rewarded with the suffect consulship before the end of the year, when the second Triumvirate was formed. These were crucial reinforcements, and Antony had also been gathering troops by enlisting slaves en route: disastrously, he had been allowed to regain military strength.[19]

Cicero had been keeping Brutus informed of events in the west and, towards the end of April, he wrote briefly to update him on the current situation: at this point, Cicero believed that Decimus and Octavian had gone together in pursuit of Antony and his followers, who had at last been declared public enemies.[20] Cicero was, in fact, misinformed about relations between Decimus and Octavian. After the siege was lifted, Decimus emerged from the town with an army weakened and depleted by months of hunger. In the aftermath of the battle, he had been unaware of exactly how events had unfolded and did not know that Hirtius had been killed. Once he learned of this, he realised that a meeting with Octavian, who was now in control of the armies of three commanders, was imperative. We do not know the proceedings of the meeting, if it took place at all, but Octavian certainly refused to cooperate with Decimus: in Appian's version of events the meeting did not happen, since Octavian declined even to speak with his father's murderer.[21] Before Decimus could take any action against Antony, he was summoned by Pansa to the camp at Bononia, but news of this consul's death reached him before he arrived. The fight against Antony, then, now rested on him and Octavian, but Decimus was fairly weak militarily: Pansa's legions of new recruits joined his weakened legions, but Hirtius' best legions remained loyal to Caesar and over the next months it emerged that they could not be induced to join the man who had betrayed him. This all clearly left Decimus in a difficult position. Cicero often appears unfairly critical of him, as, for example, when writing to Brutus in the following months, blaming Decimus for wasting too much time and having let victory slip through his hands, although acknowledging that his army was inexperienced. In early May, Decimus seems to sense Cicero's feelings on the matter, excusing himself for not having pursued Antony immediately, and explaining his quite reasonable actions on the first days after he broke out of Mutina.[22]

Decimus probably acted as hastily as his situation would allow, but Antony had already got a head start of two days: Decimus wrote to Cicero on 29 April, a week after the Battle of Mutina, from Regium Lepidi, which had been one of only three cities loyal to Antony in Cisalpine Gaul. Therefore, he had already begun his advance, if slowly, up the Via Aemilia, encamping in one of Antony's former cities, and within the next day or two had moved on to another of these, Parma. In his letter he briefly sets out his plans for pursuing Antony, displaying that he is ready for action: his aim is to drive Antony out of Italy and to block Ventidius. If Antony does manage to cross the Alps, he will station a garrison in the mountains. With an urgent tone, Decimus seeks Cicero's help in persuading Plancus, Pollio and Lepidus not to join forces with Antony, although he suspects, correctly, that Lepidus is a lost cause. By 5 May, Decimus, running out of funds, was now at Dertona (Tortona) and approaching the Alps. He had discovered that he was to the north of Antony, who had now been joined by Ventidius, meaning that he had failed to prevent these reinforcements. Uncertain, but anticipating Antony's next move, he expresses frustration with Octavian: Decimus believed that they could have cut Antony off from supplies if they had worked together, avoiding another battle. He adds that Octavian, worryingly, can neither take orders nor control his own army. Given that Decimus was Octavian's senior in both age and experience, his annoyance at such a crucial failure is easily understandable.[23]

It was not only Decimus whom Octavian was opposing, for he was also dangerously irked by the senate, which had conferred great honours upon the enemies of Caesar, while overlooking him. Cicero proposed that, for Octavian's entry into Rome, he should be granted an ovation, while Decimus was voted a full triumph.[24] Even this lesser honour for Octavian was not approved by all: friends of Brutus were among those who objected in Rome, and it can certainly be assumed, as Cicero himself did, that Brutus would be no more favourably disposed towards it. Brutus and Cassius themselves were now confirmed in the respective eastern commands that they had seized illegally, and Cassius was formally given the commission to make war on the outlaw Dolabella with the support of Brutus, while the son of Pompey, Sextus Pompeius, was given supreme command of the sea in order to support the war against Antony. A further insult to Octavian was that the legions of the dead consuls were to be placed under the command of Decimus, who was given overall command of the war, with Octavian as his subordinate: of course, in terms of seniority and experience this made absolute sense, but the young heir to Caesar reportedly felt this slight keenly. What must have caused even more resentment, in this respect, was that the senate's envoys were sent to communicate with his soldiers directly, and not with him: the army, however, refused to listen without the presence of its commander. Octavian found further support in the soldiers when two of Hirtius' best legions chose to remain loyal to Caesar's heir, ignoring the senate's ruling that they were to join Decimus, and he then also kept one of Pansa's legions from going over to Caesar's assassin. Furthermore, Decimus and Octavian were both excluded from the commission for the distribution of land to the troops, which reportedly caused yet more discontent among the legions. Octavian had also learned of the derogatory and unfortunate remark of Cicero about him: in the latter half of May, Decimus wrote to warn Cicero that someone had reported his comment to Octavian that he 'should be praised, honoured and removed'. The response of Caesar's heir was that he had no intention of being eliminated.[25] Therefore, the acts and motions of the senate understandably made Octavian feel that they were now trying to outmanoeuvre him, and this resourceful supreme mover simply could not allow such an insult. Cicero and the senate had now served their purpose, and he began to contemplate a new alliance, which they perhaps had not foreseen: a union with his recent foe, Antony, who would be similarly used and discarded in time. In the immediate moment, Octavian saw that more could be gained by making overtures to Antony and his men.[26]

Brutus, however, always had reservations about Octavian's true intentions, and repeatedly urged Cicero to be more cautious where this heir of Caesar was concerned. For the months of April to July 43 BC, we are fortunate to have a series of correspondence between Brutus and Cicero, consisting of more than twenty letters.[27] In these letters, details of the contemporary Roman political world are given, as seen through the eyes of the correspondents, and for once we hear the voice of Brutus, both through his own words and in Cicero's response to his written comments. Throughout this correspondence, Octavian became something of a bone of contention between the two men, who did not always see eye to eye on political affairs. Cicero frequently sings Octavian's praises, portraying him as something of a saviour who has rescued Rome from the mess left behind by the Liberators, blaming them once more for choosing not to assassinate Antony along with Caesar. Furthermore, Cicero unfairly finds fault with Decimus for not having pursued Antony quickly enough after the siege of Mutina, but does not mention Octavian's failure to assist in this at all. Cicero foolishly believes that Octavian has been guided by his advice so far: initially, he did seek the elder statesman's counsel, but ultimately he would always follow the path that suited his own political ends. At times even Cicero seems to acknowledge that controlling this boy will be something of a challenge, but at other times he strongly defends his position of bestowing excessive honours on him against the criticisms and cautions of Brutus, stating that Octavian has received nothing that is not due. Speaking generally in early May, Brutus accuses Cicero of getting carried away the moment that someone behaves well, concerned that all that he thus achieves is to inflame that person's arrogance and hunger for power: it may be suspected that Brutus had Octavian firmly in mind when he made these comments. A week later he was more explicitly expressing his unease that Cicero was setting dangerous precedents in giving extraordinary honours to Octavian, since he feared that he now had designs on obtaining the consulship with the backing of the senate. Indeed it soon emerged that Brutus was not at all wrong to be so troubled by this young man, of whom he said to Cicero 'if only you could see how much I fear him'.[28] In mid-June, Cicero claimed to be making an effort to dampen Octavian's ambition, blaming other people for giving him ideas above his station, without acknowledging his large portion of responsibility for it, while also recognising that Octavian's backing by the army placed much power in his hands. Cicero was evidently beginning to have some reservations, worried that others could corrupt and influence the impressionable young man, as he naively views him, leading him down the wrong path and away from the preservation of the state. For the remainder of the period of this correspondence between the two men, Cicero gradually begins to recognise and admit that Octavian is proving unreliable.[29]

A Reversal of Fortunes in the West

Despite Cicero's harsh and open criticisms of Decimus as ineffective, blaming him for having simply shifted the war to another place, rather than having made the Republic victorious in Cisalpine Gaul, as it had first beem believed in Rome, Decimus continued to do what he could and pressed on in pursuit of Antony during May. He had been made aware that Antony was aiming to cross the Alps in order to reach Lepidus and Plancus, and received a report that Antony's men were to march on Pollentia (Pollenzo) from their position on the Ligurian coast: he immediately acted on this, setting out to reach the town first. It has been suggested that this was a ploy by Antony to lure Decimus away, since it allowed him to cross with his forces into Lepidus' province. On 19 May, Cicero wrote to Decimus, who had moved northwards to Vercellae (Vercelli), with a patent tone of irritation: messages had reached the senate from Decimus, which clearly displayed his alarm at Antony's advance and, in response, Cicero admonished this 'bravest' man for his current nervousness, adding that Lepidus was not to be feared. However, it was soon to emerge that he was again showing a poor judgement of character. Furthermore, Decimus' anxiety was justified, since it was now that he learned that he did not have the forces that he had expected, because of those legions which refused to join one of Caesar's assassins. On 24 May, Decimus was still tarrying on his province's side of the Alps: he wrote to Cicero from Eporedia (Ivrea), saying that he would not cross the Alps unless instructed, because of concerns that the discontented veterans were about to stir up trouble in Rome against Cicero, including inciting Octavian. A day later brought no change in situation, but Decimus' tone was more optimistic and encouraging: he stated that the Republic had large and powerful armies behind it, and believed, erroneously, that Lepidus' attitude seemed more promising. Cicero seemed pleased with this letter, and in early June replied that, although much was afoot in Rome, Decimus should let nothing stand in the way of finishing the war in the west, assuring him that he will look into his request for money. Furthermore, Cicero agreed with Decimus that they should send for Brutus and keep Octavian to protect Italy; we may suspect that Brutus was unlikely to have thought it wise thus to employ Octavian whom, as we have seen, he did not trust.[30]

Meanwhile, Cicero and Plancus kept up their correspondence during May and June, which was in the same mutually complimentary vein as before, with Cicero encouraging Plancus to support the Republic, and Plancus sending his assurances of good faith. The impression conveyed in this correspondence is that Plancus was firmly on the side of the Republic and it is quite probable that this self-preservationist had not, at this point, decided which side he would support, as it was not yet clear who would emerge victorious. Plancus claimed to have been working on Lepidus to make war on Antony, to which Lepidus had at first allegedly responded that he would comply if he was unable to keep Antony from his province, and asked Plancus to come and join forces with him for this purpose. Plancus reported to Cicero that he had made immediate plans to set out and join Lepidus, with the hope of crushing Antony. He was also making efforts to block Lucius Antonius, who had advanced down the coast to Forum Julii (Fréjus): however, his efforts clearly failed since, within a week, Antony would join his brother there. Within a few days, Plancus was writing to inform Cicero that Lepidus' words had been false: once Plancus had set out to join him, he received a message instructing him instead to wait where he was, but initially he decided to ignore it. However, he then learned that Lepidus' soldiers were refusing to fight anymore, wanting peace after all the bloodshed between Roman citizens, and so Plancus supposedly then decided to return to defend his province and the state, and asked Cicero to send an army quickly to aid him. However, according to Plancus, Lepidus soon changed his mind once more, summoning Plancus, who finally left his camp near Cularo (Grenoble), garrisoning two forts on the river that he had earlier bridged there in order to aid Decimus' passage, and hastened to Lepidus' side. During the latter half of May, Lepidus was writing to Cicero, reporting his military manoeuvres in his province, in which he was supposedly resisting the advance of Antony. Lepidus informed Cicero that Antony had a strong cavalry force, but that many of his soldiers were deserting to him, and professed loyalty to the state but, of course, his words could not be trusted and, indeed, before the end of the month he would have joined forces with Antony. Rumours of his true intentions were obviously circulating in Rome: while Lepidus felt it necessary to write a fulsome letter to Cicero, thanking him for his continued support against this unfounded gossip, Cicero wrote to Plancus that reports of Lepidus were frustratingly contradictory. In the meantime, Lepidus was continuing to communicate with Plancus, who informed Cicero that Lepidus was waiting for his arrival as reinforcement against Antony, and assured Cicero that he would bring this war to a swift conclusion. At the end of May, Cicero anxiously sought from Plancus confirmation that Lepidus was keeping Antony at bay, as he had recently imparted to Decimus. On the last day of May, Lepidus sent an official dispatch to the senate in which, while continuing to declare his false loyalty to the Republic, he claimed that his army had mutinied and so prevented him from fighting in the interests of the state.[31]

However, news arriving in Rome from Plancus, in early June, was to clarify exactly where Lepidus' loyalties lay and the true meaning of his dispatch on 30 May, as well as proving that Decimus' fears about Lepidus' treachery were far from unfounded. Plancus had taken up a strategic position behind a river, at approximately forty miles distance from Lepidus and Antony, from where he could either make a rapid advance or easy retreat. Lepidus continued to make overtures to Plancus to join him but, following the fraternisation of his soldiers with those of Antony, and their refusal to fight each other, he eventually gave up and instead joined forces with Antony on 29 May: this was a serious blow to the Republic, which would change the fortunes of this civil war almost instantly. Antony then advanced, reportedly with fury, on Plancus, who retreated swiftly but carefully, crossing back over the bridge he had constructed before destroying it and waiting in Cularo for the arrival of Decimus, whom he expected on about 9 June. At this precarious point, Plancus requested Cicero's continued support in sending reinforcements, specifically asking that Octavian and his army be sent to join him. Decimus had learned of this situation on 3 June and, before his departure from his camp in the Alps, sent a dispatch to the senate and wrote a brief note to Cicero: he now urgently needed reinforcements, money for his troops, and Brutus to be summoned from the east.[32]

Cicero obliged by asking Brutus to return to Italy immediately, in accordance with the resolution of the senate, urging him to do so speedily for the sake of public interest in the current crisis: he told Brutus that both his strength and counsel were desperately needed, for the battle ahead and the establishment of the constitution respectively, and that all would rally to him upon his arrival. Cicero informed Brutus of the situation as it stood in mid-June: the war in the western provinces had been reignited thanks to Lepidus' treachery; Decimus and Plancus had a good and large army, but it consisted of many new recruits and Gallic auxiliaries; dissension was growing within the city of Rome; Cicero was beginning to have concerns that Octavian was being led astray; and the power of the army to control the political situation was causing grave anxiety. Indeed, by mid-July, Cicero recognised that Octavian's army was a real and dangerous threat, since they were backing their leader to become consul. There are several extant letters from Cicero to Brutus, through to the end of July, in which, conveying the perilous situation, he repeatedly implores him to return to Italy, and asks him to urge Cassius to do the same. According to Appian, messengers were also sent by the senate to Brutus and Cassius to ask for their assistance. Cicero also wrote to Cassius on the same theme, although far more briefly, summing up the crisis and stating that all hopes rested on Decimus and Plancus or, failing that, on him and Brutus, whether as a refuge or, as was more immediately needed, through their assistance in Italy. It seems that Brutus may have been taking advice on this from his mother, who still remained involved in the political world. On 25 July, Servilia summoned Cicero to a conference, along with the assassins Labeo and Publius Casca, as well as Brutus' agent, Scaptius. There, she somewhat surprised Cicero by consulting him on whether it was in her son's best interests to be called back to Italy, or whether he should delay in the east. Cicero stuck to his opinion that the chief Liberator should be recalled, but those close to him clearly had their doubts. Brutus did not comply, and was never to return to his homeland: we cannot be certain of the reasons, but it has been plausibly suggested that he had no legal command in Italy and perhaps did not wish to act thus without such constitutional backing.[33]

Once Decimus had reached Plancus in Cularo, they sent an optimistic dispatch to the senate, probably around 10 June: the note is incomplete, but it sets out their joint expressions of loyalty to the state. They inform the senate that, with the assistance of the Allobroges, a Gallic tribe of the area, and their cavalry force, they have held back the enemy. Decimus and Plancus are about to set out to reinforce them, and sound confident that they can keep Antony and Lepidus under control. However, they still require more troops and supplies. On 18 June, Cicero is in the dark about the progress of events outside of Italy: he writes to Decimus saying that he has heard neither from him nor Brutus, although he has been seeking that the latter returns to Italy, in accordance with Decimus' requests. He can add little more than that all hopes currently rest with Decimus and Plancus. Another brief note is sent from Cicero to Decimus in late June, in which he is pleased at the apparent level of cooperation between his addressee and Plancus, and urges him onwards in his mission. At about the same time, Cicero wrote to Plancus with similar encouragement.[34]

On 30 June, Lepidus was formally and unanimously declared an enemy of the state by the senate, which is unsurprising given his treacherous action in uniting forces with Antony. Indeed, Cicero claimed that he was worse and even more hated than Antony, because he had reignited the war, which it was believed would have been over if he had not lent his assistance to the latter. As an enemy of the state, Lepidus' property would be confiscated and his status would also be extended to his children. However, since Lepidus was married to Brutus' middle sister, this presented something of a problem for the chief Liberator, who understandably wished to protect his family from such condemnation. Indeed, in July 43 BC, this proved to be a major source of anxiety for Brutus, whose requests to Cicero for help in protecting the interests of his family is a theme in the correspondence between the two men. At first hoping that the rumours about his brother-in-law were unfounded, Brutus displayed a genuine depth of care and duty as an uncle. In the event that his fears about Lepidus were true, Brutus wished to be regarded as the true guardian of the children in place of their vilified father, in order to circumvent this problem. However, despite the heartfelt pleas of his dear friend, Cicero with regret felt that no exception could be made: he cited historical examples to prove that leniency was not an option, and claimed that it was Lepidus who was acting with cruel hostility towards his own family through his criminal act of betraying the state. Servilia and Junia Secunda had also apparently been petitioning Cicero, who had given them the same negative response; doubtless this was also a topic of discussion at the meeting with Servilia to which Cicero was summoned. In contradiction with his hitherto harsh stance, in the last letter of the collection, dated 27 July, he claims that he had, from the beginning, pleaded the case of the children in the senate, and expects that Brutus has already learned this from the communications of his mother. The final existing words of Cicero to Brutus are an assurance that he would always act in his interests, no matter the cost to himself.[35]

Almost a month after Lepidus was declared an outlaw, the next extant information to come directly from the western provinces arrives in the form of a letter from Plancus which, since it was written on 28 July, is also the last datable letter in this collection of Cicero's correspondence. While thanking Cicero for attending to his soldiers' interests, which helps bind them to the cause of the Republic, Plancus sounds most concerned that, although he and Decimus have very large forces, they consist of a high proportion of new recruits whom they cannot rely upon in battle. He explains that they are not in a strong enough position to engage in battle, but neither are they willing to retreat. The desperate tone of this letter suggests that the fortunes of Plancus and Decimus in the war are waning, as he urgently seeks experienced reinforcements, begging Cicero to arrange for the veteran legions from Africa to be sent. The frustrated Plancus complains that Octavian, despite sending his assurances, has not yet arrived, and blames him for the fact that the war lingers on: he seems more astute in this than Cicero who, until recently, always viewed Octavian as a saviour, choosing instead to find fault with one of his own dear Liberators, Decimus. Plancus nonetheless says that he continues to send Octavian hopeful missives seeking his assistance, although he has heard that he is preoccupied with his alarming plans to assume one of the empty consulships.[36]

The Emergence of the New Caesar

At this time, too, Cicero was beginning, regretfully, to admit to Brutus that his backing of Octavian was perhaps not so wise after all. Indeed this judgement, if a little too late, was not wrong, for the heir of Caesar now showed his true, and most un-Republican, colours, unleashing the might of his army in order to facilitate his own political power. These opinions of Plancus and Cicero signal the end of Cicero's works and correspondence meaning that, from this point on, we can no longer rely on contemporary accounts of the end of the Republic: instead, subsequent events from this momentous period of history must be reconstructed mostly from the narratives of historians who were writing at least a century later, and whose views were coloured by the intervening years of the early Empire, which was dominated by the propaganda of the so-called principate of Augustus, who, at this time, was still known by the name of Octavian. In July or August 43 BC, this future Emperor sent a group of centurions to the city to demand the consulship for their leader, as well as the payment of the promised reward for the soldiers. The senate at first refused these demands, despite the centurions' threat of armed violence. Octavian's army was incensed and demanded to march on Rome, and so the adopted son now followed in the footsteps of his father by crossing the Rubicon and entering Italy with his legions. Their approach caused a panicked concession to Octavian, allowing him to stand for the consulship *in absentia*, since there was no force in the city with which to match his troops. However, a change of heart then followed, which was bolstered when the legions from Africa arrived in the city and were able to assist its defence, for which they now prepared, and so the decrees made in haste were withdrawn. However, the people of the city began to go over to Octavian, and the African legions also defected to him, while a false rumour that two of the best veteran legions, disappointed that they had been deceived into marching against their own country, were defecting from Octavian to the state. Octavian nonetheless moved in and occupied the Campus Martius, taking control and ordering that he be given the money to pay his soldiers their due reward. He then left Rome while the elections took place and, having successfully manoeuvred the political situation in his favour through the use of armed force, on 19 August 43 BC, at the unprecedented age of nineteen, was made consul with another of Caesar's designated heirs, Quintus Pedius, chosen by him as his colleague. Octavian therefore had effectively gained complete power over the Roman state.[37]

The wily Octavian now set about arranging affairs, including making decisions working against those of the state and the Liberators, although he would always claim that he was acting for the sake of the reconstitution of the Republic. One of his first acts was to rescind the decree making Dolabella a public enemy. More serious for Brutus and the rest of the Liberators was that he immediately had his adoption by Caesar formally ratified, so that it would then be necessary for him to obey his filial duty to avenge the murder of his father. For this purpose, his colleague introduced a law, the *lex Pedia*, for the prosecution of Caesar's assassins, allowing Octavian to begin pursuing and hunting them down under the guise of justice. A tribune, Lucius Cornificius, was appointed as the prosecutor of Brutus, while Marcus Vipsanius Agrippa, who was to be Octavian's right-hand man until his death in 12 BC, indicted Cassius. Plutarch records the widespread visible distress in Rome when the name of Brutus was read out from the rostra, summoning him as one of those condemned: the crowd uttered a deep groan and the higher-class citizens bowed their heads in silence, while one juror, Publius Silicius Corona, who had voted against this, wept, and would later pay for his outburst with the penalty of death. Those assassins who were still in Rome now fled the city, including Publius Casca, who was said to have left before Octavian arrived.[38]

Focus now shifted back to events in the west. With the situation for the Republic there having suffered a reversal recently, its remaining commanders now had decisions to make about how they were to proceed. On 8 June, Pollio, still clearly a long way behind in receiving news, had written to Cicero, asking what he should do with his forces: his legions had been approached by Antony with bribes, and Pollio had, with difficulty, kept them in check, while Lepidus had been making overtures to Pollio himself. At this point, Pollio appeared to want to support the Republic but was, dangerously, uninformed of events because of his distance from the city, and so was frustrated in his efforts. When Pollio, having set out from Spain, arrived in Lepidus' province at about this time, he realised the more advantageous position of Lepidus and Antony: therefore, he chose to join forces with them, before persuading the fickle Plancus to defect as well. Decimus, therefore, found himself abandoned and effectively defeated, finally making the situation in the west no longer tenable for the cause of the Liberators. He was therefore forced to attempt to flee Gaul and reach Brutus in Macedonia, deciding to head north towards the Rhine in order to avoid Octavian, who was travelling back into Cisalpine Gaul. Decimus' soldiers gradually deserted him until he was left with no military support but a pitiful ten Gallic cavalrymen. His effort to get away was prevented when he was captured by a tribe. Their chieftain, Camulos, made a pretence of friendliness, since he was acquainted with Decimus, but simultaneously secretly got word to Antony, who ordered that he kill Decimus and send him his head. And so the man who betrayed Caesar approximately eighteen months earlier was now himself betrayed. The first of the three chief Liberators to die reportedly did so in an unbecoming fashion for a latterly victorious hero of the Republic: accounts vary, but it seems that Decimus, being afraid of death, tried to avoid his murder in some way. The Republic had now lost the west.[39]

Octavian's next move, having settled matters in the city as he wished, was to march back to Cisalpine Gaul in order to do that which he had been contemplating for some time: he would join forces with Antony, whom he realised he needed for the pursuit of his father's chief assassins, Brutus and Cassius.[40] Back in Rome, Pedius was working in Octavian's interests: he persuaded the senate to repeal the decrees making Antony and Lepidus public enemies, which then left the way open for Octavian to unite freely with these commanders in Gaul. With the recent defections to their cause, Antony and Lepidus now had a formidable force at their disposal, which would make uniting with them extremely advantageous for Octavian, whose own force was inferior by comparison. On the other hand, he possessed the name of Caesar which instilled such loyalty and devotion in the soldiers, and so Antony and Lepidus also realised the value of this union. Therefore the three generals arranged a conference on an island near Bononia, where they spent two days making their agreements in October or November 43 BC. Their principal decision was to form the political alliance known as the second Triumvirate, assuming consular power for the next five years and effectively carving the Roman world up three ways between them: ostensibly this was for the restoration of the constitution, but in reality it was, quite oppositely, an act of tyranny. Lepidus was to govern Spain and Narbonese Gaul, and Antony was to rule the rest of Gaul, while Octavian was to take Africa, Sicily and Sardinia. Noticeably, they did not include the east in their settlement, where Brutus and Cassius currently held power. Having forcibly gained the consulship only three months previously, Octavian now unconstitutionally resigned from his post before the end of November, while Lepidus was to assume the office in 42 BC, taking up the position that had been made vacant by Decimus' death. Lepidus would therefore guard Rome and Italy, while Antony and Octavian would go east to make war on Brutus and Cassius. The three generals then marched on Rome, where their new alliance was formally ratified.[41]

This compact led to the terrible proscriptions that claimed the lives of numerous Roman nobles before the end of 43 BC, and was an act of arbitrary cruelty. For, during their conference, the Triumvirs decided to follow the example of Sulla forty years earlier by writing a list of those to be condemned to death in order to help remove their political obstacles. They needed land for their veterans and to restore the depleted funds of the treasury following the wars, especially since Brutus and Cassius had been and still were collecting the riches of Asia: therefore they added many wealthy men to their list, simply in order to acquire their property and land, as well as imposing heavy taxes. They also took this opportunity to get rid of their inconvenient enemies. According to Appian, the proscription cited as its principal basis the treachery of the murderers of Caesar and those who had declared Antony and Lepidus as public enemies: they claimed that it would not be safe to leave such men behind, unpunished, while they were away in the east marching against Caesar's assassins and, ironically, that they were doing all this for the sake of the restitution of the Republic. This caused widespread terror and panic in the city, and Appian records many individual tales of men either making desperate attempts to escape, or bravely meeting their dreadful fate. Some succeeded in fleeing east to Brutus or Cassius, but most of those who got away found refuge with Sextus Pompeius.[42]

Most notable among those proscribed was Cicero: Antony was insistent that this long-term foe, who had incessantly harangued him, must go on the list above all others, while Octavian was said to have resisted this choice at first. In the end, Octavian consented and, in return, Antony agreed to have his uncle, Lucius Caesar, proscribed, while Lepidus gave up his brother, Aemilius Lepidus Paullus. However, the latter two escaped with their lives: Antony's mother protected her brother, while Paullus managed to reach safety with Brutus in Macedonia. Cicero learned of his fate while at his country residence near Tusculum. In death, as in life, Cicero was crippled with characteristic doubt and hesitation, and it was this which prevented his successful flight and so brought about his fate. According to Plutarch, although he and his brother, Quintus, began to flee with the intention of sailing to join Brutus in Macedonia, Quintus decided to turn back home in order to gather supplies for the journey, but was there executed with his son. Cicero, meanwhile, vacillated along the west coast of Italy for some time, reportedly beginning to set sail, but then changing his mind and travelling on land some way back towards Rome. He then stopped and continued to deliberate further, before resolving to go to his villa at Formiae, near the coastal town of Caieta (Gaeta), approximately seventy-five miles south of Rome. Despite omens of foreboding, Cicero tarried here until Antony's soldiers caught up with him and he fittingly faced his grisly execution with courageous resolve. Antony ordered that those parts that had most offended him through speech and writing should be removed: therefore his head and right hand were cut off. The bloody sight of these reportedly brought much joy and satisfaction to Antony and his wife Fulvia: she took Cicero's head to abuse and spit on it, before sticking a hairpin through the tongue, and Antony then cruelly had them displayed on the rostra in the forum in a most degrading manner. And so, in early December 43 BC, as the Roman Republic was in its death throes, significantly, so too, the elder statesman and stalwart of the constitution met his sad demise. According to a Plutarchean anecdote, Brutus rather coldly remarked on his friend's tragic end that he felt more shame at the cause of Cicero's death than grief at its occurrence, and he was said to have blamed his friends in Rome for allowing themselves to be turned into slaves at the mercy of tyrants who committed intolerable deeds. This political situation was far worse than at any time under Caesar, and the Roman state certainly had now become further removed from the Republican constitution.[43]

Chapter Twelve

Civil War in the East

March–December 43 BC: Preparations

It is time to return to the east, where our principal subject, Brutus, and his partner in crime, Cassius, now represented the last remaining bastions of liberty and the Republic, and were therefore busy making preparations for civil war and, indeed, were already carrying out military actions. Details of the events in the east, between March and July 43 BC, have been preserved principally in the contemporary letters between Cicero and the chief Liberators.

During the course of the correspondence between Brutus and Cicero, one pressing matter is Brutus' need of financial aid and reinforcements from Rome to aid his military activities. At the beginning of the collection, in early April, he explains that money is essential for the armies, and laments the recent loss of Asia, a province which was apparently a ready source of funds until Trebonius' recent murder at the hands of Dolabella. However, Brutus has received considerable financial aid from Gaius Antistius Vetus, the departing quaestor of Syria. Cicero's reply is a negative one, since funds in Rome were lacking, and the consul Pansa was not pleased that so many volunteers were joining Brutus: reportedly this was because he felt that there were more urgent matters closer to home, with Decimus still besieged in Mutina at this time, but Cicero hints at the suspicions existing in Rome that the Caesarian Pansa did not want to see the Republican Brutus in a position of too much strength. By the end of July, the financial situation has not changed: in the last extant letter of this collection, Cicero writes to Brutus on the general shortage of money in the city and the difficulty in raising the much-needed funds.[1]

The Execution of Gaius Antonius

One of the first missions of the chief Liberators was to deal with the two main foes currently in their respective regions in the east. When Brutus wrote to the senate in early 43 BC, declaring his possession of Macedonia, Greece and

Illyricum, he was at the point of holding Gaius Antonius besieged in the city of Apollonia. Soon afterwards he sent a further dispatch to the senate, relaying the news that Antonius had been taken captive: by the middle of March, according to Plutarch, Brutus had Antonius and his scattered troops surrounded in some marshy ground and, giving orders that they were to be spared, forced them to surrender. The troops joined the ranks of Brutus, while Antonius was kept as a prisoner. Brutus, again displaying his distaste for the unnecessary shedding of blood, treated his hostage leniently and respectfully, reportedly even allowing him to keep the insignia of his proconsular rank. Brutus also felt that, as the brother of Antony, he would have more value alive, as a potential bargaining tool, than dead.[2]

Brutus was evidently beset with doubts about what to do with his prisoner at first, and sought the elder statesman's advice on the best way to deal with Antonius: in a letter written from Dyrrachium at the beginning of April, Brutus is tempted by the pleas of Antonius to release him, although he is aware of the risk of such a move. Cicero replies in milder terms initially, advising that Antonius should be kept prisoner until they know the fate of Decimus at Mutina. However, in mid-April, Cicero adopts a tone of extreme irritation with Brutus: for two dispatches had been read out in the senate, one from Brutus and one from Antonius. The one from the latter was signed as proconsul, which caused a ripple of consternation, since the senate had annulled the distribution of provinces that had taken place at the end of November, in which he had been allocated Macedonia. Furthermore, if Brutus was acknowledging Antonius' position, it suggested the illegality of his own in usurping the governorship of the province and the criminality of the supporters of Brutus who were taking up arms against Antonius. The letter from Brutus also caused some embarrassment, since it made it apparent that he was taking too lenient an approach with regard to Antonius, and Cicero was left unsure how to respond to this in the senate. It was declared to be a forgery, although the admonishing tone of this letter to Brutus strongly suggests that Cicero believed otherwise of his all too merciful friend: he upbraids Brutus, reminding him that, while clemency is admirable, this fragile situation of war is neither the time nor the place for it, since their enemies would not show them the same consideration. Cicero declared that all three Antonius brothers were just as bad as Dolabella and should be dealt with in the same way as that public enemy, advising Brutus to take the middle line between cruelty and weakness, dealing with leaders firmly and soldiers more leniently. And so the annoyed Cicero now changed his stance on Antonius, partly blinded as ever by hatred of his brother, Mark Antony, in strongly recommending that he should be put to death. However Brutus, governed by stronger moral principles, would not execute someone on such a flimsy pretext. In letters sent from Cicero approximately a week later, he continues to argue his point of view, and we seem to be missing the intervening letter from Brutus defending his more lenient attitude, since he has no desire to take harsh vengeance on the defeated and wishes to avoid civil war. In a letter written towards the end of April, following the fall of the two consuls in Cisalpine Gaul, when Cicero has finally achieved his goal of having Antony and his followers declared public enemies, he continues to urge Brutus not to spare Antonius by adding that 'most people' interpret this outlawing as applying also to those whom Brutus himself has captured or received in surrender. In the first week of May, Brutus replies to Cicero's accusations of leniency, sternly noting that it is not for him to act as judge and jury, and so he will continue to keep Antonius in custody unless the senate and people of Rome decree that he should do otherwise: clearly he had not yet received the letter informing him that Antony and his followers were denounced as public enemies. Brutus also now begins to retort on Cicero's misjudgement and mishandling of Octavian, using a tone of irritation similar to that of Cicero when advising him.[3]

In late May, we learn of an outbreak of violence in one of Brutus' legions, in relation to Gaius Antonius: the unfortunate incomplete nature of Cicero's letter makes the context unclear, but the writer seems to side with the soldiers, suggesting that they were demonstrating against Antonius. We hear nothing further of Antonius in the correspondence between the two men. We do know that he remained in Brutus' custody for some time, despite his reported attempts to cause dissension: according to Plutarch, Antonius entered into secret negotiations with some of Brutus' officers, but the noble Liberator continued to spare his foe and pardoned his disloyal men. Dio Cassius, however, elaborates on this story and does not present Brutus as being overly merciful in his version: despite Antonius' being kept under guard and stripped of his insignia, he continued to stir up trouble, causing some soldiers to set out to Apollonia on a mission to free him; Brutus, having uncovered the plot, disguised Antonius and removed him so that the soldiers were unable to find him; in fear, they seized a hill commanding the city, but Brutus came to an agreement with them; he then executed some of the ringleaders and forced the other mutineers to kill the most seditious; henceforth, Antonius was to remain under the guard of a man named Gaius

Clodius in Apollonia. However, we do know that Brutus was finally driven to order Antonius' execution, after he learned of the horror of the proscriptions and the cruel death of his friend Cicero in December 43 BC, and possibly also motivated by Antony's attempt to rescue his brother. It was Hortensius who was to carry out these orders, and later he would pay for this with his life: at the Battle of Philippi, Antony would avenge his brother's death by slaying his killer over his tomb.[4]

Personal Matters

It was in mid-43 BC, while in the east, that Brutus suffered a personal loss of some kind. A letter in this collection, from Brutus to Atticus, whose authenticity is in doubt, makes reference to the illness of Brutus' wife, Porcia, while a more secure letter from Cicero to Brutus, written sometime in June 43 BC, consoles the addressee on his loss, and so has been interpreted as a response to the death of Porcia from her illness. However, popular legend relates how Porcia, overwhelmed with grief at the demise of Brutus at Philippi in 42 BC, was prevented by the vigilance of friends from committing suicide by the sword, and so snatched hot coals from the fire and swallowed them in order to follow her husband in death. It is easy to see how such a tale of virtue and devotion could be fabricated and attach itself to Porcia, in order to make her appear the worthy daughter of Cato and wife of Brutus, and thereby enhance the status of these noble men.[5] However, the illness and suicide are not incompatible, and it is possible that both happened in mid-43 BC, rather than after Brutus' death: as well as narrating this legendary version of her demise, Plutarch records that there was a letter from Brutus reproaching his friends for neglecting his wife in her ill health, which in turn led to her suicide. Indeed, it is generally accepted that Cicero's letter of condolences in June 43 BC is an indication of the earlier date of death for Porcia.[6] In his letter, Cicero shows all the warmth of feeling that Brutus had afforded him when his daughter had died: in effect, Cicero similarly tells Brutus that he should not grieve excessively but should pull himself together, as he has more important matters of state to which he must attend. We have no record of Brutus' reaction to the death of his wife, and so do not know if he was as deeply affected as Cicero was in his grief over Tullia, but this letter from Cicero almost has the appearance of a somewhat bitter retaliation, rather than a response to Brutus' actual behaviour. Certainly the letters that Brutus wrote subsequently display no sign of a crippling and overwhelming loss, and we may suspect that the man whose first duty was always to his state would not have been distracted from the cause of his beloved Republic for long by such personal affairs.[7]

Amid these serious matters of war and death weighing heavily on them, Brutus and Cicero still found the time to write to each other requesting favours for friends. In the latter half of May, Brutus seeks Cicero's assistance regarding a debt owed by the town of Dyrrachium to a certain Flavius. A month later he asks Cicero to support the political advancement of Vetus in return for the services he had done him: it was Vetus who supplied Brutus with considerable funds when retiring from Syria and who, resisting Dolabella in Greece, subsequently joined him, and so Brutus writes a letter to confirm his deserving loyalty to the state and, in light of this, Cicero gladly responds favourably. Brutus also requests backing for three close Republican associates in their candidacies for the college of augurs: Lucius Calpurnius Bibulus, Brutus' stepson and Cato's grandson; Ahenobarbus, one of Caesar's assassins and a devoted Liberator, who was now a commander of the Republican fleet; and Appuleius, the retiring proquaestor of Asia who had handed over money, troops and supplies to the Republican cause. Similarly, in May or June, Cicero finds it appropriate to ask both Brutus and Decimus to exert their influence on behalf of a friend in his quest for a praetorship. He also recommends to Brutus acquaintances who wish to take up appointments with him in the cause of the Republic. Notable among these is Marcus Valerius Messalla Corvinus, who was to fight on the losing side at Philippi but who would emerge safely and become a successful patron of poetry under Augustus.[8]

Brutus also frequently writes reassuring and complimentary words of praise to Cicero on the subject of his son, who was serving him well with his proactive military deeds in the region. Cicero often enquires about young Marcus' progress in these letters and mentions his expectation that he can learn much from serving as a commander under Brutus. Clearly Cicero the younger was far better suited to martial activity than his father: indeed, Brutus was not merely being polite about a friend's son since, in his dispatch to the senate in early 43 BC, he had publicly and duly acknowledged the young Cicero's valiant effort in capturing one of Antonius' legions. In the latter half of May 43 BC we learn that he was continuing to serve the Republican cause as a trusted commander: at that time, Brutus had moved from Dyrrachium to a camp on the border of lower Candavia (a mountain in Illyricum crossed by the Via Egnatia), en route to Macedonia, where he was to meet the younger Cicero, whom he had sent in advance with a squadron of cavalry.[9]

The Defeat of Dolabella

In the course of these letters, we also find Brutus deliberating over whether he should go to Asia Minor to aid Cassius in his fight against the treacherous Dolabella. On learning of the murder of Trebonius at the beginning of April, Brutus expresses his horror at the crime, as well as concern about the loss of his province, and now its oppression at the hands of Dolabella. Towards the middle of April, Cicero advises Brutus to pursue him if he continues to hold Asia, but to stay where he is if Dolabella has left there for Rhodes: Cicero has received a report that he has been refused admission to the island. Later in the month, Cicero expects news of Dolabella from Brutus, who has clearly decided to remain in his provinces rather than pursue him. On 27 April the senate confirmed Cassius in his command against Dolabella and, on Cicero's proposal, approved that Brutus himself should judge whether it was in the interest of the state for him to pursue military action against this public enemy as well. At this point in early May, Cicero's feeling is that Brutus should launch an attack against Dolabella if the latter has a stronghold anywhere, and he urges the importance of seeing him crushed so that there is no rallying point for Antony should he flee from Mutina, which at this time was misleadingly looking more promising for the Republicans. Later in May, Cicero writes to Brutus approving of his decision to have kept his armies in Apollonia and Dyrrachium until he has heard the outcome at Mutina.[10]

Meanwhile, in early May, Rome remained uncertain of Cassius' exact whereabouts and situation. However, he had been sending communications to Cicero, but these did not reach him and were presumed to have been intercepted by Dolabella. On 7 May, Cassius writes to inform Cicero that, since he has heard that Dolabella has arrived in the neighbouring province of Cilicia with his forces, he is about to set out from Syria in pursuit of him. Dolabella was, in fact, heading for Syria.[11] On 19 May, Brutus received the news that Dolabella had suffered a defeat and been put to flight by Cimber, the assassin of Caesar who had raised a fleet and supplies for the Republican cause, and King Deiotarus of Galatia, one of Brutus' allies in the east. After learning of this and the outcome at Mutina, it seems that Brutus planned to march his army into the Thracian Chersonese (the Gallipoli Peninsula) to block an attempt at an advance there by Dolabella: Cicero fully approves of Brutus' act to defend the state against this mad public enemy, and views Dolabella's aggressive move on Europe as foolish, since he was using a small force of five cohorts while, according to Cicero, Brutus had five legions, excellent cavalry and large auxiliary forces. It is understood that Brutus actually possessed eight legions, as he had since added the one that the younger Cicero seized from Antonius, and raised two more in Macedonia.[12]

At the end of May and beginning of June, Spinther, who had joined the Liberators after Caesar's assassination, sent Cicero a private letter and the senate an official dispatch. He had been quaestor under Trebonius in Asia, but had been expelled from the province when Dolabella murdered the proconsul. Now proquaestor propraetor in the absence of a governor, Spinther reports his view of the state of affairs in the east. Following his expulsion from Asia, he set out for Macedonia to seek Brutus' advice, and there discovered that Brutus' expected arrival in Asia Minor would be somewhat delayed. From Macedonia, Spinther worked for the state's restoration of the province and its revenues and, according to him, this caused Dolabella to flee Asia, but not before having plundered the province, something about which Brutus had earlier expressed concern. Spinther then decided to return to Asia to continue tax collecting there himself, raising money to send back to Rome. En route he learned that Dolabella had gathered his fleet in Lycia (a region on the south coast of Asia Minor), along with over 100 freight ships: Dolabella was preparing to transport his army to Italy to join Antony, should his advance into Syria fail. This alarmed Spinther, who promptly changed course and headed for Rhodes with a small squadron of vessels. He was outraged at the contemptuous behaviour of Rhodes, whose treaty with Rome should have determined its loyalty to the state: instead Spinther's men were denied access to both the island and supplies. Spinther succeeded in gaining entry but the Rhodians would not believe that Dolabella had been declared a public enemy, and so refused to lend aid. Spinther explains that there had been warning of Rhodes' disloyalty earlier, since the island had sent delegations to Dolabella after Trebonius' murder. Despite the obstructive attempts of the Rhodians, Spinther succeeded in causing Dolabella's fleet to flee and abandon the freighters, so that any hope of his entire army escaping to Italy was destroyed. Spinther pursued them a short way along the south coast to the edge of his province, where he learned that Dolabella's ships were scattered, with the remainder heading for Cyprus and Syria. Spinther then decided to return to his post, knowing that Cassius had a capable naval force in Syria which could take over the pursuit there. He promises to continue working in the province in the service of the state, levying taxes to send to Rome: in his letter to Cicero he eagerly, and at length, requests support to become deputy governor of Asia, setting forth his devotion to the cause of the Republic, and claiming credit for having brought the Syrian armies over to Cassius.[13]

Before he had sent his dispatch, Spinther received promising news of Dolabella's retreat from some of his soldiers who had fled from Syria to Pamphylia, from where he was writing. They reported that Dolabella had gone to the city of Antioch in Syria (now Antakya in Turkey), but had been refused admittance, despite attempts at forced entry. Having suffered hundreds of losses and casualties, Dolabella fled at night to Laodicea (Latakia), a town on the Syrian coast. Most of his troops from Asia deserted him, with many surrendering to Cassius' officers in Antioch, and the rest crossing to Cilicia. Cassius and his force were reported to be only a few days' march from Laodicea, and Spinther was confident that Dolabella would soon be crushed, unable to hold out against Cassius' sizeable army, and with nowhere to retreat. Writing to Cassius several times over the next month, Cicero notes that he has heard promising, but unconfirmed, reports regarding Dolabella, and encourages Cassius in his pursuit of this public enemy, if he has not already been defeated.[14]

On 13 June, Gaius Cassius Parmensis, one of Caesar's assassins[15] who was currently serving as quaestor and holding command of a Republican fleet, wrote to Cicero providing further details of events in the east against Dolabella. He had also launched all his available ships from the islands and coast of Asia, in pursuit of a part of Dolabella's fleet which he drove as far as Corycus (Kizkalesi) in Cilicia, where they shut themselves inside the blockaded harbour. Knowing that Cimber's Bithynian fleet was coming up behind in support, he decided it would be better for his men to make for camp. Writing from Cyprus, Parmensis reports on the treachery of Tarsus and Laodicea, who have been willingly aiding Dolabella and from where he has been able to raise an army. Dolabella had encamped in front of Laodicea, having demolished part of the wall so that the town and camp were united. However, Cassius had pitched camp with his army approximately twenty miles south on the coast: he was besieging Dolabella in Laodicea with the intention of starving him out, since the town's only hope of getting grain was by sea, and the combined fleets of Cassius, Parmensis, Cimber and Spinther would easily be able to block any chance of this getting through. Appian reports that naval battles followed, in which ships were sunk on both sides, but with Cassius' forces eventually emerging victorious. Cassius then attacked the walls of Laodicea, before managing to bribe his way into the town. Dolabella, realising that all was lost, asked his private guard to kill him.

Thus Cassius succeeded in exacting vengeance for the murder of Trebonius, although he reportedly allowed Dolabella the burial that had been denied to his fellow Liberator.[16]

Those of Dolabella's men who surrendered to Cassius received a pardon and were enrolled in his army, while he punished the chief citizens of Laodicea, plundered the temples and treasury, and levied a heavy financial toll. Tarsus was also to receive the penalty due for its treacherous act of supporting a public enemy of Rome, since they had attempted to prevent Cimber reaching and bringing aid to Cassius in his mission to bring down Dolabella and then, despite having made a truce, they refused him both entry to the city and supplies. Since Cassius learned of this while engaged in the fight against Dolabella, he sent one of his fleet commanders to the city, which surrendered without a struggle. However, the city had difficulty in raising the funds that Cassius' soldiers were demanding with violence, and was forced to put all its public property and religious treasures up for sale, before resorting to selling its people into slavery, many of whom committed suicide. When Cassius came to Tarsus after dealing with Dolabella, he took pity on the city and released it from the remainder of its due contribution.[17]

The Activities of Brutus in Asia Minor

Before Gaius Antonius' execution, when he had been left in custody in Apollonia, Brutus returned to Macedonia with the best part of his army. Despite some initial hesitation, he then made the decision to enter Asia Minor, where he reportedly gained various allies, including securing the loyalty of his old friend, King Deiotarus. While delaying in Asia Minor, Brutus was the subject of a plot, formed by Lucius Gellius Publicola, who also made an attempt on Cassius' life. However, on both occasions he did not incur punishment: as a supposed good friend of both Brutus and Cassius, and half-brother of Messalla, whom Cicero had recently recommended strongly to the Republican cause, Brutus showed him mercy; while Cassius allowed him to escape with his life because he was close to Publicola's mother, who informed him about the plot. Publicola would nonetheless eventually defect to Antony and Octavian. It was also during this absence that Brutus reportedly ordered Antonius' execution.[18]

Fearing that Antonius' death, especially combined with Antony's recent failed attempt to rescue his brother, could cause an uprising, Brutus hastened back to Macedonia. While travelling back through Thrace (an area encompassing parts of modern Bulgaria, Greece and Turkey), he took measures to secure this region: he assumed territory left to the Romans by a certain Sadalus and, with the aid of a prince named Rhascyporis, he succeeded in raiding the land of the Bessi tribe and bringing them under control. For this conquest he was awarded the title of *imperator*. At some point when Brutus was still gathering troops and funds, he acquired an unexpected windfall from Thrace: Queen Polemocratia came to Brutus, entrusting her husband's treasure and her infant son, Cotys, to him. He sent the boy to Cyzicus (a town located in north-west Turkey) until he could be restored to his kingdom, while melting the treasure down into coinage. It was during this period that Brutus is believed to have minted the well-known coin depicting his image on one side and, on the other side, the cap of liberty given to slaves upon manumission, in between two daggers. When read with the legend '*EID MAR*', a clear indication of the infamous day of Caesar's assassination, these were unmistakable and forthright references to Brutus and Cassius as Liberators of the fatherland through their notorious murderous actions.[19]

Having returned to Macedonia and consolidated his hold there, Brutus returned to Asia Minor once more, with his army. There he equipped a fleet on the coast of Bithynia and at the port of Cyzicus, and travelled across the land in his capacity as governor, settling affairs and giving audiences to local monarchs. Horace, who was a young recruit in Brutus' army, having joined him at Athens, later gives one such occasion satirical treatment in his poetry, thus offering a glimpse, albeit not serious, of Brutus the governor hearing a case. At Clazomenae, on the coast of Asia Minor (Urla in Turkey), Brutus settled a bitter dispute between a certain Persius Hybrida and Rupilius Rex. In the satire, Horace has Persius play on the name Rex, meaning 'King' in Latin, and the legendary status of Brutus' family for overthrowing tyrants, now proven in Brutus himself by his recent assassination of Caesar.[20]

Other evidence for Brutus' activities in Asia Minor comes in the form of some Greek letters, supposedly written by him to these Asian communities at about this time: the authenticity of these has been doubted, but Plutarch quotes some of Brutus' purported words, suggesting that there had been an original collection of such letters in existence. Brutus' words cited in Plutarch are fairly terse admonishments to communities which have either failed to deliver demanded money on time, or have instead aided Dolabella, so that Brutus appears to be addressing them in a rather highhanded manner.[21]

Another deed of Brutus in Asia Minor during this time was to exact punishment on one of those who had plotted the murder of Pompey. Theodotus of Chios, one of young Ptolemy's advisors, had suggested luring Pompey to Egypt to kill him. After Pompey's death, he escaped Caesar's vengeance, having fled from Egypt. However, Brutus discovered him wandering destitute about Asia and duly put him to death for his act, reportedly with 'every possible torture'. This seems somewhat uncharacteristic for the usually mild and lenient Brutus, but it is clear from the context that this man is to be viewed as getting nothing less than he deserved.[22]

Following the defeat of Dolabella, Cassius had wanted to settle scores with those places which had supported this public enemy of Rome. One of these was Egypt, where the reigning monarch was Cleopatra, former lover of Caesar and future amour of Antony. She had reportedly sent legions to Dolabella, refused aid to Cassius despite his threats, and was frustrated in her attempt to send a fleet to Antony and Octavian. For this loyalty, her son by Caesar, Caesarion, was recognised as King of Egypt. As Cassius was about to set out on a punitive expedition to Egypt, he was recalled from his mission by Brutus, who reminded him that they should be concentrating on their fight for liberty and the Republic, and not on empire building.[23]

42 BC: Brutus and Cassius Reunited

A Conference of War: Smyrna

Soon after this, in early 42 BC, Brutus summoned Cassius from Syria to Smyrna, where they were to consult on their next course of action. Their fortunes had changed much for the better since they last saw each other in 44 BC, which must have been heartening for them both. However, the chief Liberators realised that the new compact in Rome between their three foes meant for certain that civil war was approaching and that they needed to coordinate their plans. Brutus and Cassius had clearly learned from their failure to make any plans for the aftermath of Caesar's assassination, since they were now to prepare in a way fitting the demands of the pressing martial situation: according to Dio Cassius, they were eager in their plans to overthrow the Triumvirate and defend the freedom of the Roman people. At this conference they decided that they would return to Macedonia to prevent their enemy from crossing the Adriatic, but not immediately, since the Triumvirs were currently engaged in settling business in the west. In the meantime, they would use the time to continue gathering allies, troops and money throughout the east, ready for the mighty showdown that faced them.[24]

Meanwhile, in Rome, Julius Caesar was being hailed as a god: on the first day of 42 BC, the Triumvirs had the murdered dictator officially consecrated as divine. This was particularly in the interest of Octavian, his adoptee, who could now claim to be the son of a god for propaganda purposes. Dio Cassius claims that the Triumvirs were heaping honours on Caesar, with the hope of winning similar rewards for themselves in due course. They granted or observed many other honours to Caesar besides: they took an oath swearing that all his acts were to be considered binding; they laid the foundation of a shrine to him on the spot where his body was cremated in the forum, and this was to be a place of immunity for anyone seeking refuge; an image of him was to accompany that of Venus in procession at the games, while no image of him was to be permitted at the funerals of his relatives since he was to be considered truly divine and not a mere mortal ancestor; he was to receive a thanksgiving following any victory; and his birthday was to be recognised as a public celebration, while the Ides of March was to be designated a day of ill omen. The danger for the Liberators, whom the Triumvirs now sought to destroy, was patent: as the cult of the Divine Julius was clearly increasing in popularity, so their reputation was diminishing; furthermore, they had been away from the city now for far too long to exert any influence, and without anyone there looking after their interests since the death of Cicero.[25]

The ancient texts at this point imply that old tensions between Brutus and Cassius were beginning to resurface. While Appian only hints at mild disagreements over how best to proceed, Plutarch records something of a dispute: since Brutus had spent all his funds on a fleet with which they could control the Mediterranean, he asked for a part of Cassius' amassed treasure; Cassius' friends advised him against sharing what he had earned at the cost of men's hatred, so that Brutus could distribute it to earn goodwill; however, Cassius generously agreed to give him a third of it. Plutarch here takes the opportunity to contrast the character of the two men. There is a suggestion that Cassius, with his violent temper and tendency towards buffoonery in the company of friends, and despite his superior military ability, was somewhat jealous of Brutus, of whom he was keen to be considered the equal. However, Plutarch describes Brutus as popular with all because of his virtues, so much so that even his enemies found it difficult to hate him, while Cassius was said to have exerted his authority chiefly through fear. Plutarch clearly held Brutus in admiration, referring to him as remarkably gentle, and free from anger, self-indulgence and greed, while being inflexible in defence of what was honourable and just: it was this commitment to high principles,

Plutarch adds, that earned him his good reputation and the respect and affection of others. On the other hand, Cassius was known to be a man of uncontrolled passions, and men suspected that he was motivated to fight chiefly by a desire for money and power, and not the liberty of his country. Plutarch records here Antony's supposed saying that Brutus was the only one of Caesar's assassins who was driven by the nobility of the deed, while the rest were simply motivated by hatred of the man.[26]

Despite their differences, Brutus and Cassius did, nevertheless, agree on their next move: as well as gathering supplies and support, they thought that they should deal with some Caesarian sympathisers in the area who might otherwise provide Antony and Octavian with support in the east. On Cassius' suggestion, they decided to subdue those who had refused to make alliances with them, the Rhodians and the Lycians, who also possessed substantial fleets, and so, they feared, might attack them in the rear, or rebel, as they were confronting the Triumvirs. Therefore, in the spring of 42 BC, they went their separate ways so that Cassius could deal with the former, and Brutus the latter.[27]

The Suppression of Rhodes and Lycia

While Cassius was carefully preparing his fleet for opposition against the superior Rhodian naval force, Rhodes sent messengers, including his former teacher, since Cassius had pursued his education on the island, to urge him not to go up against them. As well as this personal appeal, they called on the treaty between Rhodes and Rome, but he answered that they themselves had violated this by siding with Dolabella, a public enemy of Rome. The upper-class citizens were duly concerned, but the multitude were ready for war and boldly followed this up by sailing out to the mainland to confront Cassius in a surprise attack, reportedly displaying to his army the fetters with which they were threatening to take them alive. Cassius' fleet came out to meet the Rhodians, much to their surprise. They fought in a well-matched sea battle, with Cassius' fleet, ably commanded by Murcus, who had joined the Liberators soon after Caesar's assassination, eventually emerging victorious through their superior number and ramming tactics. Once the fleet had been repaired, Cassius sailed to a Rhodian stronghold on the mainland opposite the island. From there, he sent across infantry and then surrounded the island with ships as well, ready for a simultaneous land and sea assault. At first the Rhodians resisted on both fronts, but Cassius then installed siege walls which he had prepared in advance. Realising that they could not hold out against a siege, the Rhodians entered into talks with the Romans, and Cassius himself then appeared on the island, having received no resistance, since the people remembered him fondly from his youth. Cassius ordered his soldiers to refrain from violence, and Dio Cassius claims that he did not harm the people. However, Plutarch says that he acted with undue severity, and Appian reports that he put fifty citizens to death and banished another twenty-five. He seized their ships, money and treasure, demanding individuals to pay him all that they possessed or be punished by death. The island was then garrisoned.

Cassius then demanded ten years' tribute from the rest of Asia. King Ariobarzanes, to whom Brutus had earlier lent money, was also now punished for refusing to make alliances with Cassius and Brutus. Cassius sent his cavalry into Cappadocia to arrest and execute Ariobarzanes, on the pretext of his having plotted against him: however, it is noteworthy that this enabled Cassius to appropriate his treasures and military supplies at this critical time of impending civil war.[28]

Meanwhile, as agreed, Brutus proceeded against Lycia, demanding money and soldiers from this confederacy which had been granted its freedom by Rome. The ancient accounts vary here in some details, but a general thread of events can be reconstructed. Initial resistance, under the popular leadership of a man named Naucrates, meant that Brutus met a Lycian force in battle: according to Plutarch, he sent cavalrymen in who killed 600 Lycians, while Dio Cassius reports that the opponents fled into their camp and were captured there with ease. Following this, the majority of communities in the region submitted to him, and Brutus reportedly released all captives without ransom, hoping thereby to win the people over with his clemency. The exception was the chief city, Xanthus (Kinik, in Antalya province): those in opposition to Brutus gathered here, and Appian records that they set about protecting the city by destroying their suburbs to prevent Brutus from finding supplies and lodgings nearby, and surrounded the city with an impressive trench and embankment, from which they could launch arrows and javelins. Brutus was not deterred by this and efficiently set about besieging them: encouraging his troops, he divided them into day and night forces, and brought in material from a distance, thus achieving in a few days that which the enemy believed would take months. Plutarch narrates how the Xanthians made attempts to escape by swimming out under the surface of the river, but were captured by the Romans in nets which had bells affixed to the top to alert them. Having filled in the trench,

Brutus was able to bring in the battering rams and send a steady flow of fresh infantrymen against the gates. Brutus succeeded in bringing down part of the Xanthians' fortifications, and then he ordered his men to withdraw from the gates. As he predicted, the Xanthians, believing that the Romans had deserted this part, duly made an effective sortie at night, hurling fire at the siege engines. The Romans then attacked and the light-armed Xanthians fell back to the city, but were slaughtered outside the walls, since the defenders in the city had shut the gates to keep Brutus' men out. The Xanthians then reportedly repeated this during the day, but kept the gates open this time: as Brutus' army drove them back inside the walls, some of his men gained entry. However, the portcullis fell, crushing some and trapping others inside the city with no way of retreat. From the roofs, the Xanthians threw missiles upon the men, who forced their way through to safety at a temple in the forum. Meanwhile, Brutus and his troops outside the city anxiously tried to gain access, building makeshift ladders and attempting to scale the walls. Eventually, with the aid of the neighbouring Oenandians, who were enemies of Xanthus and therefore allies of Brutus, some of the most daring succeeded in gaining entry to the city, although with difficulty. From inside they were able to attack at the portcullis more effectively, and it was finally broken down at the end of the day.

Amid all this confusion, part of the city somehow went up in flames. Plutarch records that the fire from the siege machines spread to the walls and houses, and that Brutus ordered his men to help put it out, all the while under a hail of fire from the defenders, who were also attempting to spread the fire further; Dio Cassius, on the other hand, reports that Brutus' men set some houses on fire and the Xanthians themselves then followed suit in panic. Either way, the Xanthians, unwilling to be taken captive, destroyed their city and themselves. Seeing that the entire city was ablaze, Brutus rode around outside, begging the people to save Xanthus, but they refused to listen, with many of the men killing the women and children before committing suicide. According to Plutarch, Brutus was reduced to tears on hearing tales of the tragic deaths of the women and children. He offered a prize to any soldier who managed to save the life of a Lycian, but in the end only a small number were said to have survived: the slaves, 150 men, and a few women.[29]

Brutus also met some resistance from another Lycian city: Patara, the seaport of the Xanthians, was similarly unwilling to make an alliance. Plutarch reports that Brutus was reluctant to attack the city, for fear that the inhabitants would behave in the same self-destructive way as the

Xanthians; while Appian, in contrast, narrates how Brutus surrounded Patara and threatened the inhabitants with the fate of their fellow Lycians. The ancient texts agree, however, that some attempt at negotiation was made: Brutus sent some of the captive Xanthians, many of whom were related to the Patarans by marriage, to try to persuade them to come to terms by describing their own recent plight and advising them not to follow their example. Nevertheless they continued to hold out, despite Brutus' attempts to convince them otherwise by offering each man his own relative as a gift, and auctioning the captives off: in the end, he sold only a few and then set the rest free. According to Plutarch, these captives were so full of praise for Brutus' moderation and justice that Patara was persuaded to surrender to him. Appian here again appears to be working with a tradition more hostile towards Brutus: in his version, when the Patarans refused to yield, Brutus advanced his troops forward and through this threat of violence succeeded in making them open their gates to him. The sources agree that Brutus did no harm to any of the inhabitants, but fined the city: Appian notes that, like Cassius at Rhodes, he demanded all of Patara's gold and silver, and forced private citizens to pay their wealth or be punished by death, with rewards for informers; Plutarch, however, suggests that he demanded a much smaller amount than Cassius had at Rhodes. Appian records an anecdote in which a slave informs Brutus that his master has concealed his wealth: at the tribunal, the young man's mother cried out that she was the one who had concealed the gold, the man himself remained quiet, and the slave disputed the mother's claims; Brutus reportedly approved of the man's silence, and sympathised with the mother's grief, and so set them both free, while punishing the slave with death for accusing his superiors too keenly.[30]

Plutarch preserves lines from a letter in Brutus' hand, presumably written to one of the Lycian communities, contrasting the behaviour and resulting fate of the Xanthians and the Patarans: employing a rather menacing tone, Brutus invites his addressee to choose the best course of action.[31] Unsurprisingly, other communities chose to follow the example of the Patarans. One recorded example is the town of Myra (Demre) on the Lycian coast: according to Dio Cassius, Brutus captured their general at the harbour and then released him, so that they then submitted; Appian instead records that Spinther was sent to Andriace, the port of Myra, broke the chains of the harbour, and sailed up the river to the town, where the people obeyed his commands and he was able to collect taxes to send to Brutus.

According to Appian, the Lycian confederation now sent ambassadors to Brutus, promising to form a military alliance with him and to contribute what money they could. Brutus fixed a tax rate, restored the free Xanthians to their city, and ordered the Lycians to hand over their fleet in preparation for his and Cassius' potential naval campaign against Antony and Octavian. His and the Lycian fleet then set sail northwards up the coast to Abydus (Canakkale). Here Brutus reunited with his land forces and would use the fleet to transport them across the Hellespont (the Dardanelles) to Thrace and thence to Macedonia, ready for civil war.[32]

Brutus and Cassius also took another, perhaps surprising, decision at about this time in order to secure their position in the east: they resorted to requesting reinforcements from Parthia, the arch-enemy of Rome. For this mission, they sent Quintus Labienus as an envoy to King Orodes. Labienus was the son of one of Caesar's generals in Gaul, who had later switched allegiances and fought with Pompey at Pharsalus, and had died at Caesar's last battle, at Munda. Orodes was reportedly hesitant to join forces with Brutus and Cassius, but similarly reluctant to refuse, until the outcome of events was more certain. Labienus stayed with Orodes in the meantime and, when he later learned of the defeat of the Republicans, he chose to remain with the Parthians for safety. He would later not only serve with them against Antony, but encourage them to invade the eastern Roman provinces.[33]

Reconciliation: Sardis

Before departing for Macedonia, Brutus summoned Cassius to Sardis (Sart), in June or July 42 BC, for another conference of war, in which they would also settle some of their differences and renew their friendship. Plutarch has preserved some anecdotal details of their meeting. As they reunited, their combined armies saluted them both as *imperator*. They then locked themselves away in private to discuss the mutual suspicions and accusations which had arisen against each other, thanks to the talk of men. Recriminations reportedly led to anger and tears, which alarmed their friends, who must have been listening outside. Favonius, the philosopher and follower of Cato, was determined to enter and alleviate the situation: he forced his way past those on guard, reciting a line of Homer's *Iliad*,[34] which made Cassius burst into laughter but angered Brutus, who ejected him from the room. Favonius' actions did, nonetheless, succeed in diffusing the quarrel for the time being, and Brutus and Cassius withdrew separately. Cassius later held a dinner, at which Brutus and his friends were present, although the latter became vexed once more when Favonius gatecrashed. Nevertheless, they reportedly went on to enjoy an evening of wine, mirth, wit and philosophy.[35]

On the following day, however, a conflict of opinion arose again between the two generals, when Brutus condemned and disgraced a friend, and former praetor, for embezzlement of public funds in Sardis. Cassius did not think that now was the time for such strict morals, finding his treatment irritatingly pedantic: for, a few days before, he had similarly discovered that two of his friends had committed the same crime, but instead of behaving with excessive officiousness, he had reprimanded them privately, while acquitting them publicly and allowing them to remain in his service. We may also remember Brutus' own earlier dubious financial dealings, and therefore find this a particularly hypocritical approach. Brutus' retort to Cassius was that they should not neglect justice, nor forget the Ides of March when they had assassinated Caesar in part because his power had enabled others to go about plundering; he added that it would have been better to have been judged as cowards in enduring the wrongs of Caesar's acquaintances, than accepting those of their own friends and thereby make themselves appear unjust. It may be suspected that Brutus could be a difficult character to deal with in his inflexibility and unbending principles, at least when it suited him. Nonetheless, the pair were reconciled, and proceeded to the Hellespont, ready to advance together to Macedonia to face Antony and Octavian in the decisive civil war which is known as the Battle of Philippi.[36]

Chapter Thirteen

Philippi

Summer–Autumn 42 BC

The Advance to Philippi

According to legend, the premonitions before the war were not promising for the side of the Liberators. Even before they left Asia, an ill-omened portent was witnessed: soon before they were to cross the Hellespont from Abydus to Sestus on the Thracian Chersonese, a vision appeared to Brutus. Taking the opportunity to remind us of Brutus' dedication to duty, Plutarch informs us that he was naturally wakeful and, through self-discipline, had taught himself to manage on only a few hours of sleep a night, although he would not permit himself even that until all business had been transacted. Indeed, Plutarch claims that, of all generals, Brutus was the least given to sleep. However, the magnitude of the current situation, with the impending clash of arms weighing heavily on his mind, meant that he would take a short nap after eating in the evening and work on through the night on urgent business, unless all duties were completed, in which case he would read until midnight when he received the tribunes and centurions to give his orders. Late on this particular night, when the entire camp was silent, the anxious Brutus was engaged in reflection when he thought he heard someone enter his dimly lit tent. Standing close by was a terrible and fearful apparition: when he asked what it was and what it wanted, it replied that it was his evil spirit, which he would see again at Philippi. Brutus, reportedly unperturbed, replied, 'I shall see you'. When it vanished, he called his servants, but no one had seen or heard anything, so he kept watch throughout the night. The next day he consulted Cassius who, as an Epicurean, held keen views on such matters, and easily rationalised it: he advised Brutus that it could not have been real, but must have been brought about by his current physical and mental exertions. Plutarch, on the other hand, interprets this vision as a clear indication of the displeasure of the gods at the murder of Caesar.[1]

After having subdued Rhodes, Cassius had learned that Cleopatra, who it is alleged feared him, was about to send a well-provisioned and large fleet to Antony and Octavian from Egypt. Therefore, he sent his fleet commander, Murcus, to Taenarum (Cape Matapan), the southernmost point on the Greek mainland, with a legion of the best soldiers, archers and sixty ships. Murcus was to collect what booty he could from the Peloponnese, and lie in wait. Murcus later discovered that Cleopatra's fleet had been damaged by a storm off the Libyan coast and that she had returned to Egypt. He therefore decided to sail to Brundisium and docked at an island opposite the harbour, from where he intended to block the transferral of Antony and Octavian's army and supplies across the Adriatic Sea to Macedonia. Antony, who was at Brudisium supervising the embarkation, launched the few warships he had against Murcus, but without success, and so he found it necessary to summon Octavian for assistance from the Sicilian strait, where he was currently engaged in fighting against Sextus Pompey. As Octavian approached with reinforcements, Murcus retreated a short distance so that he should not be caught between him and Antony. From there Murcus was rendered ineffective: favourable winds aided the crossing of Antony and Octavian's army, leaving Murcus unable to intervene. He nonetheless refused to give up, remaining where he was with the hope of hindering their transferral of provisions. Brutus and Cassius then sent Ahenobarbus to him in command of fifty ships, a legion, and archers as reinforcements to aid this mission. Together they sailed about harassing the enemy between Italy and Macedonia.[2]

Before the arrival of Murcus and Ahenobarbus, however, Antony and Octavian had already succeeded in dispatching an advance force of eight legions over to Macedonia. These were under the command of two men: Lucius Decidius Saxa, who had fought with Caesar against Pompey and aided Antony at Mutina; and Gaius Norbanus Flaccus, a man newly prominent in the political world, whose family were Caesarians. These men marched through Macedonia towards the Thracian mountains, and beyond the city of Philippi (now Filippoi in Greece). Here they seized the passes of the Sapaei and Corpili: these were strategically important since the Via Egnatia, the main route from Asia to Europe, ran through them, and Brutus and Cassius were, therefore, expected to march that way. These tribes were under the authority of Rhascupolis, a Thracian potentate who shared rule of the country with his brother, Rhascus. However, while Rhascupolis favoured the Liberators, his brother preferred an alliance with the Caesarians. The former had, therefore, taken up arms for Cassius, while the latter had done so for Antony. When Cassius' men consulted Rhascupolis about the best route through, he informed them that the shortest one, through the gorge of the Sapaei, was occupied by the enemy, but that the way to circumnavigate this was difficult and much longer. Brutus and Cassius, reportedly believing their enemy not to be blocking their route intentionally but to be crossing into Thrace because of a lack of provisions, marched onwards through Thracian territories. Brutus had already subdued most of these previously, and now succeeded in bringing over the remaining rulers and tribes to their side.[3]

Brutus and Cassius halted when they reached the Gulf of Melas (Gulf of Saros), so that they could conduct a review of their armies. Appian, who provides the most detailed information of events at this point, lists the size of their impressive combined forces: nineteen legions of infantry, of which Brutus possessed eight and Cassius nine, with two legions that were nearly full, totalling 80,000 infantry; Brutus had cavalry consisting of 4,000 Gallic and Lusitanian horsemen, and 2,000 Thracians, Illyrians, Parthians and Thessalians; while Cassius' cavalry was made up of 2,000 Spanish and Gallic horsemen, and 4,000 Arab, Median and Parthian mounted bowmen; Cassius also led the allied rulers of Galatia, who brought a large additional force of infantry and 5,000 cavalry. They also possessed further detachments, which they left on duty elsewhere.[4]

Before advancing on towards the enemy, Brutus and Cassius performed the lustration of the army, which was a kind of religious purification ritual carried out before battle. The generals also, at this point, took measures to secure the loyalty of their army: aware that many of the men had previously served under Caesar, and that upon the arrival of the heir who bore his name they might wish to switch sides, Brutus and Cassius now decided to distribute the promised reward to their soldiers. They then mounted a public platform to address their gathered forces, who were reportedly delighted to see their own vast number, which also served to boost the courage and hope of Brutus and Cassius. Appian here places a fictional hortatory speech in the mouth of Cassius, rehearsing the familiar reasons for their actions against Caesar and in the name of the state, as well as recalling subsequent events and explaining their current intentions and purpose, and their advantageous position. The noisy gathering was silenced by the heralds and trumpeters so that Cassius, as the elder of the two, could speak first. He successfully roused to action the troops who, despite being dismissed, remained for sometime afterwards, singing the praises of their leaders and promising to do their duty.[5]

The soldiers were then sent off by detachment on a two-day march west along the Thracian coast towards a settlement named Doriscus (Doriskos) and beyond to Mount Serrium (Cape Makri), with Brutus and Cassius following on behind. At this time, a portent of ill omen was witnessed: two eagles perched upon the silver eagles on the leading standards, either protecting or pecking at them, and they were fed by the soldiers from the public stores, travelling with them all the way to Philippi; however, once there, the birds flew away on the day before the battle. Since Mount Serrium was a promontory projecting into the sea, Brutus and Cassius here headed inland, while sending Cimber, with his fleet, a legion and some archers, to sail around the cape. While doing so, Cimber investigated and plotted suitable places for camps, and also occasionally sailed close to the coast to instil fear into Norbanus, with the hope of forcing him to abandon the Sapaean pass. Norbanus did indeed become alarmed that they might seize the pass, and summoned Saxa from the pass of the Corpili to assist him in holding that of the Sapaei. This allowed Brutus and Cassius to march through the abandoned pass with no resistance.[6]

The Sapaean pass, however, was now strongly defended by Norbanus and Saxa, making it impossible to traverse. The Republican army became disheartened at the prospect of retracing their steps and the long circumnavigation of this pass, particularly as it was now autumn and therefore approaching the end of the season. At this point Rhascupolis advised them of a route along the side of the mountain, which was difficult because of the rocks, lack of water and thick forests. However, if they could make a narrow path through, he believed that they could go undetected. This would take three days' march, but if they carried enough water, they could reach a river on the fourth day, and Philippi on the fifth. There they would surround the enemy and leave them with no way of retreat. It was decided to send Bibulus, Brutus' stepson, ahead in command of an advance detachment, accompanied by Rhascupolis, to cut a path through for the rest to follow. Some of these men came back to say that they had caught sight of the river, but on the fourth day, when the exhausted men were running out of water, they began to lose hope: panicking despite Bibulus' attempts to encourage them, they believed that Rhascupolis was deceiving them and hurled stones and abuse at him as he rode past. However, in the evening the men at the front reached the river, and their shouts of joy were passed back through the line. On hearing this, Brutus and Cassius rushed forward, leading the rest of the men along the track. However, Rhascupolis' brother, Rhascus, had also heard the shouting and so had discovered the audacious and remarkable feat achieved by the Republican army. Once he had informed Norbanus of Brutus and Cassius' impressive deed, the enemy army withdrew from the Sapaean pass by night to Amphipolis (Amfipolis). Meanwhile, Rhascupolis led the armies of Brutus and Cassius safely through some woods into the north of Philippi.[7]

Establishment of Camps at Philippi

Thus Brutus and Cassius reached the location of their final mighty showdown. Cimber also joined them there, anchoring the Republican fleet at the harbour of Neapolis (Kavala), so that the entire force was gathered in Philippi. Appian describes the site of the city: it was on a steep hill, with the woods through which the Republicans had arrived to the north, marshland extending down to the sea on the south, the passes of the Sapaei and Corpili to the east, and a fertile plain to the west. The latter sloped down towards the city of Amphipolis, where the enemy, commanded by Norbanus and Saxa, were currently encamped. Brutus and Cassius positioned themselves on two hills outside of Philippi, on either side of the Via Egnatia: Brutus took the site on the north side, and Cassius the south, with the camps joined together on their west side by a rampart which crossed the road and had a river flowing close by it. The hills were said to be ideal for their camps, because of the marshes on one side and gorges on the other, while the plain was suitable for fighting. Their fleet, based at Neapolis, was also strategically well placed for bringing in supplies from their store on the nearby island of Thasos. According to Dio Cassius, Brutus and Cassius also improved their access to provisions, by seizing Mount Symbolon from the enemy, which allowed them a shorter supply route.[8]

Reportedly, neither side offered battle to the other at this stage. Although Norbanus and Saxa sent out men and cavalry for minor skirmishes, nothing was thereby achieved, and they were more concerned to defend their camp. They now sent an urgent summons to Antony and Octavian who, up until now, had believed that Brutus and Cassius were still busy with the Rhodians and Lycians, and who had been delayed by their own engagements with Murcus and Ahenobarbus at Brundisium, and Sextus Pompeius in Sicily, respectively. The Republican army was currently superior in number, but Brutus and Cassius chose not to advance against Norbanus and Saxa when they learned that Antony was approaching.[9]

Antony marched alone to Philippi, since Octavian had been taken ill at Dyrrachium, and so had been left behind there. He arrived in Philippi with remarkable speed, reportedly astounding Brutus: indeed, Plutarch claims it was only this swift arrival that prevented Brutus and Cassius capturing the enemy forces. While they were busy fortifying their camps, Antony arrived at Amphipolis, intending to capture this advantageous site before they did. However, he was pleased to find that Norbanus already held it, and he left his supplies and one legion there, before boldly proceeding to occupy a position on the plain close to Brutus and Cassius, ready for the impending battle. Brutus and Cassius were shocked at his audacity and recklessness, especially now that the inferiority of his position was revealed: while they occupied the higher ground, he was on the open plain below; they were able to obtain fuel from the marshes, but he was forced to find it in the difficult terrain of the mountains; they had access to freshly dug wells, while his only source of water was a river; and they had a much shorter supply route than him. Antony also suffered a setback when he tried to lay ambush to some of the enemy gathering grain, but failed, meaning that both he and his men lost hope. Nevertheless, necessity forced him to press on and he fortified his camp with towers, walls, ditches and a palisade. Likewise, Brutus and Cassius completed the defence work on their camps, leaving only the cliffs on Brutus' side, and the marsh and sea on Cassius' side, exposed. Still no real fighting took place at this time, except for some minor cavalry conflicts.[10]

Learning of Antony's failed ambush attempt, Octavian became concerned at the thought of him fighting the Republican army alone. He was supposedly equally worried at the prospect of either outcome: he feared that, whichever side should emerge victorious, they would oppose him. We are told that he therefore rose from his sickbed to hasten to Philippi, carried in a litter, and arrived there ten days after Antony. Octavian's arrival reportedly buoyed the disheartened army of Antony. They decided it would be safest to encamp together within one stronghold, so Octavian set up camp on the side of the plain opposite that of Brutus, while Antony was positioned in front of Cassius. Plutarch reports that these were the largest Roman armies ever to have faced each other. Although inferior in number to Octavian's army, Brutus' was said to be impressive in appearance: while he normally instilled austerity and temperance into his men, they were now adorned with gold and silver, which he permitted because he believed that their desire to keep hold of their armour and weapons would add to their ambition and determination. However, this is in contradiction with the apparent letter from Brutus admonishing his tribunes for wearing gold fastenings at Philippi, and which certainly seems more in keeping with his stern nature.[11]

Both sides now performed lustrations of their armies. However, while Antony and Octavian carried theirs out within camp, Brutus and Cassius came out into the open field, according to custom, and were much more generous with their gifts and sacrifices. The Republican soldiers were encouraged and therefore more willing to fight than their opposite number: furthermore, they believed the enemy to be afraid because they had carried out the lustration out of sight, and this too made them more eager for battle. However, the omens in advance of the battle were not favourable for Brutus and Cassius, and these were again interpreted as signs of the displeasure of the gods at the murder of Caesar. At the lustration, the lictor placed the wreath on Cassius upside down while, at an earlier procession, the boy carrying Cassius' golden statue of Victory slipped and fell to the ground. Now many carrion birds were seen hovering over the garrison, and specifically above the heads of the conspirators, looking down upon them and screeching in a dreadful manner. Swarms of bees were also witnessed clustering within the camp, forcing the soothsayers to shut off those parts so as to avert the superstitious fear of the soldiers.[12]

With these various ill-omened signs, even the rational Epicurean Cassius began to succumb to anxiety, becoming unnerved by the portents. On the basis of this concern, he wished to delay battle. This also made the most strategic sense, since they were inferior in size to the army of Antony and Octavian: both sides reportedly had nineteen legions of infantry, but the legions of Brutus and Cassius were less full, although they had a greater number of cavalry.[13] Furthermore, the Republican army had access to a ready supply of provisions, unlike their Caesarian opponents who were reliant on the internal supplies of Macedonia and nearby Thessaly: they were blocked by Sextus Pompeius from Spain and Africa, and by Murcus and Ahenobarbus from Italy, while their only other hope, Egypt, was suffering from famine. Therefore their advantageous military position made it easier for Brutus and Cassius to prolong the war and force the submission of the Caesarian army by starving them of provisions, thereby avoiding a clash of arms.[14]

However, Plutarch here records that Brutus and Cassius were in disagreement once more, with Brutus wishing to enter battle immediately. Plutarch's Brutus, with the best of intentions, as is so often the case in his portrayal of the noble Republican, reportedly wished to bring this to a swift conclusion, either to restore freedom to his country or to spare men the various costs associated with military service. He was also encouraged by the successful preliminary cavalry forays that had been made. Another reason given by Plutarch for the Republican army preferring the battle sooner rather than later was that there were supposedly many desertions to the Caesarians, and many of Cassius' men therefore came around to Brutus' way of thinking. Dio Cassius, however, records that they were receiving new allies daily, and that this was one of their reasons to delay fighting.[15] It is quite probable that, at this uncertain stage, there were men shifting allegiances in both directions. One of Brutus' friends, Atillius, advised that they should delay until after the winter: although he was in agreement with Cassius, he angered the general and many others, for he simply gave the pessimistic reason that he wished to have longer to live. However, Plutarch's narrative contradicts the general impression of the other accounts, which present both of the Liberators as reluctant to engage in an unnecessary clash of arms, and which perhaps seems more characteristic of both men, especially Brutus. Therefore for several days, although Brutus and Cassius brought their army out into the field on the higher ground, only minor skirmishes took place between the two sides.[16]

For the same reasons that Cassius and Brutus wished to delay fighting, Antony and Octavian, as to be expected, wished to engage in battle immediately. Furthermore, the omens and sacrifices in the camp of Antony and Octavian were more optimistic than the signs given to Brutus and Cassius, and thus encouraged the desire to fight. For example, while on his way to Philippi, Octavian had been informed by a Thessalian, claiming to have met Caesar's ghost on a lonely road, that he would be victorious. Another Thessalian reportedly saw Caesar in a dream, and was told to inform Octavian that the battle would be in two days' time and that he should wear an article of clothing that Caesar himself had worn while dictator: Octavian duly put on his adoptive father's ring. According to Dio Cassius, there were also numerous supernatural signs occurring in Rome at this time, serving as a warning of the impending civil war in the east and the subsequent end of the Republic. All the recorded omens portray it as clear from the outset that Brutus and Cassius were to be defeated by Antony and Octavian in this clash and that, despite the apparently weaker military situation of the Caesarians, their victory was divinely sanctioned. There was an apparent sense of divine justice in the avenging of Caesar's murder through this battle: indeed, it was here at Philippi that Octavian vowed both a festival and a temple to the god Mars Ultor, or Mars the Avenger, in honour of his murdered father. The remains of this temple can still be seen within the Forum of Augustus in Rome.[17]

The First Battle of Philippi

The accounts of what happened next, during October 42 BC, diverge here once again: Appian's account, which has been accepted as the most likely version of proceedings, presents an accidental battle and calamitous sequence of events for Brutus and Cassius; Dio Cassius, however, presents a deliberate but reluctant decision by the Republicans to offer battle to Antony and Octavian; and Plutarch combines both aspects in his narrative.[18]

On the eve of battle, Brutus and Cassius were in contrasting moods, according to Plutarch: while Brutus was said to be relaxed, reportedly full of hopefulness and engaging in philosophical discussion over dinner before getting some rest, Cassius was uncharacteristically quiet and pensive, dining privately with only a few close friends. Plutarch records the detail that, after supper, Cassius affectionately addressed his commander, Messalla, in Greek, clasping his hand: he compared himself with Pompey before the Battle of Pharsalus, being forced to decide the fate of his country on a single battle,[19] and advised that they should bravely resign themselves to the vagaries of fortune. Cassius then embraced Messalla and invited him to dinner on the following night, which happened to be his birthday: it would also be the day of his death.[20]

Plutarch goes on to describe how, on the morning of the battle, Brutus and Cassius drew up their battle lines. A scarlet cloak, the signal for battle, was reportedly displayed before the camps, and the two generals then conversed together in the space between their gathered troops. Cassius hoped that they would be victorious, but was prepared for the worst: he asked his comrade for his view on flight and death, and Brutus supposedly responded that, as a young man lacking due experience, he had been governed by his philosophical beliefs and rashly reproached his uncle Cato for his suicide, on the basis that it was weak to run away in such a manner; in his present situation, however, he was able to see matters in a different light; this was his last stand and, if fortune was not to treat them favourably in this battle then he was ready for the end, having given his life to his country on the Ides of March 44 BC. Cassius smiled and embraced Brutus declaring, in a kind of suicide pact, that they should now face the enemy, and would either be victorious or defeated without fear. They then discussed the order of battle with their friends, with one final hint of disagreement between the pair:

Brutus wished to take command of the right wing, although this position was more appropriate for Cassius, as his senior in years and experience; however, Cassius not only acquiesced, but also put Messalla on the right wing with one of the most warlike legions. Brutus immediately led out his finely equipped cavalry, and promptly put his infantry into order.[21]

Dio Cassius portrays both sides, at dawn, spontaneously and quietly arming themselves and lining up for battle opposite each other in the middle ground between the camps. He summarises the contents of the hortatory speeches by the officers to the troops: the Republicans were encouraged by talk of liberty, democracy, and equality, with examples of the hardships borne under monarchy cited; the Caesarians were urged to exact vengeance on the assassins of Caesar, and to be filled with the desire to rule all men, with the additional incentive of a promised financial reward. The watchwords were then given, which for the Republicans was understandably 'Liberty', although another version reports that Brutus' was 'Apollo'. This was followed by trumpeters on each side sounding the notes of war, before a silence fell on the camps. Dio Cassius presents this as an entirely mutual clash, with the leaders raising the piercing battle cry simultaneously, and each section of the two sides following suit by coming together concurrently in a mighty and bloody clash of arms.[22]

However, Appian presents a different version of events. He has Antony drawing up his soldiers daily, as if ready for battle, but in reality as a ruse. According to Appian, Antony now began preliminary operations, taking action in order to try to induce a clash of arms. He decided to cut a narrow path through the marshlands to the south of Philippi, with the aim of secretly reaching the Liberators' rear, and also cutting them off from their supply base at Thasos. The reeds of the marshes kept Antony's men concealed and, after ten days, he sent a detachment of troops along the passage by night, with the mission of constructing forts to block the Liberators from the sea. However, Cassius, who was reportedly impressed by Antony's actions, swiftly countered them by building his own line of entrenchment, extending his defences, which he fortified with palisades, across those of the enemy down to the sea, and thereby cutting Antony off from his newly constructed forts and the men he had sent ahead to do this work.[23]

Cassius' move angered Antony, who now furiously led his army towards his opponent's counter-defences, carrying tools and ladders with the intention of taking them by storm and then forcing his way into Cassius' camp. Meanwhile, Octavian's men were watching events unfold on behalf of their general, who remained incapacitated on his sickbed: they expected that their Republican enemy would merely make minor sorties on Antony's entrenchment, and so were alarmed by the commotion arising there. This distracted them from Brutus' soldiers encamped opposite: seeing Antony's troops charging uphill in front of them and towards Cassius, Brutus' men were fired up for action. Brutus himself was said to be riding up and down the lines, encouraging his legions, while the watchword for battle was sent around. However, Brutus' men were so eager that, failing to wait for the watchword, they charged forward upon Octavian's camp without being given their command. Cassius, when he learned of this, was said to be somewhat displeased. This caused a disorderly surge, with Messalla's legion rushing forward first, and going beyond Octavian's left wing: they only managed to kill a few men but succeeded in breaking into the camp. Conveniently, however, Octavian was not present: his physician, Marcus Artorius Asclepiades, had obeyed a vision received of Minerva warning him to lead Octavian from his tent and place him in the line of battle. It was a narrow miss for Octavian, who only just managed to escape capture by fighting in the front line, although he was reportedly weak and barely able to stand: his empty litter, left behind, was said to have been pierced by many enemy javelins and spears, while those who were captured with the camp were killed, including 2,000 Spartan auxiliaries.[24]

Meanwhile, Brutus and the rest of his legions were engaged in fighting against the soldiers of Octavian who, in their general state of confusion, were easily overcome and routed. Brutus' troops succeeded in destroying three of Octavian's legions in hand-to-hand combat, before rushing into the camp in pursuit. However, this left parts of their line exposed, as the right wing was drawn away from the main body in their hasty pursuit: the centre of Brutus' forces resisted, holding its ground amid fierce fighting, but the left wing, unaware of what was happening and having lost its formation, was driven back into their camp, which Octavian's troops duly sacked. The centre of Brutus' forces, however, succeeded in driving back their opponents amid much slaughter. Brutus emerged triumphant in his section of the battlefield: he reportedly captured three eagles and many standards of the enemy, while Octavian's men took nothing. Indeed, Appian suggests approximately 16,000 of Octavian's men were killed.[25]

Elsewhere on the battlefield, however, Brutus' fellow commander was not enjoying the same success and his wing of the Republican army was suffering a complete reversal of fortune from that of Brutus. Although

Plutarch acknowledges, and simultaneously dismisses, a version of events hostile to Antony, in which he had supposedly abandoned his camp and hidden himself in the marshes to avoid the fighting, this not only seems wholly uncharacteristic of this skilled and experienced soldier, but other accounts present him as heavily involved in the battle, leading the attack upon Cassius.[26] For Antony, buoyed by the sight of the fighting which it had been his intention to induce, chose not to turn his men around and risk causing disarray, but pressed on with his uphill advance on Cassius' entrenchment. Although under a rain of fire, Antony reached Cassius' advance guard, which had firmly held its position. He broke through their ranks and swiftly destroyed their newly built defence works, demolishing the palisade, filling in the ditches, undermining the rampart, killing the men at the gates, and thus succeeding in breaching Cassius' fortification, before entering into combat inside the walls. Those of Cassius' troops who were working on the defences attempted to come to the rescue of their fellow soldiers, but were driven back into the marshes by Antony's men, who then turned against Cassius' camp itself. Since this was considered a strong garrison, it had been left guarded by only a few men. However, when they saw their fellow soldiers outside the camp being defeated and routed in disorderly fashion, Antony's troops easily overcame them too. Appian reports that approximately 8,000 of Cassius' men were killed which, although a large number, was about half the losses that Octavian was said to have suffered.[27]

Further ill-omened portents were witnessed at Philippi on the day of the first battle, which can possibly be dated as 23 October 42 BC.[28] As the Republican soldiers were going out to battle, an Ethiopian met them in front of the gates: this was interpreted as a sign of bad luck, and so the men immediately cut him down. Cassius himself was also subject to a terrifying vision: while standing in the battle line, he saw no less than mighty Caesar himself, wearing the purple commander's cloak and a threatening countenance, charging towards him on horseback at full speed. According to Valerius Maximus, this caused Cassius to turn in flight, crying out and asking what more could be done if killing a man was not enough.[29] While the supernatural omens of the ancient accounts suggest that there was an inevitability to the eventual outcome of this civil war, the factual details of the first battle, as they are presented, display that it was a very evenly matched affair as a battle of two halves.[30] However, it was what happened next, caused by a failure in communication between the Republican generals on the battlefield, that turned events decisively and fatally against them.

The Death of Cassius

Cassius had not simply stood by and suffered absolute defeat without putting up any resistance. However, he had reportedly acted with hesitancy instead of the required calculated and swift decision, which had allowed his troops to become enveloped and overcome by the enemy. His cavalry subsequently fled towards the sea, and Cassius, seeing his infantry likewise beginning to fall back, tried to rally them before they followed suit: he seized a standard from a fleeing standard-bearer and planted it in the ground before him. However, even his bodyguard was showing signs of giving up hope. Cassius, finding his camp had been despoiled, was forced to retreat with a small number of faithful men to higher ground, from where he could survey the plain of Philippi and the outcome of the battle. However visibility was poor, owing to the vast nature of the plain and the amount of dust that had arisen as a consequence of the conflicts and the following disarray and also, according to some accounts, since night was beginning to fall. In the confusion, the victorious of this battle were said to have assumed that their entire forces had shared the same fortune, and likewise the defeated believed that all was lost. However, Cassius reportedly sent his companion, Titinius, who was possibly one of his centurions, to investigate the situation and report back on Brutus' current position.

Meanwhile Brutus, who initially believed Cassius to have been similarly victorious, was surprised not to see his fellow commander's tent as he returned on horseback to his own camp. Some of Brutus' men were able to see men in armour moving about in Cassius' camp, but not the large number of dead bodies that would be expected from a defeat. However, Brutus was duly alarmed and so, leaving a guard in the enemy camp, he called off the pursuit of the Caesarians in order to rally his troops to Cassius' aid. Brutus sent ahead a large body of cavalry who, as they met and recognised Titinius as one of Cassius' friends, greeted him with great joy, shouting, clashing their weapons, and embracing him. However, this served to catalyse the tragedy, for Cassius, whose vision was impaired not only by the dust and darkness but by its natural weakness, believed he was witnessing the capture of his friend by the enemy and this proved too much for him to bear. Believing that he was being hunted down by the enemy, Cassius withdrew into an empty tent, taking with him his freedman, Pindarus, whom he had reportedly kept with him as a companion since the Parthian campaign, ready for such an emergency. In the manner of the beleaguered Caesar at the foot of Pompey's statue, Cassius drew his cloak over his face. He then offered his neck to

Pindarus and, in one version of events, Plutarch suggests Cassius used the very dagger with which he had killed Caesar. Cassius' severed head was later found next to his lifeless body, but Pindarus had disappeared, and so it was suggested that the freedman had murdered his master rather than aided his suicide. Meanwhile, Appian records an account proposing that it was no tragic mistake forcing Cassius to decide upon suicide, since he pursued this despite learning of Brutus' success. Whatever the circumstances, certainly here ended the life of one of Caesar's chief assassins, following the first Battle of Philippi and, reportedly, on the anniversary of his own birth.[31]

Titinius, returning to Cassius in leisurely fashion, since he knew that there was no imminent danger, was met with the cries of his distressed and grieving friends. Distraught at having tarried with Brutus' troops, when he could have returned swiftly to inform Cassius of the Republican success, and thus blaming himself for his general's demise, he killed himself over the corpse of Cassius. When Brutus in turn arrived, he wept over the body of his fellow chief Liberator, whom he called 'the last of the Romans', seemingly recognising that his beloved Republic was fast coming to an end. Brutus simultaneously reproached Cassius for his hasty actions, and envied him for his newfound freedom from the cares by which he himself was still troubled: Brutus was said to have pensively questioned where these troubles would lead him now.[32]

However, Brutus was not able to devote too long to grieving for his brother-in-law, since the war with Antony and Octavian was by no means over, and it was necessary for him to press on swiftly with practical arrangements. Fearing that a funeral on the battlefield in the presence of Cassius' men would cause too much dejection, Brutus dressed his comrade's body ready for burial, and arranged for friends to take it secretly by night to Thasos, their nearby supply island. Brutus' fellow commander, and one of the chief assassins of Caesar, was thus buried there without causing disruption to the camp.

Next, Brutus turned to the task of rallying Cassius' troops, whose cooperation would be necessary if he was to continue to fight this civil war, and who were reputed to be better disciplined than his own: certainly, Plutarch believes that Brutus would have had complete success had there not been such disorder among his own troops in the first battle. True to his dutiful character, Brutus stayed up all night, reportedly without food or care for his own person, in order to work on restoring order to Cassius' army. He assembled the troops and delivered a speech to console them. Realising that they had lost much in the destruction of their camp, he compensated them with the promise of a sum of money. This also helped to secure their loyalty: the soldiers, amazed at the size of the reward, cheered Brutus on his way, declaring him to be the only one of the four commanders not to have been defeated in the battle.[33]

Further Manoeuvres between Battles

The ancient authors here describe the somewhat precarious situation in which both sides now found themselves, both enjoying luck and misfortune in almost equal measure. What can, perhaps, be derived from this balance is that it remained quite an evenly matched war, despite the demise of Cassius, and that the outcome was by no means inevitable even at this stage.

Preparations for the next battle were thus underway, and Brutus' proactivity here displays that he had not given up all hope of winning the war at this stage. On the following day, he transferred his headquarters into the camp of Cassius, which was in a more suitable position for commanding the site. That morning, Antony and Octavian drew up their army in battle formation; according to one account, they were encouraged to action when Cassius' attendant, Demetrius, brought his master's clothes and sword to them immediately after his death. However, Brutus refused to be troubled by this show of bravado: he countered it by likewise arming his troops ready for battle, causing the enemy to withdraw. Brutus remained upbeat at this time, remarking to friends that the enemy had challenged them because they believed them to be worn down, but were too afraid to put their theory to the test. Furthermore, Dio Cassius records that Brutus, wishing to avoid joining battle with his opponents, instead set about successfully harassing them: he reportedly assaulted their camp by night, and diverted the course of a river in order to wash away part of their camp.[34]

Meanwhile, Antony and Octavian were said to be despondent about their far more significant number of losses, which was said to be approximately twice that of the Republicans. Furthermore, they were beginning to run low on supplies and, as it was late October, it was approaching the winter season, which they knew would bring them extra difficulties: given the low position of their camp, close to marshy ground, the autumn rains had already repeatedly flooded their tents with both mud and water that froze in the cold temperatures.

At this critical time, the Caesarians received news of a further blow from the Adriatic. On the same day as the first Battle of Philippi, the Republican fleet commanders, Murcus and Ahenobarbus, had succeeded in destroying a convoy of troops led by Gnaeus Domitius Calvinus, a former commander of Caesar who remained loyal to the Caesarian cause. Appian gives the most detailed account of events here. He reports that Calvinus was leading a few triremes containing two legions of infantry, including the battle-hardened Martian legion, as well as a praetorian cohort of 2,000 men, and four squadrons of cavalry. Murcus and Ahenobarbus attacked with 130 warships: only a few of the leading Caesarian ships got away, since the wind dropped and left the rest adrift at sea, and completely at the mercy of the Republicans. Despite the valiant efforts of the Caesarians to resist, they were promptly crushed: when they attempted to bind their vessels together and prevent the Republicans breaking their line, Murcus ordered flaming arrows to be shot at them causing them to free the burning ships from each other hastily, but thus then putting themselves in danger of being surrounded or rammed by the Republican triremes. Some soldiers, including those from the Martian legion, found it unseemly to die in this manner, and so killed themselves before they could be burnt to death, while others jumped aboard the enemy ships out of desperation. The disaster was so great that the men who escaped death by clinging to floating wreckage were reportedly forced by hunger to survive by chewing on the tackle and sails of their ships until they managed to reach land. Appian reports that seventeen triremes surrendered to Murcus and the men on board swore allegiance to him. Calvinus was thought to have died in the disaster, but he arrived back in Brundisium on his ship five days later.[35]

Antony and Octavian were not able, at this late stage, to transfer elsewhere, nor could they return to Italy, and so they were eager to force an engagement of arms, hoping to do so swiftly, before news of this defeat in the Adriatic spread either to their own men or their enemy. It was here that their fortunes began to change for the better since, according to Plutarch, who in this point contrasts with Appian, Brutus did not learn of his fleet's success until it was too late, reportedly twenty days after the event: in yet another tragic twist of fate, details of the matter were reportedly brought to Brutus on the eve of the second Battle of Philippi; however, it came from an enemy deserter named Clodius, who was unable to speak directly with Brutus since his information, that Octavian's very reason for wishing to force an encounter was this recent naval misfortune, was disregarded as false or idle gossip. While Appian suggests that Brutus had already been informed, Plutarch comments that, had he only known of this turn of events, he would have held out: his camp was in a much more advantageous position than that of the enemy, on higher ground and virtually impregnable; unlike Antony and Octavian, he had access to plenty of provisions to sustain his army; and he himself was also buoyed by his own recent success in the war.[36]

Appian here places fictional speeches in the mouths of the generals. Firstly, he has Brutus rousing his troops, encouraging them by recalling their success in capturing both camps on the previous day, and highlighting their clear advantage over the enemy. Since Antony and Octavian's supplies were running low, Brutus restrains his men from action, informing them that they can avoid danger by holding out and allowing hunger and exhaustion to overcome the enemy first. As well as promising that they would receive a monetary reward once they had brought the war to successful completion, Brutus now distributed a gift for their previous day's success. Brutus was also rumoured to have offered the cities of Sparta and Thessalonica (Thessaloniki) for plundering, as an incentive to the soldiers. Plutarch declares this to be the only indefensible act in the entire life of the virtuous Republican, before going on to excuse it as necessary to motivate the soldiers of Cassius, who were said to be undisciplined in camp because they lacked a personal leader, and afraid to fight the enemy because of their former defeat. Furthermore, Plutarch observes that, in any case, it was a deed paling into insignificance next to the cruel methods used by Antony and Octavian to extort land and money to reward their troops. Appian then presents the Caesarian generals as gathering and addressing their troops with a counter-speech encouraging them to force an engagement. Antony uses their refusal to fight as evidence of the enemy's cowardice and fear, adding that Cassius' suicide was proof of their feeling of defeat. He goes on to reassure them that they should not be concerned by what they lost when their camps were plundered on the previous day, for they would be able to recoup far more once they achieved victory. In contrast with Brutus, Antony urges them to hasten to battle, and promises them a reward for doing so.[37]

It was in the interest of Antony and Octavian, then, to enter into battle as soon as possible, but Brutus remained unwilling to engage, despite Antony leading his men out in battle order every day. Brutus was also keeping a line of men in order, both in preparation for a forced clash of arms and to help prevent the restlessness of Cassius' men, while he had others guard the road bringing in their supplies. Therefore, the Caesarians took measures in an attempt to force the matter. They reportedly distributed pamphlets in the Republican camp, encouraging the Republican soldiers either to transfer their allegiances, with the use of bribes, or to fight. Antony and Octavian also carried out more practical manoeuvres to try to induce a battle. Brutus had abandoned a hill near the south of the camp, which Cassius had wisely kept guarded: although it was difficult for the enemy to occupy, because it was exposed to attack from the camp, four of Octavian's legions succeeded in taking it by night, protecting themselves from arrow fire with wicker and animal hides. Securing this hill enabled the Caesarians to extend a further twelve legions in positions down towards the sea, with the aim of cutting off Brutus' supplies and breaking his lines by attack across the marsh or along the sea. However, Brutus simply countered this with the construction of fortifications opposite their camps. Thus thwarted in their plans, and becoming desperate, Antony and Octavian sent a legion of troops to Achaea (a Greek region in the Peloponnese), to gather all the food that they could find to send back to the army. In the meantime, the Caesarian troops advanced from the plains of Philippi up to the entrenchments of the Republicans, shouting insults at Brutus, thereby hoping to draw him out into an engagement.[38]

The resolute Brutus, nonetheless, had no desire to enter battle, for his situation remained advantageous, while the enemy's was becoming increasingly desperate; therefore, his plans to hold out were progressing well. However, Brutus was facing some difficulties within his own camp, with pockets of dissension arising. Despite his rousing speech, there was some dissatisfaction among Cassius' men, who were unhappy with the change of commander and resentful of Brutus' victorious troops: maintaining control of this situation was one of Brutus' reasons for keeping the soldiers under arms, despite having no intention of fighting. Brutus' own camp was filled with prisoners of war, which therefore needed heavy guarding. Furthermore, Brutus distrusted many of the slaves whom he had captured, since they were moving about suspiciously amongst his men, and so he reluctantly ordered that the majority of them should be put to death: Dio Cassius partially excuses this act with the disclaimer that necessity drove Brutus to it, adding that he was made more willing to do so since the enemy had killed all the soldiers whom they had taken alive. Plutarch also includes an act of kindness to balance this execution: Brutus released some of the freemen, declaring them to have been prisoners under the enemy but more truly free citizens of Rome in his company; however, he was forced to hide them or help them escape when he discovered that his officers and friends wished to take revenge on them. Plutarch records the anecdote that Brutus' men brought forward two prisoners, an actor named Volumnius and a clown named Saculio, who were continuing to make insolent and mocking speeches. Brutus remained distracted by other matters, but Messalla declared that they should be publicly flogged before being returned naked to Antony and Octavian. This caused amusement among the men, but Casca, who had been the first assassin to strike Caesar, disapproved of such merriment in the aftermath of Cassius' death, and demanded that Brutus duly show his respect for his dead partner in crime by suitably punishing those who were abusing his memory. Deeply offended, Brutus asked why Casca did not do what he saw fit, which was interpreted as an execution warrant for the two men.[39]

Besides all this unrest, Brutus' biggest problem was that the soldiers did not agree that they should refrain from battle: they felt that it was cowardly and lazy to hide behind the fortifications. The soldiers reportedly had less respect for Brutus than the commanding Cassius: they considered the former more of a comrade than a leader, and were willing to challenge his authority because of his mild nature. This led to the men gathering together to air their frustrations, but Brutus ignored the grumblings of discontent and did not dare to convene a meeting, perhaps having learned something of the power of the multitude from the scenes in the aftermath of Caesar's murder. The officers approved of Brutus' plan, but nonetheless thought that the army's current mood could lead to a swift victory if they engaged in battle, and so urged him to act upon this, adding that they could fall back to their fortifications if it did not go according to plan. In the meantime, some of the enemy's German contingent had defected to Brutus, while Deiotarus' general, Amyntas, and the Thracian prince, Rhascyporis, had deserted him. This reinforced a further concern weighing on Brutus: those men who had served under Caesar might soon defect to the Caesarian camp too. Therefore, supposedly declaring himself to be like Pompey before Pharsalus, commanded rather than commander, Brutus reluctantly, and disastrously, yielded to the wishes of the majority. History was, indeed, repeating itself.[40]

The Second Battle of Philippi

A few weeks after the first encounter, Brutus thus reluctantly led his army out to fight in what would be the second and final Battle of Philippi, in the middle of November 42 BC.[41] This battle also came with its share of foreboding omens for Brutus and the Republicans. On the eve of the battle, Brutus was again visited by his evil spirit, as forewarned, although this time it remained silent: Brutus nevertheless understood and accepted his fate. Publius Volumnius, a philosopher who accompanied Brutus on all his campaigns, which is further evidence of Brutus' unfailing devotion to study and learning, recorded other portents that were witnessed before the battle: the leading standard was said to be covered with bees; an officer's arm secreted oil of roses, flowers sometimes associated with death, but this could not be wiped away; and all watched in stunned silence as two eagles flew up from each camp and clashed in the space in between, with the eagle closest to Brutus giving up and flying away, and the victor returning to Octavian. Appian attributes the start of the fighting to this last sight: the enemies of Brutus supposedly raised the battle cry as they saw the eagle flee. It was clear that the outcome of the impending battle was preordained by the gods.[42]

Brutus formed his battle line before the walls of his fortifications, ordering his men to stay close to the hill, both as a place to which they could retreat, and as a strategically advantageous point from which to launch missiles at the enemy. However, they did not enter the fray immediately, with different reasons given by the ancient authors. Appian describes how, within each of the opposing armies, there was much exhortation in preparation for the battle, accompanying their general eagerness to fight: the Caesarians were driven by fear of starvation, while the Republicans were said to have felt both shame at having forced their commander to enter an engagement when he preferred delay, and fear that they may not prove as valiant as they had claimed. As Appian portrays him, Brutus himself did not now behave with sufficient leadership skills, offering little in the way of encouragement at this crucial time: riding about the men, with a solemn look, he supposedly reminded them that this was their choosing and, in response, they were raising shouts to reassure him. Antony and Octavian, on the other hand, rode through their ranks, shaking the men's hands and successfully urging them on, reminding them of the threat of hunger. Appian does suggest, however, that both sides were suitably roused to battle: forgetting that they were fellow citizens, they shouted angry abuse at one another across the lines. Plutarch's account records that there was further delay, caused by ripples of discontent among Brutus' ranks: he became suspicious that there was some treachery afoot, and saw that his cavalry were not eager to lead into battle but were hesitatingly waiting to see the infantry's moves. Finally one of his distinguished soldiers, a certain Camulatus, rode out and crossed over to the Caesarians: according to Plutarch, it was witnessing this desertion, and fear that other men would follow suit, that finally drove Brutus to confront the enemy. It was said to be about three o'clock in the afternoon.[43]

The clash was said to be a fierce one, with fighting taking place at close quarters, as each side sought to break the opposing army's line. There was much slaughter, with bodies on the front line being shifted back to allow the next line of men to move forward and attack. The commanders on both sides were to be seen busily rushing here and there throughout their ranks, rallying the troops and supporting in the action where they could. It was a long and closely matched struggle. The section of army that Brutus was commanding was immediately successful in advancing upon the retreating left wing of the Caesarians, and his cavalry came up in support of his infantry to charge upon the enemy in their disarray. However, any elation at the initial success was short-lived, for the other Republican wing was not victorious: it was extended further so that it should not become outflanked by the Caesarians, who were numerically superior, but this left it weak at the centre. The Republicans were said to have fought well and not to be at fault, but Octavian's soldiers were able to push back their line, which retreated little by little, with the troops resisting bravely until their ranks were broken and they began to fall back more quickly. The second and third ranks in the rear also began to retreat until they were all mixed in confusion, eventually being put to flight by the enemy, who continued to press them relentlessly. Following the orders that they had received from their generals immediately before the battle, Octavian's men took care to seize the gates of Brutus' fortifications, despite putting themselves at risk of being struck by missiles: in this way they were able to cut off a safe retreat for Brutus' men, who were thus forced to flee in different directions, either to the sea or through the River Zygactes to the mountains.[44]

With the enemy routed, Antony and Octavian set about bringing this civil war to its conclusion by dividing up their duties: the latter was to guard the main camp and capture any man who attempted to escape from it, while the former fiercely went about here and there on the attack, mopping up the defeated and any remaining pockets of resistance. To prevent the Republican leaders escaping and forming another army, Antony posted cavalry along the main routes and exit points from the battlefield. Rhascus the Thracian, with his knowledge of the area, led some of Antony's cavalry up the mountain. They surrounded the fortifications, tracked down those who were fleeing, and kept watch on those inside the forts overnight. Antony reportedly spent the night under arms, and we are given the grisly detail that he used the spoils and piles of dead bodies as defences, while Norbanus took over the duties of Octavian at midnight, when the latter retired because of his illness.[45]

Meanwhile other troops of the enemy, having broken through the left wing of the Republicans, proceeded to surround Brutus. True to his noble character, in the face of this crisis he was now said to have fought for victory with all the bravery possible of a soldier and commander. However, Cassius' demoralised troops contributed greatly to the downfall of the Republicans, filling Brutus' army with dejection and confusion. Nonetheless, many men continued to fight bravely, attempting to defend Brutus, and paid for this with their lives. Among them was Brutus' cousin and brother-in-law, Marcus, the son of Cato and brother of Porcia. As his line was giving way, he refused to surrender or flee, continuing to challenge the enemy boldly until he was finally overpowered. Seeing his men begin to retreat, he removed his helmet and, proudly crying aloud that he was the son of Cato, fell down dead upon the many corpses of the enemy whom he himself had killed.[46]

Another act of bravery was carried out by one of Brutus' comrades, named Lucilius. Witnessing some barbarian horsemen furiously pursuing the chief Liberator, he told them that he himself was Brutus in order to draw them away. Feigning fear of Octavian, but asking to be taken to Antony, Lucilius thus succeeded in tricking the horsemen, who duly sent some messengers ahead to inform Antony and led their captive to him by night. Some of Antony's men were said to have felt pity for the mighty Brutus, supposedly brought so low, while others considered him unworthy of his great reputation for allowing himself thus to be captured alive by barbarians. Antony himself was unsure how to receive Brutus, and hesitated, but Lucilius boldly stepped forward and proclaimed that no enemy had taken or could capture the real Brutus, and declared that he was prepared to pay with his life. Antony was so impressed by the man's loyalty and bravery that he embraced him, and told the horsemen that he would have been unsure how to treat Brutus, but that they had brought him a friend instead. He then placed him under the charge of one of his friends. Later Lucilius became a trusted aide of the Caesarian general and was to be found by his side after his defeat by Octavian at the Battle of Actium. This anecdote serves to demonstrate the nobility of the man who could thus inspire such selfless loyalty. Brutus himself was thus able to abscond from the battlefield safely. However, little hope now remained either for the noble Roman or his beloved Republic.[47]

Chapter Fourteen

The End: Death and Legacy

The End of the Republic

The Death of Brutus

With the second Battle of Philippi having been fought and disastrously lost, Brutus himself now retreated towards the mountains, from where he could see the enemy below: he kept with him a considerable force, which Appian numbered at fewer than four full legions, and with which he intended either to return to his camp during the night or to reach the sea. Deciding to address his officers instead of the troops, he was to receive a disappointingly negative response: despite having pushed Brutus into battle against his better judgement, they were now unwilling to fight their way back through the enemy's lines to reach their camp and rejoin their comrades there. They hoped instead to make terms with the enemy and, reportedly, some of them already had: according to Appian, it was this that made Brutus realise he was no longer of use to his country, and drove him to suicide. However, in Plutarch's account, Brutus did not believe that many of his men had been killed in battle, so Statilius, the Epicurean, agreed to attempt to return to the camp. Statilius had remained loyally by Cato's side until his death, and was one of the men to whom Brutus had decided it was best not to reveal the assassination plot at an early stage. However, he was now to be found serving Brutus as faithfully as he had his uncle. Having managed to reach the camp, Statilius lit a blaze as a sign that he had found safety there. Brutus expected him to return promptly, but he did not: he was killed by the enemy as he returned, remaining completely loyal to the Republican cause until the very end.[1]

All ways out were now barred to Brutus, with Antony's cavalry guarding every possible escape route. With all hope lost, Brutus advanced no further once it became dark: having crossed a brook with steep wooded banks, he sat down with some of his friends and officers in a hollow behind a large rock, remaining under arms for the night. One of his friends present was the philosopher, Volumnius, whose record of these final hours of Brutus is used by the ancient writers to produce their accounts: he recalled that Brutus, looking up at the starry sky, quoted two verses of poetry, one of which Volumnius was unable to recall, but the other being a line spoken by Euripides' tragic heroine, Medea:

Oh, Zeus, do not forget the author of these ills![2]

Appian claims that these words referred to Antony, who later repeated them himself when regretting his current partnership with the deadly Octavian, since he could have made a compact with Brutus and Cassius instead. However, they could equally have applied to Caesar or Octavian. It seems fitting that the ever-studious Brutus should have reverted from warrior to scholar in his final hours. Similarly, according to the perhaps less reliable version of events here by Dio Cassius, Brutus, on the point of suicide, also cited some words of Hercules, from an unknown ancient Greek tragedy:

Oh wretched Virtue, you were just a word,
And yet I followed you as if you were real;
But now, it seems, you were but Fortune's slave.[3]

This quotation is intended to show Brutus, in his final hopeless hours, doubtful of that which he had always held dearest, virtue. This had so often steered the path of his life, but now, at this crucial time, it was failing to be duly rewarded. Whether Brutus truly spoke these verses or not, which has been doubted in the case of the Hercules quotation,[4] it seems that he was now in a philosophical and contemplative mood: he was also said to have recalled by name each of the comrades who had fallen defending him. He was particularly affected by the suicide of Labeo, who had been involved in the conspiracy against Caesar, and the loss of Flavius, his prefect of engineers. Plutarch here records another anecdotal detail: as one of Brutus' party took a helmet to the river to fetch some water for them both, a noise was heard from the opposite direction and so Volumnius and the shield-bearer, Dardanus, went to investigate; when they returned and asked for some water, Brutus replied with a 'very expressive smile' that it had all been drunk, but that they would obtain some more; therefore, the same man was sent down to the river again, but this time he was wounded by the enemy, and only narrowly managed to escape.[5]

The ancient accounts suggest that Brutus had, for some time, been prepared to face death for the sake of his cause: we saw that he had made a kind of suicide pact with Cassius before the first Battle of Philippi, stating that he had already given his life to his country on the Ides of March; he had also supposedly written to Atticus soon before the end, declaring that he had the best fortune possible, since he would either conquer and restore liberty to the Roman people, or die and be freed from servitude; Valerius Maximus also records an anecdote in which Brutus went to the final Battle of Philippi with confidence, claiming that either all would be well or he would not be caring. Now, late into the night after this final battle, Brutus finally realised that his Republican fight was at an end. Firstly he conversed with some of those closest to him: when he sat down and talked with his servant, Cleitus, the man was unable to reply through his weeping; Brutus then spoke privately to Dardanus; finally, he addressed Volumnius in Greek, recalling their shared philosophies, before begging him to hold the sword so that he might help him end his life. However, Volumnius and the rest all refused to aid his suicide. When another member of the party suggested that they should instead quickly escape, the dignified Brutus got up and replied that they should indeed flee, but using their hands not their feet. Resigned to his fate, and reportedly smiling, Brutus shook the hand of each man, and declared his happiness that none of his friends had let him down, blaming fortune for failing his country only. Self-assured, he claimed to be in a more enviable position than his enemies, for he realised that he would leave behind a reputation for virtue which, for all their wealth and arms, would far surpass theirs; furthermore, he declared that no one would ever view such wicked men, who killed the good and the just, as fit to rule.[6]

Then Brutus, after genuinely urging his companions to save themselves, withdrew a short distance with just a few friends. One of these was Strato of Epirus, a close friend with whom Brutus had studied rhetoric, and whom he now placed next to himself. The details of Brutus' final suicidal actions vary slightly. One version has Brutus grasping his own sword with both hands and running himself through. Alternatively, it was Strato who reluctantly performed the ultimate act of loyalty for Brutus: when ordered by his friend to stab him, Strato urged him to reconsider; Brutus therefore called one of his servants, which prompted Strato to step up to the awful task; as a friend, he refused to come up short next to a servant in carrying out Brutus' final command, if he had truly reached that decision. Strato then either thrust a sword into the side of Brutus who, courageously, did not flinch or turn away, or he held the sword for him, averting his eyes as Brutus bravely ran directly onto the sword with such force that it transfixed in his breast and killed him immediately. The final details of his life are, therefore, somewhat sketchy, but he clearly chose to die by the sword, and his friend Strato was involved in some way. Furthermore, Brutus' courage and determination is apparent to the bitter end.[7]

Testament to the nobility of Brutus' character, and the admiration that he could inspire in men, is the respectful treatment of his dead body by his enemy, Antony. He and Brutus did always appear to share a mutual respect for each other and, although quite different characters, it was political circumstances that forced them into becoming enemies in war: if the pair could have reached an earlier accommodation, which at one point did seem possible until external factors, principally Octavian and Cicero, interfered, the Roman state may well have emerged somewhat differently. Indeed, Antony once claimed that Brutus was the only one of Caesar's assassins to have had honourable intentions.[8] As he stood next to his corpse, Antony is said to have gently reproached Brutus for the death of his brother, Gaius, while holding Hortensius chiefly responsible for the execution: as we learned earlier, Antony vengefully had him killed over Gaius' tomb.[9] Antony then cast his own purple military cloak, said to be of great value, over Brutus' body, instructing his freedman to attend to the cremation. When he later learned that this freedman had stolen the robe and other items for the funeral, Antony had him put to death. He then, fittingly, sent Brutus' ashes home to his mother, Servilia. Some accounts claim that Antony had only the body of Brutus, since Octavian had sent his head back to Rome to be cast down dramatically at the feet of Caesar's statue. However, misfortune befell Brutus' decapitated head, when it was thrown overboard during a storm on the sea crossing from Dyrrachium to Italy, presumably because the crew considered it to be bringing bad luck by attracting inclement weather: if this is the true version of events, it was a most undignified ending for the noble Roman of such mighty and enduring reputation.[10]

The highly principled and virtuous Brutus would have been aged just 43 when his life ended thus, far away from his beloved Rome. Indeed, when he died at Philippi, in November 42 BC, he had not seen the city since fleeing with Cassius in the wake of Caesar's assassination, two-and-a-half years previously. While Cato may have been the ultimate Republican, the death of his nephew, Brutus, would signal the absolute end of the Republican cause. With Cassius already dead, Brutus can thus, in many ways, be considered the last Republican standing and, unlike his uncle, he did die fighting for his cause, giving up and committing suicide only when he had been completely defeated, and not simply to avoid having to live life under a tyrant. Brutus must have realised, as he saw his men defecting, that the number of staunch Republicans was gradually dwindling and, without those leading figures such as Cassius, Cicero, and Decimus Brutus as a rallying point for supporters to the cause, it was a losing battle: he had made an extremely valiant effort but he now no longer felt he had the ability to defend the state.[11]

Aftermath: The Remnants of the Republicans

As we have already seen, many of Brutus' men wished to desert the Republican army in order to come to terms with the Caesarians who, by now, were clearly the victors of this war. According to Appian, Brutus' army, consisting of approximately 14,000 men, sent envoys to Antony and Octavian: they received a pardon and were divided between the armies of the two generals. Brutus' men in the forts also surrendered to the Caesarian leaders, who handed the forts and camps of their Republican enemy over to their own men for plundering.[12]

One of those officers who now received a pardon was the future Augustan poet, Horace: later, he would recall his time as a soldier at Philippi in his poetry. As a member of the circle of the literary patron, Maecenas, he would become a close associate of Octavian, or Augustus, as he would by then be known. Other men from Brutus' army took refuge on the nearby Republican supply island, Thasos, placing themselves under the leadership of Messalla, Brutus' fellow commander, and Bibulus, Brutus' stepson. Despite having access to a sizeable army, ships, money and other supplies, these two men declined the opportunity to continue to lead the fight in the name of the Republican cause, and decided instead to make an arrangement with the enemy: when Antony arrived on the island, they handed over the money, weapons and provisions stored there. Both men gained the favour of Antony. Bibulus received a naval command under Antony, and often acted as an intermediary between him and Octavian, until his death while governing Syria. Messalla remained with Antony until his relationship with Cleopatra, when he then chose to join the side of Octavian instead, and subsequently held a naval command against Antony at the Battle of Actium: Octavian later praised him for having been such a loyal supporter, despite having once been on the side of Brutus, and Messalla replied honestly that he always chose the better and more just cause. He later became a literary patron under

Augustus, once the latter had gained sole power over the Roman Empire. Plutarch records how it was Messalla who introduced Strato to Octavian, tearfully, as the man who had done the last kind service for Brutus: Octavian supposedly therefore received Strato well, and he always found him to be brave, especially at Actium.[13]

Not all of Brutus' men received a pardon from Antony and Octavian, however. Some of those distinguished men who were captured received particularly cruel treatment at the hands of Octavian: these captives, as they were led out in chains, respectfully hailed Antony as *imperator*, while fiercely abusing Octavian to his face. Among them was Favonius, the associate of Cato who had been excluded from the assassination plot because of his opposition to civil war, but who nonetheless joined the conspirators soon after Caesar's murder: he was subsequently executed.[14] Other men from the Republican army either fought on valiantly to the death, as did Cato's son, Marcus, and Cassius' nephew, Lucius, or committed suicide in the face of defeat, as did Labeo, the conspirator, and Marcus Livius Drusus Claudianus, the father of Octavian's future wife, Livia.[15]

Meanwhile others from the Republican army succeeded in escaping with their lives, fleeing by sea and assembling together elsewhere. Some fled to the island of Samothrace (Samothraki), where Atticus had reportedly sent supplies from Epirus to aid those Republicans who had survived Philippi: Atticus had succeeded in remaining neutral throughout the civil war, while giving financial support to those in need, and was said to have continued to treat Servilia with respect after the death of Brutus. Others fled to Ephesus and took sanctuary in the temple there: when Antony later arrived, he pardoned all, including Cassius' brother, Lucius; however, he did not extend this mercy to Petronius, one of the conspirators, nor to a certain man who had betrayed Dolabella.[16]

Many Republicans fled to Gaius Cassius Parmensis, one of Caesar's assassins. This Cassius had been left in command of a fleet and some troops in Asia, by Brutus and Cassius; having learned of Cassius' suicide, he selected thirty Rhodian ships and destroyed the rest to prevent a rebellion, before sailing away. He was joined by a man named Clodius,[17] whom Brutus had sent to Rhodes with thirteen ships: Clodius found the island in revolt after Brutus' suicide, and so took away the garrison of 3,000 men. Paullus, the brother of Lepidus the Triumvir, supplied additional forces which he had previously used to bring Crete under Brutus' control, and Decimus Turullius also united with them, bringing a sizeable fleet and funds which he had earlier extorted from Rhodes. Together they attracted various Republicans from around Asia, including many of those who had escaped from Philippi via Thasos by sea. This newly formed fleet sailed to the Adriatic to join Murcus and Ahenobarbus, who had enjoyed some success there with their reasonably sized force. They then split in two, with half remaining there with Ahenobarbus, while the rest were led by Murcus to Sicily, where they joined Sextus Pompeius, who became a refuge for many of the fleeing Republicans. Ahenobarbus meanwhile continued to patrol the Adriatic with his seventy ships, two legions of soldiers, and other troops including gladiators. He succeeded in devastating regions, including making an attack on Brundisium, where he captured or burned Octavian's triremes, and shut the inhabitants up inside the city while plundering the region. While Murcus was later put to death by Sextus on a false accusation of treachery, Ahenobarbus, the grandfather of the future Emperor Nero, eventually surrendered to Antony to whom he became reconciled thanks to the intercession of Pollio. He held high commands under Antony, and became consul in 32 BC. Shortly before the Battle of Actium, Antony's soldiers, disgusted by their general's relationship with Cleopatra, offered Ahenobarbus the command; instead, suffering from a fever, he chose to desert to Octavian, only to die a few days later.[18]

Among the men who fled to Cassius Parmensis, sailed to the Adriatic, and then followed Murcus to join Sextus Pompeius, was Cicero's son, Marcus. He received a military command under Sextus, but later obtained a pardon from Octavian, who made him *pontifex* by way of an apology for having betrayed his father in the proscriptions. Cicero fought with Octavian against his father's nemesis, Antony, at Actium. Later he became consul and reportedly announced Antony's demise by nailing a notice on the rostra, where once his father's head and hand had been cruelly displayed by that same man.[19]

After the battles were over, Antony and Octavian celebrated their victory at Philippi with a magnificent sacrifice, praising their armies for their success, and Antony also enlarged Philippi itself, which was now to become a Roman colony, setting up altars in honour of their victory. In order to reward the soldiers, the generals came to an agreement in which it was decided that Antony was to undertake the task of restoring order in the east, while imposing levies in order to raise necessary funds, while Octavian, still suffering from his illness, was to return to Italy to distribute lands to the veterans and settle the colonies. The troops, including those Republicans who had come over from Brutus' defeated army, were now divided up between the two generals in preparation for their respective tasks. On his travels in the east, Antony gave those places that had recently suffered at the hands of Brutus and Cassius tax relief, in recognition of their loyalty in resisting the Liberators.[20] Before they parted at Philippi, Antony and Octavian also made a renewed compact regarding the division of the provinces, manoeuvring the relatively insignificant third member of the Triumvirate, Lepidus, further out of the way, and leaving the path clear for this to become a two-way struggle for sole power, in the not-too-distant future.[21]

Therefore, the assassination of Caesar had, ironically, served only to catalyse the end of the Roman Republic, which was the exact opposite of what the Liberators, who had struck him down on the Ides of March 44 BC, had intended with their idealistic vision of a Republican state. The end of the war at Philippi, between Brutus and Cassius on the side of liberty, and Antony and Octavian fighting in the name of vengeance for Caesar, achieved nothing more than to herald a new era of civil war. It did not bring freedom or peace, nor did it restore the traditional Republican government, as Brutus had wished. For, following Philippi, Antony and Octavian would spend the next decade moving from an uneasy alliance to outright war, a situation that Plutarch claims Brutus himself had predicted.[22] This would finally come to a head at the Battle of Actium in 31 BC, with Octavian emerging victorious. Having learned from the mistakes of his dead adoptive father, he would then cautiously establish himself as the first Roman Emperor, Augustus: tyranny lived and an Empire was born, while the Republic had truly died on the battlefield at Philippi along with Brutus.[23]

Legacy

Life After Death: Birth of a Republican Hero

Brutus was dead, but his mighty reputation, thanks to his unwavering devotion to his principles, was far from over: he had acquired such renown during his lifetime that his reputation lived on in immediate history and far beyond, and still exists to this day. Despite the unsuccessful outcome at Philippi and his failure to rescue the Republic, Brutus had, in many ways, achieved his goals: he had successfully emulated the ancestors whose legendary status had pursued and driven him throughout his life.[24] For, although he had not succeeded in overthrowing tyranny, as they had, he nonetheless went down in history as one of the most famous tyrant slayers ever to have lived. Furthermore, in the years immediately following his demise at Philippi, he continued to be admired by contemporaries and their descendants living in the early Empire, while his name and reputation was often treated with caution, and even fear and contempt, by the early Emperors.

It was not only the name of Caesar, then, that had an enduring power: so too did that of Brutus. Considering that his enemy, Caesar's heir, was victorious and a master of propaganda, it is all the more surprising that Brutus' reputation was allowed to survive intact and even prevail. Octavian had portrayed Brutus and Cassius as enemies of the state, whom it was necessary to punish with death in order to avenge Caesar's murder, and he was eager to reinforce this view. Before he returned to Rome after Philippi, the people in the city voted many honours to the two conquering generals and also celebrated a thanksgiving festival for their victory, which lasted for almost a whole year. However, according to Dio Cassius, the senate, consisting of many Republican sympathisers, unwillingly did the latter: they were under the direct orders of Octavian himself, who wished to hold a festival in recognition of the vengeance that had been meted out to Caesar's assassins. Octavian was also to establish more permanent commemorations both to honour the memory of his murdered adoptive father and to celebrate his own victory over Caesar's killers. In 29 BC, following his victory at Actium, he completed and dedicated the Temple of the Divine Julius, which was erected on the site where Caesar's body had been burned by the frenzied mob in the forum. The Temple of Mars Ultor, or Mars the Avenger, was finally inaugurated in 2 BC, forty years after Octavian had originally vowed it before the Battle of Philippi if he should be victorious over his father's assassins. The remains of both of these temples can still be seen in Rome, more than 2,000 years after they were built, proving their lasting legacy.[25]

Furthermore, Octavian carefully cultivated an image of himself as the dutiful son obeying filial obligations to his father, Caesar, by avenging his murder: he thereby diminished the negative impression of his bellicose behaviour and the ensuing bloodshed, by thus justifying his actions. The literature and art of the Augustan age would be littered with imagery recalling his legendary Julian ancestry, which could be traced back to Venus through her grandson Iulus. A particular association was made between Augustus and Aeneas, son of Venus and father of Iulus, especially in Virgil's national epic, *Aeneid*: the portrayal of Aeneas carrying his father, Anchises, on his shoulders as they fled the fallen city of Troy was the ultimate symbol of filial duty.[26] Augustus himself also later set down in words his own version of the post-assassination events, including foremost how he supposedly restored the liberty of the Republic: this was always his official stance, although, in reality, he patently established the Roman Empire with his one-man rule. His funerary document recording his life's deeds, the *Res Gestae*, never mentions his enemies by name: in it, Augustus carefully refers to Brutus and Cassius as his father's murderers, whom he legally and duly punished:

> *I drove into exile those who killed my father, avenging their crime through the due process of law; and afterwards, when they waged war on the Republic, I twice defeated them in battle.*[27]

However, like Antony, Augustus also seemed to display some measure of respect for Brutus or, at least, allowed the respect of others to continue to exist. There are anecdotal tales in the ancient texts suggesting this. One such story involves Lucius Sestius, Brutus' proquaestor, who had always fought beside him: he was proscribed after he refused to betray Brutus to Antony's men, but was later pardoned and became a friend of Augustus. When, in 23 BC, Augustus finally resigned from the consulship which he had held since 31 BC, in order to symbolise a return to the Republic, he chose Sestius to replace him as suffect consul. Sestius was a suitable choice, since he always kept the Republican Brutus' memory alive by displaying images of him, and delivering eulogies on him. Augustus was said to be impressed with the man's loyalty and, when he was once visiting Sestius, instead of demanding that the images of Brutus be removed, he praised him for it.[28] Another similar tale records how Augustus enjoyed a somewhat unnerving and slightly tyrannical joke at the expense of the city of Mediolanum. The city had erected a bronze statue of Brutus, which was said to be a good likeness and of impressive craftsmanship, in honour of his lenient governorship of Cisalpine Gaul in 46 BC. When visiting the city during his reign, Augustus saw the statue of his father's murderer and defeated foe still standing: he peremptorily summoned the magistrates of Mediolanum in order to accuse them of harbouring an enemy; however he was merely toying with them and was instead said to be impressed that they had remained true to a friend, even in his misfortune; praising them, he ordered that the statue should remain in place.[29]

Augustus had this attitude towards Brutus' statue, despite it being called upon in the name of freedom and the subject being hailed as a hero, during his reign: Brutus was referred to as the founder and defender of Roman laws and liberties, a description which we can imagine that he would have proudly embraced and considered an honour.[30] Indeed his name and legend had a certain value and quality, and he assumed a status not dissimilar to that of Cato, his uncle, the staunch Republican, very soon after his death. He, along with Cato, was a man to be emulated and his Republican idealism, along with his noble virtue, made an impact on the generations immediately following his death. While Augustus apparently felt secure enough to tolerate these honours to his enemy's memory, the heroic status of Brutus nonetheless inspired fear in Augustus' successors who, with their more tyrannical natures, ruled the Empire harshly.

One modern scholar refers to the heroic status of Cato and Brutus as a kind of cult to which oppressed Romans of the early Empire could cling: such men, who objected to the tyrannical rule under which they were living, would focus and call on these two Republican stalwarts as a subtle, or otherwise, indication of their own feelings about tyranny and the current state of affairs in Rome.[31] However, the early Emperors often considered such points of view too dangerous to be expressed freely and so crushed them. One notable example of a man suffering for his supposedly subversive views was the case of the senator Aulus Cremutius Cordus, who, in AD 25, was living under the rule of Tiberius. He was a historian who had been writing since the reign of Augustus, and had compiled annals covering the civil war period down to the age of Augustus: his mistake here was glorifying the Liberators, for in his work he praised Brutus and designated Cassius the last of the Romans. In reality he had clashed with Sejanus, the infamous prefect of the Praetorian Guard who secured power for himself through his influence over Tiberius: Cordus' writings merely served as a pretext on which to accuse him, among other even flimsier excuses such as insufficient respect for Caesar and Augustus. However, Augustus, who had read these annals, had approved them, and there were others whose words about Brutus and Cassius had survived, such as those of Brutus' stepson, Bibulus, and his friend, the philosopher Volumnius, as well as the writings of Livy, Messalla and Pollio. According to the speech that Tacitus places in Cordus' mouth, he claimed in his defence that many other authors had been allowed to honour the acts of Brutus and Cassius without referring to them as parricides and plunderers, according to the current fashion, and asked what threat he could possibly be posing in thus eulogising the dead. After his prosecution, Cordus starved himself to death and his books were burned. However, his daughter, Marcia, secretly preserved copies which she was later able to republish, during the reign of Caligula, although they were censored versions omitting the offending passages.[32] Similarly, when the senator Publius Clodius Thrasea Paetus chose to withdraw from his political duties once the reign of Nero became too unbearable, accusations of treason followed. Among these was his supposed emulation of Brutus and Cassius, whose birthdays he reportedly used to celebrate. He had also, perhaps imprudently, written a life of Cato. He was duly forced to commit suicide.[33] Another man ordered to kill himself under Nero's tyranny was the poet Lucan. He fell from favour at the same time as his famous uncle, Seneca, and together they were implicated in the so-called Pisonian conspiracy against Nero in AD 65, through which the Emperor disposed of several noble Romans around him who had somehow become an inconvenience. It is notable that, in his epic, *Civil War*, Lucan described events at Pharsalus using the themes of liberty and tyranny prominently, and revering the figure of Brutus as well as openly glorifying tyrannicide.[34]

It certainly seemed necessary to the early Emperors to make an effort to silence the memory of Brutus and Cassius, even many years after their defeat and demise. This is particularly demonstrated by the funeral of Junia Tertia, the sister of Brutus and wife of Cassius, in AD 22: among the many images of her ancestry on display, those of two of her closest male relatives, her brother and husband, were missing. It seems that more than sixty years after their deaths at Philippi, the family of Junia Tertia were afraid to advertise their association with these tyrannicides because of the threat that their Republican heroism still posed to the current establishment. However, although these rulers attempted to suppress any glorified memory of these Republican heroes, Brutus and Cassius emerged with their reputations intact, if not even stronger than before: the portraits of these two men were said to be all the more notable by their absence.[35]

Clearly, then, the reputation of Brutus had a power attached to it, extending far beyond the time of his death: he had successfully emulated the heroic actions of his ancestors and in turn became a figure of inspiration to be idolised and emulated by succeeding generations oppressed by tyranny. This apparently far outweighed any of his more dubious actions along the way, since Brutus did stray from the path of righteousness more than once; however, while the ancient authors acknowledged these uncharacteristic moments, they either attempted to excuse Brutus' actions or accepted them but nonetheless could not deny his good qualities, leaving the general impression of their admiration for an inherently moral man whose intentions were most often noble. It is this version of Brutus and his unimpeachable character that has continued to exist long into the future, even passing into the world of legend: indeed, one scholar aptly described his virtue as a 'half-mythical figure'.[36] Furthermore, Brutus himself seemed all too aware of this. According to Plutarch, as he calmly prepared for suicide, he faced his death without fear, secure in the prophetic knowledge that he was leaving behind a mighty reputation for virtue. Indeed, this was to be the lasting legacy of Marcus Junius Brutus.[37]

Epilogue

Thus concludes the biography of Marcus Junius Brutus: the details of a life as far as they are discernible to us from the ancient sources. This book is intended to serve as a comprehensive survey of the life of Brutus, as far as it is possible to reconstruct. The events and episodes that make up this biography are, of course, the ones that we have according to extant ancient texts only: therefore, it is entirely likely that there are considerably more significant details that are not available to us, and so cannot be presented here. It will have become apparent that, until his later life, the details we have mainly offer a series of individual episodes from Brutus' life. Nevertheless, there are sufficient events recorded here to prove that Marcus Junius Brutus is, indeed, worthy of attention and that a fresh biography dedicated to his life has been somewhat overdue.

The historian is completely at the mercy of the surviving traditions, although at times it is possible to see where there are glaring errors. For example, the contemporary accounts of Cicero, which are assumed to be the most accurate because they were written at the time, are nevertheless subject to strong bias. However, when there is no other evidence to consult, it is necessary to take for granted the available narrations, mostly written at least 100 years after Brutus had died, and follow the most acceptable or likely version of events. It is clear from the ancient sources that there are variations on the events, especially in the wake of Caesar's assassination, but a main thread through the middle can mostly be discerned. Therefore, although we may not have entire certainty surrounding the exact details of Brutus' movements in the days, months and years after the Ides of March, his main actions and intentions should nevertheless be apparent.

The traditional impression of Brutus that has been passed down is that of the noble and virtuous man. While this remains the prevailing image of Brutus to emerge from the ancient texts, we may have discovered a new aspect to him here, by taking into account all the details and events in his life that are available in the ancient texts: Brutus was not always the upright moral character that he himself, Shakespeare and history have often led us to believe. Sometimes circumstances forced his hand, but at other times he does not seem to have been guided by his principles, even abandoning them altogether. The most prominent example of Brutus' dubious behaviour is the Salamis affair and his ruthless extortion of the city during his early career, but there are also hints that he behaved in a questionable manner at other times: however, these actions are often swept aside or excused by the ancient authors. Certainly Brutus was not perfect, and could be quite a difficult character, as Cicero and Cassius especially discovered on occasion. However, his reputation for remaining unfailingly devoted to his high moral principles outweighed these lapses in judgement and character, and also won him much respect from his contemporaries and their successors. Considering that Brutus was on the losing side, it is all the more remarkable that a predominantly favourable tradition of him has been allowed to pass down through the ages, and must be to his credit.

Brutus' dedication to liberty and the Republic certainly cannot be denied, driven, as he was, by his ancestral familial obligation, and absolute conviction in the just nature of his cause. It is clear that he was led first and foremost by his devotion to the state, and it is ironic, then, that his actions ultimately resulted in the demise of the Republic that he was so desperate to preserve. It is apparent that his life was inextricably bound up with the events of the end of the Roman Republic, making a survey of the political and military occurrences of the Roman state after the death of Caesar necessary in order to understand Brutus' actions in the wake of the assassination. It is this period of his life that is, naturally, most detailed in the ancient sources. It cannot be denied that the late Roman Republic was a particularly complicated political period: throughout this time leading politicians freely and frequently changed sides and factions, as suited their personal agenda and situation, and indeed it must have been difficult to behave otherwise in such turbulent circumstances. Brutus may well have had a strong moral Republican sense, which he never abandoned, but this was a survival tactic employed by him when the need arose too: we witnessed this, for example, when he was to be found with Pompey, his hitherto detested enemy, at the Battle of Pharsalus, only to abandon the defeated side swiftly in order to be pardoned by, and reconciled with, Caesar, whom he had similarly not held in regard up until this point. Therefore it was by no means clear that Brutus would then change his stance again and we certainly should not imagine that the assassination was something that he always had secretly planned, even taking account of his legendary ancestry and early dislike of Caesar. The indications pointing to this are merely coincidences that have been picked up on by later writers, in an irresistible and opportune fashion. The point here is that we should beware of reading Brutus' life as always leading up to the assassination: that view is imposed by the power of hindsight. For this reason, we should also try to give due attention to the other events of his life, as far as we are able to discern and reconstruct them, in order to understand Marcus Junius Brutus, the man, as a whole. It would be naive to be blinded entirely by the momentous action of his later life and, similarly, we should not be influenced by the famous literary version of this figure presented by Shakespeare.

Therefore, while the assassination of Julius Caesar will undoubtedly be the ultimate focus of any biography of Brutus, I hope that this book has suitably demonstrated that there was far more to this mighty Roman than the singular event that later seems to have defined him. From birth he was destined to be involved in the Roman political world and, indeed, he soon embarked on a public career during this most turbulent period of the late Roman Republic. Unfortunately we can never know exactly what would have come of Brutus, should he have lived beyond the age of 43, but it can reasonably be surmised that he would have remained an extremely significant figure. Had the murder of Caesar never happened, or had the Liberators been successful at Philippi, Brutus surely nevertheless would have continued to have an impact on the history of the late Roman Republic. Indeed, at many turns in this biography, we have witnessed how the course of events could so easily have turned out differently. Often, the impression is that the Caesarian victory was inevitable but, once again, this can be attributed to hindsight and the propaganda of the victor, Octavian: indeed, an examination of the ancient accounts in detail indicates the opposite was quite likely. The fight for the survival of the Republic was an evenly fought one from the beginning, until the tragic and unnecessary suicide of Cassius caused a total imbalance between the two sides. Had the Liberators triumphed, as was a real possibility, there would have been a different colour to the Roman world of the late 40s BC. However, this would undoubtedly only have served to delay the inevitable: it is extremely probable that, eventually, there would have been a battle for supremacy and the creation of a Roman Empire. History determined that this decisive battle would take place a decade later, at Actium in 31 BC, between Brutus' conquerors at Philippi, and that Octavian, or Augustus, was to emerge triumphant as the first Roman Emperor from the ashes of the Liberators and their beloved Republic.

Therefore, Brutus' death signalled the end of his beloved Republic and left the field clear for the beginning of a new chapter in Roman history: the establishment of that to which he was most opposed, a monarchy under the title of Empire. Nonetheless, this could not prevent the birth of a hero and symbol of the Republic, in the guise of Marcus Junius Brutus.

Notes

Prologue

1. On the hazards of biography, both ancient and modern, see the introduction to Grant (1999).

Chapter 1

1. Livy narrates the legend of Lucius Junius Brutus at 1.56–59 and 2.1–7, covering events from approximately 534–509 BC, the year of this Brutus' death.
2. Valerius Maximus 7.3.2 also relates this episode, with the additional detail that Lucius Brutus hid gold intended as a gift for Apollo in a hollow stick, fearing that it would not be safe to honour him openly.
3. Valerius Maximus 5.8.1 also gives a brief summary of Lucius Brutus' difficult choice to stand firm by his nation over being a father.
4. Gaius Servilius Ahala features in Livy 4.13–16, 4.21, covering the years 439 BC to 436 BC, where he quietly drops out of the pages of history. Livy goes on to narrate events concerning a Gaius Servilius Ahala becoming consul in 427 BC and master of horse to the dictator, Quintus Servilius Priscus, in 418 BC, but these are three separate figures: Broughton (1951–1960) p.618.
5. Plutarch, *Brutus* 1.5 describes Ahala as approaching Maelius as if about to begin a conversation, thus lulling him into a false sense of security before stabbing him.
6. Although Livy is silent on this, other accounts relate how Ahala was forced to go into voluntary exile due to the popular violence arising from these accusations: see Cicero, *On His House* 86, *On the Republic* 1.6; Valerius Maximus 5.3.2g. Ahala's actions are always depicted as heroic, especially by Cicero, the friend of Brutus: see also *Against Catiline* 1.3, *For Milo* 8, 30.
7. For example the Pisistratids were tyrants banished from Athens in 510 BC because of a love affair, at approximately the same time, and for a similar reason, as the Tarquins were said to be expelled from Rome.
8. Plutarch, *Brutus* 1.6–8 reports that hatred of Brutus, caused by his assassination of Julius Caesar, was the source of denials that Lucius left any children. Dio Cassius 44.12 clearly follows this hostile tradition. Plutarch also tells us that the philosopher Poseidonius upheld the tradition that Lucius had a third, infant, son.
9. MacMullen (1992) pp.296–297, n.7 observes that the derivation from Lucius Junius Brutus was already in existence in the second century BC. See also de Rose Evans (1995) p.25.
10. See especially MacMullen (1992) pp.7–10, Clarke (1981) pp.9–10, and Africa (1978) pp.616–617 on Brutus' ancestral awareness.
11. Cornelius Nepos, *Atticus* 18.3; Cicero, *To Atticus* 13.40. Atticus, who successfully remained impartial during the political struggles of the late Republic, despite his choice of close associates, was also an intimate friend of Cicero and many of the orator's surviving letters are addressed to him. On the close friendship of Atticus and Brutus, see Cornelius Nepos, *Atticus* 8.
12. Cicero, *Philippics* 2.26.
13. See de Rose Evans (1995) p.30 and Alföldi (1956) pp.66, 77.
14. For a discussion of the dating of the coins, see below, Chapter 2, pp.21–22.
15. Clarke (1981) p.10.

16. In his history of oratory, entitled *Brutus* in honour of the addressee, Cicero tells us that Hortensius was advocate for the first time ten years before Brutus was born: Hortensius first came to the bar at the age of 19, in 95 BC, placing Brutus' birth in 85 BC. However, a less reliable reference is Velleius Paterculus 2.72.1: he states Brutus' age at his death as 37 years, but he certainly died in 42 BC, after the Battle of Philippi, so this would incorrectly make his year of birth 80 or 79 BC.
17. Cicero, *For Publius Quinctius* 65. At *On the Agrarian Law* 2.89–98, he expresses his contempt for the idea that there should be a rival colony to Rome.
18. Cicero, *Brutus* 222, *For Publius Quinctius* 65–69. This was possibly Cicero's earliest case, in which he was defending Quinctius, who had inherited his brother's half of an estate and was attempting to clear debts, but was being blocked by his brother's business partner, Naevius; Brutus' father, as tribune, was asked to postpone the trial until Quinctius, whose property Naevius was seizing, returned to Rome.
19. For a useful and accessible summary of the main political events during the late Roman Republic, see Matyszak (2003). On the anti-Sullan tendencies of the Iunii Bruti during the 80s BC, see pp.243, 300 of E. S. Gruen (1968), *Roman Politics and the Criminal Courts, 149–78 B.C.*, Cambridge, Massachusetts.
20. Plutarch, *Pompey* 16; Orosius 5.22. See also Seager (2002) pp.30–32, who suggests that the elder Brutus would have been declared an enemy (*hostis*) along with Lepidus. The elder Brutus' death is often depicted as cruel and treacherous in ancient accounts: see, for example, Cicero, *To Atticus* 9.14.2; Valerius Maximus 6.2.8.
21. Appian, *Civil War* 1.35–36, 1.44.
22. Clarke (1981) p.12, however, observes that Brutus' adoptive father has not been identified with certainty.
23. Plutarch, *Cato the Younger* 21.2–3.
24. Although Plutarch, *Pompey* 44.2 mentions only two sisters.
25. See the family tree of Cato, in the genealogical tables of Syme (2002).
26. Velleius Paterculus 2.88. Appian, *Civil War* 4.50 states that his mother was also implicated.
27. Cicero, *To Atticus* 6.1.
28. Since he was about to assume the *toga virilis* on the day of Caesar's assassination: Plutarch, *Brutus* 14.4.
29. Cicero, *To Atticus* 14.20.
30. Tacitus, *Annals* 3.76; see below, Chapter 14, p.214.
31. On which, see Africa (1978) pp.603–604, 607–609.
32. Cicero, *To Atticus* 2.24.3; Plutarch, *Brutus* 5; Suetonius, *The Deified Julius* 50.
33. Suetonius, *The Deified Julius* 50 reports Cicero's witty retort to the news of Caesar reducing the price of valuable estates for Servilia: 'It was even cheaper than you think, because a third (*tertia*) had been discounted'.
34. 'καὶ σὺ τέκνον;': Suetonius, *The Deified Julius* 82.2.
35. Dio Cassius 44.19.5; Plutarch, *Brutus* 5.2; Appian, *Civil War* 2.112. For more on the identity of Caesar's possible illegitimate son, see Syme (1980); see also Africa (1978) pp.612–613.
36. Plutarch, *Cato the Younger* 3.5, 11, 15.4. For a summary of Cato's influencing characteristics and actions, see MacMullen (1992) pp.2–6.
37. Plutarch, *Brutus* 2.1.
38. See Lucan, *Civil War* 2.234ff. For more on this epic, see S. H. Braund's introduction to her 1999 translation (Oxford, first edition 1992), especially p.xxxii on Brutus.
39. Plutarch, *Cato the Younger* 3.2–4; see also Valerius Maximus 3.1.2.
40. See below, Chapter 2, pp.20–21.
41. Caesar acknowledges Cato's enmity towards himself, at *Civil War* 1.4.1.
42. Plutarch, *Cato the Younger* 22–23. For more on the conspiracy, see Sallust, *The Conspiracy of Catiline* and Cicero, *Against Catiline*.
43. Plutarch, *Cato the Younger* 24, *Brutus* 5.
44. Plutarch, *Cato the Younger* 47, *Pompey* 54, *Caesar* 28.7–8; Dio Cassius 40.50.

45. *On Illustrious Men* 82.2; Clarke (1981) p.14; Radin (1939) p.69 gives credit to this tale, adding the detail that he was said to have shared her with fellow students. Cytheris was a notorious actress whose most illustrious lover was Antony, and who was celebrated as Lycoris in the love poetry of Gallus.
46. Plutarch, *Pompey* 47.6 also mentions that a Caepio was engaged to Julia, Caesar's daughter, when Pompey married her: however, it is unlikely that this Caepio is Brutus: Syme (1980) p.422.
47. In a letter to Appius dated 4 June 51 BC (*To Friends* 3.4.2), Cicero describes Brutus as Appius' son-in-law. Cicero also refers to Appius as Brutus' father-in-law at *Brutus* 267, 324. See also Cicero, *To Friends* 3.10.10.
48. Plutarch, *Brutus* 13.3 tells us that Porcia was still young at the time of her marriage to Brutus. Cicero wrote to Atticus in June 45 BC (*To Atticus* 13.9–10), agreeing that he was concerned for Brutus and that the matter of his forthcoming second marriage was provoking gossip.
49. Bibulus, who was consul with Caesar in 59 BC, fell ill and died while fighting against him alongside Pompey in the civil war of 48 BC: Caesar, *Civil War* 3.18.1; see also Chapter 3, n.9.
50. Cicero, *To Atticus* 13.10.
51. Cicero, *To Atticus* 13.22.4.
52. Clarke (1981) pp.29–30 considers the motives for the marriage. See below, Chapter 4, pp.54–55; Chapter 6, pp.72–73.
53. Plutarch, *Brutus* 13.

Chapter 2

1. Cicero, *Orator* 34. See below Chapter 3, pp.39–40, Chapter 10, pp.125–127, Chapter 14, pp.203–204.
2. Suetonius, *On Grammarians* 13; Plutarch, *Brutus* 2.5.
3. Cicero, *Brutus* 332, *Orator* 105, 110.
4. *On Illustrious Men* 82.1; Clarke (1981) p.12. Empylus was at some point Brutus' houseguest, and wrote an account of Caesar's assassination, entitled *Brutus*: Plutarch, *Brutus* 2.4.
5. Seneca, *Moral Letters* 95.45; Plutarch, *Brutus* 2.5–8.
6. Cicero, *To Atticus* 15.9, 13.40.1.
7. Cicero, *Brutus* 120–121, 149, 332, *To Atticus* 13.25, *On the Ends of Good and Evil* 5.8; Plutarch, *Brutus* 2.1–3.
8. Plutarch, *Cicero* 4.1–3; Cicero, *Brutus* 332, *On the Ends of Good and Evil* 5.81.
9. For a full discussion of the philosophical inclinations of Brutus and the relevant schools, see Sedley (1997); see also Cicero, *Academic Questions* 2.131ff. on the views of Antiochus, with which he did not entirely agree.
10. Cicero, *Brutus* 22, 331–332. For a detailed discussion of Brutus' oratory style, and the reliability of Cicero's views of it, see Filbey (1911).
11. Quintilian, *Institutes of Oratory* 10.1.123, 12.10.11; Tacitus, *Dialogues on Oratory* 21, 25.
12. Polybius: Plutarch, *Brutus* 4.8; see below, Chapter 3, n.31. Lucius Caelius Antipater: Cicero, *To Atticus* 13.8; Brutus epitomised the Annals which this second century BC jurist wrote. Gaius Fannius: Cicero, *To Atticus* 12.5B; he was a consul in 122 BC and wrote a history, which Cicero mentions (*Brutus* 101) and which Brutus summarised.
13. Tacitus, *Dialogues on Oratory* 21; Pliny, *Letters* 5.3.5, however, describes it as an honour to follow in the footsteps of men such as Brutus in composing poetry.
14. Cicero, *Brutus* 23, 47; Plutarch, *Brutus* 1.3.
15. This is an anachronistic title bestowed on the three leaders by modern historians.
16. Cicero, *To Atticus* 2.24. Ross Taylor (1950) pp.48–51 offers an explanation of events.
17. Paullus: his brother was the future Triumvir, married to one of Brutus' sisters, and their fathers had rebelled against the Sullan constitution together; Lentulus: his father, the *flamen Martialis*, a priest of the cult of Mars, was also said to have known about this.
18. The wife of this enemy of Caesar was Porcia, the daughter of Cato whom Brutus later married.
19. Gabinius, a supporter of Pompey, became consul in 58 BC: these games were presumably to win popularity for the consulship.

20. Sulla's law against murder, the *lex Cornelia de sicariis et veneficiis*, forbade the carrying of weapons with criminal intent.
21. Lucullus was the general and statesman, a supporter of Sulla and his constitution, famous for the enormous wealth which he brought back from the east; Cicero tells us that Fannius previously backed the prosecution of his sworn enemy, Clodius; Ahenobarbus was a known opponent of Pompey and Caesar, married to Cato's sister; Piso was a quaestor in 58 BC; Laterensis was a supporter of Cicero at this time, and would become praetor in 51 BC. The point here is that all of these men are, in some way, opposed to the Triumvirate.
22. On Caesar and Servilia, see Chapter 1, pp.10–12. There also exists the view that Pompey's men were behind the fabrications, and therefore that Caesar intimidated Vettius into changing his story: see Gruen (1995) pp.95–96.
23. Suetonius, *The Deified Julius* 20 claims that Caesar poisoned Vettius.
24. Cicero, *Against Vatinius* 24–26; see also *For Sestius* 132.
25. Later ancient accounts are inconsistent on the matter: Dio Cassius 38.9 claims that Cicero and Lucullus had employed the help of Vettius in a plot against Pompey; Plutarch, *Lucullus* 42.7–8 suggests that Pompey's men had made the false charges, principally against Lucullus.
26. Literally the 'best' men: the senatorial party who had originally arisen as a group in opposition to the *populares*, the popular party.
27. See Epstein (1987a) p.43.
28. Cicero, *On His House* 65.
29. Plutarch, *Cato the Younger* 34; Cicero, *On His House* 52; Velleius Paterculus 2.45.4; although, see Badian (1965) pp.116–17 on Clodius' other motives.
30. Canidius' identity is uncertain. Ptolemy was the younger brother of the King of Egypt, Ptolemy Auletes.
31. See below, pp.22–28.
32. Plutarch, *Brutus* 3.
33. Plutarch, *Brutus* 3.4, *Cato the Younger* 36–38. Valerius Maximus does not mention Brutus in his brief summaries: 4.3.2, 4.1.14, 8.15.10.
34. Clarke (1981) pp.10, 16 opts for 54 BC; Broughton (1951–1960) p.442 simply gives the date as circa 60 BC; de Rose Evans (1995) pp.145–146 discusses the dating.
35. See de Rose Evans (1995) pp.17–19 and Alföldi (1956) p.72.
36. See de Rose Evans (1995) p.30 and Alföldi (1956) pp.66, 77.
37. Cicero, *To Atticus* 4.18, *To His Brother Quintus* 3.4.1, 3.8.4–6; Clarke (1981) p.16.
38. Quintilian, *Institutes of Oratory* 9.3.95.
39. For the suggestion that Brutus was implicated in the conspiracy precisely because of the imagery on the coins, see de Rose Evans (1995) pp.145–146: however, this means dating them much earlier.
40. Matyszak (2003) p.13 and vroma.org/~bmcmanus/romangvt.html provide useful explanations of the offices and ladder of the *cursus honorum*. See also Broughton (1951–1960) p.301.
41. *On Illustrious Men* 82.3–4: see above, Chapter 1, p.13. Radin (1939) p.68 dates Brutus' refusal to take up a military post in Gaul to 58 BC, before he went to Cyprus with Cato.
42. Radin (1939) pp.68–86 offers the most accessible and complete summary of this complicated affair.
43. By the *lex Gabinia*: Gruen (1995) pp.251–252.
44. Cicero, *To Atticus* 5.21.11–12.
45. Cicero, *To Atticus* 5.16.4, 5.17.6; see also *To Friends* 3.6.3–6 where he does, indeed, take this up with Appius.
46. Broughton (1951–1960) p.239; Cicero, *To Atticus* 5.21.10, 6.1.6, 6.2.8.
47. Cicero, *To Atticus* 6.1.6, 6.2.9, 5.21.10.
48. Cicero, *To Atticus* 5.21.10, 6.1.4, 6.1.6, 6.2.8, 6.3.5.
49. Cicero, *To Atticus* 5.21.12–13: this letter is dated 13 February 50 BC.
50. 20 February 50 BC: Cicero, *To Atticus* 6.1.
51. Cicero, *To Atticus* 6.1.6.
52. Cicero, *To Atticus* 6.1.7, 6.2.8, 6.3.7.

53. Cicero, *To Atticus* 6.2.7.
54. Cicero, *To Atticus* 6.1.7. Judging by his following letter, Cicero prided himself on his successful actions in reducing the burden of debt throughout the province: 6.2.4–5.
55. Cicero, *To Atticus* 6.2.8, 6.3.5 dated late April and May/June 50 BC respectively.
56. Cicero, *To Atticus* 6.2.9.
57. Furthermore, a fragment from a letter of Brutus, found in Quintilian, *Institutes of Oratory* 9.4.75, has been said to relate to this matter and to confirm Cato's approval of his actions: see Oost (1955) p.112, n.64.
58. Cornelius Nepos, *Atticus* 15.3. On Atticus' involvement in the Salaminian affair specifically, see Welch (1996) pp.463–466.
59. Indeed, Radin (1939) p.74 claims that Brutus had also lent money at interest while studying in Asia.
60. Cicero, *To Atticus* 5.18.4: dated 20 September 51 BC.
61. Details of this can be found at Cicero, *To Friends* 15.2.4–8.
62. Cicero, *To Atticus* 5.20.6: dated 19 December 51 BC.
63. 20 February 50 BC: Cicero, *To Atticus* 6.1.3–4.
64. Cicero, *To Atticus* 6.3.5–6.
65. Cicero, *To Atticus* 6.2.7: possibly dated to late April 50 BC; *To Atticus* 6.3.5. is written in May or early June 50 BC.
66. Cicero, *Philippics* 2.21–22. For more details, see Gruen (1995) pp.292–299, and Seager (2002) pp.133–134.
67. Initially under the *lex Pompeia de vi*, Pompey's law against force which was newly established specifically with the recent turmoil in mind.
68. Cicero, *To Atticus* 9.7.3, *For Milo* 34; Cicero's commentator, Asconius 38 Clark, claims nothing could have prevented Cicero from defending Milo.
69. Cicero, *For Milo* 1–3; Plutarch, *Cicero* 35; Asconius 41–42 Clark; Dio Cassius 40.54.
70. Cicero, *To Friends* 15.4.12; Velleius Paterculus 2.47; Asconius 53–54 Clark.
71. Cicero, *For Milo* 6; Asconius 41 Clark.
72. Quintilian, *Institutes of Oratory* 3.6.93, 10.1.23, 10.5.20; Scholia Bobiensia 112 Stangl; Asconius 41 Clark.
73. As Clarke (1981) p.17.
74. Cicero, *Brutus* 22, 230, 324; Plutarch, *Brutus* 2.5.
75. Without Cicero's knowledge and much to his displeasure and embarrassment: *To Friends* 3.10.5, 3.12, 8.6.
76. Cicero mentions Brutus and Pompey's support: *To Friends* 2.13.2, 3.10.2, 3.11.3, *To Atticus* 6.2.10.
77. The less reliable source, *On Illustrious Men* 82.4, claims that Brutus was defending Appius on an extortion charge (*repetundae*), but this seems unlikely given the information with which Cicero supplies us at *To Friends* 3.11.1–3, 3.12.1: Gruen (1995) p.352, n.194. On Appius' trials, see Gruen (1995) pp.352–354.
78. On the acquittal, see Cicero, *To Friends* 3.11; on the censor role, see *To Friends* 3.10.3, 3.10.11. It is in this last passage to Appius that Cicero describes Brutus as having been a leader among his contemporaries for some time, and hopefully soon to reach the same distinction in the state.
79. There is some uncertainty over the year of Appius' death: this date is given by Kleine Pauly I vol. 1207. Keil *Grammatici Latini* 1.367.
80. Cicero speaks of this in his letters to Brutus: *To Brutus* 1.5.3, 1.15.8.
81. Cicero, *Brutus* 211–212. This was written in early 46 BC, shortly before Metellus Scipio's death.
82. See Broughton (1951–1960) p.254 and Ross Taylor (1942) p.405.

Chapter 3

1. For a detailed and accessible study of this, see Fields (2008), especially pp.121–122, 144–162. For Pompey's perspective, see Seager (2002) pp.133–168; for Caesar's, see Gelzer (1969) pp.146–194.

2. For more on Crassus' Parthian campaign and death, see Plutarch, *Crassus* 16–33.
3. All ancient authors seems to agree on this: Plutarch, *Caesar* 28.1–2, *Pompey* 53; Velleius Paterculus 2.47.2; Dio Cassius 40.44.2–3, 41.57.4; Valerius Maximus 4.6.4; Lucan, *Civil War* 1.98–120; Florus 2.13.13–17; see also the summaries of Scullard (1984) p.119 and Seager (2002) pp.130–132. However, Gruen (1995) pp.449–497, warning against the temptations of hindsight, disagrees with this evidence and traces events in depth in an attempt to prove that the coalition continued to exist and so civil war was not inevitable following the deaths of Crassus and Julia.
4. See above, Chapter 2, pp.28–29.
5. Dio Cassius 40.51. Metellus Scipio's daughter, Cornelia, the widow of Crassus' son, married Pompey in 52 BC.
6. Plutarch, *Caesar* 29, *Pompey* 56; Dio Cassius 40.59; Suetonius *The Deified Julius* 28–30.
7. Dio Cassius 40.60–64; Plutarch, *Pompey* 58. Gaius Scribonius Curio the younger had previously been an opponent of Caesar (see above, Chapter 2, pp.17–18); however, Caesar later took advantage of his financial difficulties, and bought his support by clearing his debts.
8. For an explanatory summary of events leading up to this decision, see Bringmann (2007) pp.251–253; Fields (2008) pp.144–149; Syme (2002) pp.45–49. See also Plutarch, *Caesar* 29–31.
9. Caesar, *Civil War* 1.2, 1.5; Dio Cassius 40.60.1, 41.1.4, 41.3.4; Velleius Paterculus 2.49.4; Suetonius, *The Deified Julius* 30.3; Plutarch, *Caesar* 31–32. During his first consulship, in 59 BC, Caesar took measures either to ignore or override his optimate colleague, Bibulus, causing the latter to withdraw and leave Caesar effectively with a sole consulship, meaning that the rest of his legislation was not valid. This was the year in which the consuls were said to be 'Julius and Caesar': Suetonius, *The Deified Julius* 20.2; see also Gelzer (1969) p.79.
10. See Gilliver, *et al.* (2005) pp.111–148 for a detailed summary of the various events of the civil war.
11. Plutarch, *Pompey* 59.1; Dio Cassius 40.65–66; Caesar, *Civil War* 1.2, 1.9.4; Cicero, *To Atticus* 7.4.
12. Appian, *Civil War* 2.41.1; Dio Cassius 41.8.5–6; see also Gelzer (1969) p.189. Gaius Marius, a powerful Roman statesman who held seven consulships, and a general who made important reforms to the Roman army, was married to Caesar's aunt.
13. For example, Cicero, *To Atticus* 7.13.
14. Plutarch, *Caesar* 33–34, *Pompey* 60–61.
15. Some of Pompey's letters to Ahenobarbus, dated around mid-February, are preserved in Cicero: *To Atticus* 8.12B-12D. Ahenobarbus was consul in 54 BC. Caesar, *Civil War* 1.15–23 narrates events of the siege from his perspective.
16. Caesar, *Civil War* 3.3–5.
17. Cicero, *To Atticus* 10.4.8; Plutarch, *Caesar* 35, *Pompey* 62.1–2; Appian, *Civil War* 2.41; Pliny, *Natural History* 33.56; Dio Cassius 41.17.2, 41.19–25; Caesar, *Civil War* 1.34–87, 2.1–22.
18. Caesar, *Civil War* 1.30–31, 2.23–44; Dio Cassius 41.26–35, 41.40–42. Antonius was the brother of Mark Antony, and Dolabella was the son-in-law of Cicero.
19. Plutarch, *Caesar* 37; Caesar, *Civil War* 3.6–19; Dio Cassius 41.44.
20. Caesar, *Civil War* 3.41–72; Plutarch, *Pompey* 65, *Caesar* 39; Dio Cassius 41.49–52.
21. Caesar, *Civil War* 3.78–80; Plutarch, *Pompey* 66–68, *Caesar* 40–41; Dio Cassius 41.55.
22. Plutarch, *Pompey* 68–73, 77–80, *Caesar* 42–45; Caesar, *Civil War* 3.88–94; Dio Cassius 42.2. Caesar himself offers a factual, and rather brief and cold, report of his rival's demise at *Civil War* 3.102–104.
23. See also MacMullen (1992) pp.3–4.
24. Caesar, *Civil War* 1.9.5; Plutarch, *Pompey* 58.4–5; Scullard (1984) p.122.
25. Plutarch, *Brutus* 4.1–3, *Pompey* 64.3. See Epstein (1987a) pp.23–24, 43, 75 and nn.89–91.
26. Cicero, *To Atticus* 9.14, March 49 BC. However, we should note that the reference in Cicero is to M. Brutus, and this could have been either our Brutus' father or his namesake who committed suicide off Lilybaeum (Marsala in Sicily), rather than falling into Pompey's hands: given the social and political circles of both Cicero and Caesar, it seems quite probable that the most relevant man here would be Brutus senior, but either way such claims by Caesar would surely have reminded Brutus of his father's demise.

27. See Epstein (1987a) p.34, and Africa (1978) pp.612–613.
28. Plutarch, *Comparison of Dion and Brutus* 3. See also Africa (1978) p.613.
29. Plutarch, *Brutus* 4.3–5.
30. Cicero, *To Atticus* 11.4A, dated June 48 BC.
31. Plutarch, *Brutus* 4.6–8. Polybius was a Greek historian of the Hellenistic era, flourishing in the second century BC, whose *Histories* charted the rise of Rome and its eventual domination of the Greek world.
32. Plutarch, *Brutus* 6.1.
33. Plutarch, *Brutus* 5.1, *Caesar* 46; Suetonius, *The Deified Julius* 30.4; see also Scullard (1984) p.122.
34. Gelzer (1969) p.243.
35. Plutarch, *Brutus* 6.2, *Caesar* 57.4–5, 62.3–4, *Comparison of Dion and Brutus* 3. On Caesar's clemency more generally, see Dio Cassius 41.62–63; Cicero, *To Atticus* 8.16.2, 10.4.8; Caesar, *Civil War* 3.98.
36. Plutarch, *Brutus* 6.3–5; Caesar, *Civil War* 3.106; Clarke (1981) p.21.
37. *The Alexandrian War* 67–68; Dio Cassius 41.63.1–3; Cicero, *For King Deiotarus* 8–9, 14, 36.
38. Cicero, *Brutus* 21; Dio Cassius 42.48.3; Plutarch, *Brutus* 6.6; however, Plutarch's version appears slightly confused since he states that Brutus was defending a King of Libya. See Magie (1950) pp.413–414; Gelzer (1969) p.261.
39. Plutarch, *Brutus* 6.8–9.
40. *magni refert hic quid velit, sed quicquid vult valde vult*: Cicero, *To Atticus* 14.1.2; Plutarch, *Brutus* 6.7.
41. Cicero, *Brutus* 21; Tacitus, *Dialogues on Oratory* 21. See Chapter 2, pp.15–17 on Brutus' style.
42. The *For King Deiotarus*, delivered to Caesar at his house.
43. Plutarch, *Caesar* 29; Dio Cassius 40.59.1; Appian, *Civil War* 2.25–26.
44. Cicero, *Brutus* 248–250.
45. This no longer exists, but is described in Seneca, *On Consolation: To My Mother Helvia* 8–9.
46. Dio Cassius 40.59.1.
47. Cicero, *Brutus* 155–157.
48. See above, Chapter 2, p.31.
49. Hendrickson (1939) pp.411–412; Cicero, *To Atticus* 13.10.3.

Chapter 4

1. Caesar, *Civil War* 1.30; Plutarch, *Cato the Younger* 53; Dio Cassius 41.41. According to Caesar, Cato reproached Pompey for abandoning him in Sicily, and for undertaking an unnecessary war without making due preparation.
2. Plutarch, *Cato the Younger* 54–55.
3. Plutarch, *Cato the Younger* 56, *Caesar* 52.1.
4. Plutarch, *Caesar* 52–53; Appian, *Civil War* 2.95–97; Dio Cassius 43.2–9; for details of the African campaign, see *The African War* and Gilliver, *et al.* (2005) pp.148–153 who offer a summary of events.
5. Plutarch, *Cato the Younger* 58.
6. Plutarch, *Cato the Younger* 59–66; *The African War* 87–88.
7. Plutarch, *Cato the Younger* 64–71; Appian, *Civil War* 2.98–99; Dio Cassius 43.10–11; *The African War* 88.
8. Cicero, *On Duties* 1.112; Plutarch, *Cato the Younger* 66, 72, *Caesar* 54; Appian, *Civil War* 2.98–99; Dio Cassius 43.10–12.
9. Appian, *Civil War* 2.101.
10. Plutarch, *Brutus* 40.6–9. See below on Brutus' own suicide, Chapter 13, p.189, Chapter 14, pp.203–207. For views on Cato's suicide, see MacMullen (1992) pp.4–5.
11. Cicero, *Orator* 35. MacMullen (1992) p.5 attributes this request specifically to Brutus' anger at the insensitive triumphal images, but Cicero's *Cato* seems to have been written by July, while the triumph probably took place later, in September: see Gelzer (1969) p.284.
12. Plutarch, *Caesar* 54; Cicero, *On Topics* 94, *To Atticus* 12.40.1, 12.41.4, 12.44.1, 12.45.2, 12.48 (letters dated to May 45 BC and mentioning both Caesar's *Anti-Cato* and the one which Caesar commissioned Hirtius to write). See Gelzer (1969) pp.301–304.

13. Cicero, *Orator* 35; a correspondent of Cicero, Aulus Caecina, accuses Cicero of shielding himself thus: *To Friends* 6.7.4. Elsewhere Cicero himself expresses reservations about eulogising Cato without offending Atticus' friends (*To Atticus* 12.4.2), but a month later claims to be pleased with the work he has produced (*To Atticus* 5.2 in July 46 BC).
14. Cicero is unable to disguise how affronted he feels: *To Atticus* 12.21.1.
15. As Plutarch's comments suggest, *Caesar* 54.
16. Lucius Cornelius Balbus showed Cicero a letter from Caesar containing these comments: *To Atticus* 13.46.2.
17. Suetonius, *The Deified Augustus* 85.1.
18. MacMullen (1992) pp.18–41, speaking of both Brutus and Cato, refers to their Republican influence living on after their deaths as a kind of cult: see Chapter 14, pp.213–215 below.
19. Plutarch, *Brutus* 6.10–12; Appian, *Civil War* 2.111.
20. On the *cursus honorum*, see Chapter 2, n.40. Cicero remarks on Caesar's generosity towards the former Pompeians: *To Friends* 6.6.10.
21. See above, Chapter 1, p.9.
22. In his *Brutus*, which can safely be dated as shortly before the Battle of Thapsus, Cicero mentions that the addressee will soon be in Gaul (171). A year later, Cicero writes (*To Atticus* 12.27.3) of his wish to avoid Rome, where he will be expected in order to receive Brutus formally upon his return, which he estimates will be 1 April; Broughton (1951–1960) p.301.
23. Cicero, *To Friends* 13.10 warmly recommends him to Brutus. He apparently openly and mockingly prophesied Antony's fitting death shortly before his own: Velleius Paterculus 2.71.2.
24. See Cicero, *To Friends* 13.11–14.
25. Cicero, *Orator* 34.
26. Radin (1939) p.111.
27. See above, Chapter 2, pp.22–26. Plutarch, *Brutus* 6.10–12.
28. See below, Chapter 14, pp.212–213.
29. Plutarch, *Brutus* 6.12.
30. Cicero, *To Atticus* 11.5–22. He was also distressed about family matters: he had become estranged from his younger brother, Quintus, who appears to have been actively working against his precarious political position; he was also much concerned for his daughter, Tullia, trapped in an unhappy marriage to Dolabella.
31. Cicero, *Brutus* 11–13, 330.
32. On Brutus' less friendly approach, see above, Chapter 2, pp.23–28; Cicero, *Brutus* 330 summarises the contents of the letter.
33. Hendrickson (1939) p.412.
34. Plutarch, *Cicero* 39.3–5; Cicero, *For Ligarius* 7, *For Marcellus* 13, *To Friends* 14.20.
35. See above, Chapter 3, pp.42–43. Hendrickson (1939) proposes this in a detailed discussion, while Clarke (1981) p.138, n.1 argues against this view.
36. Cicero, *Brutus* 13–15.
37. Cicero, *Brutus* 10, 147, 190, 211, 266, 300, 324.
38. Cicero, *Brutus* 284.
39. Cicero makes this clear in several places, and also claims reluctance to carry out the task: *To Atticus* 14.20.3, *Orator* 1–2, 35, 52, 140, 174, 238.
40. Cicero, *Brutus* 285; Clarke (1981) pp.25–26.
41. Clarke (1981) p.27; Cicero, *To Atticus* 14.20.3.
42. Cicero, *On the Ends of Good and Evil* 1.8, 3.6; see also Chapter 2, pp.15–17 above.
43. Cicero, *On the Ends of Good and Evil* 1.8, *Disputationes Tusculanae* 1.1, 5.1, 5.121.
44. Cicero, *To Atticus* 12.13–14, 12.36.2, 13.11.1, 13.23, 13.35–36, *To Brutus* 1.9.
45. On this marriage, see also above Chapter 1, pp.13–14 and MacMullen (1992) p.6.
46. Cicero, *To Atticus* 13.9.2, 13.10.3, 13.22.4.
47. Clarke (1981) pp.29–30.
48. See Cicero, *To Friends* 15.15.

49. Clarke (1981) p.22 thus speculates on the reasons for Brutus' decisions.
50. Dio Cassius 43.10.4–5; Plutarch, *Cato the Younger* 66.3.

Chapter 5

1. On the *cursus honorum*, see above, Chapter 2, n.40.
2. Plutarch, *Brutus* 7.1–5, *Caesar* 57.5, 62.4–5; Appian, *Civil War* 2.112. On their rivalry, see also Epstein (1987) pp.567–568 and (1987a) p.52.
3. Plutarch, *Brutus* 7.6.
4. Cicero, *To Atticus* 13.44.1.
5. Cicero, *To Atticus* 13.39.2. Although the exact nature of Brutus' journey is not specified by Cicero, that he was welcoming Caesar home seems to be the general consensus: Clarke (1981) p.33; Radin (1939) p.119; Gelzer (1969) p.304.
6. Cicero, *To Atticus* 13.40.1.
7. Plutarch, *Brutus* 8.4, *Caesar* 62.4; Cicero, *To Friends* 12.2, *Philippics* 8.27; Velleius Paterculus 2.56.3.
8. Plutarch, *Brutus* 7.7, 8.5.
9. Plutarch, *Brutus* 14.4; Cicero, *To Atticus* 14.20.
10. Suetonius, *On Grammarians* 13.
11. Appian, *Civil War* 4.67–68; Dio Cassius 47.33.4; Plutarch, *Brutus* 9.1–4, 8.5.
12. Plutarch, *Crassus* 18.4–5, 20.2, 22.4, 27.5.
13. Velleius Paterculus 2.46.4; Dio Cassius 40.25, 40.28–29; Cicero, *To Atticus* 5.20.3, *To Friends* 2.10.2. Cassius' claims to have brought an end to the Parthian war were, according to Cicero, somewhat bold and overstated (*To Atticus* 5.21.2, 6.1.14): however, Cicero was openly in a state of anxiety about the threat of a Parthian offensive at the time, because he was proconsul of neighbouring Cilicia and feared invasion.
14. *On Illustrious Men* 83.4. Not to be confused with Quintus Cassius Longinus, who was probably Cassius' cousin, and a Caesarian tribune that year.
15. Cicero, *To Atticus* 7.21.2; Caesar, *Civil War* 3.5.3, 3.101.
16. Plutarch, *Brutus* 6.5, *Caesar* 57.5, 62.3; see also Chapter 3, pp.40–41 above. Appian's report, *Civil War* 2.88, that Cassius came upon Caesar on the way to the Hellespont and immediately surrendered to him, appears to be confusing him with his brother, Lucius Cassius Longinus: Cassius' flight from Sicily would be at a different time from Caesar's voyage through that area, as reported reliably by Caesar himself: *Civil War* 3.101.
17. Cicero, *To Atticus* 11.13.1, *To Friends* 6.6.10, 15.15, *Philippics* 2.26.
18. For example, Cicero, *To Friends* 15.14.
19. Cicero, *To Atticus* 7.23–25.
20. Cicero speaks to Cassius of his new philosophy in rather mocking terms: *To Friends* 15.16–18. Cassius responds at *To Friends* 15.19. See also Sedley (1997).
21. Plutarch, *Brutus* 7.1–5, 34–35; Dio Cassius 47.35.1.
22. Plutarch, *Brutus* 7–8.
23. Cicero, *Philippics* 2.26. See also Radin (1939) pp.126–127 who considers his time fighting against Parthia as a further motivation for hatred of monarchy.
24. As Gelzer (1969) p.301. Cicero, *To Friends* 15.19.4: *malo veterem et clementem dominum habere quam novum et crudelem experiri.*
25. See Balsdon (1958) pp.92–94, and MacMullen (1992) pp.6–16.
26. Plutarch, *Comparison of Dion and Brutus* 3.
27. For a useful and accessible discussion of the incidents following Pharsalus, which act as a background to the conspiracy and are aptly collected under the subtitle 'The State of the Dictator Caesar', see Bringmann (2007) pp.262–275. See also Gelzer (1969) pp.277–278, 289–294, 299–324; Fields (2008) pp.174–182; Lintott (2009); Grant (1999) pp.35–49; le Glay *et al.* (2009) pp.157–158. Gardner (2009) provides a balanced defence of Caesar's actions.
28. See Gelzer (1969) pp.187–188 for a brief summary of Caesar's poor relationship with the nobility.

29. See above Chapter 2, p.29.
30. One disgruntled reaction is recorded at Suetonius, *The Deified Julius* 80.3.
31. Dio Cassius 43.46; Plutarch, *Caesar* 58.1–3. The two consuls were Quintus Fabius and Gaius Trebonius; when the former died, Gaius Caninius Rebilus was the man appointed for the last few hours of the year.
32. Cicero, *To Friends* 7.30; Suetonius, *The Deified Julius* 76.2.
33. On the unconstitutional role of Oppius and Balbus, Caesar's close and trusted agents who unofficially ran Rome in his stead, see Grant (1999) pp.39–42, and Lintott (2009) pp.75–76.
34. Suetonius, *The Deified Julius* 41.2, 76.2–3; Dio Cassius 43.47–48; Nicolaus of Damascus, *Life of Augustus* 20.
35. Caesar was reported to have said that Sulla did not know his political ABC: Suetonius, *The Deified Julius* 77.1.
36. See above Chapter 4, p.46. Plutarch, *Caesar* 56.7–9; Dio Cassius 43.42.1–2.
37. Dio Cassius 43.14; Plutarch, *Caesar* 57.1; Appian, *Civil War* 2.106; Suetonius, *The Deified Julius* 76.1.
38. This is why each of the Roman Emperors was an *imperator*, with the word 'emperor' deriving from this. Dio Cassius 43.44.2–5; Suetonius, *The Deified Julius* 76.1.
39. Cicero, *On Duties* 3.83, *To Atticus* 16.1.1; Appian, *Civil War* 2.106; Suetonius, *The Deified Julius* 76.1; Dio Cassius 44.4.4, 44.5.2–3, 45.7.2.
40. Dio Cassius 43.43–45, 44.4.4–5, 44.6; Appian, *Civil War* 2.106; Cicero, *Philippics* 2.110, *For King Deiotarus* 33–34; Suetonius, *The Deified Julius* 76.1; Plutarch, *Caesar* 57.4.
41. Plutarch, *Caesar* 59; Suetonius, *The Deified Julius* 76.1; Appian, *Civil War* 2.106; Dio Cassius 44.6.1, 44.6.3.
42. Suetonius, *The Deified Julius* 6; Dio Cassius 43.43.2–5. On familial propaganda, see de Rose Evans (1995), especially Chapter 2.
43. Plutarch, *Caesar* 60.4–8; Suetonius, *The Deified Julius* 78; Dio Cassius 44.8; Appian, *Civil War* 2.107; Nicolaus of Damascus, *Life of Augustus* 22.
44. Plutarch, *Caesar* 60.3, 61.8–10, *Brutus* 9.8–9; Suetonius, *The Deified Julius* 79.1–2; Dio Cassius 44.9–10; Velleius Paterculus 2.68.4–5; Appian, *Civil War* 2.108; Nicolaus of Damascus, *Life of Augustus* 20.
45. Suetonius, *The Deified Julius* 76.1, 79.2; Dio Cassius 44.6.2, 44.11; Cicero, *Philippics* 2.85–87, 3.12, 5.38, 13.17, 13.41; Plutarch, *Caesar* 61.1–7, *Antony* 12; Velleius Paterculus 2.56.4; Appian, *Civil War* 2.109. Nicolaus of Damascus, *Life of Augustus* 21 suggests that Cassius was involved in encouraging Caesar to accept the diadem.
46. Cicero, *On Divination* 2.110; Plutarch, *Caesar* 58.6, 60.1–2; Suetonius, *The Deified Julius* 44.3, 79.3; Dio Cassius 43.51.1–2, 44.4.6; Appian, *Civil War* 2.110.
47. Dio Cassius 43.41.3. See Bringmann (2007) pp.273–275 on the similarities here with the Hellenistic ruler cult. See also Gelzer (1969) pp.277–278.
48. See above, Chapter 3, p.43. For Servius' comments, see Cicero, *To Friends* 4.5.2 and Gelzer (1969) pp.300–301.
49. Suetonius, *The Deified Julius* 77; Cicero, *To Brutus* 1.16.3. See Gelzer (1969) pp.274–275.
50. Plutarch, *Caesar* 57.2–3, *Comparison of Dion and Brutus* 2; Dio Cassius 44.3, 44.7.2–3; Nicolaus of Damascus, *Life of Augustus* 20. Lintott (2009) pp.76–77 notes that the ancient authors are almost casting Caesar as the tragic Agamemnon, tricked into hubris by his calculating wife Clytemnestra.
51. Epstein (1987a) pp.56–58 discusses Caesar's monarchical designs in terms of the *invidia* (envy) and *inimicitiae* (enmity) which it provoked and attracted.

Chapter 6

1. On the role of Brutus' heritage in the assassination, see especially MacMullen (1992) pp.7–10.
2. See above, Chapter 5, p.66 on the two tribunes hailed as Brutuses.
3. Plutarch, *Caesar* 62.1–2, *Brutus* 9.5–8.

4. Plutarch, *Brutus* 1.1; Dio Cassius 43.45.4. Although, as Clarke (1981) pp.35–36 observes, Lucius did not actually kill Tarquinius.
5. Suetonius, *The Deified Julius* 80.3.
6. Plutarch, *Brutus* 9.5–8; Appian, *Civil War* 2.112; Dio Cassius 44.11–12. On the death of Lucius' sons, see Chapter 1, pp.4–5.
7. Cicero, *Brutus* 331–332, *Paradoxes of the Stoics* 12, *Tusculan Disputations* 4.2 and compare also 4.50. A decade earlier, Cicero was already writing about Lucius Brutus' deposition of the Kings of Rome: *On the Republic* 2.43–46. Elsewhere this work displays Cicero's views on tyranny: for example, 1.50, 1.65, 1.68; similarly, see *For Milo* 80. See also Balsdon (1958) p.91.
8. Cicero, *To Atticus* 13.40.1.
9. Cicero, *Philippics* 2.25–28.
10. Plutarch, *Brutus* 11. The biographer seems to be mistaken in referring to him as Gaius instead of Quintus.
11. See above, Chapter 5, p.58.
12. Plutarch, *Brutus* 10.1–2, *Caesar* 62.8; Nicolaus of Damascus, *Life of Augustus* 19.
13. Plutarch, *Brutus* 10; Appian, *Civil War* 2.113.
14. Dio Cassius 44.13.1; Appian, *Civil War* 2.112.
15. Plutarch, *Caesar* 62.1–6.
16. Plutarch, *Brutus* 13, *Cato the Younger* 73.4; Valerius Maximus 3.2.15; Dio Cassius 44.13–14.
17. MacMullen (1992) pp.10–12; Clarke (1981) pp.35–36, 49; Radin (1939) pp.125–126.
18. Cicero, *For Milo* 80.
19. Thucydides, *History of the Peloponnesian War* 6.56–59; Aristotle, *The Athenian Constitution* 18. Similarities between certain details of this tale and that of the conspiracy against Caesar are notable, displaying the ancient historical narrative tradition. See also Lintott (2009) pp.72–73: he interestingly records that a Republican statue of Aristogeiton was found on the Capitol in Rome.
20. Dio Cassius 47.20.4.
21. See Sedley (1997) pp.49–53, discussing Brutus specifically and offering a useful summary of Antiochean philosophy. See also Lintott (2009) p.74, and MacMullen (1992) pp.11–12. On Brutus' philosophical persuasion, see above, Chapter 2 pp.16–17. See also Plato, *Republic* 8.564a; Cicero, *To Brutus* 1.16–17; Plutarch, *Brutus* 10.4, 29.9; Dio Cassius 44.1.2, 44.19.2, 44.21.1; *Memnon of Heraclea* Fragment 34 in *Brill's New Jacoby*.
22. Bringmann (2007) p.262.
23. Plutarch, *Brutus* 12.1, *Comparison of Dion and Brutus* 4; Appian, *Civil War* 2.113; Cicero, *Philippics* 2.26–27; Velleius Paterculus 2.56.3; Dio Cassius 44.14.4.
24. Suetonius, *The Deified Julius* 80.4; Cicero, *Philippics* 2.26; Nicolaus of Damascus, *Life of Augustus* 19.
25. Plutarch, *Caesar* 64.1; Dio Cassius 44.14.4; Velleius Paterculus 2.58.1, 2.60.5; Suetonius, *The Deified Augustus* 10.2; Appian, *Civil War* 2.143, 2.146, 3.2, 3.16; Nicolaus of Damascus, *Life of Augustus* 19, 22.
26. Plutarch, *Brutus* 12.5–7; Appian, *Civil War* 2.122.
27. Epstein (1987) p.568; Dio Cassius 43.46.2; Suetonius, *The Deified Julius* 76.2; Plutarch, *Brutus* 19.5; Appian, *Civil War* 3.2; Velleius Paterculus 2.69.1.
28. Cicero, *Philippics* 2.34; Plutarch, *Antony* 13.1. See also below, Chapter 7, pp.83–84, where Cicero speaks of an assassin supposedly sent to Caesar by Antony (*Philippics* 2.74), although caution should be urged where Cicero is accusing this foe.
29. Plutarch, *Antony* 11.3, *Caesar* 62.10, *Brutus* 8.2.
30. Cicero, *Philippics* 2.26–27, 2.30.
31. Cicero, *To Friends* 6.12; Plutarch, *Brutus* 17.3, 19.5; Appian, *Civil War* 3.2; Seneca, *Moral Letters* 83.12.
32. Cicero, *Philippics* 2.27: *longum est persequi ceteros*. Dio Cassius makes a similar comment: 44.14.3.
33. Suetonius, *The Deified Julius* 80.4 and Nicolaus of Damascus, *Life of Augustus* 19 respectively.
34. Appian, *Civil War* 2.113; Dio Cassius 43.47.5.

35. The other names mentioned by Appian, *Civil War* 2.113 are: the brothers Caecilius and Bucilianus (or Bucolianus); Rubrius Ruga; Marcus Spurius; and Sextius Naso. Limited information is available about these men.
36. Cicero, *To Atticus* 14.21.3; Suetonius, *The Deified Julius* 50.2.
37. Caesar, *Gallic War* 3.1–6, 8.50; Dio Cassius 39.5.2–4, 39.65.2; Suetonius, *Galba* 3.2–3.
38. *The African War* 89; Cicero, *For Ligarius*, *To Friends* 6.14, *To Atticus* 13.19.2, 13.20.2, 13.44.3; Plutarch, *Cicero* 39.6–7.
39. Plutarch, *Brutus* 12.4–6.
40. Plutarch, *Brutus* 12.1–4, *Cicero* 42.1–2. For a full discussion of this episode in philosophical terms, see Sedley (1997). Favonius had been involved in the defence of Milo.
41. Nicolaus of Damascus, *Life of Augustus* 19 recounts the motives of these men, although it should be kept in mind that he was an Augustan author and so offers a biased version of events. For a list of the motives of the main conspirators, see Epstein (1987), who considers personal enmity to be the principal driving force for the assassination.
42. Plutarch, *Brutus* 12.8; Appian, *Civil War* 2.114; Dio Cassius 44.15.1–2; Nicolaus of Damascus, *Life of Augustus* 23.
43. See above, Chapter 1, p.9.
44. Plutarch, *Brutus* 18.2–6, *Antony* 13.2; Appian, *Civil War* 2.114, 3.33; Velleius Paterculus 2.58.2; Dio Cassius 44.19.2; Nicolaus of Damascus, *Life of Augustus* 25. See also MacMullen (1992) p.13.
45. Cicero, *To Atticus* 14.12.1, 14.14, 14.21.3, 15.4, 15.11.2, *To Brutus* 2.5.1, *To Friends* 12.4 (to Cassius) and 10.28 (to Trebonius), *Philippics* 2.34. Clarke (1981) p.39 believes that the decision not to kill Antony as well was a major factor in the failure of the conspiracy.
46. Plutarch, *Brutus* 14.1–3; Suetonius, *The Deified Julius* 80.4; Nicolaus of Damascus, *Life of Augustus* 23.
47. Plutarch, *Brutus* 14.1; Dio Cassius 44.16; Appian, *Civil War* 2.114; Nicolaus of Damascus, *Life of Augustus* 23.
48. Plutarch, *Pompey* 52.4; Cicero, *On Duties* 2.57; Dio Cassius 39.38.
49. Plutarch, *Brutus* 14.2–3, *Caesar* 66.1; Nicolaus of Damascus, *Life of Augustus* 23.

Chapter 7

1. Cicero, *On Divination* 1.119, 2.36–37. There are also brief accounts of this in: Plutarch, *Caesar* 63.4; Suetonius, *The Deified Julius* 81; Dio Cassius 44.17.3; Appian, *Civil War* 2.116.
2. Suetonius, *The Deified Julius* 81.2 has Spurinna warn Caesar that the danger will not come later than the Ides; Plutarch, *Caesar* 63.5; Velleius Paterculus 2.57.2.
3. Suetonius, *The Deified Julius* 81.1–3; Plutarch, *Caesar* 63. The poet Ovid also sings of many omens in his *Metamorphoses* 15.761–798 but, as this belongs to the more creative genre of epic poetry, portraying the gods discussing Caesar's approaching fate, much of it can be disregarded as purely fictional.
4. Balbus had also been close to Pompey, and a supporter of the Triumvirate who managed to stay out of the civil war. Along with Gaius Oppius, he effectively managed many aspects of Rome's affairs in Caesar's absence, which was yet another source of displeasure to the optimates: see above, Chapter 5, n.33.
5. See above, Chapter 5, p.65.
6. Suetonius, *The Deified Julius* 81.2–3; Plutarch, *Caesar* 63, recording a report from Strabo, the Greek geographer, historian and philosopher who lived through this period and into the early Roman Empire.
7. Cicero, *For Marcellus* 21–23, *Philippics* 2.74.
8. See above, Chapter 6, p.76.
9. Plutarch, *Caesar* 62.6–10, *Antony* 11.3, *Brutus* 8.1–3.
10. Cicero, *To Atticus* 14.1.2, 14.2.3. See also Bringmann (2007) p.275.
11. Plutarch, *Caesar* 57.7; Velleius Paterculus 2.57; Suetonius, *The Deified Julius* 84.2, 86; Dio Cassius 44.5.3, 44.7.4; Appian, *Civil War* 2.109, 2.124, 2.145; Nicolaus of Damascus, *Life of Augustus* 22.

12. Suetonius, *The Deified Julius* 87: he was reading the biography of the founder of the Achaemenid Empire, the *Cyropedia* of Xenophon, an Athenian soldier and student of Socrates.
13. Plutarch, *Caesar* 63.7; Suetonius, *The Deified Julius* 86–87; Decimus appears in Appian's account: *Civil War* 2.115. See also Gelzer (1969) p.328 and Clarke (1981) p.39.
14. Calpurnia was the daughter of Lucius Calpurnius Piso Caesonius who, as consul in 58 BC, had been instrumental in bringing about the exile of Cicero for Clodius. He is also the conjectured owner of the famous Villa of the Papyri in Herculaneum.
15. Plutarch, *Caesar* 63.8–9; Suetonius, *The Deified Julius* 81.3; Dio Cassius 44.17.1–2; Appian, *Civil War* 2.115; Velleius Paterculus 2.57.2.
16. Plutarch, *Caesar* 63.10–12; Suetonius, *The Deified Julius* 81.4; Appian, *Civil War* 2.115; Velleius Paterculus 2.57.2.
17. Plutarch, *Caesar* 64, *Brutus* 15.1; Suetonius, *The Deified Julius* 81.4; Dio Cassius 44.18.1–2; Appian, *Civil War* 2.115; Nicolaus of Damascus, *Life of Augustus* 23–24.
18. Plutarch, *Caesar* 64–65; Dio Cassius 44.18.2–3; Velleius Paterculus 2.57.2; Suetonius, *The Deified Julius* 81.4; Appian, *Civil War* 2.116; Nicolaus of Damascus, *Life of Augustus* 19.
19. Plutarch, *Caesar* 63.5–6; Suetonius, *The Deified Julius* 81.4; Appian, *Civil War* 2.149, 2.153; Dio Cassius 44.18.4.
20. Plutarch, *Brutus* 14.4–7; Dio Cassius 44.16.2; Appian, *Civil War* 2.115; Nicolaus of Damascus, *Life of Augustus* 26a.
21. Plutarch, *Brutus* 15–16; Appian, *Civil War* 2.115–116.
22. Plutarch, *Brutus* 15.5–9. The contrast in Porcia is observed by Clarke (1981) p.38.
23. Cicero, *To Friends* 10.28.1, *Philippics* 2.34, 13.22; Plutarch, *Antony* 13.2, *Brutus* 17.2, *Caesar* 66.4 (where it is incorrectly stated that Decimus Brutus kept Antony talking outside); Dio Cassius 44.19.1–3; Appian, *Civil War* 2.117, 3.15.
24. Plutarch, *Brutus* 17.1–4, *Caesar* 66.5–6; Suetonius, *The Deified Julius* 82.1; Appian, *Civil War* 2.117; Dio Cassius 44.19.1–4; Nicolaus of Damascus, *Life of Augustus* 24.
25. Plutarch, *Brutus* 17.4–7, *Caesar* 66.7–11, 66.14; Suetonius, *The Deified Julius* 82.1–3; Appian, *Civil War* 2.117; Dio Cassius 44.19.4–5; Nicolaus of Damascus, *Life of Augustus* 24.
26. See above, Chapter 1, pp.10–11: 'καὶ σὺ τέκνον;' is recorded by Suetonius, *The Deified Julius* 82.2.
27. Plutarch, *Caesar* 66.12; Suetonius, *The Deified Julius* 82.2; Appian, *Civil War* 2.117; Dio Cassius 44.19.5.
28. Cicero, *On Divination* 2.23; Plutarch, *Brutus* 14.2–3, 17.2, *Caesar* 66; Appian, *Civil War* 2.117; Nicolaus of Damascus, *Life of Augustus* 19, 23–24. As well as the site of the murder, there is a Republican temple complex located at Largo Argentina, which is also home to the Torre Argentina Cat Sanctuary, looking after many Roman strays; visitors to the site will usually be able to see some of these felines wandering, or sunbathing, among the ruins: www.romancats.com
29. Antony apparently used this as evidence that Cicero had known about the plot. Cicero, *Philippics* 2.28–30; Dio Cassius 46.22.4; see also MacMullen (1992) pp.9–10. For a view of Caesar's death mostly in a tragic light, and a summary of his policies and their legacy, see Gelzer (1969) pp.328–333.

Chapter 8

1. Plutarch, *Caesar* 66.9, 67.1, *Brutus* 18.1; Appian, *Civil War* 2.118; Dio Cassius 44.20; Nicolaus of Damascus, *Life of Augustus* 25.
2. Plutarch, *Caesar* 66.10–14; Suetonius, *The Deified Julius* 82.3–4; Cicero, *On Divination* 2.23; Appian, *Civil War* 2.118; Nicolaus of Damascus, *Life of Augustus* 26.
3. Cicero, *Philippics* 2.88–89; Plutarch, *Antony* 14.1, *Brutus* 18.6, *Caesar* 67.2; Appian, *Civil War* 2.118–119; Dio Cassius 44.19.2, 44.22.2.
4. Cicero, *To Atticus* 14.10.1, 14.14.2, *Philippics* 2.89; Plutarch, *Caesar* 67.3, *Brutus* 18.7, *Antony* 14.1; Velleius Paterculus 2.58.2; Appian, *Civil War* 2.119–120; Dio Cassius 44.20–21; Nicolaus of Damascus, *Life of Augustus* 26a. There also exists a brief and excited

note of congratulations from a joyous Cicero to one of the conspirators, Minucius, possibly written on the Ides of March: *To Friends* 6.15.

5. Plutarch, *Caesar* 67.3–6; Appian, *Civil War* 2.119–120; Dio Cassius 44.20–21. Other men mentioned are: Marcus Aquinus, a legate under Cassius from 43–42 BC; Quintus Patiscus, proquaestor in 43 BC, who fought alongside Spinther; and Gaius Octavius.
6. Cicero, *Philippics* 2.79–84, 2.99, 3.9, 5.9; Velleius Paterculus 2.58.3; Plutarch, *Antony* 11; Appian, *Civil War* 2.119, 2.122; Dio Cassius 43.51.8, 44.22.1.
7. Bringmann (2007) p.280; see also Clarke (1981) pp.38–39.
8. Cicero, *To Atticus* 14.10.1, 14.14.2.
9. Cicero, *To Atticus* 15.1A, 15.3.2, 15.4.3; Plutarch, *Brutus* 18.9–13, *Caesar* 67.7; Appian, *Civil War* 2.120–122, who suggests that only Brutus and Cassius descended from the Capitol; Nicolaus of Damascus, *Life of Augustus* 26a. On the tribunes, see above, Chapter 5, p.66.
10. Broughton (1951–1960) pp.320–321; Plutarch, *Brutus* 18.13–14, *Caesar* 68.5–6; Dio Cassius 44.50.4; Appian, *Civil War* 2.121–122; Nicolaus of Damascus, *Life of Augustus* 22.
11. Appian, *Civil War* 2.123–125.
12. Cicero, *Philippics* 1.1, 1.31, 2.89, 13.7–8, 13.15; *To Atticus* 14.14.2, 16.5.4, 16.11.8; Plutarch, *Brutus* 19.1; Velleius Paterculus 2.63.1; Appian, *Civil War* 2.126, 132; Dio Cassius 44.22, 44.50, 44.53.6–7.
13. Cicero, *Philippics* 1.1–3, 1.16–25, 1.31–32, 2.89–92, 2.100, 5.7–10, 5.38–41, 10.17, *To Atticus* 16.16C.2; Plutarch, *Brutus* 19.1, *Caesar* 67.8–9, *Antony* 14.2, *Cicero* 42.3; Velleius Paterculus 2.58.4; Appian, *Civil War* 2.124–129, 2.132–135, 2.142; 3.5, 22, 34; 4.94; Dio Cassius 44.22–33, 44.53.6–7, 45.23.4–8; Suetonius, *Tiberius* 4.1.
14. However, Clarke (1981) p.41 suggests that Appian could be using the published speech of Brutus as a basis for his text here, therefore making it a more reliable account.
15. Dio Cassius 44.34.1–3; Appian, *Civil War* 2.130–131, 2.137–142.
16. Cicero, *Philippics* 1.2, 1.31; Plutarch, *Antony* 14.2, *Brutus* 19.2–3; Velleius Paterculus 2.58.3; Appian, *Civil War* 2.142, 3.15; Dio Cassius 44.34.4–7; Nicolaus of Damascus, *Life of Augustus* 17, 27.
17. Plutarch, *Caesar* 67.9, *Brutus* 19.4–20.2; Suetonius, *The Deified Julius* 83.1; Velleius Paterculus 2.59.1; Appian, *Civil War* 2.135–136; Cicero, *To Atticus* 14.10.1, 14.14.3.
18. Plutarch, *Brutus* 20.3, *Caesar* 68.1; Suetonius, *The Deified Julius* 83.2; Appian, *Civil War* 2.143, 2.146; Dio Cassius 44.35.2–3; Velleius Paterculus 2.59.1; Cicero, *Philippics* 10.15.
19. Pacuvius was a second-century BC Roman tragic poet, the nephew of the Latin poet Ennius. The line, spoken by Ajax, is from *The Judgement of the Arms*: for more on this, see pp.96–97 of A. J. Boyle (2006), *Roman Tragedy*, Abingdon.
20. Cicero, *Philippics* 2.90–91; Plutarch, *Antony* 14.3–4, *Brutus* 20.4, *Caesar* 68.1, *Cicero* 42.4; Suetonius, *The Deified Julius* 84.2; Appian, *Civil War* 2.143–146, 3.35; Dio Cassius 44.35–49; Quintilian, *Institutes of Oratory* 6.1.31.
21. Cicero, *Philippics* 1.5, 2.91, *To Atticus* 14.10.1; Plutarch, *Antony* 14.4, *Brutus* 20.5–11, *Caesar* 68, *Cicero* 42.4; Suetonius, *The Deified Julius* 84–85; Appian, *Civil War* 2.147–148, 3.15, 3.35; Dio Cassius 44.50–52.
22. Cicero, *To Friends* 11.1.
23. Cicero, *Philippics* 2.31; Plutarch, *Brutus* 21.1–3, *Caesar* 68.7, *Cicero* 42.5; Appian, *Civil War* 2.148.
24. See above, Chapter 6, pp.79–80 and n.45.

Chapter 9

1. Plutarch, *Brutus* 21.1–2, *Caesar* 68.7; Cicero, *To Brutus* 1.15.5; *Philippics* 1.6 notes the Liberators' absence from Rome at the beginning of June.
2. Cicero, *To Atticus* 14.6.2, 14.10.1, 14.20.4, *To Brutus* 1.15.5, *Philippics* 2.107, 10.7, *To Friends* 12.16; Appian, *Civil War* 3.2.
3. Cicero, *To Atticus* 14.1. An invaluable secondary source, which acts as an accessible guide through the complicated political period of the downfall of Republican Rome, is Rice-Holmes (1928).

4. Cicero, *To Atticus* 14.1–4.
5. Cicero, *To Atticus* 14.2.2, 14.5.1; see also *To Friends* 11.27–28.
6. Cicero, *To Atticus* 14.4, 14.6.1, 14.11.1, 14.13.3, 14.14, 14.15.1, 15.12.1, *Philippics* 2.114.
7. Cicero, *To Atticus* 14.2.1; compare also 14.3.2.
8. Cicero, *To Atticus* 14.6.
9. Cicero, *Philippics* 1.3–4, 1.32–33, 2.91, 2.115, 5.10; Dio Cassius 44.51.2; Appian, *Civil War* 3.37. See also Rice-Holmes (1928) pp.187–188.
10. Cicero, *To Atticus* 14.7.1, 14.8.1.
11. Cicero, *To Atticus* 12.49, 14.6.1, *Philippics* 1.5; Appian, *Civil War* 3.2–4, 3.16, 3.36, 3.57. See Rice Holmes (1928) p.5 for the view that Antony was unable to tolerate a rival.
12. Cicero, *To Atticus* 14.1.2, 14.7.1, 14.8.2, 14.12.3, 14.17A.5.
13. Cicero, *To Atticus* 14.6.2, 14.9.2, 14.10, 14.12.1, 14.13.6, 14.13A, 14.13B, 14.14, 14.17.6, 14.18.1, 14.19.2, 14.21.3, 14.22.2, 15.4, 16.16, *To Friends* 12.1, *To Brutus* 1.15.4, *Philippics* 1.16–26, 2.35, 2.92–98, 2.100, 3.30, 5.11–12, 7.15; Dio Cassius 44.53, 45.23–25, 45.32.4, 45.47.3–4, 46.23; Velleius Paterculus 2.60.4; Plutarch, *Antony* 15.2; Appian, *Civil War* 3.5.
14. Cicero, *To Atticus* 14.14.7.
15. Cicero, *Philippics* 1.5, 1.30, 2.107, *To Atticus* 14.15, 14.16.2, 14.17A (= *To Friends* 9.14), 14.18.1, 14.19, 14.20.4, *To Friends* 12.1.1; Appian, *Civil War* 3.3; Dio Cassius 44.50.3.
16. Cicero, *To Atticus* 14.18.3–4, 14.19, 14.20.2–3, 15.1.3, *To Friends* 12.1.
17. Gaius Asinius Pollio was a writer and would become a literary patron under Augustus. His historic works reputedly provide the basis for some of the extant accounts of the period that we are using here.
18. Cicero, *To Atticus* 14.1.2, 14.4–5, 14.8.2, 14.9.3, 14.10.1, 14.13.2, 14.17.2, 14.20.2–3, 14.21.2–3, 14.22.2, 15.1.2, 15.20.3, 15.21.3, 15.22, 15.29.1, 16.1.4, 16.4.1–2, *Philippics* 2.43, 2.100–108, 5.17, 8.25–26, *To Brutus* 1.15.4, *To Friends* 11.2; Appian, *Civil War* 3.2, 3.5–6, 4.84; Dio Cassius 45.10; Velleius Paterculus 2.73.2. See also Rice-Holmes (1928) pp.190–191.
19. Cicero, *To Friends* 12.1, *To Atticus* 14.20.4, 14.21, 14.22.1, 15.1, 15.4, 15.5.1, 15.6, 15.22. For another contemporary negative view of the assassins, see Matius' comments in *To Friends* 11.28.
20. Cicero, *To Atticus* 14.5.3, 14.6.1, 14.10.3, 14.11.2, 14.12.2, *To Brutus* 1.17.5; Plutarch, *Cicero* 45.1–2; Nicolaus of Damascus, *Life of Augustus* 16–18; Appian, *Civil War* 3.9–12; Dio Cassius 45.3.
21. On the illegal nature of the adoption, see Gardner (2009) pp.66–69.
22. On the expectation that a Roman should avenge wrongs done to his family, see Epstein (1987a) pp.23–24; Bringmann (2007) p.283.
23. Cicero, *To Atticus* 14.20.5, 14.21.4, 15.2.3, 15.3.2, 15.12.2; Appian, *Civil War* 3.13–20, 3.28; Dio Cassius 45.4–6; Suetonius, *The Deified Augustus* 95; Velleius Paterculus 2.59–60; Nicolaus of Damascus, *Life of Augustus* 17, 28; Plutarch, *Antony* 16.1–2, *Brutus* 22.1–3; Florus 2.15.2. Antony famously taunted Octavian that he was the boy who owed everything to his name, as Cicero records at *Philippics* 13.24: *et te, o puer, qui omnia nomini debes.*
24. Cicero, *To Atticus* 15.12.2; Appian, *Civil War* 3.21; Nicolaus of Damascus, *Life of Augustus* 28.
25. Cicero, *To Atticus* 14.22, 15.1.5, 15.3–5, 15.6.2, *To Friends* 11.2, *Philippics* 1.6, 1.25, 2.6, 5.9–10, 10.7.
26. Cicero, *To Atticus* 14.9.3, 14.14.4, 15.4.1, 15.5, 15.10, *Philippics* 1.6, 1.19, 2.108–109, 5.7; Velleius Paterculus 2.60.5; Appian, *Civil War* 3.8, 3.27; Nicolaus of Damascus, *Life of Augustus* 30. The law was the *lex de permutatione provinciarum*, or *lex tribunicia de provinciis.* See also Rice-Holmes (1928) pp.188–90, 192–196.
27. Cornelius Nepos, *Atticus* 8, 11.1.
28. Syme (2002) p.116.
29. Cicero, *To Atticus* 15.9–11, 15.12.1; Appian, *Civil War* 3.6.
30. Cicero, *To Atticus* 14.5.2, 14.7.2, 14.10.1, 14.12.2, 14.13.4, 14.14.6, 14.15.2, 14.16.3, 14.19.6, 14.18.4, 14.22.2, 15.5, 15.8.1, 15.11.3–4, 15.15.4, 15.17.2, 15.18.2, 15.19.1, 15.20, 15.21.3, 15.22, 15.25, 15.26.3, 15.28, 16.1.3–4, 16.2.4, 16.3–4, 16.5.3–4, *To Friends* 7.20, 11.29, *Philippics* 1.6, 2.76; Plutarch, *Cicero* 43.1–3.

31. Cicero, *To Atticus* 15.11.2, 15.12.1, 15.17.2, 15.18.2, 15.26.1, 15.28, 16.1.1, 16.4.1, 16.5.1, 16.2.3, *Philippics* 1.36–37, 2.31, 10.7–8; Plutarch, *Brutus* 21; Appian, *Civil War* 3.23–24 reports that the response of the people was quite the opposite; Dio Cassius 47.20.2 incorrectly records the urban praetor as being Cassius.
32. Cicero, *To Friends* 11.27.7, 11.28.6, *To Atticus* 15.2.3; Augustus, *The Achievements of the Divine Augustus* 15; Suetonius, *The Deified Augustus* 10.1, *The Deified Julius* 88; Appian, *Civil War* 3.21–23, 3.28–30; Dio Cassius 43.22.2–3, 45.6–8; Nicolaus of Damascus, *Life of Augustus* 28–29; Plutarch, *Antony* 16.2–3; Ovid, *Metamorphoses* 15.848–850; Pliny, *Natural History* 2.92–94. On the role of the soldiers in controlling the relationship of Antony and Octavian in the aftermath of Caesar's assassination, see Keaveney (2007) pp.47–48.
33. Cicero, *To Atticus* 15.12, 15.16A, 15.19.2, 15.20.2, 15.21.1, 15.26.2, 15.29, 16.1, 16.2.4, 16.4.4, 16.5, *Philippics* 10.8. Rice-Holmes (1928) pp.21, 197 believes that Brutus and Cassius collected their fleets for the corn commission, and possibly as protection against the danger of pirates, but not in preparation for war.
34. Rice-Holmes (1928) p.22.
35. Cicero, *To Atticus* 16.3.6, 16.6.1–2, 16.7.1, *Philippics* 1.6–8; Plutarch, *Cicero* 43.3–4; Velleius Paterculus 2.62.3; see also Ramsey (2001).
36. Cicero, *To Atticus* 16.7, *Philippics* 1.9–10, 1.14–15, 2.31, 2.97, 5.19 10.8, 11.27–28, *To Friends* 11.3, 12.2.1, *To Brutus* 1.10.4, 1.15.4–6; Plutarch, *Brutus* 19.5; Appian, *Civil War* 3.8, 3.12, 3.16, 3.35–36, 4.57; Florus 2.17.4; Dio Cassius 45.32.4, 46.23.3, 47.21.1; Rice-Holmes (1928) pp.196–197.

Chapter 10

1. Plutarch, *Brutus* 23, quoting Homer *Iliad* 6.429–430, 6.491. These anecdotes reportedly came from the memoirs of Brutus which Porcia's son, Bibulus, wrote: see Plutarch, *Brutus* 13.3.
2. Cicero, *Philippics* 10.8, 11.28; Cornelius Nepos, *Atticus* 8.5; Nicolaus of Damascus, *Life of Augustus* 30.
3. See above, Chapter 6, pp.73–74. Dio Cassius 47.20.4.
4. Theomnestus belonged to the Academy, the Platonic school of philosophy to which Brutus subscribed, but little else is known about him. Cratippus of Pergamum was of the Peripatetic school, whose teachings derived from those of Aristotle, and he was a friend of Cicero and teacher of many prominent Romans of the era.
5. Plutarch, *Brutus* 24.1–3, *Cicero* 45.3; Cicero, *Philippics* 10.8, 11.27, *To Brutus* 2.3.6; Cornelius Nepos, *Atticus* 8.5–6; Nicolaus of Damascus, *Life of Augustus* 30. The young Marcus Cicero was a pupil of Cratippus: Cicero, *To Friends* 12.16.2, 16.21.3–5. Horace, *Epistles* 2.2.43–49, *Satires* 1.6.48, *Odes* 2.7.1–16, 3.14.27–28; Suetonius, *The Life of Horace*.
6. See Raubitschek (1957) p.8.
7. Plutarch, *Brutus* 24–25; Cicero, *Philippics* 10.13, 10.24, 11.27, 13.32, *To Brutus* 1.7.2, 1.11, 2.3.5, *To Friends* 12.13.3; Dio Cassius 47.21.3; Velleius Paterculus 2.62.3; Appian, *Civil War* 3.6, 3.63, 4.75.
8. Plutarch, *Brutus* 24.5–7; Homer, *Iliad* 16.849; Valerius Maximus 1.5.7 records that 'Apollo' was instead the password of the Caesarians at Philippi; Appian, *Civil War* 4.134 has this taking place at Samos. See also Moles (1983) and Gosling (1986).
9. Rice-Holmes (1928) pp.23–44 provides a useful summary of these events.
10. Cicero, *Philippics* 1.11–13, 2.110, 5.19, *To Friends* 10.1.1, 12.2.1; Plutarch, *Cicero* 43.5–8.
11. Rice-Holmes (1928) pp.198–199; Cicero, *To Atticus* 15.13.1–2, 15.13A.3, 16.11.1–2.
12. Cicero, *Philippics* 2.19, 2.25–36, 2.42, 2.74, 2.112, 5.19–20, *To Friends* 10.2, 12.2, 12.25.3–4. On the supposed earlier conspiracy, see above, Chapter 6, p.76.
13. The Latin inscription read *parenti optime merito*.
14. Cicero, *To Friends* 12.2, 12.22, 12.23.3, *Philippics* 2.31. See also Stockton (1971) pp.287–288 on Cicero's flaws and short-sightedness with regard to Antony; Bringmann (2007) p.287 aptly sums it up when he notes how Cicero lost 'every sense of proportion for the political consequence of their personal feud'.
15. Plutarch, *Antony* 16.2; Appian, *Civil War* 3.31; Dio Cassius 45.6.2–3; Suetonius, *The Deified Augustus* 10.2.

16. Followed by Rice-Holmes (1928) pp.26–28.
17. Cicero, *To Friends* 12.23.1–2, *To Atticus* 15.13A.2, 16.11.5, *Philippics* 3.19; Suetonius, *The Deified Augustus* 10.3; Seneca, *On Clemency* 1.9.1. Other ancient sources tend not to believe it was true: Nicolaus of Damascus, *Life of Augustus* 30; Appian, *Civil War* 3.39; Plutarch, *Antony* 16.4; Velleius Paterculus 2.60.3.
18. See above, Chapter 9, pp.116–117 Appian, *Civil War* 3.37; Cicero, *To Atticus* 15.13.2.
19. Cicero, *To Atticus* 16.8–15.
20. Cicero, *To Friends* 12.23.2, 12.25.4; Augustus, *The Achievements of the Divine Augustus* 1; Plutarch, *Cicero* 44.1–45.1, *Antony* 16.3; Appian, *Civil War* 3.40–45; Nicolaus of Damascus, *Life of Augustus* 31; Dio Cassius 45.12–15, 45.20.3–4; Velleius Paterculus 2.61.2; Suetonius, *The Deified Augustus* 10.3; Tacitus, *Annals* 1.10.
21. Appian, *Civil War* 3.41–42, 3.58; Dio Cassius 45.12.3–6, 45.38.3–4.
22. In the event it seems that Octavian did not obstruct Casca's tribuneship, doubtlessly waiting for a more suitable time to begin punishing Caesar's assassins: Cicero, *Philippics* 13.31.
23. Cicero, *Philippics* 3.3–7, 3.10–11, 4.3–7, 5.22–23, 5.42–44, 13.18–19.
24. Cicero, *Philippics* 3.6–7, 3.15–17, 3.19–26, 4.5–6, 5.4, 5.23–24, 5.46, 5.52, 13.19, *To Friends* 10.28.1, 11.7.2; Appian, *Civil War* 3.45–46, 3.56; Dio Cassius 45.13.3–5, 45.38.5, 45.42.1; Velleius Paterculus 2.61.2. See also Rice-Holmes (1928) pp.199–200.
25. Cicero, *To Atticus* 14.13.2, *To Friends* 11.4–7; Velleius Paterculus 2.60.5; Suetonius, *The Deified Augustus* 10.2; Appian, *Civil War* 2.124, 3.2, 3.6, 3.37–38; Dio Cassius 44.14.4.
26. Cicero, *To Friends* 11.1.1, *To Atticus* 15.4.1, 15.10.
27. Cicero, *Philippics* 3.13, 3.25, 3.37, *To Friends* 11.6A; Dio Cassius 45.15.3; Appian, *Civil War* 3.27 claims that the senate secretly asked Decimus to guard the province against Antony's martial moves.
28. Cicero, *Philippics* 3.8–11, 4.7–9, 5.28, 5.35–37, 6.2, 6.8–9, *To Friends* 10.28, 11.8.
29. Cicero, *Philippics* 3.1–7, 3.13–14, 3.31, 3.37–39, 4.1–9, 4.16, 5.24, 5.27–30, 6.1–2, 7.11, 7.24–25, 10.23, 12.9, 13.21, 14.20, *To Friends* 12.22A.1, 12.25.2; Nicolaus of Damascus, *Life of Augustus* 28; Dio Cassius 45.15.2.
30. Cicero, *Philippics* 5.1–4, 5.24–31, 5.34–37, 5.46, 5.50–51, 7.14–15, 7.26, 13.20, 14.4, *To Brutus* 2.3.4; Appian, *Civil War* 3.47–49; Dio Cassius 45.14–15, 46.34–36. Dio Cassius provides a version of Cicero's fifth *Philippic* at 45.18–47: see especially 45.34–39, 45.42–45.
31. Appian, *Civil War* 3.54–61; see also Dio Cassius' version of the speech of Quintus Fufius Calenus, Pansa's father-in-law, who proposed sending the envoy to Antony, against Cicero and in favour of Antony: 46.1–29.
32. Cicero, *Philippics* 5.53, 6.2–9, 6.15–19, 11.4, 11.20, *To Brutus* 1.15.7, 2.3.4; Augustus, *The Achievements of the Divine Augustus* 1; Appian, *Civil War* 3.50–61; Dio Cassius 45.17, 46.29; Velleius Paterculus 2.61.3; Plutarch, *Antony* 17.1, *Cicero* 45.4; Suetonius, *The Deified Augustus* 10.2–3; Tacitus, *Annals* 1.10.
33. Cicero, *Philippics* 1.37, 7.1–3, 7.8–15, 7.21–27, 8.5–6, 10.16, 10.21, 11.21–24, 14.4–5, *To Friends* 12.24.2; Dio Cassius 46.29.5.
34. Cicero, *To Friends* 11.8.
35. Cicero, *Philippics* 7.2–3, 8.17, 8.21–28, 9.15, 12.11–13, 13.21; Appian, *Civil War* 3.61–63; Dio Cassius 46.30–31.
36. Cicero, *To Friends* 10.28.1, 12.4.1.
37. Cicero, *Philippics* 8.1–6, 8.17, 8.20–22, 8.33, 9.7, 10.19, 12.14–18, 13.32, 14.20, *To Friends* 12.25.2.
38. Cicero, *Philippics* 9.7, 9.15.
39. Cicero, *To Friends* 12.5.2, *Philippics* 10.10, 12.10; Dio Cassius 46.35–36. Parma had been sacked and captured by Antony's brother, Lucius: Cicero, *Philippics* 14.8–9, *To Friends* 10.33.4, 11.13B.
40. Presumably one of Brutus' two associates who went by that name, and who were both involved in his moneylending activities a decade earlier.
41. Cicero, *To Friends* 12.4.2, *To Atticus* 15.13.4, *Philippics* 10.14. Clarke (1981) p.50 interprets the absence of Cicero's correspondence concerning Brutus as an indication that Brutus was acting alone, and was out of touch with the Republicans based in Rome.

42. See above, Chapter 9, p.117.
43. See above, Chapter 2, p.30.
44. This is the same Vatinius who was involved in the Vettius affair.
45. Plutarch, *Brutus* 25–26; Cicero, *Philippics* 3.26, 7.3, 10.9–14, 10.24, 11.26–27, 13.30, 13.32; Velleius Paterculus 2.69.2–4; Dio Cassius 45.9.2, 47.21; Appian, *Civil War* 4.75. On the possible timing of Brutus' departure from Athens to Macedonia, see Raubitschek (1957) pp.6, 9.
46. Cicero, *To Friends* 12.5.1. On the illegality of Brutus' actions, see Clarke (1981) pp.52–53, Magie (1950) pp.418–419, and Raubitschek (1957).
47. Cicero, *Philippics* 10.4–7, 10.9–12, 10.14–17, 10.23–26, 11.37–39, *To Brutus* 2.3.4; Dio Cassius 46.29.4, 47.22.1–2; Appian, *Civil War* 3.63.
48. See above, Chapter 9, p.110.
49. Cicero, *Philippics* 11.1–10, 11.15–16, 11.26–32, 12.21, 12.25, 13.22–23, 13.35–39, 14.8, *To Friends* 12.7, 12.15.4, *To Brutus* 2.3.1, 2.3.5, 2.4.2; Appian, *Civil War* 3.26, 3.61; Dio Cassius 47.29, 47.30.6.
50. See above, Chapter 5, pp.58–59.
51. Cicero, *To Friends* 12.2.3, 12.3.2, 12.4.2, 12.5.1, 12.7, 12.11–12, 12.13.3, 12.14.4–6, *Philippics* 11.30, 11.32, 11.35, *To Brutus* 2.3.3, 2.4.5; Dio Cassius 47.20.3–21.2, 47.26–28; Velleius Paterculus 2.69.1–2; Appian, *Civil War* 3.6, 3.77–78, 4.58–59; Nicolaus of Damascus, *Life of Augustus* 28, 31.

Chapter 11

1. Cicero, *Philippics* 12.1–7, 12.11–17, 12.24, 12.30, 13.47; in 14.20, however, he claims that he never voted for an embassy. Dio Cassius 46.32.3–4.
2. On the character of these three men, see Syme (2002) pp.165–166.
3. Cicero, *To Friends* 10.6.1, 10.31, 10.32.4, *Philippics* 13.7–10, 13.13–17, 13.43, 13.49–50. Pollio remained cut off from news for several months: he wrote with the same frustrations at the beginning of June in *To Friends* 10.33.
4. Cicero, *Philippics* 13.22–26, 13.30–48; Caesar, *Civil War* 3.34–35.
5. Cicero, *Philippics* 13.43–44, *To Friends* 10.6, 10.27, 10.31.4.
6. Cicero, *To Friends* 10.1–5, 10.7–8, *To Atticus* 15.29.1.
7. Cicero, *To Friends* 10.10 (written on 30 March, before Cicero and the senate received Plancus' letters), 10.12 (written on 11 April, in response to Plancus' dispatches received four days earlier).
8. Cicero, *To Brutus* 2.2.
9. Cicero, *To Brutus* 2.1–2, *To Friends* 12.6.2; Appian, *Civil War* 3.64–65; Dio Cassius 46.35–37.
10. Cicero, *To Friends* 10.30.
11. On the date and sources, see Rice-Holmes (1928) pp.208–210.
12. Cicero, *Philippics* 14.26–28, 14.36–37, *To Friends* 10.33.3–4, 11.13.2; Appian, *Civil War* 3. 66–70; Dio Cassius 46.37.4–7; Orosius 6.18.
13. Cicero, *Philippics* 14.1–12, 14.15–16, 14.20–25, 14.29–38; Dio Cassius 46.38.1–2; Ovid, *Fasti* 4.673–676: the poet Ovid, incidentally, was born during this period of civil chaos, on 20 March 43 BC.
14. Cicero, *To Brutus* 1.3, *Philippics* 14.12–19. See also Stockton (1971) p.315.
15. See Rice-Holmes (1928) p.210.
16. Cicero, *To Friends* 10.33.4, 11.10.1, 11.14, *To Brutus* 1.4.1, 1.15.8; Appian, *Civil War* 3.71–72; Velleius Paterculus 2.61.4; Suetonius, *The Deified Augustus* 10.2–3; Florus 2.15.
17. Cicero, *To Friends* 10.33.4, 12.25A.1, *To Brutus* 1.3A, 1.6.2, 1.15.8; Augustus, *The Achievements of the Divine Augustus* 1; Appian, *Civil War* 3.71, 3.75–76; Dio Cassius 46.39.1, 46.40.2; Velleius Paterculus 2.61.4; Suetonius, *The Deified Augustus* 10.4–11.1; Tacitus, *Annals* 1.10; Plutarch, *Antony* 17.1; Eutropius 7.1; Orosius 6.18; Florus 2.15 records a version in which Octavian was wounded in battle; Valerius Maximus 5.2.10.
18. Cicero, *To Friends* 10.9 on 27 April, 10.11 a few days later, and 10.14 is Cicero's encouraging response.

19. Cicero, *To Friends* 10.33.4, 10.34.1, 11.9.1, 11.10.3, 11.11.1, 11.12, 11.13.2, *To Brutus* 1.10.2, *Philippics* 12.23, 14.21; Appian, *Civil War* 3.66, 3.72, 3.80, 4.2; Velleius Paterculus 2.61.4, 2.65.3; Dio Cassius 47.15.2.
20. Cicero, *To Brutus* 1.3A, 1.5.1; Velleius Paterculus 2.64.4; Dio Cassius 46.39.3; Appian, *Civil War* 3.63.
21. Appian, *Civil War* 3.73.
22. Cicero, *To Brutus* 1.10.1–3, *To Friends* 10.33.5, 11.13.1–2, 11.14, 11.19.1.
23. Cicero, *To Friends* 11.9–10, 11.11.4, 11.13B.
24. It is unclear whether Octavian's ovation was actually decreed: see Keaveney & Madden (1983).
25. *laudandum, ornandum, tollendum* (Cicero, *To Friends* 11.20.1; see also 11.21.1): *tollendum* has the double meaning of 'to be extolled' and 'to be got rid of'.
26. Cicero, *To Brutus* 1.5.1–2, 1.15.8–9, *To Friends* 11.14.2, 11.18.3, 11.19.1, 11.20, *Philippics* 13.50; Dio Cassius 46.39–41, 46.50.1; Plutarch, *Cicero* 45.4–6, *Brutus* 27.1–3; Velleius Paterculus 2.62, 2.73.2; Appian, *Civil War* 3.63, 3.74–76, 3.80, 3.82, 3.86–89, 4.84; Suetonius, *The Deified Augustus* 12.
27. The authenticity of two letters in the collection, *To Brutus* 1.16–17, supposedly written from Brutus to Cicero and Atticus respectively, has been doubted. The main theme of these letters is the purported author's ranting irritation that Cicero is apparently willing to see Octavian become Caesar's replacement as tyrant. Although these are perhaps not his words, they nevertheless display the impression of Brutus' opinion that has been formed and generally accepted. For arguments against authenticity, see D. R. Shackleton Bailey (ed.), (1980), *Cicero: Epistulae ad Quintum Fratrem et M. Brutum*, Cambridge, pp.10–14, and (2002), *Cicero – Letters to Quintus and Brutus*, London, pp.204–205; and arguments for can be found in Moles (1983a) p.765, n.6.
28. Cicero, *To Brutus* 1.4A.3: *quod utinam inspectare posses timorem de illo meum!*
29. Cicero, *To Brutus* 1.3.1, 1.4.3, 1.4A, 1.10, 1.14.2, 1.15.3–4, 1.15.7–9, 1.18.3–4, 2.5.1–2; Plutarch, *Brutus* 22.4–6, *Cicero* 45.1–2, 46.1.
30. Cicero, *To Friends* 11.11–14, 11.18–21, 11.23–24. Rice-Holmes (1928) p.59.
31. Cicero, *To Friends* 10.13, 10.15–21, 10.34–35, 11.14.3.
32. Cicero, *To Friends* 10.23, 11.26; Appian, *Civil War* 3.83–84; Velleius Paterculus 2.63.1; Plutarch, *Antony* 18; Dio Cassius 46.38.5–7, 46.51.1–2.
33. Radin (1939) p.202. Cicero, *To Brutus* 1.9–10, 1.12, 1.14.2, 1.15.12, 1.18, *To Friends* 12.8–10; Appian, *Civil War* 3.85; Dio Cassius 46.51.5.
34. Cicero, *To Friends* 10.22, 10.26.1, 11.13A, 11.15, 11.25.
35. Cicero, *To Brutus* 1.12–13, 1.14.2, 1.15.9–3, 1.18.2, 1.18.6, 2.2.1, *To Friends* 10.15.1, 12.8–10; Velleius Paterculus 2.64.4; Dio Cassius 46.51.4.
36. Cicero, *To Friends* 10.23.6, 10.24, 11.25.2; Appian, *Civil War* 3.85.
37. Cicero, *To Brutus* 1.18.3–4; Appian, *Civil War* 3.86–94; Dio Cassius 46.41–47, 56.30.5; Augustus, *The Achievements of the Divine Augustus* 1; Suetonius, *The Deified Augustus* 26.1, 31.2; Velleius Paterculus 2.65.2; Tacitus, *Annals* 1.10, *Dialogues on Oratory* 17.
38. Plutarch, *Brutus* 27; Velleius Paterculus 2.69.5; Augustus, *The Achievements of the Divine Augustus* 2; Appian, *Civil War* 3.94–95, 4.27, 5.48; Dio Cassius 46.47–49, 47.22.4; Suetonius, *Nero* 3, *Galba* 3.2.
39. Cicero, *To Friends* 10.32; Appian, *Civil War* 3.81, 3.96–98; Velleius Paterculus 2.63–64, 2.87.2; Plutarch, *Antony* 18.4; Dio Cassius 46.53; Seneca, *Moral Letters* 82.12; Valerius Maximus 4.7.6, 9.13.3.
40. For a summary of Octavian's possible motives, see Rice-Holmes (1928) pp.214–215.
41. Appian, *Civil War* 3.80–81, 3.96, 4.2–4, 4.7, 5.43; Suetonius, *The Deified Augustus* 12, 96.1; Eutropius 7.2; Dio Cassius 46.41.5, 46.43.6, 46.51–52, 46.54–56, 47.1–2, 47.15.2, 48.22.1; Augustus, *The Achievements of the Divine Augustus* 1; Plutarch, *Brutus* 27, *Antony* 19.1, *Cicero* 46; Velleius Paterculus 2.65; Florus 2.16.1–3; Orosius 6.18.
42. Appian, *Civil War* 4.5–18, 4.21–32, 4.35–51, 5.143; Valerius Maximus 5.7.3, 6.7.2–3, 6.8.5–7, 9.5.4, 9.11.5–7; Dio Cassius 47.3–13; Velleius Paterculus 2.66–67; Suetonius, *The Deified Augustus* 27.1–2; Florus 2.16; Orosius 6.18.

43. Plutarch, *Cicero* 46–49, *Antony* 19–20, *Brutus* 28.2; Appian, *Civil War* 4.19–20, 4.37; Dio Cassius 47.8, 47.11.1–2; Velleius Paterculus 2.64.3–4, 2.66.2–5; Valerius Maximus 1.6.4, 5.3.4; Tacitus, *Dialogues on Oratory* 17; Martial, *Epigrams* 5.69; Juvenal, *Satires* 10.118–126.

Chapter 12

1. Cicero, *To Brutus* 1.11, 1.18.5, 2.3, 2.4.4.
2. Cicero, *Philippics* 10.9–13, 11.26; Plutarch, *Brutus* 26.3–6; Dio Cassius 47.21.7; Appian, *Civil War* 3.79, 4.75.
3. Cicero, *To Brutus* 1.2A.2, 1.3.3, 1.3A, 1.4, 1.15.10, 2.3.2, 2.4.3, 2.5. On Brutus' views of Octavian, see above, Chapter 11, pp.151–152.
4. Cicero, *To Brutus* 1.2.3; Plutarch, *Brutus* 26.7–8, 28.1, *Antony* 22.4; Dio Cassius 47.22.4–24.4; Appian, *Civil War* 3.79; Seneca, *On Consolation: To Polybius* 16. See also Keaveney (2007) pp.86–87.
5. As Clarke (1981) p.59 has also observed.
6. Africa (1978) p.621 has noted that another indication that Porcia was dead by the time of Brutus' suicide is that Antony sent his ashes to Servilia rather than her: see below, Chapter 14, p.206.
7. Cicero, *To Brutus* 1.9, 1.17.7; Plutarch, *Brutus* 53.5–7, *Cato the Younger* 73.4; Valerius Maximus 4.6.5 (on which see Moles (1983a) pp.765–766); Appian, *Civil War* 4.136; Martial, *Epigrams* 1.42; Dio Cassius 47.49.3. See Hershberg (1970) pp.22–23.
8. Cicero, *To Brutus* 1.6.4, 1.7–8, 1.11, 1.12.3, 1.15.1–2, *To Friends* 11.16–17.
9. Cicero, *To Brutus* 1.4A.4, 1.6.2, 1.12.3, 1.14, 2.3.6, 2.4.6, 2.5.2, 2.5.6, *To Friends* 12.14.8.
10. Cicero, *To Brutus* 1.2A.1, 1.5, 2.3, 2.4.2–3.
11. Cicero, *To Brutus* 1.5.2, *To Friends* 12.12.1, 12.12.5.
12. Cicero, *To Brutus* 1.2, 1.6.3; Appian, *Civil War* 3.79.
13. Cicero, *To Friends* 12.14–15, *To Brutus* 2.2.3.
14. Cicero, *To Friends* 12.8.2, 12.9, 12.10.2–3, 12.14.4, 12.15.7.
15. Velleius Paterculus 2.87.3.
16. Cicero, *To Friends* 12.13.3–4; Appian, *Civil War* 3.78, 4.60–62; Dio Cassius 47.30; Velleius Paterculus 2.69.2.
17. Dio Cassius 47.30.7–47.31.4 depicts a far more merciful Cassius here than Appian, *Civil War* 4.62, 4.64.
18. Dio Cassius 47.24.
19. Dio Cassius 47.25; Appian, *Civil War* 4.75.
20. Horace, *Satires* 1.7.
21. These letters are preserved in R. Hercher (1873), *Epistolographi Graeci*, Paris, pp.177–191. For a summary of their contents and discussion of their doubtful authenticity, see Magie (1950) p.422 and n.54. Plutarch, *Brutus* 2.5–8, 28.3.
22. Plutarch, *Brutus* 33, *Pompey* 77, 80.6. Appian, *Civil War* 2.90 has Cassius kill Theodotus.
23. Appian, *Civil War* 4.63, 5.8; Dio Cassius 47.31.5; Plutarch, *Brutus* 28.3–5.
24. Plutarch, *Brutus* 28.6–7; Dio Cassius 47.32; Appian, *Civil War* 4.63, 4.65: indeed, Appian suggests that Antony and Octavian were already crossing the Adriatic with several legions, but Brutus and Cassius would surely have acted more urgently and defensively if that had been the case.
25. Dio Cassius 47.18–19. See also Rice-Holmes (1928) p.75 and Pelling (1996) p.5.
26. Plutarch, *Brutus* 29–30, *Comparison of Dion and Brutus* 3; Appian, *Civil War* 4.65.
27. Plutarch, *Brutus* 30.3; Dio Cassius 47.33.1–2; Appian, *Civil War* 4.65; Velleius Paterculus 2.69.6.
28. Appian, *Civil War* 4.63, 4.65–74; Dio Cassius 47.33; Plutarch, *Brutus* 30.3, 32.4; Valerius Maximus 1.5.8.
29. Plutarch, *Brutus* 30–31; Appian, *Civil War* 4.76–80; Dio Cassius 47.34.1–3; Velleius Paterculus 2.69.6. Both Plutarch and Appian note that the Xanthians had once before destroyed themselves, when facing the Persians in 546–545 BC: it is most likely that Herodotus' account of these events (1.176) influenced the narration of Brutus' dealings with the same city.

30. Plutarch, *Brutus* 32; Appian, *Civil War* 4.81; Dio Cassius 47.34.4–6.
31. Plutarch, *Brutus* 2.8. See above, p.172 and n.21 on the collection of letters which Plutarch may have been quoting. If the authenticity is to be accepted, Brutus shows a less merciful side in this correspondence: see Rice-Holmes (1928) p.79, n.4, and Rawson (1986) pp.107–108.
32. Appian, *Civil War* 4.82; Dio Cassius 47.34.6; Plutarch, *Brutus* 32.4.
33. Dio Cassius 48.24–27; Velleius Paterculus 2.78.1; Florus 2.19. See also Magie (1950) pp.430–432.
34. *Iliad* 1.259, where Nestor says to Achilles and Agamemnon: 'Be ruled by me, young men, I have more years and wisdom than you'.
35. Plutarch, *Brutus* 34; Dio Cassius 47.35.1.
36. Plutarch, *Brutus* 35. On Brutus' moneylending activities, see above, Chapter 2, pp.22–28.

Chapter 13

1. Plutarch, *Brutus* 36–37, *Caesar* 69.6–11; Appian, *Civil War* 4.134; see also Florus 2.17.6–9. Valerius Maximus 1.7.7 describes a similar vision appearing to Cassius Parmensis, considered the last of Caesar's murderers to die, soon before his death.
2. Appian, *Civil War* 4.63, 4.74, 4.82–86, 4.99, 5.8; Dio Cassius 47.35–46, 48.17–19; Velleius Paterculus 2.72.4–5.
3. Appian, *Civil War* 4.87–88; Plutarch, *Brutus* 38.1.
4. Appian, *Civil War* 4.88–89.
5. Appian, *Civil War* 4.89–101. See also Keaveney (2007) pp.49–52, 87.
6. Appian, *Civil War* 4.101–102; Plutarch, *Brutus* 37.7.
7. Appian, *Civil War* 4.103–105; Dio Cassius 47.35.2–4; Plutarch, *Brutus* 38.2.
8. Appian, *Civil War* 4.105–106; Dio Cassius 47.35.5–36.1.
9. Dio Cassius 47.36, 48.18; Appian, *Civil War* 4.106.
10. Appian, *Civil War* 4.107; Dio Cassius 47.37.2; Plutarch, *Brutus* 38.3.
11. Dio Cassius 47.37.3–6; Plutarch, *Brutus* 38.3–7; Appian, *Civil War* 4.108; Pliny, *Natural History* 33.39.
12. Plutarch, *Brutus* 39.1–6; Appian, *Civil War* 4.134; Dio Cassius 47.38.4, 47.40.7–8; Florus 2.17.6–7.
13. Appian, *Civil War* 4.108 reports that Brutus and Cassius had 20,000 cavalry over Antony and Octavian's 13,000, although he previously stated that the Republicans possessed 17,000 (4.88: see above, p.183). Dio Cassius 47.38.2 suggests that Brutus and Cassius had weaker soldiers, but were superior in number.
14. Plutarch, *Brutus* 39.6–7; Appian, *Civil War* 4.108–109; Dio Cassius 47.37.5–38.3.
15. Dio Cassius 47.38.3. One of these defectors was Quintus Dellius who, having deserted from Dolabella to Cassius, now defected to Antony, and later would go over to Octavian at Actium: Velleius Paterculus 2.84.2.
16. Plutarch, *Brutus* 39.8–11; Appian, *Civil War* 4.108–109.
17. On the Via dei Fori Imperiali. Appian, *Civil War* 4.108; Dio Cassius 47.37.5–38.3, 47.40.1–6, 47.41.1–2, 48.32.4; Florus 2.17.9; Suetonius, *The Deified Augustus* 29.1–2, 96.1; Ovid, *Fasti* 5.567–579.
18. See Rice-Holmes (1928) pp.85–86. Plutarch, *Brutus* 39.11; Dio Cassius 47.38.4.
19. Although see below, p.199, where Appian, *Civil War* 4.124 instead places these words in the mouth of Brutus.
20. Plutarch, *Brutus* 40.1–4.
21. Plutarch, *Brutus* 40.5–12; Velleius Paterculus 2.71.1. On the probable historicity of the suicide pact between Brutus and Cassius, see Moles (1983a) pp.767–771. On Brutus' attitude to suicide, see Sedley (1997) pp.51–52.
22. Dio Cassius 47.42–44; Plutarch, *Brutus* 24.7.
23. Appian, *Civil War* 4.109; Plutarch, *Brutus* 41.1.
24. Appian, *Civil War* 4.110; Plutarch, *Brutus* 41, 43.1, *Antony* 22.2; Suetonius, *The Deified Augustus* 91.1; Dio Cassius 47.41.3, 47.46.2; Velleius Paterculus 2.70.1; Valerius Maximus 1.7.1; Florus 2.17.9–10; Orosius 6.18.
25. Plutarch, *Brutus* 42.1–5; Appian, *Civil War* 4.110, 4.112.

26. Plutarch, *Brutus* 42.3, *Antony* 22.3. Pliny, *Natural History* 7.148.
27. Appian, *Civil War* 4.111–112.
28. Rice-Holmes (1928) p.85, n.3; Syme (2002) p.205, n.2.
29. Appian, *Civil War* 4.134; Florus 2.17.8; Plutarch, *Brutus* 48.5; Valerius Maximus 1.8.8.
30. Dio Cassius 47.45–46; Plutarch, *Brutus* 42.4; Florus 2.17.10–11.
31. Plutarch, *Brutus* 42–43, *Caesar* 69.3, *Antony* 22.3; Dio Cassius 47.45–46; Appian, *Civil War* 4.113; Velleius Paterculus 2.70.2–3; Florus 2.17.11–13; Valerius Maximus 6.8.4 presents Cassius as needing Pindarus' help to kill himself because he was too afraid.
32. Plutarch, *Brutus* 43–44; Appian, *Civil War* 4.113–114; Dio Cassius 47.46–47; Valerius Maximus 9.9.2.
33. Plutarch, *Brutus* 44; Frontinus 4.2.1; Appian, *Civil War* 4.114; Dio Cassius 47.47.2.
34. Dio Cassius 47.47.2–3; Appian, *Civil War* 4.114; Plutarch, *Brutus* 45.1–2.
35. Appian, *Civil War* 4.115–116; Plutarch, *Brutus* 47.1–3; Dio Cassius 47.47.4.
36. Plutarch, *Brutus* 47.4–9; Dio Cassius 47.47.5; Appian, *Civil War* 4.122–123.
37. Appian, *Civil War* 4.117–120; Plutarch, *Brutus* 46.
38. Appian, *Civil War* 4.121–122; Dio Cassius 47.48.1; Plutarch, *Brutus* 45.3.
39. Plutarch, *Brutus* 45; Appian, *Civil War* 4.123; Dio Cassius 47.48.3.
40. Appian, *Civil War* 4.123–124; Dio Cassius 47.48.2. Moles (1983a) pp.771–772 discusses the improbability of Brutus' comparison of himself with Pompey. See above, p.189, where this comparison with Pompey is attributed to Cassius.
41. At the time of Tiberius' birth, according to Suetonius, *Tiberius* 5.
42. Plutarch, *Brutus* 48, *Caesar* 69.13; Valerius Maximus 1.4.7; Appian, *Civil War* 4.128; Dio Cassius 47.48.4.
43. Appian, *Civil War* 4.125–128; Plutarch, *Brutus* 49.1–4.
44. Plutarch, *Brutus* 49.5–6; Appian, *Civil War* 4.128; Dio Cassius 47.48.4–5.
45. Appian, *Civil War* 4.129–130; Dio Cassius 47.48.5.
46. Plutarch, *Brutus* 49.7–10, *Cato the Younger* 73.3; Appian, *Civil War* 4.129, 4.135; Velleius Paterculus 2.71 and Valerius Maximus 4.7.4 name other noblemen who died in this war.
47. Plutarch, *Brutus* 50, *Antony* 69.1; Appian, *Civil War* 4.129.

Chapter 14

1. Plutarch, *Brutus* 51.5–6, *Cato the Younger* 65–66, 73.4; Appian, *Civil War* 4.130–131: according to Appian, he addressed his officers on the following day, but according to Plutarch his suicide took place on the same night as the battle.
2. Plutarch, *Brutus* 51.1–2; Appian, *Civil War* 4.130; Dio Cassius 47.49.1; Euripides, *Medea* 332. Euripides was one of the three great tragedians of classical Athens, in the fifth century BC. Medea was the mythological heroine and sorceress of Colchis who committed the infamous deed of killing her own children in revenge for the infidelity of her husband, Jason.
3. Appian, *Civil War* 4.130; Dio Cassius 47.49.2. For a detailed discussion of these purported final words of Brutus, see Moles (1983a) pp.772–773, 775–779.
4. See Clarke (1981) pp.71–72 and Moles (1983a) pp.775–779.
5. Plutarch, *Brutus* 51.2–4. This passage is discussed in detail by Moles (1983a) pp.773–775.
6. Plutarch, *Brutus* 29.9, 52.1–5; Valerius Maximus 6.4.5.
7. Plutarch, *Brutus* 52.6–8, *Caesar* 69.14; Appian, *Civil War* 4.131; Velleius Paterculus 2.70.4–5; Dio Cassius 47.49.2; Florus 2.17.14–15.
8. Plutarch, *Brutus* 29.7. Syme (2002) p.106 acknowledges Antony's respect for Brutus.
9. See above, Chapter 12, p.166.
10. Plutarch, *Antony* 22.4, *Brutus* 53.4, *Comparison of Dion and Brutus* 5; Valerius Maximus 5.1.11; Dio Cassius 47.49.2; Suetonius, *The Deified Augustus* 13.1; Appian, *Civil War* 4.135.
11. Plutarch, *Comparison of Dion and Brutus* 3 suggests that Brutus still had other options open to him, although his *Brutus* narrative presents a situation devoid of all hope.
12. Appian, *Civil War* 4.135.
13. Appian, *Civil War* 4.38, 4.135–136, 5.113; Velleius Paterculus 2.71.1; Plutarch, *Brutus* 53.1–3.
14. Suetonius, *The Deified Augustus* 13.1–2; Dio Cassius 47.49.4.

15. Appian, *Civil War* 4.135; Velleius Paterculus 2.71.2; Dio Cassius 48.44.1.
16. Cornelius Nepos, *Atticus* 11.2–4; Appian, *Civil War* 5.4, 5.7.
17. This Clodius may be identified either with the man who kept Gaius Antonius under guard, or with the enemy deserter who tried, but failed, to bring news of the Caesarians' naval disaster to Brutus.
18. Appian, *Civil War* 4.37, 4.138, 5.2, 5.15, 5.25–26, 5.70; Dio Cassius 47.49.4, 48.7.4–5, 48.19.2–4; Suetonius, *Nero* 3; Velleius Paterculus 2.72.3–5, 2.76.2, 2.77.3; Plutarch, *Antony* 63.2–3.
19. Appian, *Civil War* 4.51, 5.2.
20. On Antony in the east, see Magie (1950) pp.428–429.
21. Suetonius, *The Deified Augustus* 13.3; Plutarch, *Antony* 23.1; Appian, *Civil War* 5.3, 5.7, 5.12–13, 5.22; Dio Cassius 48.1–3, 48.22.2, 48.30.2, 48.32.4, 54.9.6; Velleius Paterculus 2.74.1; Strabo 7, fragment 41; Suetonius, *Tiberius* 14.3. See also Rice-Holmes (1928) pp.218–219.
22. Plutarch, *Brutus* 29.10–11. Moles (1983a) pp.763–765 discusses the authenticity of this comment, and observes that such a vision of the future does not seem astounding, given Antony and Octavian's uneasy relationship.
23. Tacitus, *Annals* 1.2 views the deaths of Brutus and Cassius as signalling the end of the Republic. See also Dio Cassius 47.39.
24. MacMullen (1992) pp.1, 7–10.
25. Dio Cassius 48.3.2; Augustus, *The Achievements of the Divine Augustus* 21.
26. Virgil, *Aeneid* 2.705ff.
27. Augustus, *The Achievements of the Divine Augustus* 2.
28. Dio Cassius 53.32.4; Appian, *Civil War* 4.51 speaks of 'Publius', which has been suggested is a mistake on the author's part: Broughton (1951–1960) pp.362–363. Publius Sestius was Lucius' father.
29. Plutarch, *Comparison of Dion and Brutus* 5.
30. Suetonius, *On Rhetoricians* 6, describing the words of Gaius Albucius Silus of Novara, an Augustan rhetorician and orator.
31. MacMullen (1992) pp.18–19.
32. Tacitus, *Annals* 4.34–35; Dio Cassius 57.24.2–4; Seneca, *On Consolation: To Marcia* 1; Suetonius, *Tiberius* 61.3, *Caligula* 16.1; Quintilian, *Institutes of Oratory* 10.1.104. See also MacMullen (1992) pp.19–20; Scullard (1984) pp.349–350.
33. Tacitus, *Annals* 13.49, 14.48–49, 15.20–23, 16.21–35; Juvenal, *Satires* 5.36–37; Dio Cassius 62.15; Suetonius, *Nero* 37.1. See also MacMullen (1992) pp.21–23; Scullard (1984) pp.310–311.
34. Tacitus, *Annals* 15.56–57, 15.70; Suetonius, *The Life of Lucan*. See also MacMullen (1992) pp.23–27 and Clarke (1981) pp.82–83 who briefly discuss some of the relevant passages from Lucan's *Civil War*.
35. Tacitus, *Annals* 3.76.
36. Hendrickson (1939) pp.401–402.
37. Plutarch, *Brutus* 52.5. Brutus' virtue features heavily in the overall assessment of his character by the ancient sources, for example: Appian, *Civil War* 4.132–133, 4.138; Plutarch, *Dion* 1–2, *Brutus* 1.3; Velleius Paterculus 2.72.1–2. For a modern summary of his character, see Clarke (1981) pp.72–78, 84.

Bibliography

Ancient Sources
Appian, *Civil War*
Augustus, *The Achievements of the Divine Augustus*
Julius Caesar, *Civil War*
Cicero, *Letters to Atticus*
— *Letters to Brutus*
— *Letters to Friends*
— *Brutus*
— *Orator*
— *Philippics*
Cornelius Nepos, *Atticus*
Dio Cassius, *Roman History*
Florus, *Epitome of Roman History*
Livy, *The Early History of Rome*
Lucan, *Civil War*
Nicolaus of Damascus, *Life of Augustus*
Orosius, *Seven Books against the Pagans*
Plutarch, *Antony*
— *Brutus*
— *Caesar*
— *Cato the Younger*
— *Cicero*
— *Comparison of Dion and Brutus*
— *Pompey*
Suetonius, *The Deified Julius*
— *The Deified Augustus*
Tacitus, *Annals*
Valerius Maximus, *Memorable Doings and Sayings*
Velleius Paterculus, *Compendium of Roman History*

Secondary Sources
Africa, T. W. (1978): 'The Mask of an Assassin: A Psychohistorical Study of M. Junius Brutus', *Journal of Interdisciplinary History* 8.4: 599–626
Alföldi, A. (1956): 'The Main Aspects of Political Propaganda on the Coinage of the Roman Republic', pp.63–95 in R. A. G. Carson & C. H. V. Sutherland (eds.), *Essays in Roman Coinage presented to Harold Mattingly*, Oxford
Badian, E. (1965): 'Cato and Cyprus', *Journal of Roman Studies* 55: 110–112
Badian, E. (1972): *Publicans & Sinners – Private Enterprise in the Service of the Roman Republic*, Oxford
Balsdon, J. P. V. D. (1958): 'The Ides of March', *Historia: Zeitschrift für Alte Geschichte* 7.1: 80–94
Bringmann, K. (2007): *A History of the Roman Republic*, Cambridge (1st edition 2002, Munich)
Broughton, T. R. S. (1951–1960): *The Magistrates of the Roman Republic,* Volume 2, New York
Clarke, M. L. (1981): *The Noblest Roman – Marcus Brutus and his Reputation*, London

Coulter, C. C. (1940): 'Marcus Junius Brutus and the "Brutus" of Accius', *Classical Journal* 35: 460–470
Drathman, A. R. (1946): 'How Cicero and Brutus Hated the Nones of July', *Classical Journal* 42: 92
Epstein, D. F. (1987): 'Caesar's Personal Enemies on the Ides of March', *Latomus* 46: 566–570
Epstein, D. F. (1987a): *Personal Enmity in Roman Politics, 218–43 BC*, Beckenham
Fields, N. (2008): *Warlords of Republican Rome – Caesar versus Pompey*, Barnsley
Filbey, E. J. (1911): 'Concerning the Oratory of Brutus', *Classical Philology* 6: 325–333
Gardner, J. F. (2009): 'The Dictator', pp.57–71 in M. Griffin (ed.), *A Companion to Julius Caesar*, Oxford
Gelzer, M. (1969): *Caesar – Politician and Statesman*, Oxford (1st edition 1968)
le Glay, M., Voisin, J.-L., & Le Bohec, Y. (2009): *A History of Rome*, Chichester
Gosling, A. (1986): 'Octavian, Brutus and Apollo: A Note on Opportunist Propaganda', *American Journal of Philology* 107: 586–589
Grant, M. (1999): *The Twelve Caesars*, London (1st edition 1975)
Gruen, E. S. (1995): *The Last Generation of the Roman Republic*, Berkeley (1st edition 1974)
Gilliver, K., Goldsworthy, A. & Whitby, M. (2005): *Rome at War – Caesar and his Legacy*, Oxford
Haskell, H. J. (1943): 'The Senate's Summons to Brutus', *Classical Journal* 39: 29–30
Hendrickson, G. L. (1939): 'Brutus *De Virtute*', *American Journal of Philology* 60: 401–413
Hershberg, D. (1970): 'Porcia in Golden Age Literature: Echoes of a Classical Theme', *Neophilologus* 54: 22–30
Holland, T. (2012): *Rubicon – The Triumph and Tragedy of the Roman Republic*, London
Horsfall, N. (1974): 'The Ides of March: Some New Problems', *Greece & Rome* 21: 191–199
Keaveney, A. (2007): *The Army in the Roman Revolution*, Abingdon
Keaveney, A. & Madden, J. A. (1983): 'An *Ovatio* for Octavian?', *Phoenix* 37: 245–247
Lintott, A. (2009): 'The Assassination', pp.72–82 in M. Griffin (ed.), *A Companion to Julius Caesar*, Oxford
MacMullen, R. (1992): *Enemies of the Roman Order – Treason, Unrest and Alienation in the Empire*, London (1st edition 1966)
Magie, D. (1950): *Roman Rule in Asia Minor*, Princeton
Matyszak, P. (2003): *Chronicle of the Roman Republic – The Rulers of Ancient Rome from Romulus to Augustus*, London
Moles, J. (1983): 'Fate, Apollo, and M. Junius Brutus', *American Journal of Philology* 104: 249–256
Moles, J. (1983a): 'Some "Last Words" of M. Iunius Brutus', *Latomus* 42: 763–779
Oost, S. I. (1955): 'Cato *Uticensis* and the Annexation of Cyprus', *Classical Philology* 50: 98–112
Pelling, C. B. R. (1986): 'Plutarch and Roman Politics', pp.159–187 in L. S. Moxon, J. D. Smart, & A. J. Woodman (eds.), *Past Perspectives – Studies in Greek and Roman Historical Writing, Papers Presented at a Conference in Leeds, 6–8 April 1983*, Cambridge
Pelling, C. B. R. (1996): 'The Triumviral Period', pp.1–69 in A. K. Bowman, E. Champlin, & A. Lintott (eds.), *The Cambridge Ancient History*, 2nd ed., Volume 10, Cambridge
Radin, M. (1939): *Marcus Brutus*, Oxford
Radin, M. (1943): 'The Senate's Summons to Brutus', *Classical Journal* 39: 30–31
Ramsey, J. T. (2001): 'Did Mark Antony Contemplate an Alliance with His Political Enemies in July 44 B.C.E.?', *Classical Philology* 96: 253–268
Raubitschek, A. E. (1957): 'Brutus in Athens', *Phoenix* 11: 1–11
Rawson, E. (1986): 'Cassius and Brutus: the Memory of the Liberators', pp.101–119 in L. S. Moxon, J. D. Smart, & A. J. Woodman (eds.), *Past Perspectives – Studies in Greek and Roman Historical Writing, Papers Presented at a Conference in Leeds, 6–8 April 1983*, Cambridge
de Rose Evans, J. (1995): *The Art of Persuasion – Political Propaganda from Aeneas to Brutus*, Michigan (1st edition 1992)
Ross Taylor, L. (1942): 'Caesar's Colleagues in the Pontifical College', *American Journal of Philology* 63: 385–412

Ross Taylor, L. (1950): 'The Date and the Meaning of the Vettius Affair', *Historia: Zeitschrift für Alte Geschichte* 1: 45–51
Scullard, H. H. (1984): *From the Gracchi to Nero – A History of Rome from 133 B.C. to A.D. 68*, London (Reprint of 5th edition; 1st edition 1959)
Seager, R. (2002): *Pompey the Great*, Oxford (1st edition 1979)
Sedley, D. (1997): 'The Ethics of Brutus and Cassius', *The Journal of Roman Studies* 87: 41–53
Simpson, C. J. (1977): 'The Date of Dedication of the Temple of Mars Ultor', *The Journal of Roman Studies* 67: 91–94
Southern, P. (2010): *Mark Antony – A Life*, Stroud
Stockton, D. (1971): *Cicero – A Political Biography*, Oxford
Syme, R. (1980): 'No Son For Caesar?', *Historia: Zeitschrift für Alte Geschichte* 29: 422–437
Syme, R. (2002): *The Roman Revolution*, Oxford (1st edition 1939)
Welch, K. E. (1996): 'T. Pomponius Atticus: A Banker in Politics?', *Historia: Zeitschrift für Alte Geschichte* 45: 450–471
Wistrand, E. (1981): *The Policy of Brutus the Tyrannicide*, Göteborg

Index